$14.–
X3

THE WHITE SEPARATIST MOVEMENT IN THE UNITED STATES

THE WHITE SEPARATIST MOVEMENT IN THE UNITED STATES

"WHITE POWER, WHITE PRIDE!"

Betty A. Dobratz
and
Stephanie L. Shanks-Meile

The Johns Hopkins University Press
Baltimore and London

To visionaries with dreams of a better world

Printed in the United States of America on acid-free paper

Originally published in hardcover by Macmillan Library Reference, USA, Inc., 1997
Johns Hopkins Paperbacks edition, 2000
9 8 7 6 5 4 3 2 1

The following groups requested credits for the material they provided:

The Christian Guard, John Standring, P.O. Box 9963, East Ridge, TN 37412

Day of the Sword/White Terror Records, P.O. Box 7419, Minneapolis, MN 55407

14 Word Press—Wotansvolk, HC01 Box 268K, St. Maries, ID 83861

Knights of the Ku Klux Klan, P.O. Box 2222, Harrison, AR 72607

White Aryan Resistance, P.O. Box 65, Fallbrook, CA 92088
and phone hot line (619) 723-8996

Wolfpack Services, P.O. Box 212, South St. Paul, MN 55407

The Johns Hopkins University Press
2715 North Charles Street
Baltimore, Maryland 21218-4363
www.press.jhu.edu

Library of Congress Cataloging-in-Publication Data

Dobratz, Betty A.
The white separatist movement in the United States: white power, white pride!/
Betty A. Dobratz and Stephanie L. Shanks-Meile.
p. cm.
Originally published: New York : Twayne Publishers, c1997.
Includes bibliographical references and index.
ISBN 0-8018-6537-9 (pbk. : alk. paper)
1. White supremacy movements—United States—History—20th century.
2. Whites—United States—Politics and government. 3. United States—Race relations.
I. Shanks-Meile, Stephanie L. II. Title.

E184.A1 D63 2000
305.8′00973—dc21 00-030211

A catalog record for this book is available from the British Library.

Contents

Map and Figures

Preface to the Johns Hopkins Edition

We have written a book about the contemporary white separatist movement in the United States, providing historical background and identifying characteristics of and changes in the movement. The book is meant for a general audience that includes undergraduate students as well as social scientists. It is intended to analyze a social movement rather than serve as a social psychological profile of individuals, although we interviewed movement adherents as sources for information on the movement. We expected the research and writing of the book to take considerable time, effort, and resources; however, it was more demanding than we had anticipated.

We originally titled the book *"White Power, White Pride!"*, a much-used chant of white separatist movement supporters; these words, we believe, reflect significant motives of people in the movement. We, however, accepted the publisher's request to begin the title of the book with *The White Separatist Movement in the United States* to emphasize its social movements dimension. We continue to believe that *white separatist* is an appropriate term to describe this movement; it is indicative of what those in the movement advocate, and separatism itself is an important sociological concept used by those who study race relations. For example, S. Dale McLemore and Mary Romo in their text *Racial and Ethnic Relations in America* (1998) and Tamotsu Shibutani and Kian Kwan in *Ethnic Stratification* (1965) discuss separatism as an anti-assimilationist ideology. Emory Bogardus (*Sociology and Social Research,* Jan./Feb., 1933:265–71 and Nov./Dec., 1958:127–35) studied the degree of separateness between and among ethnic groups by developing a scale to measure social distance. The item that represented the greatest amount of social distance was based on agreement with the statement that a group should be excluded from one's country. Movement supporters frequently advocate such exclusion and/or the creation of a white separatist homeland.

A few readers may have thought we were justifying the movement and others perhaps thought we should have condemned it. They may have reacted more from what they wanted to read than from what we actually wrote. In contrast, others recognized our efforts by giving the book three awards: a *Choice* Award for an Outstanding Academic Book of 1998, a Distinguished Scholarship Award from a section of the American Sociological Association, and the Scholarly Achievement Award of the North Central Sociological Association.

We spent over six years in the field interviewing Klan members, neo-Nazis, and skinheads associated with a variety of religious beliefs, including Christian Identity, Odinism/Wotanism, and the Church of the Creator. Prior to engaging in fieldwork, we collected movement publications, videos, and music from archives, through subscriptions and other sources over a nine-year period so that we would have some understanding of the terminology and worldviews of movement respondents. Although other researchers studying the white power movement continue to rely solely on movement newspapers, magazines, and other written materials as secondary data for propaganda analysis, we find empirical data from primary interviews in the field to be more useful for studying this ever-changing, complex social movement.

We realize that some countermovement activists and academics argue that the empirical study of the white power movement serves to legitimize its ideologies and that value neutrality is impossible when studying these groups (Perlstein, *Lingua Franca,* Nov./Dec., 1995:79–83). However, others support the use of ethnographic research to avoid distorting knowledge and placing too much emphasis on the ideologies of the movement's leaders without understanding the diverse beliefs of the rank-and-file, which often diverge from organizational philosophies (pp. 81–83). Since ethnography is a primary methodological choice for researchers studying "deviant" or underground groups and behaviors, we are puzzled by sociologists who argue against interacting with these research subjects.

People in our society have often formulated caricatured images of how white separatists look and act, so we assumed the challenge of studying the movement from a sociological perspective in order to present our research subjects as we saw them in real-life situations. Given our social identity as white women, we were able to obtain the necessary entree into the movement to study this social world. Goffman said that individuals are categorized into "particular social identities" and those identities serve "gate-keeping functions" in social situations (*Stigma*, 1963:67). Irving Zola coined the term *socioautobiography* to stress the phenomenological importance of the sum total of a person's life experiences in the process of reflexivity or *verstehen* (understanding) (*Socio-Medical Inquiries*, 1983).

Our interviews have enabled us to experience many persons in the movement as real human beings, at times already living in social isolation from the multicultural world. The desire to be separate, coupled with their views about race and the importance of maintaining whiteness, illustrates their dissatisfaction with other races, with members of the white race who do not support them, and with the U.S. government. Achieving a greater understanding of the movement's ideologies through an ethnographic methodology does not mean that we are personally sympathetic. Erving Goffman used the term *courtesy stigma* to refer to sociologists who study deviant groups and become socially tarnished by their association with their research subjects, or "guilty by association."

After attending about twenty rallies or get-togethers of varying types across America, we did achieve a better understanding of white separatism and those ascribing to that worldview. Indeed, our use of the term *white separatism* evolved from the field research. We had initially assumed that the label *white supremacy*, which has been used to describe this movement through much of the twentieth century, was still appropriate in the 1980s and 1990s. However, the ideology of the movement is constantly being constructed and reconstructed, and the way movement members frame their discourse affects their actions. If indeed the Klan of the 1920s shared many beliefs of society in general, the views of the contemporary movement are less socially accepted and more stigmatized.

This contemporary ideology is being framed toward support of separatism as a means to disengage from what movement members see as a multicultural and integrated society. We learned that most of the white power activists we encountered were separatists, although the degree of separatism desired varied. The contemporary members of the movement typically do not support the old style white supremacy of domination through segregation or slavery, which they believe has not worked well in preserving the purity of the white race. The more militant white separatists want to completely remove themselves from people of color or have people of color completely removed from all or at least part of the United States. We therefore decided that the term white separatism accurately describes the movement's ideological position, its strategy, and its vision for the future. Separatism is key to their achieving Order member David Lane's "14 Words": "We must secure the existence of our race and a future for White children."

One criticism raised about our book was that we underplayed race hatred, anti-Semitism, and violence. We would like to reiterate that this book was intended for a general readership. We have made presentations about the movement to students and general audiences and realize people become upset by the racist content. People who belong to the movement, the watchdog groups who challenge the movement, and the researchers who constantly study the movement may become accustomed to the material or, some might say, desensitized, making it difficult to determine the impact of the racist material on those not frequently exposed to it. We feel we achieved a balance between a description and an understanding of the racist material and the beliefs in the movement.

Even now there is still little social-scientific literature available that has tried to examine this movement as an entity. We pointed out the confluence of economic, political, and cultural forces that has shaped this movement, using a political economy framework. We grow weary of newspaper and television statements about how well this economy is doing when it is doing well only for those at the top, especially the top 5 percent. Eighty percent have made little if any gain and the bottom 20 percent are becoming even more disadvantaged. Economic inequality is not declining. Many Americans believe that they have not benefited from the growing concentration of wealth in the hands of a few, a perception also expressed by most of our research subjects. (See Andrew Hacker's 1997 book *Money* for a detailed discussion of these trends.) True, not every person joins the movement because of feeling economically disadvantaged, but financial loss and job insecurity have motivated many to seek the movement for a sense of collective identity. This is in response to what they perceive as a multicultural society that has forgotten white people, rejects "white power, white pride," and forces integration by government edict.

We as authors recognize that many unanswered questions about the movement remain for social scientific study. Perhaps we added to the questions, but we believe that in this book we have discussed topics in an intellectually honest attempt to understand this movement. We hope readers find valuable information herein on movement history, ideology, protest and violence, and linkages to the mainstream within a broad political economy perspective.

Acknowledgments

We wish to thank all those who contributed to this project even though they are too numerous to mention. We especially appreciated those scholarly books already available on the topic, although we wish there had been more of these publications. Conducting interviews provided us with the most valuable information on the movement. Our interviewing was primarily funded by us with Betty teaching overload extension courses and Stephanie receiving limited Indiana University research and travel grants. Betty also was awarded a grant from the American Philosophical Society to examine research materials about the movement at selected library collections. We owe our greatest debt of thanks to all those in the movement who talked with us and shared their views. Some labored separately, filling out a detailed questionnaire. We greatly appreciate their time and effort in helping us to understand this movement. The hospitality we received from several of them was extremely generous and kind. Not only did many movement participants talk with us, but they provided us with a great deal of written material as well. We also received valuable information from a variety of other sources including journalists, other researchers, and those at organizations working against the movement.

We would like to thank Rob Benford, the series editor, for his helpful comments. During our research and writing, our publisher went through numerous changes as Twayne ultimately became part of Simon & Schuster. Then the bombing in Oklahoma City occurred, and given the media's not particularly careful discussions of the relationship of white supremacist and militia labels (see George and Wilcox 1996:chapter 18 for possible examples), our potential book appeared even more timely. We realized the possibility of publishers exploiting the Oklahoma bombing as a marketing strategy when we learned that the most recent reprint of *The Silent Brotherhood* by Kevin Flynn and Gary Gerhardt changed the subtitle from *Inside America's Racist Underground* to *The Chilling Inside Story of America's Violent Anti-Government Militia Movement*. Since authors do not control the marketing of a book, including its cover, we want to clearly state that this book is not about militias, nor are we making any connections between our research subjects and the tragic Oklahoma City bombing.

Betty was fortunate to have her sociology department fund a number of honors undergraduate research assistants—Rita Townsend, Roberta Bachelder, Doug Wubbin, Ann Engelen, Brenda Patton, Barbara Leih, and Ann Grienke—over the years we collected material. Their work was greatly appreciated by us both. Iowa State University (ISU) also provided considerable support for phone, mailing, and copying of Betty's materials. Our colleagues provided numerous helpful and encouraging comments as did three former graduate students of Betty's who showed great interest in the project although they weren't directly involved—Tim Buzzell, Pete Conis, and Lisa Waldner-Haugrud. Betty would also like to thank ISU graduate student Pat Hipple for taping hot lines while she was on leave. Most significantly, LaDonna Osborn handled all kinds of secretarial tasks (and unreasonable requests), including transcribing most of our interviews and cataloging the material, with the utmost ability. Without her support this book could not have been completed. Our families endured through the agony of our time constraints and seeing us go places that they didn't really want us to. Betty would like to extend her gratitude to her parents, brother, and other relatives for their encouragement as well.

Stephanie would also like to thank a number of people who made significant contributions to the development of this manuscript. Leona Lashenik, the departmental secretary, provided general assistance and encouragement and worked with Margaret Wheeler in transcribing interviews that were often taped under nearly impossible audio conditions. Cheryl Watkins, an interested student, volunteered her time filing boxes of newspaper articles and movement publications. Several departmental assistants also made contributions over the years—John Krampien, Margaret Wright, Jacqueline Jennings, and Kathleen Thomas. Thanks also go to Brooke Boroughs for her editorial insights on numerous projects over the years and Ellen Wolske for her supportive friendship and help with transcriptions and filing. Professor Daniel Stern, a sociologist at Northeastern Illinois University, was also extremely helpful to this project by sharing a massive amount of historical materials on the movement from his personal collection. Stephanie would also like to acknowledge the role that her parents played in the development of an interest in the study of race relations. Most importantly, she thanks her husband and soul mate, Richard Meile, for his continued intellectual and emotional support and her daughter, Amalia, who has spent her toddler and preschool years saying goodbye as her mother traveled across the country collecting data with Betty. Thank you, Amalia, for knowing in your little heart that your mother would be home soon and for your enormous reception upon her return. Know that you bring a richness to your mother's life that is beyond words.

We realize there will be critics of this book for both omissions and commissions. Time and space restrictions meant we could not always give justice to certain issues. We often had to rely on secondary sources, and even the statements of individuals pro- and antimovement whom we talked to and/or interviewed may not always be true. Some will say we were too sympathetic to the movement, and some will argue we were biased against it from start to completion. Whether pro- or antimovement, sociologist or not, we ask that you present your views to us in a way that can stimulate discussions, and ultimately we can all learn more about the movement from the discourse. Our interest in the movement does not end with this publication.

Abbreviations

ACLU	American Civil Liberties Union
ADL	Anti-Defamation League of B'nai B'rith
AFA	Ásatrú Folk Assembly
AFDC	Aid to Families with Dependent Children
AIDS	Acquired Immune Deficiency Syndrome
aka	also known as
AN	Aryan Nations
ANC	African National Congress
ANP	American Nazi Party
ARI	American Research Institute
AWOL	Absent Without Leave
AYM	Aryan Youth Movement
BATF	Bureau of Alcohol Tobacco and Firearms
BCE	Before Common Era
CASH	Chicago Area Skinheads
CDL	Christian Defense League
CDR	Center for Democratic Renewal
CEO	Chief Executive Officer
CHD	Coalition for Human Dignity
CIA	Central Intelligence Agency
CIO	Congress of Industrial Organizations
COINTELPRO	Counter Intelligence Program
COTC	Church of the Creator
CRA	California Republican Assembly
CRAP	Judeo-Christian Right Wing Anti-Communist Patriots
CSA	Covenant, the Sword, and the Arm of the Lord
CWP	Communist Workers Party
FBI	Federal Bureau of Investigation

GANPAC	German American National Political Action Committee
GATT	General Agreement on Tariffs and Trade
GOP	Grand Old Party
HRT	Hostage Rescue Team
HUAC	House on Un-American Activities Committee
IQ	Intelligence Quotient
IRA	Irish Republican Army
IRS	Internal Revenue Service
ISF	International Separatist Front
JFK	Just For Kicks
KKK	Ku Klux Klan
KKKK	Knights of the Ku Klux Klan
LSU	Louisiana State University
NAACP	National Association for Advancement of Colored People
NAAWP	National Association for Advancement of White People
NAFTA	North American Free Trade Agreement
n.d.	no date
n.p.	no page
NRP	National Renaissance Party
NSDAP/AO	Nationalsozialistische Deutsche Arbeiterpartei Auslands- und Aufbauorganisation
NSLF	National Socialist Liberation Front
NSPA	National Socialist Party of America
NSRP	National States Rights Party
NSV	National Socialist Vanguard
NSWPP	National Socialist White Peoples Party
PAIN	Pan-African Inter-National Movement
PLO	Palestine Liberation Organization
POW	Prisoner of War
PRA	Political Research Association
RAHOWA	Racial Holy War
RICO	Racketeer-Influenced and Corrupt Organization(s)
RNC	Republican National Committee
ROTC	Reserve Officer Training Corps
SHARP	Skinheads Against Racial Prejudice
SPLC	Southern Poverty Law Center
SS	Schutzstaffel (German for Protection Squad)
SWAT	Special Weapons and Tactics
UKA	United Klans of America
UN	United Nations

WAPA	White American Political Association
WAR	White Aryan Resistance
WASH	White American Skinheads
W.O.T.A.N.	Will of the Aryan Nation
WSA	White Student Alliance
WYA	White Youth Alliance
ZOG	Zionist Occupational Government

Many of these listed are organizations in the movement. For a listing, a classification, and an address of a group typically considered to be right wing, we suggest *Guide to the American Right: Directory and Bibliography*, 21st edition, compiled by Laird Wilcox, Editorial Research Service, PO Box 2047, Olathe, KS 66061. It is checked more-or-less annually for deletions and corrections.

THE WHITE SEPARATIST MOVEMENT IN THE UNITED STATES

Chapter One

Introduction

In this book we examine the American white separatist movement, which is composed of many different elements, some of which are formal organizations and others that are not. Analyzing this movement in the United States is especially difficult because some activities, events, and even groups are not open to the public, and some are underground or secret. In drawing a picture of the movement, we look at its history, ideology, strategy, and tactics. At times movement groups use protest; other times they pursue more mainstream paths to power. Various groups and leaders disagree about important issues, and we consider some of the major cleavages that exist, although sharp distinctions in groups or their ideological beliefs cannot always be made. We conclude by discussing the relationship of this movement to the political and economic situation in the United States. Although we have tried to achieve a balance between making generalizations about the movement and noting its variations, we realize that movement activists may feel we have glossed over significant differences between groups, and those on the outside may feel perplexed by the number of groups and differing beliefs the movement comprises.

The mass media refers to the groups we are studying as the white supremacist movement or as hate groups. Participants have typically been pictured as believing that the white race is superior to other races and wants to dominate minorities. However, as we studied the movement, we realized that several, but not all, leaders and members of the associations within the movement reject the labels of "white supremacist" and/or "hate groups." Some tend to see themselves as belonging to white racialist groups advocating the need for whites to assert or regain their power in an America that has become too multicultural, favoring minorities over whites and allowing too much immigration. Most use the term *white separatist* to describe their beliefs because they want the races to be separate, and some of these would seek to achieve this by creating a separate white nation. For example, the northwestern part of the United States has been viewed by some as an excellent location for the beginning of an all-white nation. A number of people in the movement maintain that advocating separateness does not necessarily mean that one group is superior to another; separateness would allow each group to maintain its own culture and one group would not be dominating another. Movement participants often describe themselves as racialist, stressing love of their own race. *Racialist* is sometimes used to challenge the media's label of them as racist.

Social scientists have not often analyzed extreme right-wing movements (Lo 1982:107). Although recently there have been several accounts of certain aspects of this movement, few have examined the movement overall. Often what exists are journalistic accounts rather than social scientific ones. In spite of these concerns, we have had to rely heavily on the work of others. This means that, unfortunately, errors made previously could well be made again in our book.

Since little social scientific writing on the current movement exists, we at times used the observations of organizations directly opposed to the movement. The most prominent ones that publish their own materials are the Anti-Defamation League of B'Nai B'rith (ADL), the Center for Democratic Renewal (CDR), Coalition for Human Dignity (CHD), Political Research Associates (PRA), and the Southern Poverty Law Center (SPLC) with its Klanwatch Project. In a sense, we consider these groups to be "watchdog" organizations that engage in claims making, promoting the "assertions of grievances and claims with respect to some putative conditions" (Spector and Kitsuse 1977:75). Claims makers not only draw our attention to certain conditions but also "inevitably choose to focus on particular aspects of the condition" (Best 1989:xx). In giving attention to certain causes, they are setting particular agendas. What the "watchdog" groups focus on is at least partially influenced by the fact that these organizations depend on public financial support, and the public is likely to contribute to groups that they perceive are struggling against some major threat to America. We relied on SPLC and ADL reports for general information, but we have noted differences between the way events have been reported and what we saw at those rallies. For instance, events were sometimes portrayed in *Klanwatch Intelligence Reports* as more militant and dangerous with higher turnouts than we observed. Also, "watchdog" groups promote "claims" that are compatible with their political agenda and neglect other ones as they attempt to wield political influence among policymakers. The general caution that the literature on the movement needs to be read with care seems to be particularly relevant here.

After reading and analyzing white power publications from a variety of organizations on and off for several years, we decided to gain a greater sense of white separatism in the real world. As sociologists, we were aware of the limitations of understanding ways of life and divergent philosophies by relying solely on published propaganda that is far removed from social interaction and can provide only one aspect of the public face of a social movement. Goffman (1959) suggested that people present themselves in face-to-face relations much like actors on a stage, in order to manage their identities and appearances in everyday life. In attempting to go beyond the stereotyped images, propagandistic publications, and our superficial understanding about white separatism, we decided to conduct interviews of movement people. Aho (1990:26) pointed out that "few sociologists have gone into the field to speak with right-wingers themselves," although they have frequently studied "other regions equally alien to the security of academia."

If one is to really understand subjects, it seems particularly important for researchers to conduct fieldwork in social settings that are far afield from their everyday lives. We attended public and private rallies, congresses, benefit dinners, and cross lightings, and we conducted face-to-face interviews in private and public places.[1] To be cost-effective, we traveled to movement events so that we could conduct numerous interviews at each site. Since travel to a locale for one interview was financially prohibitive, we also utilized telephone interviews and mail questionnaires, which, at times, led to the development of "pen pal" relationships. From these experiences, we interviewed or received questionnaires from approximately 125 movement people, including both key leaders and rank-and-file members.[2] Typically those interviewed gave their own opinions and answers to our questions rather than as representatives of their organizations. We also collected publications, videotaped materials (popular and movement media sources), and audiotaped speeches and interviews.

"You Stereotype Me, I'll Label You"

Our early impressions of the white separatist movement and its participants differed somewhat from each other originally, yet evolved together through our shared experiences and mutual understandings. Early in the fieldwork, it became clear that our extensive reading about the movement was inadequate to function effectively in the white separatist world. We were unaware of the social rules that governed interaction in their world and did not know how to gain entrée to those settings. As academic researchers, we also encountered difficulty with how we were defined by law enforcement as well as by movement supporters. Researchers are in a "no person's" land because they are not readily classified and recognized as media, who are typically allowed special entry to public rallies. On the other hand, white separatists may categorize all people writing about the movement as "Jewsmedia" and initially may be reluctant to allow unknown "outsiders" into their world. White racialists are heavily stigmatized and participate in organizations that are constantly undergoing surveillance by law enforcement. In attending two of Thom Robb's Knights of the Ku Klux Klan (KKKK) public rallies in Dubuque, Iowa, and Janesville, Wisconsin, we became aware of difficulties in gaining access to rallies. In Dubuque we were treated like the media, but in Janesville we were not. We came to believe that having press credentials was our best route to enter public rallies in which the police determine which "outsiders" can enter the events. In preparation for a public rally in Gainesville, Georgia, on Labor Day weekend 1992, we sought Georgia press credentials. This took approximately two months to get through the state bureaucracy since our request that press credentials be given to academic researchers appeared atypical. We also wanted to attend the private rally later in the day that was to be held in Lawrenceville, replacing the historic rallies at Stone Mountain that could no longer be held there.

Since we were new to the research field, we had to establish relationships with our subjects to gain entrée. Prior to our journey, Shanks-Meile contacted Thom Robb, who was listed as a keynote speaker at the rally, and requested permission to attend the rally. However, Pastor Robb said that Dave Holland of the Southern White Knights was the actual organizer of the event. Holland was encountering legal difficulties resulting from the Forsyth County march in 1987 in which Klansmen counterdemonstrated a civil rights march that led to several injuries.[3] We did not know about Dave Holland's legal difficulties or his changing status within his organization. He resigned from the position of Grand Dragon during that period to deal with his appeal of the court decision and other financial and legal problems stemming from the episode. Ezekiel (1995:108), a social scientist who was doing research on the movement, noted that the legal problems had worn on Holland. Shanks-Meile called Holland without this information and was unprepared for his suspicions and rejection of us as "Jewsmedia." In retrospect, it was understandable that Holland would be resistant given his legal status. Dobratz had been in contact with Dr. Ed Fields, editor of *The Truth at Last,* who was also listed as a speaker at the rally and was willing to be interviewed at the event. We expected this would give us access to the private event.

We traveled to Gainesville in the rain for the public rally, where we showed our press credentials and entered with the journalists. Three skinheads began heckling us during the speeches. Although no contact occurred, a young woman suggested that they kick Shanks-Meile's "fat ass" and a young man was disturbed by Dobratz's pointed "Jewish nose" and began calling us the all-too-familiar "Jewsmedia." Although we knew sociologically that the public rally was a front-stage theater-type production, we were not prepared for the verbal assault. After speeches were given in downtown Gainesville and the public event ended without incident, we drove in the rain to the private rally site. When we arrived at the entrance to the private rally field, we parked near the road because we were afraid of getting stuck in the mud and also wanted to be able to leave if trouble arose. In retrospect, we realize the influence that media images of white separatists had on us. The rains grew even heavier and eventually flooded the field, prohibiting the rally and "cross lighting." Some of the participants' cars sank into the mud down in the rally field. When we finally walked up to a house near the gate to find out if anything further was planned, the young skinhead woman we had encountered earlier in the day was on the front porch. Since we were entering the private event without the media baggage and were joining their world, she was quite retiring.

In Pulaski, Tennessee, the birthplace of the Ku Klux Klan (KKK), David Mehus, a member of the Confederate Knights, told us in 1993 that the public rallies are a show for curious white people. He became attracted to the Klan after reading an article on a rally in Chapel Hill, North Carolina, and told us: "I was vaguely aware something was wrong, and I think it took seeing a bunch of idiots in funny looking robes walking down the street while hundreds of people jeered at them to really focus." To him rallies were the way to take the "struggle to the masses" who do not want to hear "ideological talk" with "a lot of words with 18 letters in it. They want to see pure action, who's got the biggest reproductive organs." In keeping with Goffman's assumptions, we saw that movement participants act differently at public rallies, which are media events, than they do at private events amid the "folk."

Another flash of insight regarding public versus private behavior occurred as a result of the July 1995 Aryan Nations (AN) World Congress in Hayden Lake, Idaho. Michael Moore was producing a segment of "TV Nation," so a film crew and singers were positioned on the road at the entrance to the AN headquarters. Several white separatists attending the Congress evidently had walked down to the gate. We arrived at the compound after the media and "TV Nation" had dispersed because we had learned from our early experiences to avoid possible connections to the media so we would not be labeled "Jews-media." There was talk of someone spitting at Michael Moore's crew, but we did not know who was involved until watching the segment, which was aired in August 1995. During the Congress, we interviewed a number of people, including the person who turned out to be the "spitting skin." Shanks-Meile had approached him because he seemed friendly and "laid back," which turned out to be accurate perceptions in that social setting as he was quite cooperative about the interview. When he was among movement people, it would have been difficult to imagine that this mild-mannered young man had been the infamous skinhead that we saw later in the televised segment.

Goffman's (1963:2) classic work *Stigma* suggests that "society establishes the means of categorizing persons and the complement of attributes felt to be ordinary and natural for members of each of these categories." Individuals characterize each other prior to knowing that person and impute certain qualities that are transformed into demands, or normative expectations. These characterizations are called the "virtual social identity," differing from a person's "actual social identity," which consists of attributes that really exist. Stigma occurs when a person has an attribute that is socially discredited. The world of white separatism is highly stigmatized. In developing a "virtual identity," media images would lead us to expect white power people to be hostile, violent, criminal, antisocial, and ignorant. However, the individual world of the "actual identity" presents contradictions from the social expectations tied to the labels of "white supremacist," "Nazi," "skinhead," and "Klansman."

Stemming from the social stigma associated with white separatism, people in the white power movement acquire a deviant master status that

> overrides all other statuses and have a special priority. . . . Possession of one deviant trait may have a generalized symbolic value, so that people automatically assume its bearer possesses other undesirable traits allegedly associated with it. (Becker 1963:33)

Gordon Kahl's life provides an excellent example of the salience of a master status and the wide variety of behaviors a person exhibits that run counter to deviant labels. In the midst of controversy stemming from two shoot-outs with law enforcement and a long personal history of refusal to pay taxes, Gordon Kahl was labeled a fugitive and criminal. However, a glance into his personal life, or backstage behavior as Goffman (1959) would describe it, revealed a compassionate man. Corcoran (1990:3) said, "Kahl didn't look like a killer. Rather, he looked like someone's grandfather." In the "movement" biography, Joan Kahl Britton (Turner and Lowery 1985) recalled incidents that run counter to her husband's master status as a "cop killer and tax protestor." She described a situation on a stormy and bitter cold afternoon in North Dakota when Gordon took her and their two-year-old son to the hardware store to purchase some nails. Joan and their son waited "for over two hours in the car in 30 degrees-below-zero weather, a long time even with the heater going" (Turner and Lowery 1985:xiii). When Gordon emerged from the store, he told Joan that he had found a woman's wallet full of cash and had tracked her down from the information on the driver's license. Gordon returned the wallet and refused the dollar reward she offered even though the Kahl family was living on $33 per month, which was his 30 percent disability pension from a World War II injury. Joan said that dollar would have allowed them to buy much-needed staples such as sugar and bread. Friends also knew Gordon as an excellent mechanic who worked on their cars for free (Turner and Lowery 1985:xiii–xiv). These personal accounts point to contradictions between Kahl's highly stigmatized virtual social identity and his actual social identity manifested in private settings.

Somewhat similarly, Aho (1994) points out that Randy Weaver, who was involved in a siege on Ruby Ridge that resulted in the death of his son, his wife, and a U.S. marshal, was known for helping local residents, including a woman needing wood during the winter. She commented: "Randy cut me a load and wouldn't let me pay him for it. You know what he wanted for cutting that wood and hauling and delivering it? A cup of hot coffee, because it was cold that day" (Aho 1994:68).

As a result of our fieldwork experiences, we modified some of our stereotypical assumptions. Like any research subjects, the behaviors and qualities of some movement people fit stereotypes while others varied from mainstream expectations. For example, Shanks-Meile expected the women in the movement to be subservient with ill-defined political goals. Some women did fit that stereotype, but we encountered others who were far from that image. Katja Lane, the wife of David Lane (who was a member of the Silent Brotherhood), is an extremely articulate person holding a bachelor's degree in Spanish and Portuguese literature and a master's in economics. When we saw her for the first time, she was speaking fluent French to a skinhead couple from Canada. Currently, Mrs. David Lane (Katja) facilitates her husband's movement work while he is in the federal penitentiary by helping run Wotansvolk—14 Word Press out of St. Maries, Idaho. We met women from a variety of occupations such as construction worker, nurse, and manager. Although some women fit the stereotypical "procreator," there is clearly variability in women's roles both in the movement and society at large.

Popular press images also suggest that "white supremacists" are "criminal." Although many have been tried and convicted of a range of offenses, we encountered behaviors that ran counter to their infamy. For instance, during the 1995 AN World Congress, Shanks-Meile realized, after several hours, that she had lost her file folder containing questionnaires and notes. We canvassed the grounds asking people if they had seen it. When we went back into the church, the file folder was untouched and positioned on the same chair exactly where it had been left. One would not be able to leave unattended valuables in too many settings and expect to see them again. After the Congress, we attempted to buy a newspaper from a machine that a movement person had just tried. We noticed that there was a quarter still in the machine and called out for him to retrieve his money, but he said that he had found the quarter and left it there since it was not his. On several occasions, we enclosed payment for written materials valuable to us in our research, and the money was returned if the person decided not to share materials with us as "outsiders" or no longer had them. Some people sent money back because they felt that the materials they sent to us did not warrant that much generosity. Thus the label of criminal or thief runs counter to those experiences.

Characterization of the Movement

We originally thought the term *white supremacy* would be most appropriate in the title of the book and were surprised by the number of labels that the movement members used to identify the movement, such as *white separatist, racialist, white power, white nationalist, Pan Aryan, white civil rights,* or *white survival movement.* We were also struck by the use of slogans in the movement that capture the self-definitions and spirit of their protest such as "What do we want? White Power! When do we want it? Now!" "Hail Victory!" and "White Revolution, The Only Solution." We took a chant that we heard often, "White Power, White Pride," and added the concept of white separatism to title this book. From our discussions with movement people, it seemed they preferred the term *white separatist* to other possible identifiers, and we felt that term best reflected the contemporary core ideology of much of the movement, especially the more militant part. Langer (1990:83) also was not completely comfortable with the term *white supremacist* as the generic label of the movement:

> The problem with this usage, it seems to me, is not that it is wrong but that it does not go far enough, retaining an old-fashioned, unduly Southern and narrowly political flavor that fails to reflect the modern racialism that comes to us directly from the Nazi era and that I think is the essential characteristic these groups share.

She preferred to label the entire movement neo-Nazi but noted that this label had "varying degrees of applicability" (Langer 1990:83). We believe that within the movement there are enough people and groups that want to distance themselves from Hitler and National Socialism that neo-Nazi is not the best label to describe the entire movement. While the extent of desired separateness varies within the movement, virtually all reject marriage outside "the white race." Some of those who belong to the movement prefer separation of the races within the U.S. borders; others prefer a separate nation.

We altered our perceptions over time to note possible distinctions between white supremacy and white separatism, although both terms are applied to the movement. Both *The Oxford English Dictionary* (Simpson and Weiner 1989:268 Vol. 20) and *A Dictionary of Americanisms* (Mathews 1951:1861) define *white supremacy* as domination by whites. Cell (1982) entitled his book *The Highest Stage of White Supremacy: The Origins of Segregation in South Africa and the American South*. In a speech at the Portage, Indiana, rally in May 1996, Barry Black of the Keystone KKKK used the word *supremacist* to characterize his beliefs, which include the view that whites will take back power:

> Be proud to be white. Be proud of what America stands for. The Ku Klux Klan does not stand for hatred. It stands for heritage. It stands for the love of the white race. I am a racist and I am a prejudiced person and I am proud to be a white supremacist and I have no doubt in my mind. I don't apologize for anything that's happened in the past because the past has a way of repeating itself and it will repeat itself again. America will wake up and the white race will survive and take over—take back what's rightfully ours.

The separatist may well believe that his or her race is superior to other groups; however, we believe there can be a distinction between the supremacist desire to dominate (as in apartheid, slavery, or segregation) and complete separation by race. Some members of the movement argue that this is the case. For example, J. B. Stoner told us in our interview:

> Well, I'm a racial separatist, but I just don't know enough people would understand what is meant, and I wouldn't know whether all the people who call themselves white separatists know what they mean either. . . . Do you want to have segregation? Do you want to have it within the United States or do you want to have it on a geographical basis? Where there would only be white people here in the United States because that's the difference, lastly, between white racism and white supremacy. White supremacy says it's okay for the niggers to be here as long as the white man is supreme but I'm a white racist so I don't want the niggers here at all.

To some in the movement the term *white supremacist* suggests domination of "inferior" minority groups, whereas the white separatist, like his black nationalist counterpart, does not want to associate with other races.

An interesting movement story about "Whitey Revolutionary" (Kerling 1995:8–9) helps illustrate other views on separation and supremacy. As Whitey was being introduced to separatist beliefs, he found that

> White Separatists were not the booze guzzling, illiterate losers television and movies portrayed them as. Rather, most were intelligent men and women, who were not simply haters, as the media termed them, but rather White Separatist because they believed the races should not be mixed.

Later in a conversation between Whitey and his wife, Ann, she states that

> "I have always been told that the high Black crime rate, welfare dependency, illiteracy, and illegitimacy were because Blacks did not live next to, go to school with, work with, or got the break Whites did."
>
> "Now that is White Supremacy!" Whitey declared. "To say non-Whites have to be like and with Whites to succeed is the highest form of White Supremacy."

This is a reinterpretation of white supremacy to include some type of "forced" integration.

Although we are concerned that our use of the term *white separatism* may be viewed as "taking sides" by some, we hope that the term will be seen as a social scientific concept useful in analyzing the current movement. Claims makers or "watchdog" groups are likely to question the use of the term *white separatism*. In its description of movement leader Dr. William Pierce of National Alliance, SPLC (1994a:4) notes that *separatist* is "a claim made by many contemporary white supremacists who have abandoned hope of bringing back racial segregation and white dominance of American society." CDR (1992:189) believes the term *white separatist* is "media gloss" used by movement members while Crawford et al. (1994:A-8 published by CHD) define it as a label "adopted by individuals and organizations in order to obscure or present a more benevolent facade to their belief in Jim Crow segregation and neo-Nazism." Certainly any movement tries to give a positive spin to its beliefs, but it seems to us that many movement supporters tend to believe a return to the past system of segregation is unlikely and not even the preferred alternative.[4] For example, Tom Metzger (1996a:11) of White Aryan Resistance (WAR) maintains that "races which live in the same proximity, no matter what the prevailing standards, will eventually mix." Louis Beam, a well-known movement proponent, points out:

> We do not advocate segregation. That was a temporary measure that is long past. . . . Our Order intends to take part in the Physical and Spiritual Racial Purification of ALL those countries which have traditionally been considered White lands in Modern Times. . . . We intend to purge this entire land area of Every non-White person, gene, idea and influence. (Capitalization in original) (taken from CDR 1996:7)

Such a statement does not seem particularly benevolent or illustrative of media gloss.

Although segregation may still exist in American society,[5] the massive overarching legal structure of segregation is no longer in place. As historian C. Vann Woodard (1966:191) put it: "The year 1965 . . . did not mark the solution of a problem, but it did mark the end of a period—the period of legally sanctioned segregation of races. As a legal entity Jim Crow could at last be pronounced virtually a thing of the past. If Jim Crow was dead, however, his ghost still haunted a troubled people." Omi and Winant (1996) argue that the right wing is not simply demanding a return to segregation and that indeed the racial upheavals of the 1960s made such a return unlikely. They also suggest that:

> The far right was attempting to develop a new white identity, to reassert the very meaning of *whiteness,* which had been rendered unstable and unclear by the minority challenges of the 1960s. Nor was it clear what "rights" white people had in the wake of challenges to their formerly privileged status. (Omi and Winant 1996:120)

Movements adapt to changing political and economic conditions all the time, and we believe that for much of the current movement, white separatist is the most appropriate characterization. Indeed, the term *black separatist* has been used for a number of years to describe blacks who want to separate. White separatism will be discussed more fully in chapter 3, as will "the ideological notion of biological, genetic, intellectual or other inherent superiority of whites over other population groups" that has been used to define white supremacy (Crawford et al. 1994:A-8; very similar definition in CDR 1992:189). We believe that particular definition is best viewed as racism on the part of whites. The domination of whites over other groups because of control of various institutions in American society is an important indicator of white supremacy.[6]

An additional issue about characterizing this movement is whether or not this is actually a "movement." There are numerous definitions of *social movement,*[7] and we view a social movement "as organized efforts to promote or resist change in society that rely, at least in part, on noninstitutionalized forms of political action" (Marx and McAdam 1994:73). Marx and McAdam (1994) acknowledge that this definition implies more coherence and organization than what may exist in the early period of a movement. We recognize that analyzing white separatists as participants in *one* movement is fraught with pitfalls. In part this is because different types of groups have somewhat different beliefs and strategies, which makes it difficult for them to exhibit solidarity. Even though elements of this movement have been in existence for a long time, a great deal of coherence may not exist in the movement today. There has also been stereotypical labeling of the groups.

The use of the word *organized* in the definition of social movements normally suggests social movement organizations. However, in this movement there is heated debate about whether some form of organization that has a "paper trail" is desirable or whether some form of leaderless resistance should be followed at this particular juncture of time. In our interview, Harry Schmidt, a state chairman of the Populist Party, acknowledges the movement diversity:

> The movement has many aspects. There are some which are more reactive—reactionary, violent. There are others which are more long-term. There's some that are organizational. There are others that are leaderless. And I think that they're all important and valid. And I think that they all in one way or another work towards the greater good . . . if they're not infiltrated—if they're done with pure heart and they allow self-discovery.

Several people we consider to be in the movement prefer to be characterized as participants in the resistance and question the mainstream's reference to them as part of the right-wing movement. Some in the movement argue they are adopting a third position that is neither right nor left. These splits will be discussed further in chapters 3 and 6.

The movement includes many factions—so many in fact that we asked our interviewees: "Some suggest there are too many factions and divisions in the movement. What do you think about this? Why?" Some see the factions as relatively typical of any movement. For example, K. A. Badynski of the Northwest Regional Office of Thom Robb's KKKK stated: "Most factions or division in the Movement concern themselves with specific issues, so it is not a problem. It is no worse than Marxists or race-mixers who have many different groups."

Other responses about the numerous factions, such as the following comment from John Murphy of the Bedford Forrest Brigade of the KKK, illustrate the potential disadvantages: "It is true. It is probably because of a lack of a cohesive philosophy and recognized national leadership." Another person who wished to remain anonymous was more negative characterizing the movement as "fractured, poorly led, glutted with egotists, Fakirs and 'wanna be' Hitlers." A third person, Bill Werner of the Templar KKKK in Wisconsin, identified the strong individualism in the movement when he responded: "It only expresses the number of individual viewpoints within the movement. We need one powerful union of sorts. But everyone wants to have it their way. We need compromise." This centralization could be helpful as David Mehus of the Confederate Knights of America told us in our interview:

I've always wondered what could happen if some kind of central command was in place—that could produce a book or a piece of literature on like Thursday and have it be in all these PO boxes on Friday or Saturday. Wasted resources because, you know, they get along—they march with each other and stuff. At the higher levels there is really not a lot of coordination. . . . It's not like there's a central organization. I think that's what gets us more notoriety is these people have this vision like a Mafia. This huge octopus with tentacles all over the place, you know, and one centralized control. If we had it, the whole situation, I believe would be different, but we don't have it. And the system makes sure that we'll never have it.

Matt Hale, then of the National Socialist White American's Party and now leader of the World Church of the Creator (COTC), believed that later the movement will become more unified:

Well, I think ultimately these factions will slip away in a sense. And I believe that will happen when times get bad enough in this country. . . . And I believe that when that happens, some leader or maybe a few leaders will rise above the others and will have strong effective organizations and that they will rise as far as membership and popularity in their areas etc. and people will take notice. The small splinter groups will start to join them. And I think that that's what eventually is gonna happen.

David A. Neumann, Imperial Wizard of the KKKK based in Michigan, saw factions as helpful and recognized the positive role the leadership could play:

I believe that factions represent the specific ideals of their particular memberships. I believe that this in fact is beneficial as people gravitate where they fit in best. This helps to keep people within the movement, and the leadership of separate groups can then work together to co-ordinate.

Others also stressed the advantages of the factions, at least at this historical time period. For example, William J. Murray of SS Action Group wrote to us:

I don't think there are too many factions. There are as many factions as there are ideas, and this diversity is not necessarily bad. No one person or group has all the answers. Another point is that it is better to be de-centralized due to the repressive nature of our government. It makes it harder to bring us down when you have so many groups to attack. Morris Dees was able to bring down the largest Klan group in the U.S. because of this. Had they stayed split into smaller local, and autonomous cells, this wouldn't have occurred.

Andrew Jones of The Flaming Sword, KKKK Inc. (New Jersey) thought new factions were a sign of growth:

Personally, I think it's great that there are so many because every time the government smashes one little organization then it seems like two or three more sprout up in its place. . . . It's a good sign, I believe, when we see more and more little Klan groups sprouting up all over the country and other groups that could eventually become something good like the Klan was in the 1920s. I think it's a good wave that's coming about.

In general, participants believe a number of factions exist but that this can be advantageous as well as disadvantageous. Some believe the divisions suggest the movement is not as powerful as it could be if there were more unity. The quality of the leadership is sometimes questioned as well. On the other hand, having numerous factions allows the movement to recruit people with rather diverse views. It also makes it much more difficult for the government to bring the entire movement down.

Not everyone agreed, however, that this was a movement. A person who wished to be anonymous recounted:

> There is no "movement". There are millions of dissatisfied people but there is no single unifying force or leader. The fear of revolution is paranoid thinking by people who know their rotten acts deserve [to be] overthrown and wishful thinking by people who don't know what to do but wait for someone to bring about desired change. There is no North-South thinking nor a single set of issues that unify. Only economic chaos might produce a leader who could provoke meaningful resistance.

David Lane, who is now imprisoned for his participation in the Silent Brotherhood, also questioned whether the white separatist movement existed. In an untelevised interview for ABC's "Turning Point" with Meredith Vieira, August 30, 1995, Lane discussed Robert Mathews and Lane's association with him and others. Lane indicated:

> I spent years should we say penetrating the alleged or ostensibly racial groups in this mythical and non-existent movement. . . . If something has absolutely no validity, if it gets nowhere, if it constantly goes backward and loses, I wouldn't even give it the name of movement. A movement has dynamic. . . .
>
> I had an association with all kinds of groups. I had to find out why nothing worked. . . . Probably the best known group Aryan Nations, once a year with luck can draw 300 people. There's 300 people that go down to the local corner and watch a porno movie. That's no movement.

Lane focused on actions and progress as well as numbers in deciding what a movement was. He felt saddened by the lack of mass interest in and concern about what he perceives as the death of his race.

Later in our telephone interview with David Lane, he talked about preparing for the *revolution* rather than using the term *movement.* He acknowledged that being in jail meant he was in a disadvantaged position to judge what was happening, but he did indicate that: "I think we're getting more talent and I think that's inevitable that that will continue to rise until we really get some young fellows out of college who see they have no future and are ready to risk something." Later he also indicated: "I believe that as more and more realize that our kind is being exterminated and that there's no choices—I believe we'll get more talent." His famed "14 Words," which are "We must secure the existence of our race and a future for White children," illustrate the core of the movement's ideology.

Although there is disagreement about whether or not this is a movement, more than three-fourths of those we surveyed actually believed the movement was growing in influence, which seems to suggest some positive activity, at least, at this point or some sense of optimism. One person using the name POPEYE, Order of the Sword, White Knights of Amerika, noted: "The movement has grown in a number of Organizations, Quantity of publications, Quality of publications, and an influx of Active people who are new to the Movement particularly to the Skinhead Movement and National-Socialist Movement." An anonymous respondent referring to himself as "Skinhead" from California said it was growing in influence but not in a dramatic way. He cited a number of examples, including his belief that ideas in David Duke's platform had been taken by certain Republican candidates and that the media and opponents of the movement seemed to be using movement terms such as white separatist and race-mixer. The movement's influence, he felt, could also be seen because the U.S. government had formulated hate laws particularly to stop skinheads. He stressed that skinhead influence in Europe is already quite strong, especially in Spain, France, Italy, and Germany. "Skinhead" believed that in 5 to 10 years, everyone will have been in contact with the movement's message and that the situation in the United States will have worsened both socially and economically. The factions would then come together and fall behind new leaders in the movement.

Although there may be debate over whether this is a movement, we suggest that a movement does exist, which focuses especially on the issue of race and typically advocates separation of the races because of the perceived differences among the races. Lenny Zeskind (1985:25), formerly of CDR, wrote that the "nazi-right is fluid and changing. It should be considered more of a movement than any particular series of organizations."

A Look at Theoretical Frameworks Related to Social Movements

There are several theoretical frameworks on social movements, and we draw on their sociological concepts to help us understand the white separatist movement. Resource mobilization and political process models concentrate on the political aspects of social movements. These approaches are macro- or societal-level frameworks that view social movements as rational and goal-oriented activities that involve conflict to gain realistic advantages (Skocpol and Campbell 1995:285; Jenkins 1995:289). The relatively powerless have the ability to group together to try to improve their position by forming social movements. Resource mobilization theories stress the key role of resources (e.g., money, skills) in aiding the emergence of a movement. Political process theorists focus on the "broad economic, demographic or political processes that serve to enhance the political leverage of previously powerless groups" (Marx and McAdam 1994:85). McAdam (1982) maintains that resource mobilization is more of an elite model that emphasizes the role of resources outside the movement (e.g., from those more influential) while the political process model is more Marxist in orientation and stresses the resources available from participants in the movement. Marx and McAdam (1994) also seem to believe that the need for resources is fundamental to the former perspective while increasing political power is primary for the latter.

The resource mobilization approach maintains that potentially aggrieved people or groups need to attain some sense of solidarity in order to form a movement (Skocpol and Campbell 1995:285). Following an open-systems perspective,[8] the outcomes of movements involve both strategic choices within the movement and factors in the larger political environment (e.g., the position of those in power and the support or opposition from other movements and organizations) (Jenkins 1995). Economic changes and political realignments can be relatively independent of movements but significantly influence the movement (Marx and McAdam 1994).

The political process model advocated by McAdam (1982) identifies three sets of factors significant in generating insurgency. One is the structure of political opportunities or possibilities for a challenging group or movement to be successful; it varies over time and depends not only on the group itself but the broader political system as well. A second factor is the indigenous organizational strength of the aggrieved population that potentially provides a base from which the social movement emerges. This includes the following: (a) members who are typically recruited along established patterns of interaction; (b) an "established structure of solidary incentives," which means "the myriad interpersonal rewards that provide the motive force for participation in these groups" (McAdam 1982:45); (c) a communication network; and (d) leaders. In addition to structure of political opportunities and indigenous organization strength, there is cognitive liberation, which refers to the development of a consciousness that the current situation is unjust and the oppressive conditions can be changed through collective action.

Klandermans (1991:8) argues more attention should be paid to "grievance interpretation" since "interpretations of reality rather than reality itself guide political actions." Coercion by authorities may be seen as oppression by those who disagree with a government while those who support a government may see its actions as simply enforcing the law. Klandermans (1991:9) further suggests: "Because social reality is complex enough to allow for completely different interpretations of what is happening, one situation can produce a variety of definitions, sponsored by competing actors." Snow et al. (1986:464) have noted how important "framing" one's grievances are to the study of social movements. They use Goffman's definition of frames as "schemata of interpretation" that enable people "to locate, perceive, identify, and label" grievances and related factors that are associated with the movement. Social movements "frame, or assign meaning to and interpret, relevant events and conditions" (Snow and Benford 1988:198).

The "new social movement theorists" examine individual motivations and the shared "identities" of participants in the movement. Although this has typically been applied to newly defined social identities, cultural meanings, and supposedly new ways of viewing the world (e.g., environmentalists, lesbian feminists) (Skocpol and Campbell 1995), Taylor and Whittier (1995:353) argue that collective identity is an important concept for all social movements. They single out three key concepts in studying collective identity: boundaries, consciousness, and negotiation. Boundaries are "the social, psychological, and physical structures that establish differences between a challenging group and dominant groups" (Taylor and Whittier 1995:347). Consciousness draws upon McAdam's cognitive liberation and Snow et al.'s frames to mean "interpretative frameworks that emerge from a group's struggle to define and realize members' common interests in opposition to the dominant order" (Taylor and Whittier 1995:349). Blame or discontent is placed on cultural, structural, or systemic factors rather than on individual deviance or personal failures. Negotiation, the third concept, involves the use of symbols and everyday actions of social movement groups to resist or restructure the current system, including trying to change symbolic meanings of certain key concepts. Taylor and Whittier (1995:351) believe that negotiation is different from what is typically discussed as strategy and tactics in a social movement; however, these authors argue that negotiation should be considered as part of the strategy associated with the ideology of a movement.

Although not part of the social movement literature per se, the labeling framework in the study of deviance is useful in analyzing this movement as well. As Schur (1980:402) has pointed out, labeling theory has been misunderstood to mean that there is only "direct, negative sanctioning or stigmatizing of specific individuals"; instead, the terms a "definitional approach" or "social reactions approach," which focus attention "on processes of definition-reaction (meaning-production and ascription)—at all levels of the social system," may be more appropriate. Labeling refers to the "process that transforms one's conceptions of self from normal to deviant" (Davis and Stasz 1990:46). While there is the primary deviation in which one misbehaves or breaks the rules, this deviance and the reasons for it are not the focus of the approach. Rather, the secondary deviation happens when the behavior is observed by the authorities or control agents who surveil, intervene, or punish (Davis and Stasz 1990). Based on Lemert's description, secondary deviance refers to the behavior of the person labeled as a response to the problems caused by the label itself (Clinard and Meier 1992:106–7). Labeling leads to stereotypes and can cause the norm breakers to view themselves negatively. It can encourage the deviant to seek out others similar to themselves for protection. Labeling also restricts the image that people in general have of the deviants because they focus only on the negative stereotypes[9] (Davis and Stasz 1990:46–48). Drawing on Kitsuse's ideas, Clinard and Meier (1992:107–8) suggest that whereas secondary deviants are rather passive recipients of their labels who try to adjust to the labeling process, tertiary deviants actively protest their labels, "reject the rejectors," and sometimes join social movements to reaffirm their self-worth and fight against the negative self-images.

Application of the Theories to This Movement

The theoretical frameworks just discussed contribute to our understanding of various facets of the white separatist movement. A resource mobilization approach emphasizing the importance of attracting resources from those not formally part of the movement may help explain why this movement is not particularly influential at this time. White separatists do not seem to have a great deal of financial resources, although this varies somewhat from group to group. It is very difficult to determine whether some elites outside the movement proper may be supporting the movement currently.

Jerry Thompson, a reporter for *The Tennessean,* infiltrated the KKKK headed by Don Black of Birmingham, Alabama, and The Invisible Empire of the KKK for more than a year, from 1979 to 1980. He reported attending a meeting that included both Klansmen and non-Klansmen held in February 1980 at the home of a prominent Birmingham area physician. Another well-known physician was in attendance as well. Thompson (1980:9) concluded: "FIRST, AND sadly, there is surprising, latent sympathy for the Klan movement among many 'respectable' citizens who shun KKK membership" and "Second, Klan leaders are quick to exploit any racial incident—a police shooting, a school confrontation or an affirmative action controversy involving blacks and whites—to try to build membership and sympathy for the Klan's regeneration." He indicated that it is impossible to determine how many professionals support the Klan financially, socially, or personally. Thompson participated in a Klan roadblock on Highway 79 in Birmingham trying to solicit donations; he recounted how many whites dropped money into his container. The cars that stopped were of various models, including Cadillacs, Lincolns, Fords, Chevies, and Toyotas. In our interview, Thompson suggested that the Klan has what they call "secret members" who are known only to the top leadership. Secret members might, for example, help finance the start of a new chapter in a town.

In addition, David L. Sadler of the National Socialist Party of North America informed us: "We are financed by some very rich people who prefer to stay in the background. They basically agree with our racial ideals" and their "main goal is to bankroll us and working people do all the labor such as literature distribution, demonstration etc." Eric Hagen Watts, an independent in the movement, also noted a similar phenomenon: "The people who the system works for—the rich, they stay on the sidelines, they send checks through the mail—the poor are more apt to get active, working class active, they've got nothing to lose."

Not only is it impossible to know the number of very well off who support the movement, it is hard to assess the amount of support the movement receives from the general population. Seltzer and Lopes (1986) surveyed residents of Chattanooga, Tennessee, in 1981. In 1980 Chattanooga had witnessed the shooting of five elderly black women by three members of the Justice Knights of the Ku Klux Klan following an initiation ceremony. The Klansmen were charged with attempted murder. Two were acquitted by an all-white jury and one received a nine-month jail sentence, which led to a black riot in protest of the verdicts. Seltzer and Lopes (1986) found that 32.3 percent of white respondents approved of the Klan. Nineteen and two-tenths percent felt very favorable or somewhat favorably toward the Klan with an additional 13 percent saying that there were things about the Klan that they approved of. Thirty-six and three-tenths percent of the respondents who favored the Klan did so because of its racial policies, 28.6 percent said that the Klan "consisted of good people" or did charitable work, and 32.9 percent supported the Klan because of its "vigilante activities that purport to enforce the law and public morality" (Seltzer and Lopes 1986:101). Seltzer and Lopes (1986:95) also noted Gallup poll data that found 3.5 percent of the U.S. population favorable to the Klan in 1965, but this increased to 9.8 percent in 1979. There is clearly more broad-based support for organizations in the movement than membership figures would reflect.

Two nationwide opinion polls taken in 1968, one of blacks and one of whites, asked respondents about their support for separatism (Feagin 1971). One question asked whether it would be a good idea for blacks to have a separate country made up of some of the states in the United States and another asked about blacks having a separate country outside the United States. Whites were much more positive toward these solutions than were blacks. Twenty-six percent of the whites believed it was a good idea to have separate states in the United States while 36 percent favored a separate country outside the United States. Only 1 in about 20 blacks supported either idea. Feagin (1971:177) also found that the whites who tended to favor separatism were most likely to view blacks negatively, consider them less civilized than whites, and see blacks as attempting to take over the cities. Generally, controlling for socioeconomic status did not greatly reduce the relationship between approval of separatism and antiblack attitudes (Feagin 1971:179). A 1990 National Opinion Research Center study found a majority of whites did not support racial intermarriage. Two-thirds indicated that they did not approve of a close relative marrying a black. Also, about 20 percent of the whites supported a law prohibiting intermarriage of whites and blacks (Feagin and Vera 1995:137).

These opinion polls tend to suggest some support by whites for the Klan and for the idea of separatism as well as opposition to racial intermarriage that goes well beyond the size of the movement's membership. CDR (1996:1) suggests that "what is really significant is not the number of actual members but the number who endorse their message." On the other hand, the agreement with certain beliefs that the movement espouses does not necessarily translate into actual support for movement groups. Feagin and Vera (1995:161) point out that many whites who have stereotyped images of blacks try to distance themselves from racist groups like the Klan or skinheads. As we noted, movement organizations are highly stigmatized, and even their benefactors are not likely to desire recognition. Sometimes people lose resources or the potential for acquiring resources by virtue of joining the movement and being stigmatized. A few people in the movement told us they had lost jobs and housing because of their participation, and others indicated that they were concerned about losing jobs. Although resource mobilization may view movements as emerging or growing due to an influx of resources, we believe the white separatist movement potentially grows in hard economic times. Our respondents tend to support this view. For example, an anonymous National Socialist told us: "With more and more people getting sick and tired of the way our government is being run—low paying jobs, unemployment, immigration, and gun control, all of these issues help us recruit and find new supporters and members." Charlotte Pipes, unit coordinator for Robb's KKKK, also argued that "people are gettin' fed up" and the government is providing more economic benefits to illegal immigrants and those in foreign countries than to Americans:

> I've worked all my life, paid taxes, didn't play the welfare game. . . . we've got all these illegal aliens coming over here, getting every damn thing handed to them. . . . Let's take care of America first. We've got people, you see it on TV all the time—of people living out in the streets—you don't see them air-dropping them any food or medical supplies.

William J. Murray of SS Action Group maintained: "Take away a man's ability to provide a decent existence for his family, especially after he's been used to it for so long, and he will of course naturally be unhappy. How unhappy remains to be seen, but if he's as mad as we are, then he will more than likely pick up a gun and join us." Altogether about a third of our respondents volunteered poor economic conditions as a reason for the perceived growth of the movement.

The political process model is especially appropriate in helping to understand certain aspects of the white racialist movement. For example, political opportunities for success have changed over time. One could argue that the Ku Klux Klan (KKK) was partially successful after the Civil War. The whites in both the North and the South eventually desired harmonious or peaceful relations with each other, so Jim Crow laws and segregation were implemented. In the early 1920s the Klan was quite strong, although for a short period of time. Political opportunities were limited in the 1960s as the white supremacist movement advocating segregation suffered while the civil rights movement achieved several successes.

We have already noted the role of hard economic times, but there are sociopolitical concerns like affirmative action, growing crime rates, and racial unrest in the schools that have influenced the political opportunities of this movement. According to Bobby Norton, who we interviewed in Pulaski in 1993 and we met again at AN:

> When I became involved in the movement, we were attracting mostly middle-aged to older people with the Klan message, you know. But as the Skinhead movement has come to the forefront over the past few years, so now we are attracting middle-age to young people. . . .
> I think that . . . the system has forced race-mixing on our young people . . . we had four blacks in high school so I grew up in a school that was pretty settled. There was not a lot of violence in school and you could get an education if you wanted. I think as the younger people come up there . . . they are forced into schools that have a great deal of violence. . . . I think that they are pushed to the back of the benefits. . . . And I think they are intimidated. . . . And in turn, I think [this] causes them to rebel.

Bob Martin of AN noted that a wide variety of factors encouraged him to join the movement, including the economic situation and seeing "a lot of anti-white legislation" and "how unfair the whites were being treated" in the workplace and in schools. He had been a white child in a predominantly black school who "was made to be submissive or subject to the majority [blacks]. I knew that wasn't right—right off the bat. I also watched the city that I grew up in go from the shopping center of the county . . . to a slide down into the slums as the blacks became more powerful and had more babies. . . . You can't even walk on the streets anymore." Another respondent, Bill Werner of the Templar

KKKK in Wisconsin, told us "We're living in a very exciting lifetime. Racism, New World Order, corrupt government, eternal deficit, crime. You bet. America isn't and never should have been a melting pot. America is a pressure pot waiting to explode and we will witness this."

In addition to changing political opportunities, another key concept of McAdam's political process model is indigenous resources. Estimates of the number of white separatist organizations and members are available, but the actual numbers are not known. In part this is due to the underground nature of this movement but also because many organizations guard their membership lists closely. Some groups do not even consider themselves formal organizations with members and argue that having large numbers of people is not necessarily beneficial. Rather, they want a few good people who are very committed. In addition, rapid change occurs among these groups due to the rise and fall of leaders in the movement, the prosecution of some, the infiltration by government, and the traffic of members in and out of groups.

CDR (1992; 1996) estimates the number of hard-core white supremacists in this country to be about 25,000. The largest group would be composed of 14,250 to 15,500 Christian patriots, Identity, and others, followed in size by members of the various Klan factions with 5,500 to 6,500. Skinheads and neo-Nazis would be about 3,500 to 4,000 with another 500 to 750 members of other groups who see themselves as National Socialist. CDR also estimated there are an additional 150,000 to 175,000 active sympathizers who buy literature, make contributions, and attend periodic meetings. Bennett (1995:442) pointed out there is no consensus regarding the number of people in the movement, but he indicated there were probably less than 100,000 people in various groups at any particular time. A SPLC report (1994b:1) on Klanwatch's law enforcement strategy suggested an increase of 3,000 since 1990 to a total of 25,000 members in white supremacist organizations. The number of groups had also increased by a quarter to around 300 organizations (including Klan, skinhead, neo-Nazi, and militant tax protest groups). The 1996 year-end edition of the *Klanwatch Intelligence Report* (SPLC 1997a:18), however, maintained that the number of organized hate groups had declined from 300 in 1992 to 241 in 1996.

While members are a potential resource, the quality of the membership and their commitment to the cause are important. As with other movements, some people may join for the wrong reasons. In his telephone hot line message of June 9, 1996, Metzger (1996b) mentioned his concerns about some skinheads in the movement but then generalized:

> This is not merely young people either. It reaches into the older age groups also. Too many pseudo racial activists, whether they're Skins, Klan, National Socialist, or from some other group, have not committed to themselves as racial separatists. But they're looking for a quick fix to their screwed up lives. Yes, they're out there, weak men trying to join organizations to make them strong, which it never does. Uniforms, drinking parties, and rallies provide a quick fix for this type of person. These people never last since they need another high as soon as the present one wears off. If everyone who claims to be a racial soldier in the struggle was actually doing what it takes to assume power, our status would be improved 100 fold.

Some participants in the movement seem to be involved for only a short period of time as we have frequently seen many new groups starting and others closing their post office boxes. Others are very committed even in the face of persecution, loss of jobs, and/or imprisonment.

In our interviews we tried to obtain some sense of the perceived social class background of the membership. We asked, "Would you say your organization appeals more to those who are rich, middle class, working class, or poor?"[10] More than 20 percent indicated all the categories that we had listed (rich, middle class, working class, and poor). Richard Kelly of the Invincible Empire KKKK told us "We have white collar people and blue-collar. We probably have poor people. I'd say it's more predominantly . . . middle-class people, but we do have a range from all different kinds." Kelly also explained how his organization may be the only Klan group where one doesn't have to give one's name to join: "We give you a military number, in other words, on one's card. If you want to be like a police officer or a teacher . . . or a businessperson and you don't want to give your name and have it laying around in somebody's house on literature—we don't need your name. We don't check you out or anything because we're not doing anything wrong."

The working class was the most likely to be identified as the class the movement groups obtained support from. More than 30 percent indicated working class alone, and another 30 percent indicated working class in some combination with other categories. According to Matt Hale, then of National Socialist White Americans' Party and now Pontifex Maximus of World COTC:

I would say working class if I had to pick. Because the working class people really are losing the most. I mean, they have the most—in a sense they had the least to lose—and it's well, they don't have a lot of money so they can get involved in our movement without much retaliation for example. But, at the same time, they are the ones who are really getting the shaft more than anybody else. When we send jobs overseas, for example, it's not the rich who hurt, you know, because the rich—a lot of them are actually sending the jobs overseas. But the working class hurt and the working class know what it means to work, to be a productive citizen and they don't like the fact that their livelihood is being taken from them. And they also don't like the fact that there are people on welfare who are just living off them. So, I would say, at looking over our rolls, our membership rolls in my head, that most of our members are working class.

According to our data, the middle class was mentioned about a third of the time and the poor were mentioned about 40 percent of the time. If these perceptions are correct, the movement tends to be more working class but also cuts across classes considerably.

In addition to perceiving members as an indigenous resource, interpersonal rewards help create feelings of solidarity. Beth Helen Reynolds of SS Action Group and the Klan informed us: "I believe that we need the Movement to defend our Race and Nation, plus I really enjoy the Comradeship and friendship of all the people that we meet. Believe [it] or not, they are some of the smartest and nicest people that I have ever met in my life." An anonymous National Socialist indicated a different kind of reward: "People feel angry and want to belong to 'something' that they can be in to try to help understand what's happening and why. Some actually want to help change things too." Thus people feel good about taking part in an important endeavor such as saving the white race, gaining a better understanding of how things work, and developing important friendships.

Effective communication between groups is another indigenous resource. Almost 90 percent of those we interviewed indicated having some links with other organizations and most felt that these linkages were important in facilitating communication. Sean Haines, a skinhead, indicated a particularly powerful reason to maintain communication:

Everyone's gotta work together. . . . If everyone's . . . getting along and they have good communication between each other, it's harder to infiltrate. You know. Cause a lot of times we've seen in the history of the movement that an

> infiltrator will just go from group to group because he might get found out and get kicked out of this group—but this group's . . . got a problem with the Church of the Creator—so he'd just hop right on over to the Church of Creator because no one will ever tell the Church of Creator—you know—hey, watch out for this guy.

Excellent communication between groups could reduce the number of infiltrators, and it might also be a means to limit some of the deception and false rumors that may be spread in the movement.

Some groups have telephone hot lines with messages changed weekly, or more often if major events occur, and have gained access to local public cable television, putting on various programs. Many groups put out newsletters and often trade their publications with each other. Some organizations have public rallies that various other groups attend to show their solidarity; others have more private functions. Communication and possible recruitment has been facilitated by the Internet system with its World Wide Web sites. Barney (1996:1) suggests that white separatists "have turned to the 'Net in droves, creating an interconnected world of paranoia, hate and violence." He claims that there is a wide array of sites that are "effective in recruiting new members and uniting the various splinter groups" (Barney 1996:8). It should be pointed out though that even in the mid-1980s white separatist groups were using the computer network to communicate and recruit members (ADL n.d.a.; King 1985).

Many groups now have their own Web pages, and various movement supporters have extolled the benefits of communicating on the Internet and provided advice on how to use it. For example, "Thorsson" (1996:9) urged white people to wake up to the possibilities of the Internet arguing "communication belongs high on the list of necessary tools to achieve victory in battle." "Thorsson" (1996), Kaldenberg (1996:2) and McAleer (1995) all noted the problems "the Jews" were having controlling this form of communication. According to Kaldenberg (1996:2): "The Net is the only place in the world where free speech is a reality and the Jews hate it. They are so used to controlling speech that whenever they can't get their claws on our thoughts, they see it as a hate crime." McAleer (1995:19) too proclaimed the Internet's potential because of "its speed, number of users, and their [the Jews] inability to control its content" and urged supporters to buy a computer, get on-line, and "fire the shot that is read around the world!"

The final indigenous resource to be considered is leaders. We have already discussed some concerns about the capabilities of leaders in the movement. One person, Christopher Johnson, Imperial Klaliff, KKKK based in Michigan, commented: "The movement is very factionalized. Leaders put their egos in the way of progress. They would trade a title for white victory." Because of government repression, infiltration, and the number of legal suits against some organizations and/or their leaders, a strategy of leaderless resistance has been adopted by some elements in the movement. Others in the movement prefer the hierarchical style of an organization. Frank DeSilva, a member of the Silent Brotherhood who was released from prison in April 1995, commented on both the different types of movement leaders and the need for organization as well as ideology:

> Leaders in the "movement" fall into several categories. There are those that "honestly" believe in what they must do, and there are those who believe, but are not fully aware or sincere. Then, of course, you have those leaders who are not what they appear to be. The latter may in fact be provocateurs from one or many diverse origins, yes, and even paid provocateurs by the government—and not necessarily our national one. The end result, of course, is the disruption of the whole.
>
> Leadership in the movement is weak on several fronts. One major source of weakness is that only those, just like on a national level, who own a larger market share of the printed media share, accordingly, a disproportionate amount of "leadership." The continuous libel of one "leader" against the other serves no other purpose than to inflame petty rivalries and egos. Of course, all clamor for the light of the sun, and struggle is the way of life, it seems to me that a coordinated test of philosophies must be presented, coupled with a viable Organization(s) which will then absorb finances, recruitment, and social control over that of the host its seeks to educate and lead. It is the Corporate mentality. A mentality that most "leaders" have neither the ability nor the inclination to emulate. This is a true lack of leadership, and shows all to [sic] well the weakness of a organism without organization. The duality of *form* and *function*.

DeSilva recognizes that the movement has been infiltrated and also lacks sound leadership. He argues for leadership similar to that of corporations rather than informal means of communication.

The importance of developing a sense of consciousness is recognized by McAdam's (1982) political process model, the framing process (Snow et al. 1986), the interpretation of reality (Klandermans

1991), and the new social movements approach that has been extended by Taylor and Whittier (1995). Jack Wikoff, editor and publisher of *Remarks,* a movement publication, noted the importance of consciousness as a means to unify the movement: "The white racial nationalist movement is made up of individuals and groups of widely varying ideals. It is not monolithic. Nevertheless, we are all contributing toward a higher consciousness of race, being, and identity. . . . Some day our collective consciousness will create effective political unity." Jeremy, a second lieutenant of AN, also stressed the need for unity in spite of the fact that there were many groups:

> Politically they're basically the same and religiously they are drastically different. And I believe that all white, European Aryans wherever they live who have National Socialist or similar beliefs—irregardless of their spiritual beliefs should all band together because we're all in the cause for the same goal being—you know—white unity and Aryan brotherhood and a national state of our own.

Ron McVan of Wotansvolk—14 Word Press also pointed out how important it was to make people aware of their heritage in order to develop consciousness: "We should understand our ancestral background, the customs and traditions of our people. . . . If we don't understand who we are . . . and think with our blood . . . it would be hard to go in any direction because we'll just continue fighting each other. . . . You have to have that cohesiveness . . . and your racial family is the first step in building that foundation."

Skinheads often stress international solidarity, staying bonded (Northern Hammer Skinheads, #3 February), and maintaining a "racial tribe of tightly knit, like minded brothers and sisters. . . . We support our Skinhead brothers and Kinsmen before all others" ("We Are the Law" n.d., #4:2). At the same time, however, skinheads make it clear they desire educated dedication rather than blind loyalty. It may be that tension exists between their individualism and their group allegiance.

Bill Werner of the Templar KKKK believed the O. J. Simpson verdict of not guilty was not fair and would help make whites more racially conscious: "Hopefully due to this trial of misjustice with O. J. Simian White America will begin to open their eyes to reality and come to a conclusion that race is a major factor in this nation and White America was disgusted with the verdict. If this present trend continues with injustices the movement will indeed gain momentum." His view illustrates how the Simpson verdict and the large differences in opinion between blacks and whites about the verdict could potentially be a political opportunity that stimulates the development of white consciousness. The declining economic conditions we already mentioned could arouse awareness as well. Our finding that most people we surveyed believed the movement is growing can be interpreted as a sign of possible consciousness. Several of our respondents noted the potential for the movement to come together. In this sense consciousness could be developing in the movement, but at the same time the differences and divisions in the movement are great and are recognized as such by many of its members.

Not only is consciousness an important ingredient, but the interpretation of events and grievances is crucial in understanding the white separatist movement. The movement has been stigmatized, and boundaries have been constructed, separating it from the mainstream. One need only attend a typical rally to see how physical barriers are constructed to keep a movement group separate from those protesting the demonstration. Social boundaries are constructed in the labeling process. Movement groups are pictured as hate groups in the mainstream media. One possibility suggested in the labeling framework is that movement members will not be passive but reject the rejectors. We found this to be the case. For example, one of our interviewees, Nathan Pett of the Battle Axe Skinheads and *Hail Victory* publication, stated in our phone interview: "Especially . . . with the way things are now in this country—we're like the most hated group there is—in my opinion. . . . We're the most outcast group." Instead of accepting the label of hater, he saw the movement as being hated. How language is used by movement members to distinguish themselves from the rest of society is explored in chapter 3.

Mr. Pett had been involved in the movement for about five years and explained how some people in the movement react to the labeling process: "You pick up a complex like a persecution complex and although it is true to a certain extent—it makes you more hostile to people that would ask you about your beliefs—you become defensive—you know." We also discussed the government's infiltration of various movement groups. He pointed out:

> There's a lot of paranoia because there are people that get persecuted by the government. . . . We are persecuted because of our beliefs, but you can only take—you know—you can take precaution to an extreme where it's like

> you're paranoid and you start to sound like you're a nut. And, sometimes people—there's a lot of people in the movement now accusing all these different people of being informants, snitches—some of them are—but there's others that aren't.

Aho (1990:30) believes that the paranoia movement members exhibit is partially because of the "conflictual situations in which they often find themselves with liberal reporters, self-righteous academics, the police, and civil rights activists."

Symbols as well as words take on different meanings in the movement than in the media. The white separatist movement uses the term *cross lighting* rather than the legal and media term *cross burning.* According to the KKKK, the Klan "lights" the cross as part of its ceremony rather than "burns" it. *White Patriot*'s special issue "This is the Klan" (n.d.a.:4) maintains that the mass media calls it "burning" the cross to give the Klan a negative image. Rather, the light of the cross is to symbolize the light of Christ dispelling darkness and ignorance. The KKKK say the Klan adopted the fiery cross from old Scottish traditions where the lighted cross was a symbol of freedom from tyranny. In preparing the cross for Klan lightings, the cross is wrapped with such things as burlap or carpet that are soaked with kerosene. When the fire is ignited, the wrappings around the cross are burnt but the freshly cut wood of the cross should not be burned very much. Ron Edwards, Grand Dragon of the Federation of Klans, told us how important it was to see the cross lighting, "which is very religious to us and it's not for hatred. They don't light a cross to tell somebody to do something wrong. Cause we won't do that. . . . They pray to Jesus Christ who died upon a cross." On the basis of our observations of several cross lighting ceremonies, the cross is an integral part of a solemn ritual designed to promote feelings of unity. With the contemporary blending of Klan and Nazi symbols among certain eclectic organizations, "swastika lightings" are also conducted, sometimes in conjunction with a Klan lighting. This defining or redefining of symbols is one example of what Taylor and Whittier (1995:351) have referred to as negotiation.

The theoretical frameworks have provided us with a number of concepts that help us understand the movement, including the socioeconomic conditions, changing political opportunities, resources, consciousness, labeling, framing, interpretations of reality, boundaries, and negotiation of the meaning of symbols. More detailed information on the white separatist movement is given in the remainder of the book. Chapter 2 provides a historical perspective, especially on four key elements of this movement: the Ku Klux Klan, the National Socialists or neo-Nazis, the Christian Identity, and the skinheads. The ideology of the movement is discussed in chapter 3, and areas of agreement and disagreement in the movement are noted. Chapter 4 considers protest activities that are typically regarded as noninstitutionalized forms of behavior, followed by chapter 5's examination of linkages between the movement and mainstream politics. The book concludes by placing the movement within a broad political economy framework.

Chapter Two

Historical Overview

To understand the white separatist movement, it is helpful to develop some historical perspective. It was the KKK that began after the Civil War that initially provided the basis for the movement. Most people are acquainted with the original Klan, but fewer know about the number of divisions in today's Klans. The impetus for the second ingredient of this movement would occur with the defeat of Germany in World War I. Thus another key component of the movement would arise, the National Socialists that are commonly labeled neo-Nazi. Probably lesser known is the rise of Christian Identity in this country. In the 1980s we saw the development of skinheads in American society. These two components have helped reinvigorate this movement.

Dividing the movement into the elements of KKK, neo-Nazi or National Socialist, skinheads, and Christian Identity is not nearly as neat and straightforward as the distinction might suggest. Memberships in these groups overlap considerably, and some prominent figures have been involved in some groups and then have moved on to others or created their own groups. Specific organizations may also fall into more than one of these categories, which are overlapping rather than mutually exclusive. A few groups do not fit well into any of the specific classifications. Although we use this classification scheme of KKK, neo-Nazi or National Socialist, skinheads, and Christian Identity to simplify our discussion, it should be remembered that the pieces of the movement are complexly intertwined to form the current white separatist movement. First we look at these four groups' historical roots and then discuss their development and present-day forms. A major split between the current movement groups is also discussed.

The Ku Klux Klan and Related Organizations

Post–Civil War The KKK was founded in Pulaski, Tennessee, by former Confederate soldiers in late 1865, less than a year after the Civil War ended.[1] In 1917 the United Daughters of the Confederacy commemorated the founding of the Klan by unveiling a plaque in Pulaski that read "KU KLUX KLAN ORGANIZED IN THIS THE LAW OFFICE OF JUDGE THOMAS M. JONES, DECEMBER 24TH, 1865. NAMES OF ORIGINAL ORGANIZERS CALVIN E. JONES, JOHN B. KENNEDY, FRANK O. MCCORD, JOHN C. LESTER, RICHARD R. REED, JAMES R. CROWE." The United Daughters of the Confederacy had little reason to anticipate the kind of controversy that would arise over this plaque in the late 1980s and 1990s. In 1989 Don Massey, owner of the building, had the plaque, which was bolted to the exterior of the original building, turned around so that the inscription could not be read. This was done more in response to the 1989 Aryan Nations (AN) rally that was held in Pulaski than to Thom Robb's Knights of the Ku Klux Klan (KKKK) annual rallies (Harrington 1992) that had begun in 1986. Since then Klan rallies in Pulaski have urged that the plaque be returned to its proper position.

According to several sources, the name Ku Klux came from the Greek word *kuklos* meaning circle, band, or wheel. The reasons why the six Confederate veterans chose it are not known. It may have been simply to suggest that they would be a small closed, or secret, circle of friends, or they could have taken it from the name of a popular fraternal organization, Kuklos Adelphon (Newton and Newton 1991:vii). Such interpretation fits with the idea that the group was formed for social and entertainment reasons by young men who were rather bored. Ackridge (1978) suggests that the founders wanted to surround their organization with mystery and thus devised an oath that bound the members to absolute secrecy about Klan activities and who the other members were. The wearing of the robe and hood may have been for entertainment purposes as part of a farcical initiation ceremony into this secret organization. It may later have been used to protect their identity as they scared both whites and blacks.

In looking for a pleasant-sounding name, the founders may have changed *kuklos* to "Ku Klux" and added "clan" but spelled it "klan" to match the spelling of "Ku Klux." *Clan* could have been thought of because the founders were Scotch-Irish men who may have had romantic visions of the old Scottish clans portrayed by Sir Walter Scott, one of the South's most popular authors at the time (Tucker 1991:19). One source (Romine and Romine 1934), however, suggests that the name *Ku Klux* may have come from *Cukulcan,* who in Mexican mythology was the god of light. Some of the original founders could have heard that name from their fathers or uncles who had fought in the Mexican War. Members of the Klan at times called themselves "sons of light." Klan literature of today (*An Introduction to the KKKK,* Realm of Illinois undated leaflet) suggests that *kuklos* was selected because it illustrated some of the unique characteristics of the White (or Aryan) race. The wheel could be taken as a symbol of creativity and more specifically the creativity of the white race. The circle represents a symbol of unity. Within that context, *kuklos* would mean white racial brotherhood.

The Klan spread rapidly within Tennessee and also Mississippi and Alabama. In early 1867 the Pulaski leaders requested each den (individual organization) to send delegates to a national convention in Nashville, Tennessee. General Nathan Bedford Forrest, a famous Confederate cavalry leader, was elected Grand Wizard, the leader of the national organization. Evidently it was here that the name "invisible empire," meaning the territory where Klans existed, was coined. The territory was divided into dominions, dominions into provinces, with the provinces having local klans called dens. Many former Confederate officers of high rank played important roles, including General Albert Pike, prominent in the Scottish Rite Masonery, who became chief judicial officer. Klan units were organized to oppose various activities associated with Reconstruction.

At the Nashville convention "the maintenance of the supremacy of the White Race in this Republic" was the main and fundamental objective of the KKK (ADL 1988a:75), but there were also calls for support of the U.S. Constitution, helping the injured and oppressed, and protecting the weak and innocent. In 1868 General Forrest estimated total Klan membership at 550,000 (ADL 1988a:76) while Newton and Newton (1991) estimate half a million members in a dozen states at its peak in the late 1860s.

Interpretations of the nature of officially organized Klan activities vary by how favorably disposed one is to the Klan. A very positive view of the Klan would say that "from this humble beginning the Klan arose, in a few years, like a Phoenix from her ashes, to dominate the South during reconstruction times, to eventually expel the carpetbagger and the scalawag from her State governments, and to recapture for her people the rule of law and the courts" (Ackridge 1978:17). On the opposing side, the KKK has been labeled the "world's oldest, most persistent terrorist organization. . . . the Ku Klux Klan was actively harassing, torturing and murdering in the United States. Today the members remain fanatically committed to a course of violent opposition to social progress and racial equality" (Newton and Newton 1991:vi).

Certainly there were masked night riders and "ghosts" scaring blacks. Some Klansmen went beyond this, using more violent tactics including whippings and murders. But there were those who didn't belong to the Klan who wore the Klan regalia while they committed crimes in order to cast suspicion on the Klan (Tucker 1991:20). In 1869 General Forrest formally disbanded the Klan, but that did not mean its activities stopped. There have been differing interpretations of why he dissolved the Klan formally. Some argue it was because Southern whites were regaining their control of the states, and others suggest it was because things had gotten out of his control with many upper-class Southerners concerned by the excesses of the Klan (Tucker 1991:20). Beam (1983:3), a former Texas Klan Grand Dragon and AN ambassador-at-large, points out in his *Essays of a Klansman* that Forrest may have broken up the Klan to protect himself and others from being charged by the government for things the Klan did. When Forrest and other Klan leaders were called to testify to the U.S. Congress about the Klan, they were able to point out that the Klan had been officially dissolved.

The Klan in the Early 1900s The second Klan, and by far the largest, was started in 1915 by "Colonel" William Simmons. Before that, Thomas Dixon wrote a trilogy, including *The Clansman,* about Reconstruction in the South and the role of the Klan. Dixon's work provided much of the basis for D. W. Griffith's silent movie *The Birth of a Nation* that premiered in 1915. In a nutshell, the movie shows that the first Klan was a significant factor in saving the South and preserving its way of life. The film generated great controversy, including egg throwing at the screen and a near riot in a Northern city. In Southern cities its debut was warmly received.

Indeed, Simmons used the premiere of the film in Atlanta to help him found the second Klan. On Thanksgiving Eve 1915 Simmons took several of his supporters to Stone Mountain, Georgia (not far from

Atlanta), to give rebirth to the Klan and conduct a cross-lighting ceremony. On December 7 Simmons placed an advertisement announcing "The World's Greatest Secret (Social, Patriotic, Fraternal, Beneficial) Order" adjacent to an announcement of *The Birth of a Nation*. According to Beam (1983:3), the popularity of the film was "the spark which helped ignite the flame of the Klan in the 1920's." Indeed the film grossed more than $60 million (Newton and Newton 1991:51).

"Colonel" Simmons, who was never a colonel in the military, did serve in the Spanish American War. He was a circuit-riding Methodist preacher who was defrocked in 1912 on the grounds of inefficiency and "moral impairment" (Newton and Newton 1991:520) and later became a fraternal organizer. Simmons is responsible for the development of certain Klan rituals and changing many of the titles of Klan officials at the local level to begin with "kl" (e.g., "Kligrapp" for "secretary," "klabee" for "treasurer") (Beam 1983:4). The flaming cross symbol was probably first used by this second Klan. Some writers, including ones supportive of the Klan, have thought that the flaming cross idea came from Scottish tradition when it was used to rally or warn clans in the old Scottish Highlands. However, its use may well be related more to Simmons's background as a Methodist, because the Methodist Church uses imagery of the cross and fire (Tucker 1991:20).

Simmons lacked good organizational skills, so in 1920 he signed a contract with Edward Young Clarke of Atlanta to raise money and attract new members. Clarke, in conjunction with his coworker Elizabeth Tyler, increased membership from a few thousand to 100,000 in a year and a half. Then in October 1921 the U.S. House of Representatives Committee on Rules conducted hearings on the Klan at which Simmons repeatedly stressed the benevolent and fraternal aspects of the Klan. As a result, the Klan was overwhelmed with letters from people who wanted to start their own local organizations. The Klan may have gained 1.1 million new members in the next year. Simmons claimed, "Congress made us" (Rice 1972:8).

In spite of the rapid gain of members, all was not well within the leadership structure. Some wanted Simmons replaced, possibly because of his health problems (including heavy drinking), questionable organizing skills, or his corrupt policies. Simmons claimed he was tricked into not putting his name up for reelection; Hiram Wesley Evans became Simmons's successor. Evans introduced certain reforms including: (1) Each Klan functionary was given a modest salary rather than receiving substantially greater amounts from initiation fees and sales of Klan regalia, (2) Klansmen who were not behaving in a moral way were to be expelled and background checks of applicants were made, (3) acts of terrorism or vigilantism were condemned, and (4) the Klan should try to become a powerful factor in local, state, and national politics (Rice 1972:10–11). Supporters had been upset at the rich lifestyles of Klan leaders like Simmons, who reportedly was making $1,000 a month with unlimited expense accounts and had been given a $33,000 home and two high-priced cars by supporters (Rice 1972:11). Many other Americans became concerned about the Klan's desire to play significant political roles, including running for office.

Estimates of membership in this second Klan vary somewhat, but it is clear that it was a mass movement. Zerzan (1993:48) mentions that estimates ran between 2 and 8 million. Goldberg (1981:vii) states at its height it could have been as much as 6 million members. Others (Newton and Newton 1991:ix; Rice 1972:13) estimate around 4 million. Membership was not something reserved for the South but was actually greater north of the Mason-Dixon line, with particular success in the Midwest.

There are numerous examples of famous people who at one time belonged to or supported the Klan. President Warren Harding was initiated into the Klan in the Green Room of the White House by William Simmons and others. The Klansmen evidently forgot to bring their Bible, and Harding used the White House Bible to administer the final oath (Newton and Newton 1991). Supreme Court Justice Hugo Black was a member of the Klan during the early 1920s.

President Truman may have joined or nearly joined the Klan in the early 1920s. In a supposed meeting with a Klan organizer, Truman was asked to state that he wouldn't hire Catholics if elected. Truman refused and apparently his $10 initiation fee was returned. McCullough (1992:165) explained Truman's original decision to join:

> It had been a grievous mistake ever to have said he would join in the first place. . . . In his [Truman's] defense later, it would be said that the Klan in 1922 seemed still a fairly harmless organization to which a good God-fearing patriot might naturally be attracted, that it offered a way for those who felt at odds with the changes sweeping the country to make known their views.

President Woodrow Wilson had a private screening of *The Birth of a Nation* and declared, "It is like writing history with lightning, and my only regret is that it is all so terribly true" (Wade 1987:126). The next day Supreme Court Chief Justice Edward White, a former Klan member, and other Washington dignitaries previewed the film. Wilson and White endorsed the film but later recanted when the film generated so much controversy.

Support for the Klan seems to have fallen precipitously in the late 1920s and 1930s. Although several reasons can be suggested, it remains difficult to understand why its decline was so rapid. There were major internal conflicts in the Klan and several leaders were indicted for a variety of crimes related to corruption or immorality. The arrest and conviction of Indiana's Grand Dragon D. C. Stephenson for the rape and mutilation of a woman who shortly thereafter took poison and died is an excellent example of the type of problems certain Klan leaders had. It may also be that people became increasingly aware of and concerned about the violent activities of the Klan. Although some Klan leaders had been successfully elected to public office, they found it much more difficult to live up to the promises they had made while campaigning. In 1939 Hiram Evans resigned the leadership of the Klan and James Colescott took over. In 1944 the Internal Revenue Service (IRS) proclaimed the Klan owed $685,000 in back taxes. Colescott then officially disbanded the KKK.

What did the Klan of the 1920s represent and who were the members? One could answer this easily if one simply followed the stereotypes of the Klan that have been offered by journalists and social scientists alike. That portrayal would stress how the second Klan extended their antiblack beliefs to include anti-Semitism, anti-Catholicism, and anti-immigrant views. Typically Klansmen would be uneducated rednecks from small towns and rural areas, Protestant fundamentalists, and narrow-minded extremists on the fringe of society. Some would maintain they suffered from extreme status anxiety and felt they were losing their place in American society.

Such a description has been challenged recently by revisionist historians who point out that the picture is much more complex. Many Klan members came from urban areas, and although they were Protestant, they often were not fundamentalists. In fact, the average Klan member was much like the average American. The Klan's concerns varied a great deal by locality, although typically important was the government's failure to enforce Prohibition. The Klan often thrived in places that had a *small* percentage of minorities. The thesis of the revisionist scholars seems to be thus: "The Klan's racist, nativist, and often violent rhetoric was a poor guide to its behavior; KKK members primarily engaged in scrupulously legal battles against local politicians and businessmen—the great majority also being native-born Protestants—who were lax about enforcing Prohibition and financing more and better public schools" (Kazin 1992:140). L. Moore (1992:24) points out in his review article of historical interpretations of the Klan: "There can be no argument that the Klan's racist, anti-Catholic, anti-Semitic ideology was offensive and threatening to many Americans during the 1920s. To describe such ideas as extremist and pathological, however, is to paint a rather distorted picture of mainstream racial and ethnic attitudes." Blee's work on women in the 1920s Klan also points out how well the Klan's racism fit into the white Protestant culture of the Midwest that valued religious and racial homogeneity and distrusted outsiders. The Klan not only mirrored the racist attitudes of the majority, but it "provided an organizational means to transform fears and resentment into political action" (Blee 1991:155).

Rather than seeing the KKK simply as an aberration in American society in the 1920s, one should understand how in certain ways it agreed with much of the values in American society. Recognizing this not only gives us a more accurate view of the Klan but also tells us much about the United States at that time. In explaining why the Klan of the 1920s has often been pictured as deviant, Ribuffo (1983:xviii) notes that most scholars, whether they emphasize conflict or consensus in their writings, share a common flaw in that they hesitate "to take seriously groups that retard 'progress.' " Kazin (1992:136) puts it another way: "Historians like most people are reluctant to sympathize with people whose political opinions they detest," so they often avoid doing scholarly research projects about such movements.

In trying to characterize the Klan movement as a whole, L. Moore (1992) believes that the word *populist* may be most appropriate and better than *extremist, terrorist,* or *nativist. Populist* for him refers to the desire for greater popular control socially and politically. Further, L. Moore (1991:11) maintains in his book *Citizen Klansmen* that the largest state Klan of the 1920s (Indiana) engaged in "a movement that was united by a temporary but powerful outpouring of ethnic nationalism, and that concerned itself primarily not with ethnic minorities but with promoting the ability of average citizens to influence the workings of society and government." The Klan was an interest group for average white Protestants who believed their values should dominate over those of the elite in society. Both Kazin and L. Moore agree that the Klan's chief conflict was with elites who typically were white. The revisionist approach has never gained dominance and also has its critics. For example, Maclean believes such an approach denies the Klan's inherently violent nature, doesn't fully recognize its racism, and becomes an apology for the Klan (Moore 1990:357).

Post–World War II Klan and Related Activists After World War II, Klan activity by basically independent Klan groups was limited until the civil rights movement grew in strength. In the *Brown vs. Board of Education* (of Topeka) Supreme Court decision, schools were to be desegregated. White Citizen Councils were formed and the Klans grew as well. During the time of the civil rights movement, the National States Rights Party (NSRP) was significant. It was formed in 1958 with Ed Fields and Jesse B. Stoner playing significant roles. At one time, Stoner was a KKK Kleagle while Fields was a Grand Dragon of the New Order, KKKK. Stoner ran for political office several times, including in 1970 for governor of Georgia on the NSRP ticket, receiving less than 3 percent of the vote. In 1972 he gathered 40,600 votes in a race for U.S. Senate and then 71,000 votes in a race for lieutenant governor of Georgia (Newton and Newton 1991:544–5). Based on our interview with him at an AN World Congress meeting and other sources of information, Stoner is very adept at coining some memorable racist and anti-Semitic phrases. In 1945 he founded the Stoner Anti-Jewish party, wanting to "make being a Jew a crime, punishable by death" (ADL 1988b:159). In 1946 he claimed Adolf Hitler was "too moderate" (Newton and Newton 1991:545). In one of his campaigns he stated: "You can't have law and order and niggers, too" (ADL 1988b:159). According to a document of a *New York Times* article submitted to the House on Un-American Activities Committee (HUAC 1965) investigation of the Klan, Stoner proclaimed at a Klan rally in Jacksonville, Florida, on May 3, 1964: "People in other parts of the country like to think of niggers as human beings because they have hands and feet. So do apes and gorillas have hands and feet . . . the only good nigger is a dead nigger" (HUAC 1965:3686).

In 1977 Stoner was indicted and then charged as a "conspirator" in the 1958 bombing of a Birmingham church. George and Wilcox (1992:383) point out that while many may have believed that the church was one in which several black children were killed, the indictment reads that the church was empty at the time. Although the charges came about 20 years after the event, Stoner was convicted and lost an appeal. He served three and a half years and was released in 1986. He then founded Crusade Against Corruption, which featured his slogan "Thank God for AIDS." Crusade Against Corruption (n.d.) literature helps explain his reasoning: "God is intervening on earth with AIDS to destroy His enemies and to rescue and preserve the White race. **AIDS is a racial disease** of jews and negroids that also eradicates sodomites."

Fields, who has never run for political office, founded NSRP and was essentially the organization person of the party. The ADL (1988b:44) states that "NSRP has been a significant anti-Black, anti-Jewish organization functioning as both a propaganda mill and a political party. Ideologically hybrid, it was a bridge between the Ku Klux Klan and the American neo-Nazi groups." The constitution and bylaws of the NSRP illustrate its anti-Semitism: "Jew-devils have no place in a White Christian nation. When our party is elected . . . the Government will expel the Jews and confiscate their ill-gotten wealth for the benefit of the American people. Communism is Jewish" (taken from George and Wilcox 1992:364).

When Stoner was in jail, there seems to have been problems between some supporters of Stoner in NSRP and Ed Fields. Fields left the party but retained control of *The Thunderbolt,* its monthly newspaper. Fields later changed the name of the newspaper to *The Truth at Last,* and NSRP eventually faded away. Fields and others are now involved in the America First Party, which is described in their brochure as "America's new Third Party with a Platform of ACTION to protect the rights of the majority. The two major parties have become captives of political action committees, special interest lobbies and of the organized minorities. The voice of the majority is no longer heard in Washington" (America First Party Inc. n.d., received 1994).

In the 1950s the U.S. Klans' KKKK led by E. L. Edwards was probably the strongest Klan. Edwards incorporated the U.S. Klans in 1955 in Georgia and in 1956 had one of the largest Klan rallies in years, drawing about 3,000 to Stone Mountain. He was never able, however, to unify the various independent Klans (ADL 1988b:81). In 1960 membership in the U.S. Klans was estimated between 15,000 and 23,000 (with a total Klan membership of 35,000 to 50,000) (ADL 1988b:92). Splintered Klan groups met in 1960 to form the National Klan Committee that seemed to unite in part on the basis of their opposition to Edwards. The confederation of Klan groups became known as the National Knights of the Ku

Klux Klan. James Venable, an Atlanta attorney, led the organization with an estimated 7,000 to 9,000 members, mostly in Georgia.

Robert Shelton was a state leader for the U.S. Klans until he was removed after disagreements with Edwards (although some sources indicate Edwards later reinstated him). Shelton consolidated numerous local Klans in the Alabama Klan. When Edwards died in 1960, there was considerable infighting and a new group emerged called the Invisible Empire, United Klans, Knights of the Ku Klux Klan of America, Inc. Their name was shortened to United Klans of America (UKA) with Shelton becoming Imperial Wizard in 1961. This organization then became the largest Klan group; during the 1960s it was estimated to have about 26,000 supporters from Klans directly affiliated with it or semiautonomous. The UKA has been regarded as one of the more militant and violent Klans following the traditional ideas of the Klan as a secret organization.

When the U.S. Congress House on Un-American Activities Committee (HUAC 1965) investigated the Klan in the 1960s, it called more than 180 witnesses, including officers of the major Klans. Most of these Klan refused to answer the questions, pleading the Fifth Amendment. Shelton refused to give the Committee some internal Klan documents, including membership lists, and was sentenced to federal prison for contempt of Congress.

Figure 1 shows the U.S. Congressional Report diagrams of the general Klan structure, the UKA, and the National Association of Knights. The model Klan pictured in part A stresses the connections of the national level to the state and more local levels. The Imperial Office represented the highest level of the Klan organization and was ideally elected at a national convention. At the next highest level is the realm, with its leader, the Grand Dragon, being elected by a state convention (klorero) unless there aren't sufficient local units (klaverns), in which case positions are appointed by the Imperial Wizard. The UKA structure presented in part B shows how the Grand Dragons of 17 different states were linked with Imperial Wizard Shelton. The designation of realm is used for the eight Klans regarded as large enough to elect their own leaders. In part C, the National Association of KKKK is composed of relatively autonomous organizations that existed in certain states in the form of a confederation. The association headed by Venable met about three times a year to discuss mutual problems. In addition, there were independent Klan organizations, of which the most important was the White Knights of the KKK, located only in Mississippi.

A. MODEL KLAN ORGANIZATION CHART[1]

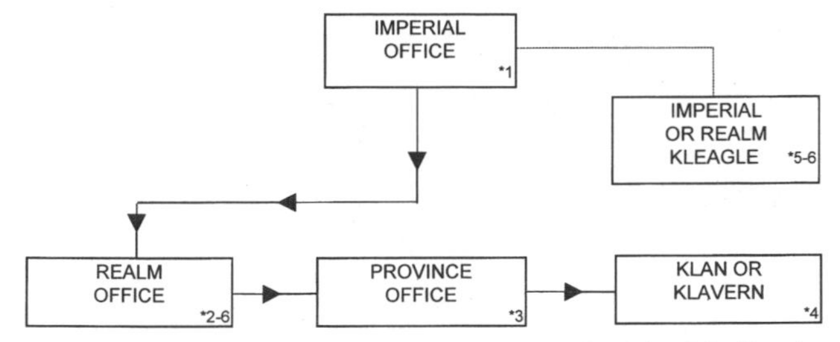

*1 Compares with National Offices - positions filled by vote of delegates, to Imperial Klonvokation or National Convention.

*2 Compares with State division of National Office - is not autonomous body. Offices filled by vote of delegates to a Klonero or State Convention.

*3 Provinces conform to the boundaries of a Congressional District. Provinces are as many as Congressional Districts assigned a given state. Officers filled by vote of delegates to Klonverse or District Convention.

*4 Compares with a club of a National or State organization. Offices filled by election of club membership.

*5 Organizer appointed by Imperial Wizard or Grand Dragon - receives portion of Klectokon or initiation fee paid by new member until Klavern has 25 members.

*6 Realm officers and Kleagles are appointed by the Imperial Wizard until membership has grown to strength sufficient to hold elections.

[1]House on Un-American Activities Committee (HUAC) House of Representatives, Activities of Ku Klux Klan Organizations in the U.S. (Exhibit #2)

B. UNITED KLANS OF AMERICA[2]

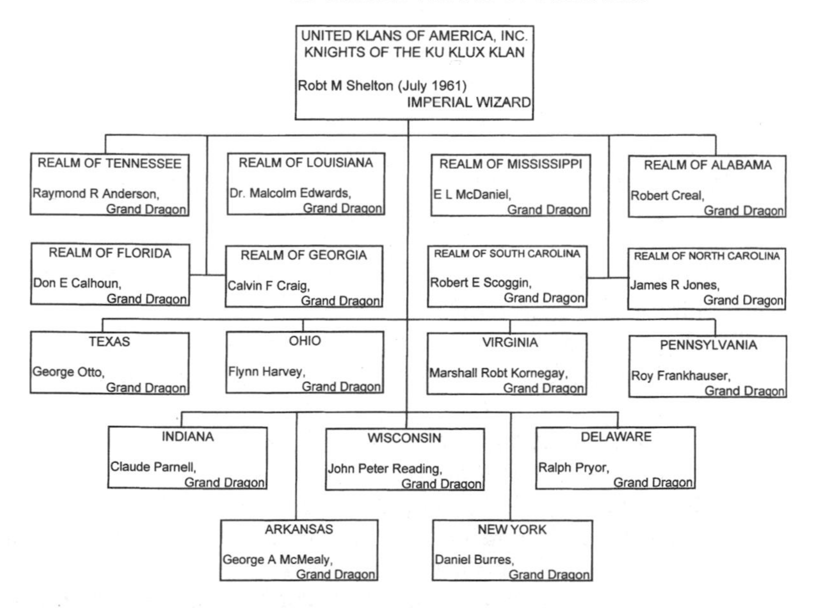

[2]**HUAC, Exhibit #7, p. 1542**

Figure 1. Klan Organizational Charts in the 1960s.

C. NATIONAL ASSOCIATION OF KNIGHTS OF THE KU KLUX KLAN[3]

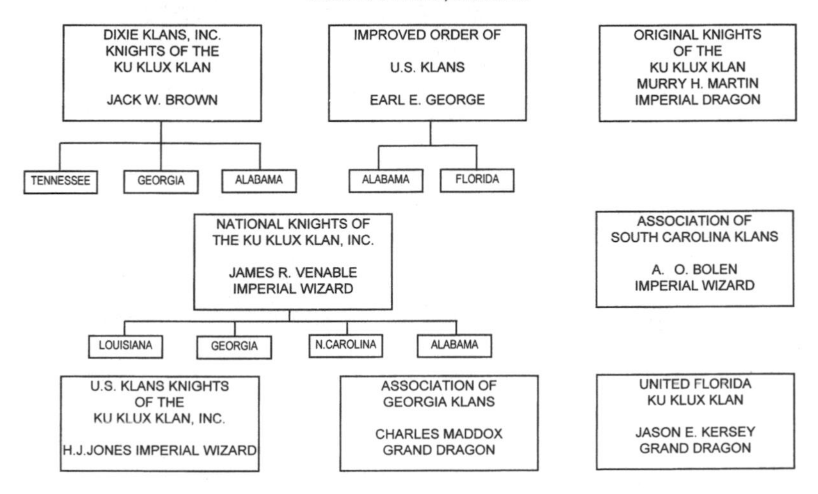

[3]HUAC, Exhibit #8, p. 1544

Figure 1. (*continued*)

On November 9, 1965, the chair of the U.S. House of Representatives, Subcommittee of the Committee on Un-American Activities (HUAC 1965:2330–32) declared the following:

1. The Klan is not a monolithic movement but has about a dozen different organizations.
2. Before the investigation Klan membership had been estimated at about 10,000 but it's now believed to be four or five times greater.
3. The largest Klan group is the UKA which has not fully reported its income nor paid taxes as it should have.
4. Klans have used innocent sounding cover or front names such as hunting, fishing or sportsmen's groups or civic association to hide their klaverns and their bank accounts.
5. A considerable number of Klan members have criminal records, carry weapons, and use cross burnings for intimidation. Klan units have training schools to teach members how

to use rifles and other weapons as well as make demolition devices, Molotov cocktails, etc.

6. There are secret Klan organizations using names like The Vigilantes or Black Knights that carry out violent or terrorist acts.
7. Only a small minority of law enforcement support the Klan.
8. "There are some basically good and decent American citizens who have apparently been deceived into joining the Klan by its patriotic and noble sounding propaganda."

In addition to the Congressional investigation, the government attempted to disrupt the Klan as part of the FBI's Counterintelligence Program (COINTELPRO) against right and left extremist groups. Starting in 1964 and "officially" concluding in 1971, COINTELPRO engaged in many activities to make life difficult for the Klan. According to Wade (1987:361) "COINTELPRO was essentially a Hoover-hatched scheme of cheap psychological warfare and dirty tricks." Of 404 proposed activities against 17 Klan groups and 9 white racist groups, 289 were used (Finch 1983:158). Some of these were legal but others were more questionable, including a smear campaign of Shelton. Postcards were sent to secret Klansmen stating, "Klansmen—Trying to hide your identity behind a sheet? You received this—somebody knows who you are!" or "Which Klan leader is spending your money tonight?" (Finch 1983:16; Wade 1987:362). In addition, FBI agents provided money to Klansmen to form independent Klans. Agents strongly encouraged employers of Klansmen to let them go. Informers or infiltrators often tried to harass Klansmen including sleeping with wives of Klan leaders to get information and to create marital strife. The FBI also developed a letter sent to the wives of Klansmen telling them their husbands were having affairs with other women (Wade 1987:362).

O'Reilly (1989:198) maintains that COINTELPRO not only wanted to see that Klansmen were punished for their activities but also that the Klan would be brought "into disrepute" to make the American public aware of the evils of the Klan. Informants had so penetrated the Klan that in 1965 the FBI had more than 2,000 informants in the various Klans, including the Grand Dragon of one realm and high-ranking officers in seven organizations (Newton and Newton 1991:194). Wade (1987:362) points out that "at its very worst, COINTELPRO may have actually provoked Klan violence in order to arrest its perpetrators." The most-cited example of this is how two paid informants "set up" Thomas

Tarrants by persuading him to bomb the home of a Jewish businessman in Mississippi in 1968. Tarrants was severely wounded, being shot several times, and his companion, Kathy Ainsworth, a schoolteacher, was killed by the police (Newton and Newton 1991:195; Wade 1987:363). When newsman Jack Nelson in his book *Terror in the Night* described the FBI's role in setting up Tarrants, FBI Director Hoover tried to spread unfounded rumors about Nelson and have him fired (Newton and Newton 1991:195). COINTELPRO and the Congressional investigations were extremely successful in reducing the strength of the Klan. From 1967 to 1973 the Klan lost a large part of its membership and many klaverns folded. George Wallace's presidential campaign also attracted previous or potential members of the Klan (Wade 1987).

In the 1970s some members of Shelton's UKA were involved in racial episodes in Talledega County, Alabama, and in the hanging of a young black teenager, Michael Donald, in 1981. In addition to the criminal case involving the death of Donald, an Alabama civil suit was filed against the UKA organization by the SPLC. There was a $7 million damage award in 1987, with the UKA being forced to surrender its national headquarters building in Tuscaloosa, Alabama, to help pay part of the damages. Since then the UKA has not been publicly active.

In the mid-1970s David Duke took over the leadership of the KKKK in Louisiana. David Duke did not fit the typical Imperial Wizard image because he had a college degree, was young, very good looking, and quite articulate. He told his supporters: "We've got to get out of the cow pasture and into the hotel meeting rooms" (Wade 1987:368). He attempted to mainstream the Klan and to attract the young by recruiting on college campuses. Duke was supposedly the first in Klan history to accept women as equal members and also encouraged Catholics to join (ADL 1988b:84). He organized various local Klan units in a number of states and used the media to gain attention for his cause. In spring 1978 Duke went on a political tour of Great Britain, where his racist presentations irritated many. The Home Secretary in Britain ordered Duke to be deported, but he managed to avoid Scotland Yard for some time before he returned to the United States.

In 1980 Duke resigned from the KKKK. According to some sources, Duke had offered to sell his membership lists to a competing Klan organization for $35,000, in part because he allegedly wanted to found a new organization that appealed more to the middle class. Duke never admitted he tried to sell the list, but he left the Klan and founded the National Association for the Advancement of White People (NAAWP), which describes itself as a civil rights organization that "maintains that there should be equal rights and opportunities for all, including Whites! It believes that White people need to defend and preserve their civil rights, heritage, and basic interests, just as Blacks and other non-Whites do" (NAAWP 1992a:6). After Duke, Paul Allen became president of NAAWP. SPLC (1997a) found that NAAWP increased from 8 chapters in 1995 to 18 chapters in different states in 1996. "Prime Time Live" featured the organization in a May 1997 program. David Duke was scheduled to speak at the third annual rally of the NAAWP in 1997.

Duke chose legitimate political means to attract attention and garner support. He ran for political office several times, the first time in 1975 when he was a member of the Klan, although he did not mention his Klan connections. In 1988 and 1992 he was a candidate for the presidency of the United States. When Duke announced his candidacy for president in 1988 in Georgia, Ed Fields was there. Ralph Forbes, a member of Rockwell's American Nazi Party (ANP) from 1959 to 1967, became Duke's campaign manager.

When Duke left the Klan, his Alabama Grand Dragon, Don Black, took over. However, Black was arrested and sentenced to three years for planning to invade Dominica, a Caribbean island, and then overthrow its government. Although he tried to retain leadership, the organization split, with a second faction led first by Stanley McCollum and then by Thom Robb. Robb's organization became the largest Klan after the fall of the Invisible Empire in 1993. In 1994 the KKKK experienced serious splits, especially within the Midwest. Robb's literature stresses how his Klan has achieved higher status than many others:

> We do want to mention that the Knights of the Ku Klux Klan, under the leadership of Thomas Robb has grown to be the largest and most professional White Rights organization in America. There are, however, others who have used the name Ku Klux Klan is [*sic*] less than honorable ways. Just because you have seen someone claiming to be a member of the Klan does not mean that they are a member of The Knights. Other "Klan" groups are usually very small, have poorly educated "leadership" and are an embarrassment to the memory of the original Klan. (KKKK n.d.a.)

SPLC (1997b) identified chapters of the KKKK in only five states in 1996.

At one time, Tom Metzger was also a member of Duke's national Klan but left it and formed his own California Klan. He ran for political office in 1980 as a Democratic congressional candidate, receiving 33,000 votes in the primary and winning the nomination. In the election, his vote total remained about the same while his opposition received about 254,000 votes. Metzger later left his own Klan and then campaigned for the U.S. Senate, receiving 75,313 votes, about 2.8 percent of the votes cast in California. The first organization he created after his withdrawal from the Klan was the White American Political Association (WAPA). He changed it to the more militant-sounding White American Resistance in 1983, with a publication of the same name, and explained the ideological significance of the name change:

> The name of our new group was White American Resistance. It was an ideological change. And I liked the acronym: WAR. When you choose words, it is very important to choose strong ones. WAR was a deliberate move to scare off the weak-kneed people from my group. It worked.
>
> With WAR, I became even more serious in my political endeavors. Rather than trying to work with the system, as I had done with WAPA, I shifted my stance and became more anti-system than ever. I condemned the federal government, the idle rich, the one-party political system, the "minorities," and the white public at large, for being worthless hypocrites. (Metzger 1996c:160)

Later in 1984 he changed the name to White Aryan Resistance (WAR) because American could include Hispanics, Jews, and others who lived in the United States.

Zia (1991:25) suggests that *WAR* may "represent the most naked expression of white supremacy." Similarly, George and Wilcox (1992:375) have noted that the publication contains "some of the most outspoken and vehement racist and anti-Jewish rhetoric in the neo-Nazi movement. There are no subtleties or nuances. Metzger's views are right up front." Although Metzger initially had Klan ties, he has broken from much of the traditional racial right wing and stresses his own philosophy of resistance.

Tom Metzger and his son John lost a civil suit against themselves and WAR for the beating death of an Ethiopian male, named Mulugeta Seraw, by skinheads in Portland, Oregon; the judgment totaled $12.5 million. George and Wilcox (1992:376–7) and Diamond (1995:269) pointed out that Morris Dees of SPLC argued in the lawsuit that Tom and John Metzger were responsible for Seraw's death because they had given Dave Mazella, a skinhead organizer, instructions to organize and motivate Portland skinheads. Skinheads other than Mazella were the ones involved in the actual death of Seraw. The doctrine Dees advocated is an argument of vicarious liability, which is of concern to many civil libertarians. Even some liberal and leftist papers expressed concern about the decision and about the veracity of Mazella's testimony (George and Wilcox 1992:376; Diamond 1995:269). The Metzgers appealed their case but lost, and the Supreme Court refused to hear it. Metzger (1996c:205) summarized his views of the case in his autobiography:

> I feel that the First Amendment's right to free speech should have protected us against liability. I believe that Judge Haggerty made legal errors during the trial. And I know that David Mazzella committed perjury on the witness stand.

WAR continues to operate a newspaper, a telephone hot line, and the *Race and Reason* TV programs, as well as distribute books, videotapes, compact discs, and cassettes.

At one time Bill Wilkinson also belonged to Duke's Klan but quarreled with Duke and left to form the Invisible Empire, KKKK in 1975. It was Wilkinson who claimed that Duke had offered to sell him the Knights' membership list in 1980. In 1981 the press reported that Wilkinson had been a paid FBI informer since 1974. Wilkinson claimed that he only revealed things that were typically already known and had appeared in the newspapers; however, needless to say, his organization lost membership. Then in 1983 he declared bankruptcy due to an IRS lien for back taxes and a lawsuit filed by the SPLC growing out of the 1979 Decatur, Alabama, riots in which four people were shot.

Wilkinson was succeeded by James Blair, who resigned due to ill health. James W. Farrands of Shelton, Connecticut, a Roman Catholic tool and die maker, was selected as Imperial Wizard in 1986. He eventually moved the Invisible Empire headquarters from Shelton, Connecticut, to Gulf, North Carolina. With the decline of the UKA, the Invisible Empire probably became the largest Klan organization. The SPLC also became involved in a suit against the Invisible Empire. The Invisible Empire disbanded in 1993 based on an agreement made in the U.S. District Court in Atlanta. Originally the Invisible Empire and the Southern White Knights were found guilty of depriving Forsyth County, Georgia, marchers of their civil rights and ordered to pay damages. The Invisible Empire, estimated at having 4,000 members (ARI 1994:6,7), was ordered to give up their rights to the name Invisible Empire Knights of the Ku Klux Klan, to Empire Publishing and to their newspaper *The Klansman,* and to destroy their mailing list. They were ordered to pay $37,500 and surrender more than $25,000 in office equipment and unsold Klan merchandise.

At the time of the dissolution of the Invisible Empire, a new group was formed, called the Unified Ku Klux Klan, which clearly rejected ties to skinheads and neo-Nazis. According to Farrands, "No Klansman or Klan group will associate with any Neo-Nazi's [*sic*] or Skinheads or any other group that associates with Skinheads or Nazi's [*sic*]" and "A Klansman is a Klansman pure and simple" (*The Klansman* n.d.:1). Since it appeared that Farrands was trying to evade the 1993 court order by simply changing the name of his organization, SPLC lawyers returned to court. In July 1994 the federal court in Atlanta approved a decree that ordered Farrands to dissolve the corporation and no longer operate or participate in any white supremacy organization or activity (SPLC 1994c:7).

The Bedford Forrest Brigade is one of the Klan groups that had been a regional affiliate of the Invisible Empire before it was disbanded. John Murphy, the commander of that independent Florida-based group, wrote us that it was a small group that did not actively recruit, so they could be very selective in their membership. Small numbers meant they were "more secure." Murphy shared some general information on his membership:

> The typical Klansman in our organization is between 20 and 40 years old, male, skilled worker, blue collar worker, fundamentalist background, structured personal habits, regular churchgoer, stable family relationships (divorce is rare). He has strong values and is frustrated by changing social trends. He tends to resent government intrusion. Is conservative politically. Most are southerners many from farming or rural stock. We do admit women and have some professional people, but the stereotype holds most of the time.

While organizations like Robb's and Farrands's Klans and the American KKKK in Indiana have taken positions against National Socialists and skinheads or at least some National Socialists and skins who display Nazi symbols, other Klans may work with them and attend each other's rallies. Two quite significant events help illustrate linkages between Klan and neo-Nazis. In the late 1930s there was talk of merging the Klan and the German-American union, or organization, referred to as the Bund. On August 18, 1940, there was a joint rally at the Bund's 200-acre compound, called Camp Nordland, near Andover, New Jersey. Supposedly about 800 Bundsmen greeted 200 Klansmen and several hundred of their friends. Afterward this meeting attracted a great deal of national attention and concern, followed by a congressional investigation that was particularly critical of the Bundsmen (Wade 1987:271–72).

The second major event was the November 3, 1979, Greensboro, North Carolina shoot-out between Communist activists and a group of both neo-Nazis and Klansmen. Five Communist Worker Party (CWP) activists were killed at what was to be a "Death to the Klan" rally. The Klansmen and neo-Nazis were tried twice but acquitted. At one of the trials it came out that Bureau of Alcohol Tobacco and Firearms (BATF) agent Bernard Butkovich had infiltrated a unit of the American Nazi party but failed to inform the police of the planned confrontation. In addition, an FBI and Greensboro police-paid informant, Edward Dawson, was active in the Klan. On November 6, 1985, Dawson and several others were found liable for $394,459 in a civil suit (George and Wilcox 1992:186–189).

The Klan has changed considerably over time. While it started as one organization, it has split into numerous groups. According to the SPLC's (1995a) listing of hate groups in different states in the United States, there were 98 Klan groups in 1994, 94 in 1995 (1996a), and only 73 in 1996 (1997b). According to SPLC (1997b), the International Keystone Knights of the Ku Klux Klan has the most chapters (13) in different states. The Klan has also had links with other groups, including National Socialists, which we will now consider.

National Socialists or Neo-Nazis in America

Rather than use "neo-Nazi" loosely to categorize people because they are anti-Semitic or overbearing and authoritarian, we follow George and Wilcox's (1992:351) definition of "neo-Nazi" as referring to an organization or party that typically uses Nazi symbolism, calls themselves Nazi, or National Socialist, and shows high regard for Adolf Hitler and the Third Reich. The swastika, described as an even or equilateral cross, the arms of which are bent at right angles, is the most well known symbol of Nazi Germany. Although the origins are unknown, it signifies good luck and for thousands of years appeared as a symbol of the sun, of infinity, and of continuing re-creation in places like China, Egypt, Greece, Scandinavia, and North and South America. It has been found in the relics around the site of Troy, the catacombs of Rome, and the textiles of the Inca period. In *Mein Kampf,* Hitler declared that the swastika represented "the fight for victory of Aryan man and of the idea of creative work, which in itself eternally has been anti-Semitic and eternally will be anti-Semitic" (Fried 1980:677). In 1935 the black swastika on a white circle with a crimson background became the national flag of Germany. Because of the close association of the swastika with Hitler and National Socialism, the leaders of the Allied occupation of Germany ordered it removed from public view after World War II.

For many Americans the swastika triggers feelings of fear, hatred, or revulsion; yet the National Socialists in America continue to use the symbol. SS Action Group (n.d.a.), in a flier entitled "Why We Use the Swastika," acknowledges that its members have been told, "You'd go a lot further a lot faster if you would just drop all the 'Nazi' stuff and try a more American approach." Their response, however, is that they use it first "because it is the symbol of the National Socialist movement, and for us not to use it or use anything else would be dishonest." Second, the swastika is viewed as the most ancient symbol of the white race, and people must be educated to learn the importance of the symbol. Third, using the swastika gives them a tactical advantage because when people see it, they pay attention. The boldness of the symbol is viewed as keeping people who are weak-willed and cowardly away from the movement.

Our informal conversation with Charles Hall, the commander of White Aryan Legion, and three of White Aryan Legion's supporters confirmed the influence of the swastika and other German symbols on these National Socialists. When asked how they got involved in the movement, Dan explained:

I have always felt that the white race was the master race. Ever since I was a very small child. When I saw documentaries on TV about World War II and Hitler and things like that—I was totally fascinated—totally fascinated. And I thought well, I guess this is what children sometimes think is that if it's forbidden fruit, then you must taste it to see why it's forbidden.

But I've always had a very positive attitude towards Nazism and the Third Reich and Adolf Hitler. I don't know. I felt it deep inside me, always, that there was something good about this and some people were spending an awful lot of time and energy to make it look the other way. So, I had to find out why it was. Once I started doing heavy research into it and that's when I realized that Adolf Hitler was right the whole time.

Charles Hall indicated he felt pretty much the same way, saying that when he played war as a child he wanted to be a German, and commented: "You know, a true white separatist—a true National Socialist . . . always felt the same way. Was always attracted to the swastika and, you know, the iron cross and stuff. . . . The swastika without a doubt is the most hated symbol, but it should be the most loved and cherished symbol that there is. . . . When you put . . . a swastika on your skin or you wear it on a shirt, you've separated yourself from 99.9 percent of the population."

Thus we see how for some in the movement the swastika is used as a major symbol, in spite of the fact that it has been rejected by most in American society. National Socialists are rejecting the rejecters.

Pre–World War II Nazis in America Canedy (1990), in *America's Nazis: A History of the German American Bund,* argues that to understand the Nazi influence in America, one must first look at World War I and its effects. The U.S. Census of 1910 found 8,282,618 German Americans (born in Germany or of German-born parents) in a population of about 92 million. Although the large majority were loyal to the United States, some were not. Particularly after the United States entered the war, Germanophobia swept the United States. Anti-German sentiment could be found in such things as rumors that German-speaking Red Cross workers put bacteria in medical supplies and meat packers ground glass into the sausages. The names of streets and towns were changed and sometimes the German language was not allowed to be spoken in churches, schools, and public places. German shepherd dogs were called Alsatians, the frankfurter was renamed the hot dog, and sauerkraut became liberty cabbage. Canedy (1990:13) maintains that the National Socialist "German American Bund that emerged prior to World War II was as much a product of the harsh treatment of German Americans during the World War as it was an arm of the Nazi movement." Bundist ideology was triadic in nature, trying to sound pro-American, strongly National Socialist, and also generally Germanic (Canedy 1990:74).

It is difficult to know the number of members in the German American Bund because many documents were destroyed to protect its members. At one time its leader, Fritz Kuhn, said membership was 8,299, but the Justice Department found only 6,617, of which an estimated 4,529 were in New York City. A Committee to Investigate Un-American

Activities and Propaganda reported in 1939 that a uniformed force of 5,000 was possible. By 1938 the German American Bund faced various problems, including its lack of support from Germany, investigations from the United States, declining economic strength, rivalries within its own organization, and inability to expand its support. It continued to try to superficially Americanize itself. At its 1938 convention it passed a program calling for the following:

1. A socially just, white, Gentile-ruled United States.
2. Gentile-controlled labor unions free from Jewish, Moscow-directed domination.
3. Gentiles in all positions of importance in government, national defense, and educational institutions.
4. Severing of diplomatic relations with Soviet Russia, outlawing of the Communist Party in the United States.
5. Immediate cessation of the dumping of all political refugees on the shores of the United States.
6. Thorough cleansing of the Hollywood film industries of all alien, subversive doctrines. (Canedy 1990:191–92)

On January 5, 1938, Attorney General Cummings actually reported that the FBI investigation could *not* find evidence against the Bund for any wrongdoing. HUAC, however, examined the Bund's relationship with National Socialist and other groups such as the KKK, Knights of the White Camellia, and the Silver Shirt Legion of America and concluded:

The testimony which our committee has heard reveals a widespread cooperation between half a hundred of these Nazi-Fascist groups. Interchange of speakers and literature is common. On several occasions in recent months they have endeavored to come together in some kind of a permanent federation. So far these efforts have been frustrated by organizational jealousies, but the search for a "man on horseback" goes on. (Canedy 1990:219)

This was supposedly used to prove the existence of a fascist united front, but Canedy (1990:219) points out there was no evidence regarding the Bund to support such a claim. Canedy (1990:224–25) further maintains that the German American Bund "was tried and convicted on the basis of the perception it engineered." Under the First Amendment, its activities should have been protected by the Constitution.

What happened to the German American Bund happened to other groups that were labeled as having extremist views of either the right or the left. Goodman (1968:22) states that not only was there anxiety over the parading Nazis, but the spirit of HUAC and of America itself included "the suspicion of the foreigner and nervousness over foreign ideologies" (Goodman 1968:116). The German American Bund voted to disband itself the day after Pearl Harbor, December 8, 1941.

Remak (1957:41) offers a different view of the German American Bund. He believes that had the Bund not existed, American opinion might well have reacted less strongly to German Americans than it did. The image of uniformed young men bearing the swastika while marching in Madison Square Garden added fuel to the rumors of the Nazi menace. The Bund "supplied the perfect ammunition to any anti-Nazi publicist in America who cared to use it."

Post–World War II

George Lincoln Rockwell and the American Nazi Party

The first neo-Nazi party to emerge after World War II was the National Renaissance Party (NRP), founded by James Madole in 1949. The NRP eventually associated with other National Socialist and Klan groups, including celebrating the birthday of Adolf Hitler with the KKK and the White Action Movement in 1972. According to ADL (1988a:24), George Lincoln Rockwell "launched" the American version of the post–World War II neo-Nazi movement in 1958 when he started the American Nazi Party (ANP), which he later named the National Socialist White People's Party (NSWPP). According to a White Lightning (n.d.) leaflet of Rockwell's biographical sketch, Rockwell was born in 1918 in Bloomington, Illinois, and served in the U.S. Navy during World War II. Later he was recalled for the Korean War in 1950 and trained Marine and Navy pilots. At that time he became deeply concerned about Communism and was aware of Hitler's statement that Communism is Jewish.

Rockwell's experiences illustrate an excellent example of the divisions within the movement overall. While he originally worked with numerous "right-wing" organizations, Rockwell (1966:2) eventually concluded the following: "The typically southern 'States' Rights' organizations, the 'Birch' type 'conservatives', and even the Klan, were too old-fashioned, feeble and/or unradical, I believed and still believe, to be able to attract the masses of the enraged people, once the Reds, Jews and Blacks have pushed hard enough."

Rockwell believed that it was time for the "White Man" to take America back from aliens, minorities, and terrorists. Rockwell (1977:50) wrote *White Power* to explain why: "Too many Americans are doing everything possible to hasten the death of our civilization, to welcome inferior barbarians who openly organize to murder and destroy our kind forever, all in the name of 'Brotherhood' and 'Freedom.' " The solution he proposed was white power: "Make no mistake about it I am advocating total and complete WHITE POWER in this world!" (Rockwell 1977:462). This would be achieved by whites standing together. National Socialism was viewed as a program for all people rather than just for the middle and upper classes and combined concerns for the purity and protection of the white race with a commitment to stop further "mongrelization" of whites. Rockwell spoke on college campuses and was able to get widespread media attention. The ANP often engaged in street actions and marched in military formation wearing Nazi uniforms. In August 1967 John Patler, whose artistic skills were used in the ANP publications, assassinated George Lincoln Rockwell in the parking lot of a laundromat. Patler evidently was a disgruntled party member whom Rockwell had expelled (George and Wilcox 1992:357).

Matt Koehl and the NSWPP

After Rockwell's death, Matt Koehl, who had at one time or another been a member of the NRP and NSRP, became the leader of the NSWPP. According to George and Wilcox (1992:357–58), the party experienced modest growth and stability in spite of some internal squabbling. William Pierce and Frank Collin were dismissed in 1970 and later formed their own organizations. Joseph Tommassi headed a unit of NSWPP but quit the party to form the National Socialist Liberation Front (NSLF), which was one of the more militant and underground organizations. He published the periodical *Siege* for a short time but was murdered by an NSWPP member in 1975. James Mason, who had previously been a member of NSWPP, helped revive the NSLF and *Siege* in 1980. Eventually he left NSLF but continued the publication of *Siege,* which focused on revolutionary philosophy and strategy, until 1986 (Jenkins 1992). Mason's book *Siege* (1992) is a compilation of his own writings on topics like NSLF, National Socialism, conservatism, the system, leaders, and, finally, the Universal Order, which is associated with the ideas of Charles Manson.

Over time the NSWPP under Koehl lost strength. Eventually the *White Power* newspaper ceased publication, although the *NS Bulletin* continues to be published. The organization changed its name to New Order, and the party moved to New Berlin, Wisconsin. ADL (1988a:26) states that the New Order is the most direct descendant of Hitler's party among American neo-Nazi groups and the present-day successor to Rockwell's organization, with an active core of 25 and membership of about 100.

Dr. William Pierce and National Alliance

William Pierce is a Ph.D. physicist who once taught at Oregon State University. He joined the John Birch Society and then in 1966 joined the ANP under Rockwell, editing *National Socialist World,* which was directed toward intellectuals and the academic community. After Dr. Pierce left Koehl's NSWPP, he associated with the National Youth Alliance. Later, part of it became National Alliance, directed by Dr. Pierce, which seems to appeal to the more intellectual people in the movement. Its brochure "What Is the National Alliance?" (National Office of the National Alliance 1993:2) summarizes its beliefs:

> We see ourselves as a part of Nature, subject to Nature's law. We recognize the inequalities which arise as natural consequences of the evolutionary process and which are essential to progress in every sphere of life. We accept our responsibilities as Aryan men and women to strive for the advancement of our race in the service of Life, and to be the fittest instruments for that purpose that we can be.

The group publishes *National Vanguard* and *Free Speech* and has put out a comic book called "New World Order Comix #1" (National Vanguard Books 1993), which tells the story of White Will, a high school student who is struggling against "multiculturalism" and "forced mixing" in the school. At the end of the comic, students are encouraged to write for free information from the "most politically incorrect organization," the National Alliance.

In the April 1994 issue of its *Klanwatch Intelligence Report*, SPLC (1994d) stated that, after years of decline, the National Alliance was the fastest growing neo-Nazi organization in North America and in its May 1996 report (1996b) said it was North America's largest neo-Nazi organization. It had chapters in 10 different states in 1996 (SPLC 1997b). In May 1996 attorneys for the SPLC (1996c) were successful in obtaining an $85,000 judgment against William Pierce for his involvement in a plan to hide the assets of another movement group, Church of the Creator (COTC). COTC had sold Pierce its headquarters for considerably less than its market value when COTC was involved in a lawsuit because one of its members had killed a black Gulf War veteran, Harold Mansfield. Pierce resold the former COTC property, gaining $85,000 profit, but a federal court ruled that the $85,000 should be awarded to Mansfield's family.

Perhaps the most well known publication that labels the white separatists the "good guys" is *The Turner Diaries* (1980), a novel by Andrew Macdonald (which is a pseudonym for Dr. William Pierce). Some view this book as a racial fantasy, whereas others like ADL (1987:10, 16) suggest that it provided the blueprint for the violent activities and robberies of the Silent Brotherhood. Pierce (Harrison 1990:A25) has denied instigating violence and stated: "It's clearly not a blueprint or a plan" and "It's a novel in which the action and characters serve as a vehicle for the presentation of ideas." On the other hand, the FBI has called the book "the bible of the racist right" (Macdonald 1980:back book jacket). In the novel, Earl Turner is the hero who provides a record of the days leading up to the Great Revolution, which results in the white liberation of North America and eventually the world. He becomes a member of the Order, the secret part of the Organization. White Patriots like Turner fight against the hated Equality Police and use terrorist techniques to free the Aryans. The United States is eventually purged of non-Aryans and of those whites disloyal to the white cause.

National Socialist Party of America

Frank Collin was expelled from the NSWPP when an FBI-instigated smear campaign revealed Collin's name was Cohn and he was half Jewish. Collin then founded the National Socialist Party of America (NSPA) based in Chicago. NSPA and Collin received considerable notoriety when they planned to hold a rally in Skokie, Illinois, a largely Jewish suburb, in 1977. The proposed rally became a First Amendment issue and went to the Supreme Court. Collin was told he had the right to march in Skokie but instead rallied at the Federal Building in Chicago where he faced several thousand counterdemonstrators on June 24, 1978. On July 9, 1978, in Marquette Park, Collin and about 25 NSPA members and associates held a rally where there were police with riot helmets, several hundred counterdemonstrators, and 2,500 spectators.

Harold Covington used the Skokie controversy to attract attention for his NSPA activities in Raleigh, North Carolina. It was members of his organization that were involved in the Greensboro deaths of Communist Workers Party members in 1979. Also in 1979, Covington went to the NSPA headquarters in Chicago and found films and pictures of young boys that suggested Collin was taking indecent liberties with them. When Collin returned, he was arrested, and Covington became the national leader of NSPA in 1980. However, some of the things that occurred related to the trials of Klansmen and NSPA members in the Greensboro murders led some of Covington's supporters to question whether Covington was an undercover informant. Covington appointed a successor and went underground for several years (George and Wilcox 1992:361–62) but then went to the Seattle, Washington, area in 1994 (Crawford et al. 1994:i.9) and later returned to the East Coast.

National Sozialistische Deutsche Arbeiterpartei/Auslands-und Aufbauorganisation (NSDAP/AO)/National Socialist German Workers Party/Overseas Organization

Gary Rex Lauck, also known as Gerhard Lauck, was once associated with Frank Collin's NSPA in Chicago and founded the National Sozialistische Deutsche Arbeiterpartei/Auslands-und Aufbauorganisation (NSDAP/AO) in late 1972 or 1973. The organization distributes neo-Nazi literature and material not only in the United States but abroad, seeing itself as a global propaganda machine and publishing National Socialist newspapers in 10 languages. According to ADL (1988b:118), NSDAP/AO is the largest distributor of neo-Nazi material in West Germany, where circulation of the material is a criminal offense. NSDAP/AO is an international organization dedicated to promoting a worldwide National Socialist–led white revolution for the restoration of white power in all-white nations (NSDAP/AO 1994a:8). Much of the organization is in Germany in underground cells attempting to overcome the ban against National Socialism, to reform the NSDAP as a legal political party, and to gain powers by legitimate means through elections. Ultimately NSDAP/AO wants to create a "National Socialist state in a sovereign and united German Reich" (NSDAP/AO 1994a:8).

The NSDAP/AO does not maintain that it is the official continuation of the original NSDAP, because the party ended in 1945. However, it sees itself as an orthodox National Socialist organization that acknowledges Hitler as the Führer and *Mein Kampf* as the primary source of the ideological foundation. Although the major activities have been oriented toward Europe, Michael Storm attended and spoke at the 1994 AN World Congress, which was attempting to develop linkages between Christian Identity religion, National Socialism, and Odinism, a pre-Christian Nordic religion.

In March 1995 Lauck was arrested in Denmark on an international arrest warrant issued by Germany (Associated Press 1995). In spite of pleas to "Free Gerhard!" from NSDAP/AO (NSDAP/AO 1995:1–2), Lauck was extradited to Germany (Associated Press Berlin 1996a) and convicted of inciting racial hatred and distributing illegal propaganda in Germany on August 22, 1996. Lauck and his attorney argued that the things he was charged with were not crimes in the United States. As he was being led out of the courtroom, Lauck shouted: "Neither the Communists nor the Nazis would ever have dared kidnap an American citizen. The fight will go on" (Randal 1996:A23). Lauck was sentenced to four years, a verdict that Christian Tomuschat, an international law professor at Berlin's Humboldt University, suggested "at first glance appeared somewhat harsh," pointing out that manslaughter frequently carries a similar penalty (Randal 1996:A24).

SS Action Group

The SS Action Group, led by Edward "Ted" Dunn, has chapters in several cities and publishes the *SS Action Group Michigan Briefing* and *Aryans Awake!* According to SS Action Group (n.d.b.) promotional material from *Aryans Awake!*, "Who We Are and What We Are All About":

> The SS Action Group is an organization of men and women volunteers who are fighting for the rights of White Americans. We believe that this country was built by White people, and that minorities, non-white crime, and racial treason are ruining this nation. We are witnessing the virtual destruction of our White Aryan culture and heritage in every aspect of daily living.... We are laying the groundwork for a revolution which will return power to the White Race.

Concerning estimates on the number of National Socialist groups, the SPLC *Klanwatch Intelligence Report* (1995a:10–14) listed 76 "neo-Nazi" locations, some groups being in more than one city in 1994 (e.g., AN, National Alliance, Nationalist Movement, SS Action Group, and WAR), and 92 in 1995 (SPLC 1996a:5–6). After this growth, the number of National Socialist organizations declined to 67 in 1996 (SPLC 1997a:18). Mostly, National Socialist groups are small but have received considerable media attention. The 1980s witnessed the growth of rather nontraditional neo-Nazi or hybrid organizations such as WAR, AN, the Mountain Church, and the Silent Brotherhood (George and Wilcox 1992). Illustrative of how movement groups overlap, Aryan Nations, Miles's Mountain Church, and the Silent Brotherhood will be discussed under Christian Identity, although they could be discussed in this section as well.

Skinheads

When one hears the name *skinheads,* one may think of young men with shaved heads and swastikas engaging in violence. ADL (1990a:2) points out that not all skinheads are racist and that in fact those who are *not* are actually more numerous. Skinhead organizations that are vehemently opposed to racism are called "Skinheads Against Racial Prejudice" (SHARP). The skinheads began in Great Britain in the 1960s and developed in the United States during the 1980s.

British Skinhead Origins According to Brake (1974:180), "skinhead" refers to a traditional British working-class delinquent subculture that is predominantly drawn from the semiskilled and unskilled manual working class. In the late 1960s, a skinhead style developed that celebrated traditional working-class values and was concerned about the economic and social issues facing the working-class community (e.g., dead-end jobs, lack of housing, poor education). Big boots, a certain style of jeans, and short cropped haircuts were often means of identification of a skinhead. Brake (1974) suggests that the hair style may have been a reaction to that of the longhaired, more middle-class hippies. According to Hamm (1993:25) "short hair was a rejection of elitist acid rock, Carnaby Street fashion, and exotic drugs such as marijuana, hashish and LSD." Territoriality of skinheads can be seen through allegiance to their local soccer (football) team, which could reflect values of collective solidarity and toughness. Skinheads perceived their community being threatened by immigrants and engaged in racial attacks, particularly against Pakistani immigrants ("paki-bashing") (Tanner 1978:360).

Music helps define the white power skinheads. According to Moore (1993:40), punk rock provided the subcultural foundation for the development of the skinheads in England and America. Skinheads, however, came to distinguish themselves from punkers. Hamm (1993:29) maintains that punk violence was more abstractly expressed so that they could attack anybody, but white skinheads had particular targets (hippies, Pakistanis, homosexuals, etc.).

The emergence of skinhead music is largely associated with Ian Stuart Donaldson, who dropped his surname and became known as Ian Stuart. In 1977 Stuart renamed his band Skrewdriver and came to view punk and reggae as too left wing (Hamm 1993:32). In 1979 Stuart aligned with British National Front, which is regarded as a neo-fascist organization. In spite of some hard times, Stuart and Skrewdriver became internationally renowned. An example of Stuart's music is "White Power," whose first verse is: "I stand and watch my country, going down the drain, we are all at fault now, we are all to blame, we're letting them take over, we just let them come, once we had an empire, and now we've got a slum" (Coplon 1989a:86–87). In 1987 Stuart founded the publication *Blood and Honour* as the independent Voice of Rock Against Communism. In September 1993 Stuart was killed in an automobile crash; as part of the tribute to him, the *Blood and Honour* British publication (1994:n.p.) commented on the importance of his music:

> The music of Ian Stuart has had a profound effect on the World and will quite possibly have a greater effect after his untimely death. His records do not merely contain a collection of songs, more so, they are musical testimonies to our times and the ongoing struggle for White racial freedom. . . . The hope continues in the bands that will continue to pick up the guitars and persevere down the road of White Power Rock n Roll.

Skinheads in the United States Although in Great Britain skinheads were tied closely to working-class culture, that linkage is not as strong in the United States; there are numerous middle-class skinheads (ADL 1993a; Moore 1993). The shaved head image does not always characterize skinheads. ADL's (1995:9) worldwide survey of skinheads suggested that some skinheads are intentionally letting their hair grow long and changing their clothes styles, making it more difficult for them to be observed by law enforcement. In Hamm's (1993) sample of 36 people, only 32 percent of those he labeled "terrorists" shaved their heads, whereas more than half of the nonterrorists did. Quite possibly one of the first neo-Nazi skinhead groups formed was Romantic Violence, which benefited financially from the selling of skinhead paraphernalia such as T-shirts, tapes, and records (Moore

1993). Now various groups market their material before or after public or private rallies. On the eve of November 9, 1987 (49th anniversary of Nazi Germany's *Kristallnacht*), Romantic Violence members smashed glass doors, painted red swastikas on the walls of three synagogues, and tore up two Kosher markets, a Jewish bookstore, and other businesses. Its leader, Clark Martell, beat up his girlfriend and eventually was arrested and jailed. Romantic Violence splintered, with some members creating Chicago Area Skinheads (CASH) and others going to Milwaukee (ADL 1988a:30). Moore (1993:63) believes that by the late 1970s skinheads were part of the punk rock movement, but they operated more at an individual level than as organized groups.

The handout "Skinheads" (undated flier, archives, Political Research Associates 1989) characterizes skinheads of America as working-class Aryan youth who "oppose the capitalist and communist scum that are destroying our Aryan race. . . . We never run away, back down, or sell out. . . . Skinheads believe in the virtues of hard work." Skinhead music has been associated with "Oi," a powerful, hard-driving style of rock and roll that is distinct from punk rock, hardcore, or heavy metal. Oi has a crisp beat with melodic tune variation, and the lyrics of most Oi bands contain proud racial statements. In Cincinnati, White American Skinheads (WASH n.d.) developed and put out a brochure entitled "What Is a Skinhead?" which also makes it clear skinheads are "NOT *IDIOTIC* PUNK ROCKERS." Further, "WE ARE PART OF A WORLD-WIDE WHITE NATIONALIST MOVEMENT OF YOUTH. WE OF W.A.S.H. ARE PROUD TO BE WHITE, GENTILE, AND AMERICAN. WE WOULD PREFER TO SMASH THE PRESENT ANTI-WHITE, ZIONIST (JEW), PUPPET RUN GOVERNMENT WITH A HEALTHY, NEW, WHITE MAN'S ORDER!"

A well-known skinhead group developed in the Haight-Asbury district of San Francisco, once known as the peace and love area of the hippies. Bob Heich, who had gone to London and learned about the British skinhead style, organized the skinhead American Front in 1985. Heich described that summer to Coplon (1989a:87) as a "bitchin' summer" with fights with hippies, blacks, punks and anarchists: "Kids were coming in from the suburbs, and other skins from Los Angeles and Seattle, and everyone was hanging on Haight Street—it was like a big party. And any time anyone gave us any lip, we just bashed 'em, because this was *our* street." Shortly thereafter, however, the police were pressured by local merchants to watch the skinheads. Heich suggested that police routinely pulled them over, took them in for questioning, or both. Eventually he and the American Front went to Portland.

The Hammerskins are significant groups under one broad organizational umbrella in the movement. They are sometimes considered the elite of skinheads and are located in different geographic regions, calling themselves Confederate, Northern, or Eastern Hammer Skinheads. An interview with three Hammerskin Skinheads at a White Aryan Legion celebration of Adolf Hitler's birthday shed light on the self-perceptions of the special nature of Hammerskins. John Pizii explained, "The Hammerskin Nation has not one leader. There's not one leader that guides us all. There's different chapters who have spokesmen, who have directors, and we all pretty much follow the same goal, and we all have the same beliefs." Later in the interview he added, "You haven't seen us hand out one flier. The Hammerskin Nation will build itself, because people know that this is a great Skinhead organization. The greatest. And if they want—if they want to be members—if they want to know something about it, they'll come to us. We don't need to go to them." George Courtney Jr. identified the essence of the Hammerskins as "Pure white—pure Aryan culture—no exceptions. That's what Hammerskins are all about—100 percent. . . . But in this country it's cultural attrition. They're weeding out the European culture for a so-called multi-racial nightmare." Chris Welch also indicated, "Family is what we're about. I mean, that's our heritage. That's our bloodline . . . our people. And if you don't love your family and your own people, then what can you love?"

The Northern Hammer Skinheads (n.d.) do not see themselves as a transient group that will burn itself out or as unconcerned about advancing their own folk, or as overly indulgent in alcohol. They question the need to march and place their faces in the limelight and would rather be low-keyed, trying to find like-minded people to associate with. Statements on their business cards help illustrate their beliefs: "Earth's most endangered species: THE WHITE RACE. Help preserve it" and "A Declaration of War Against the Existing Order."

Numerous skinhead bands in North America help promote the white power music scene. Their names are intriguing, including Angry White Youth, Extreme Hatred, JFK (Just For Kicks), Aggravated Assault, Aryan, Nordic Thunder, Bound for Glory, Max Resist, New Minority, and RAHOWA (Racial Holy War). The lyrics of the song "My Honor, My Pride" by Nordic Thunder illustrate what it means to be a skinhead:

As a Whiteman on the street, many thoughts in my mind
Thoughts of my Race, and the answers I seek to find
I am loyal to my people, my Race and family
For I am a skinhead with pride and dignity
I am part of the few, a strong and powerful force
To my enemies I'll have no remorse
They try to break my will, they try to destroy my cause
But their efforts have been in vain for I will always stand tall.

As skinheads have been searching to find their own identity and their place in society, various groups in the movement have tried to recruit them. Skinheads have been referred to variously as the security forces and the foot soldiers in the movement. Our interview with the three Hammerskins revealed that they disagreed somewhat with that perception of Hammerskins. Chris Welch pointed out some of the Klan groups and, at one time in the past, WAR had viewed skinheads as foot soldiers, but any "Skinhead with a brain in his head and on his shoulders is going to know better." George Courtney Jr. referred to the Hammerskins as a "Leadership of generals. Everybody is well-versed. Everybody's been around the block. Everybody knows what's going on. We're all hard-core. You can talk to anyone of us and we're well-versed in what we believe in, what we're for, where we've been, what we're going towards, our movement. So, basically you don't have any foot soldiers in Hammerskins. We're all men of honor."

Hamm (1993:42) goes into great detail about WAR and Metzger's role in recruiting skinheads, describing his central hypothesis as the following:

> Were it not for Tom Metzger—the Fallbrook, California, TV repairman who subscribed to Ian Stuart's newsletter *Blood and Honour* back in the winter of 1985—the American neo-Nazi skinheads would never have become more than scattered, short-lived groups led by disturbed individuals.

After examining his survey results to a number of questions about Metzger; use of Metzger's telephone hot line; exposure to *Race and Reason,* which is a videotaped series on public access TV, and to *WAR;* and receipt of WAR rewards, Hamm (1993) concluded that the results didn't support his hypothesis: "Tom Metzger is not, as hypothesized earlier, *solely* [italics ours] responsible for the spectacular increase in the number of racist skinheads in the United States during the late

Figure 2. Hammer Skinhead Insignia (with permission of Mike Streicher of the Hammerskins).

1980s" (Hamm 1993:152). Hamm (1993:151) believes this is probably because "Metzger failed to develop a coherent subculture that would respond to his material incentives." On the other hand, in such a complex social movement as this with numerous divisions and subdivisions and pressured by external forces (e.g., the government, groups opposed to the movement, etc.), it would have seemed very strange to find Tom Metzger or anybody else solely responsible for the growth of American skinheads. Skinheads are often very individualistic, and, as Metzger acknowledged in our interview, "Skinheads didn't have much discipline. It's very difficult, the discipline. That's why it's sort of funny when they said I was a skinhead leader. They went 15 different ways . . . very difficult to control."

Tom Metzger and his son John did, however, do a great deal to recruit skinheads, especially through the Aryan Youth Movement (AYM) and White Student Union. In the 1960s there was the White Student League, but it declined in the 1970s. Greg Withrow reenergized the movement beginning in 1979 and incorporated AYM into the White Student Union as a "militant extension of the student struggle" (Aryan Youth Movement White Student Union n.d.:3). In 1986 Withrow broke with Metzger, denounced Metzger's views, and apologized for his own racist activity. (One story suggests that Withrow's girlfriend changed his views.) Withrow was beaten once and then later attacked, slashed with a razor blade, and nailed to a board. In May 1987 John Metzger was declared president of the AYM.

After the Portland court had ruled against the Metzgers and WAR in a $12.5 million civil suit concerning the murder of Seraw by skinheads, Metzger declared:

> The movement will not be stopped in the puny town of Portland. We're too deep. We're embedded now. Don't you understand? We're in your colleges, we're in your armies, we're in your police forces, we're in your technical areas, we're in your banks. Where do you think a lot of these skinheads disappeared to? (Dees and Fiffer 1993:273)

There were indeed other white separatist groups that tried to (and did) attract skinheads. For example, a 1990 Roundtable Discussion on Skinheads (The Governor's Racial, Religious and Ethnic Intimidation Advisory Committee et al. 1990) indicated that the groups most active in recruiting skinheads were WAR, COTC led by Klassen (now deceased), the Nationalist Movement headed by Richard Barrett, and Aryan Nations (AN) led by Pastor Richard Butler. Beginning in 1989 through 1996, AN held Aryan Youth Festivals on the weekend nearest to Hitler's birthday at Butler's Hayden Lake, Idaho, property. The April 1994 festival, according to SPLC (1994e), had the largest crowd of skinheads in years due in part to the leadership of Tim Bishop, who was then the chief of staff. A total of about 150 skinheads and other white power representatives were estimated to have attended. Butler has characterized the "Skinhead phenomenon as a 'natural biological reaction' of white teenagers banding together after being taught that 'non-white kids are great and white kids are scum' " and that "Skinheads would eventually 'clean up the streets' after receiving 'the proper guidance' " (Moore 1993:104).

The NSDAP/AO devoted an issue of its paper *New Order* (NSDAP/AO 1989) to an "Action Program for Aryan Skinheads" trying to help skinheads fight the race war and a world Aryan revolution that will create an Aryan new order. Skinheads are perceived to occupy the pivotal position between the adult racist group and the masses of white youth. Some do's and don'ts of conduct are suggested; for example, if the local situation is very unfavorable, one should not participate in public demonstrations. Private rallies and Oi concerts on private property tend to be better. If the situation does allow, though, one definitely should get involved in public activities. Skins should work with organizations like SS Action and the Klan, who have been quite effective in generating publicity and gaining new members by holding public rallies. Skinheads are also advised not to talk to the police or the press.

Although some groups have been very active in recruiting skinheads, some organizations, particularly Robb's KKKK and Farrand's former Invisible Empire, backed off because of some of the violent activities of skins and possibly the open display of National Socialist material. Barkun (1990:135) has noted internal disagreements in the Christian Identity movement about the desirability of recruitment of skinheads.

A prowhite music company, Resistance Records, has been founded by George Eric Hawthorne and is "forging a new destiny for white power music" (*Resistance Magazine* 1994a:n.p.). In our interview with Hawthorne, he explained: "We are not affiliated with anybody. . . . One of our policies is that we stay totally nonpartisan. . . . We don't alienate members of any given group that may disagree with some of the ten-

Youth displaying a combination of neo-Nazi and Klan regalia at a public rally in Pulaski, Tennessee, January 8, 1994.

ants of a particular political organization or whatnot." Later as we discussed the role of Resistance Records in the movement he indicated:

> For young people to be healthy and havé a clear-cut sense of who they are—they have to understand their place in history and ah—really every other race really does promote these things for their own kind. I chose to promote that for the white youth and so our role in this movement is to publish music that speaks to young people in a language in a way that they understand. . . . We aren't going to censor bands or doctor the lyrics to recreate them in our own image of what we think they should be saying.

Resistance Records also puts out *Resistance Magazine,* which Hawthorne told us tries to combine "the elements of entertainment with the elements of the ideological education." He pointed out that the magazine has to be vibrant and exciting to keep young people interested and also has to promote concepts that keep people thinking. This magazine regularly carries interviews with various white power bands and a number of special features on topics such as the origins of skinheads, what is racism, blind nationalism, the passion of white power, and gun control. Contributors include such well-known movement figures as Dr. William Pierce of National Alliance; James Mason, the author of *Siege;* David Lane, a Brüder Schweigen "P.O.W."; and David Duke, former candidate for the president of the United States. The magazine's covers are in color and issue four mentioned a circulation of 13,000.

Hawthorne (1994: inside cover), the vocalist of the white power band RAHOWA (Racial Holy War), recognized the potential of the music as well as the problems bands were having receiving recording money and the difficulties young people encountered finding out where to buy white power recordings. Since the record company started, approximately in early 1994, it has signed a number of bands. The band sales report for fall 1995 indicated the top bands were Bound for Glory with the album "The Fight Goes On," followed by RAHOWA's "Declaration of War" and Nordic Thunder's "Born to Hate." All three of these had received initial commission payments (*Resistance Magazine* 1995:49).

Resistance Records has received a great deal of media attention, such as being featured on A&E television programs, including an investigative report on "The New Skinheads" and "Hate Across America" as part of the Twentieth Century series. SPLC (1995b:3) suggested: "Resistance Records is far more than a mere record label for racist rock bands. It is a growing skinhead organization that aims to unite young white supremacists in North America under its banner." Further, the article indicated that the skinhead movement "could be poised for a revival" if those who organized the record company (especially Hawthorne and Mark Wilson) were successful.

The number of racist skinheads in the United States has grown over time, although Moore (1993) makes the point that their notoriety has risen more than their numbers. In February 1988 ADL (1993a:5) estimated 1,000 to 1,500 skins in 12 states. In both June 1989 and June 1990, estimates suggested 3,000 members, but in 31 states in 1989 and 34 in 1990. The June 1993 estimate is 3,300 to 3,500 in 40 states. ADL (1995) suggests those numbers have been relatively steady since then, although according to the American Research Institute Report (1994), the number of skinheads has declined the last couple of years, but their activity level has stayed about the same. SPLC (1995b:3) has also observed a decline in the number of skinhead groups from its high of

144 in 1991 to 34 in 1994 and 30 in 1995 (SPLC 1996a:6–7). Then there was a modest increase in groups to 37 in 1996 (SPLC 1997a:18). John Pizii, a Hammerskin, suggested that the number of skinheads was increasing and told us the following: "Now I've been seeing more and more of younger people becoming skinheads. If they remain a skinhead for the rest of their life, then we have accomplished something. If they sell out by the time they're 16, 17, 20—then we've done nothing for them."

In trying to understand the skinheads, one must be aware that social scientists seem to know very little about the skinheads, and some of what social scientists think they know is contradictory or at least not very consistent. For example, Hamm (1993:203) found skinheads devoted to conventional family values and who were hard-core drug abstainers. However, the Governor's Racial, Religious and Ethnic Intimidation Advisory Committee et al. (1990:3) mentioned a vacuum of values existing in violent individuals like the skinheads. Moore (1993:85) and ADL (1993a:1) noted skinheads' drug use. Zeskind suggested skinheads may be alienated from mainstream society when he stated: "We now have the first generation of young white kids who don't expect to live better than their parents, and [they] are looking for scapegoats" (cited in Hamm 1993:5). Hamm (1993:163–66) found that skinheads were alienated in regard to politics and economics but *not* about their future. Also, a *low* level of alienation was associated with *strong* antiminority sentiments. Moore (1993:75) found skinheads antiauthoritarian (against discipline; unable to submit to higher authority), although 21 of 22 who were labeled terrorists in Hamm's (1993:122) research agreed with the statement "What the youth needs is strict discipline. . . ." It seems relatively safe to conclude that we need extensive social scientific research with shared definitions of terms as well as more comparisons of racist and nonracist skinheads.

Christian Identity Religion

Barkun (1990:121) believes that the white separatist movement has certain relatively recent tendencies that mark a change in the characteristics of the movement. For him the "novel religious character" of much of the current movement is rooted in the "Christian Identity" religious position, a kind of "New Age Fascism" (Barkun 1990:136). Zeskind (1986:7) sees Identity as a "theological undergirding for racist violence," and Larson (1992:23) calls it the "uniting force among many white supremacist groups." It has definitely attracted certain Klan and skinhead participants.

Origins of Identity Like the skinheads, Identity's beginnings can be traced back to Great Britain but to an earlier time period—the mid–nineteenth century. The theological roots of the Identity movement are in British Israelism or Anglo-Israelism, although Aho (1990:51) maintains it is virtually impossible to pinpoint the origins of the doctrine of Christian Identity. Some historians refer to Scotsman John Wilson's *Lectures on Our Israelitish Origins* that appeared in 1840 or Edward Hine's writings that started in the late 1860s. Both men were searching for the descendants of the 10 lost tribes of Israel. British Israelism maintains that the lost tribes eventually migrated over the Caucasus Mountains to become the various Anglo-Saxon peoples while orthodox Protestantism suggests that the lost tribes became guest peoples of nations in the Middle East that assimilated and disappeared (Aho 1990:51–52). If the 10 tribes are racial in character rather than religious, the appearance of these tribes could indicate an uninterrupted link to Biblical prophecies (Zeskind 1986:18). In other words, the British would be God's chosen people who would fulfill the Biblical prophecies (Barkun 1990:122). British-Israelism and Identity maintain that the Anglo-Saxon-Celtic people have a racial destiny that would involve the "divine right, to dominate and colonize the world" (Zeskind 1986:19). British-Israelism was not especially anti-Semitic, although Christian Identity is.

Beginnings in the United States Barkun (1994:ix) suggests that three men were particularly significant in the early formation of Christian Identity in the United States. Mentored by Edward Hine, Charles A. L. Totten, a Yale military science instructor, may have been the first American to convert to British Israelism around 1885. Howard Rand, originally a construction company manager, began first as an American representative of the British-Israel World Federation based in London. Starting in New England, Rand's travel and recruitment ultimately resulted in numerous Anglo-Saxon branches. He evidently met the third significant person, William J. Cameron, at Federation meetings in Detroit in 1930. Cameron was linked to Henry Ford and also to British-Israelism. He had been the editor of Ford's *Dearborn Independent,* a notorious anti-Semitic publication. Beginning in 1920 until 1922, the newspaper carried a number of versions of anti-Semitic articles, including *The Protocols of the Elders of Zion,* which purports to be a secret Jewish plan to dominate the world. The famous article "The International Jew" provided the title of a four-volume book that later contained most of these articles. Through the Anglo-Saxon Federation, Cameron and Rand were involved in the first systematic link of British-Israel religious beliefs with the political right in the United States. In large part because of Cameron's activities, a movement was formed in which racists and anti-Semites could feel comfortable. Rand himself lived until age 102 but always viewed Identity as a deviation from British Israelism and disagreed with many of Identity's theological arguments (Barkun 1994).

The Transformation to Christian Identity

American Identity has been associated with several preachers who knew the right-wing politician and anti-Semite Gerald L. K. Smith. It is, however, not clear if Smith was actually an Identity believer (Barkun 1994:56). Particularly significant were Bertram Comparet, Wesley Swift, and William Potter Gale in putting the racialist and anti-Semitic ideas together with certain aspects of British Israelism. In the post–World War II period Wesley Swift may have been the most significant person in the early history of Identity despite never having published any extended statement of his religious views. He was involved in trying to rejuvenate the Klan in 1946 and may have formed his first church about then in Lancaster, California. He later renamed it the Church of Jesus Christ Christian, which indicated his view that Jesus was not a Jew (Barkun 1994:63). One of Swift's famous quotations is "IF YOU BELIEVE THE BIBLE, YOU ARE GOING TO BE A SEGREGATIONIST" (Zeskind 1986:29). Swift died in 1970.

Comparet, educated at Stanford, was a lawyer and served as legal adviser to the California Anti-Communist League that Swift headed. He wrote Identity tracts such as *Your Heritage* (Comparet n.d.a.) and *The Cain-Satanic Seed Line* (Comparet n.d.b.). He died in 1983. One of Swift's protégés was William Potter Gale, although they later had a falling out. Gale was not only actively involved in Christian Identity as a preacher but played an important role in organizing a Posse Comitatus group called United States Christian Posse Association and the Committee of the States. In 1987 Gale and four other members of the Committee of the States were convicted of conspiring to threaten the lives of IRS agents and a state judge. He died before his appeal could be heard. Seymour (1991), in her book *Committee of the States,* provides a detailed accounting of Gale's organization and trial as well as information on Christian Identity. Her (1991:377–81) discussion with Attorney Rommel Bondoc suggests that the case against Gale involved the issue of "vicarious responsibility" and First Amendment rights, somewhat like that of WAR and the Metzgers.

Current Identity and Related Organizations Although the doctrine of Identity is indeed complex and not all Identity supporters agree on all aspects of the religious tenets, Barkun (1994:vii–ix) has identified three core beliefs of much of Christian Identity:

1. White "Aryans" are the offspring of the tribes of Israel according to the Bible.
2. Rather than being tied to the Israelites, Jews are the children of the Devil. This is traced back to the sexual relationship between Satan and Eve in the Garden of Eden.
3. The world is on the verge of a final apocalyptic struggle between good and evil with Aryans battling a Jewish conspiracy to try to save the world.

Perhaps the most well known Christian Identity organization is AN Church of Jesus Christ Christian. Butler, who attended Swift's congregation, maintains that his church is a continuation of Swift's Lancaster one, although this is somewhat controversial. Butler received his formal education in southern California, including aeronautical engineering at Los Angeles City College, and is coinventor for rapid repair of tubeless tires, holding the American and Canadian patents on them. In 1968 he became senior manufacturing engineer for Lockheed Aircraft Co. He later resigned to devote full attention to the Identity movement. In 1973 he moved to northern Idaho and established his church near Hayden Lake.

Basic tenets of the Identity religion include the following:

WE BELIEVE in the preservation of our Race, individually and collectively, as a people as demanded and directed by Yahweh. We believe our Racial Nation has a right and is under obligation to preserve itself and its members.
WE BELIEVE that there is a battle being fought this day between the children of darkness (today known as Jews) and the children of light (Yahweh, The Everliving God), the Aryan Race, the true Israel of the Bible. Revelations 12:10–11.

Pastor Neumann Britton (left) and Pastor Richard Butler (right) of Aryan Nations prepare for the Soldiers' Ransom at Aryan Nations, July 23, 1995.

WE BELIEVE that the present world problems are a result of our disobedience to Divine Law.
WE BELIEVE that there is a day of reckoning. The usurper will be thrown out by the terrible might of Yahweh's people, as they return to their roots and their special destiny. We know there is soon to be a day of judgment and a day when Christ's Kingdom (government) will be established on earth, as it is in heaven. (Aryan Nations n.d.a.)

In 1979 Butler began holding annual conferences and then in 1989 added annual youth meetings as well. AN also has a prison ministry and puts out a special prison newsletter, "The Way," as well as their own "Calling Our Nation." AN may well have reached its height in the mid-1980s and then declined. However, in April 1992, SPLC (1992b:1) noted that AN was "showing ominous signs of life" with "Richard Butler's militant Identity group recruiting neo-Nazi Skinheads and planning a base in the Southeast." After that, some of its leaders (e.g., Carl

Franklin Jr. and Floyd Cochran) left AN, but Tim Bishop became chief of staff for a while, handling many of the everyday activities for the aging Butler. SPLC's March 1995 article "Aryan Nations: A Long History of Hate and Violence" suggests that after Carl Franklin and Wayne Jones left AN in mid-1993, "Aryan Nations' phenomenal resurgence began" (SPLC 1995c:7). Another article in the same issue noted its growth from being in 3 states in 1993 to adding 15 new ones in 1994[2] (SPLC 1995d:1, 5–7). In 1996 it had chapters in 27 different states (SPLC 1997b).

Until the death of Robert Miles in 1992, his Mountain Church of Jesus Christ near Cohoctah, Michigan, was in certain respects the Midwest equivalent to the western AN. Miles believed in dualism, which some have said is a variant of Christian Identity. According to Miles's brochure, "The Identity of Dualism and the Duality of Identity" (n.d.a), dualism existed before the "Christian Era," arguing that there are two forces at war with each other—the force of light, coming from all-good, ever pure God, versus the force of darkness, an evil presence admitted into the world through the rebellion of the adversary to God, Satanael. Angels were godly creations under the dominion of Lucifer, who was originally loyal to God, but after the seventh day (the day God rested from the creation), Lucifer rebelled. Dualism maintains it was one of the rebellious angels, serving the devil, who seduced Eve while Identity believes that the devil himself seduced Eve. Identity holds that the 10 lost tribes crossed the Caucasus Mountains and southern Russia to get to Europe, while dualism believes that the white race originally descended to earth in Europe. Dualism and Identity agree on the following: (1) God is white; (2) it is the divine mission of the white race to conquer this earth; (3) the white race is special, a chosen people; (4) the white race needs to unify; (5) racial purity and genetic cleansing of the racial pool is necessary; and (6) man must fight and not simply wait for Jesus to come.

James K. Warner was a disciple of Swift's and associated with Rockwell, NSWPP, NSRP, and Odinism (Barkun 1994, ADL 1988b). He started the New Christian Crusade Church in 1971 in Los Angeles; in 1974 or 1975 Tom Metzger was ordained as a minister in Warner's Church. According to Barkun (1994:210), Metzger met Duke at James Warner's home. In 1975 Warner became director of information for Duke's Klan. He also assumed the director of the Christian Defense League (CDL) and moved it and his church to Louisiana in 1976. Warner's *CDL Report,* a publication of the New Christian Crusade

Church (1993:16), offers "the facts suppressed by the rest of 'our' national news media" and "is your only source for a penetrating analysis of the Jewish question." A special issue of *CDL Report* (The New Christian Crusade Church n.d. Issue 137:7) states: "As White society is mesmerized by the theatrics of enraged Blacks, Zionists slip a few hundred thousand more Orientals and Hispanics in, slip a few billion dollars more to Israel, etc."

Barkun (1994:200) points out that Christian Identity has given rise to numerous forms of political action, some of which are legitimate, some not, and others more ambiguous. Within the "gray" area are survivalists who want to be self-sufficient and have limited contacts with the larger society; possibilities for violent confrontation exist when this occurs. Violence may also occur when local political groups believe that only local political authorities are legitimate. Probably the most well known of these is the Posse Comitatus (Latin for "power of the county"); not all Posse Comitatus members belong to Identity, but certainly Identity leaders have played prominent roles in the Posse. The basic tenet of Posse philosophy is that the local sheriff is the supreme political authority in the county and should not be constrained by the state or federal government. The Posse maintains that the U.S. Constitution forbids collecting federal income tax, that the Federal Reserve is part of an international banking conspiracy, and the U.S. government should be isolationist in their foreign policy (Ridgeway 1990:20). According to Aho (1990), Christian constitutionalists, such as members of the Posse Comitatus and John Birch Society, see an abstract group behind the conspiracy to destroy America; Identity Christians believe it is a Jewish conspiracy.

The Order, or the Silent Brotherhood, founded by Robert Jay Mathews in 1983 is an organization that engaged in illegal activities. Some of its members were Odinist or belonged to several Klan and Identity groups as well as the National Alliance. The different beliefs and organizational backgrounds of the Order members illustrate the diversity of viewpoints in the movement. Mathews was killed in a shoot-out in 1984 and 24 Order members were convicted or pleaded guilty to racketeering charges. (Chapter 4 provides much greater detail on the Silent Brotherhood.) The activities of the Order also provided the basis for charges of seditious conspiracy to overthrow the U.S. government. Among those indicted were certain members of the Order and Butler, Miles, and Beam. All were acquitted after a three-month trial in 1988 at Ft. Smith, Arkansas. David Lane, a member of the Silent Brotherhood and a person who had at one time been involved in the Klan and AN, has founded 14 Word Press and Wotan's Volk with his wife, Katja, and friend Ron McVan.

In the late 1980s and into the 1990s, some parts of the Identity movement became very concerned about the paramilitary image of Identity. Pete Peters, pastor of The LaPorte Church of Christ in Colorado, emerged as a major figure trying to develop new methods for the Identity Movement to expand. His outreach ministry is called Scriptures for America. Peters has a radio ministry and each summer offers family-oriented Bible camps with numerous Identity speakers. In addition, he has engaged in numerous speaking activities across the country. Some of his services had been attended by Silent Brotherhood members before their arrests.

It is important to realize that Identity is not organized as denominations might be under Protestantism. Like other parts of the movement, Identity is fragmented. In our interview, Pastor Barley of America's Promise Ministry in Sandpoint, Idaho, explained the divisions this way:

> That Identity or the Christian Israel Covenant People fellowship groups is still evolving. We're still growing. We're still changing. So, what we may be today does not necessarily mean we're going to be that 10 years from now. Right now, we believe it is better for us to have our own independent, individual churches and fellowships. And we will fellowship and unite and have conferences—um—and be a united group when we are together, but we all maintain our special, unique Identity and we all have our statements of faith that we have drawn up. There is no united, universal statement of faith that you could go to to find out what Identity is.

Illustrative of this is the fact that Barley's ministry is only about 30 miles from that of Butler's, but they have important areas of disagreement. As Barley put it:

> Again, I don't hate Richard Butler, it's just—there's differences of opinion. He has a different interpretation or a different slant on his interpretation of the Scriptures than I do in certain areas and right now I think that they're—those differences are so big and also the fact that he tends to glorify a little bit more on Hitler than I care to.

According to Crawford et al. (1994:3.12) in their book *The Northwest Imperative,*[3] Barley tried to "formulate a kinder and gentler Identity rhetoric, which he began to call the 'Kingdom' message."

Another key development has occurred in Christian Identity: "Contemporaneous with the rising influence of Colorado Identity leader Pete Peters as the movement's key figure of the 1990s, is the rise in stature of the Midpines, California-based *Jubilee.* This bimonthly tabloid has fast become the flagship publication of the Identity movement" (Crawford et al. 1994:3.18). Those associated with the publication hold annual Jubilation conferences that have included prominent figures like Pete Peters and Louis Beam as well as public officials such as California state representative Republican Don Rogers and Richard Carver, a Nye County, Nevada county commissioner (Crawford et al. 1994:3.19–3.20). Randy Weaver, whose son and wife were killed on Ruby Ridge, answered questions at the banquet at the 1996 Jubilation, which was attended by more than 500 people (SPLC 1996d). The *Jubilee* (1996a:19) challenged the definition of Christian Identity that appeared in a SPLC publication and countered with its own definition:

Christian Identity—Anglo Saxon, Scandinavian, Germanic and kindred people (Christians) who have learned their true identity as descendants of Jacob (Israel). Contemporary Jews are descendants of Esau (Edom) and were *not* the offspring of "Satan and Eve." Blacks and other non-whites are creations of God and to be treated with respect as strangers in the land.

As already pointed out, it is important to recognize that not all those who believe in Christian Identity share the exact same beliefs.

Rough estimates of the number of people involved with Identity range from 2,000 to more than 50,000 (Barkun 1994:viii). SPLC (1996d) estimated 35,000 supporters in the United States. In its decade review of the 1980s, SPLC (1989:26) listed 38 different Identity groups as currently active. SPLC representatives (1995a:11) explained that since 1990 they have not counted Identity groups because they have frequently kept their activities low-key and often work underground. For their 1994 calculation, Identity groups were included in the "other" list that rose from 48 in 1993 to 66. For 1996 SPLC (1997b:22) again listed Identity groups separately, naming 12 of them. Groups like Aryan Nations, with its 27 chapters in different states, and Christian Defense League were listed as neo-Nazi rather than Identity.

As we have already noted, for the movement's comparatively small size, there are a number of groups that exist with differing views. According to the "watchdog" organizations like SPLC, a group may seem to grow rapidly but then decline relatively quickly. We will now consider a major split in the current movement.

A Fundamental Division: The Movement versus the Resistance

The American Research Institute (ARI) (1994) identified three distinct groupings in the white separatist movement. The first includes those who strongly advocate a white separatist nation and tend to use the term *resistance* to describe themselves.[4] WAR's Tom and John Metzger, Louis Beam, and John Baumgardner belong to this segment. It also includes some who discuss worldwide revolution and forming a global army, such as Gerhard Lauck of NSDAP/AO (ARI 1994:2). This element tends to be quite militant as it tries to awaken whites in America to the perceived threats to their race. The second distinct grouping that ARI identifies is the political branch that believes change through new and different political parties is the key. Its supporters are upset with the current political officials who occupy the government but are not critical of American democracy as originally conceived. Ed Fields is the "undisputed leader of this group" (ARI 1994:3), and Thom Robb's KKKK belongs to this part. The third part is an underground movement that is least understood and that we do not really directly explore here. This part typically involves individuals who act on their own, following the late Bob Miles advice, "Run silent. Run deep" (ARI 1994:3). Some of these individuals may also be referred to as lone wolves.

On WAR's hot line, frequent references are made to the differences in strategy between WAR and the less militant groups of the political branch. Tom Metzger (February 7, 1993a, taping) cautioned against organizations meeting in large groups so that they could be infiltrated and have their members photographed. Specifically they should "quit operating like a bunch of Hollywood people marching around in the street." On the other hand, our interview with Ed Fields indicated his interest in the political process, including his support for the stands of people like David Duke and Bo Gritz (who ran on the Populist Party ticket for U.S. president). He believes that only whites should vote, preferably going back to the Constitution with only white male property owners voting. He sees democracy as an invention of the white race, suggesting it has only been successful among white-ruled nations. Fields clearly places himself within the right wing that Metzger has rejected. His paper *The Truth at Last* (n.d. Issue 366:1, 8) described a June 12, 1993 meeting "as conferring on the future of the Right-Wing movement" (p. 1). It resulted in the creation of the "America First party" because neither of the two major parties represent the majority of the people; Ed Fields was elected secretary of the organization.

Trying to clarify the difference between "the Right-Wing Movement" and "White Resistance," Dennis Mahon, Oklahoma WAR Consultant, pointed out:

> By the "Movement," we mean the activities and ideology of most Judeo-*C*hristian, *R*ight-Wing, *A*nti-Communist, *P*atriotic groups (C.R.A.P.). The CRAP usually consist of most Klan groups, patriotic christian churches, patriotic veterans groups, and so on. By Aryan or White Resistance we mean groups like White Aryan Resistance, National Alliance, Church of the Creator, skinhead groups, and some radical white survivalist groups. . . .
>
> CRAP movement people believe that the masses of sheep, called the American people, have the courage and intelligence to fight for their own destiny. Resistance people study history and know that it's the 1 or 2% of revolutionary zealots who change history, while the sheep follow and obey those who wield power. (Mahon 1994:6)

John Baumgardner, formerly a member of Farrand's Invisible Empire, has aligned with the International Separatist Front (ISF) (no date), which is not a traditional organization. Baumgardner (n.d.) too distinguishes between movement and resistance:

> Most of us who have come to understand the need for resistance came out of that movement. Therefore, it stands to reason that the movement has not been a total failure. In the movement we saluted the flags of nations. For the resistance there is no flag as we have begun to deeply root ourselves under the surface in every facet of life. . . . We cannot recruit from the movement for it is not possible to recruit into the resistance. One must hear the call in this war for racial liberation. . . . Such an attitude cannot be recruited but must be developed through suffering, failure, and loss. The movement serves such a purpose today—to weed out the weak followers from those who are generals of themselves. . . . The movement seeks to halt the repression and racial genocide through political means. How long will the movement accept failure while maintaining a hope of change by these means? The resistance understands that repression is what is needed to turn the tide against the system.

According to this terminology, the movement is different from the resistance, but it may have some utility for the resistance since it provides a setting for people to experience shared problems and potentially grow to become part of the resistance.

Many of those in the resistance do not have formal hierarchical organizations with membership lists nor do they hold public rallies. They avoid leaving a paper trail (such as corporate accounts and records), possibly making it more difficult for the government to identify leaders and hold them responsible for the activities of their members. However, as Baumgardner pointed out in our interview, "You can be organized without being an organization. . . . I don't think the IRA puts signs up in Belfast that say join the IRA, contact PO Box such and such you know . . . that's not how revolution works."

In stark contrast to the resistance strategy, Robb has been trying to change the image of the Klan from crude hooded night riders to a more-polished political image (Fruhling 1992:5A). According to Robb: "We're setting our sights on government power" (Riley 1992:26) and "Louisiana has one David Duke. We plan to give America 1,000 of them" (Riley 1992:25). The KKKK are portrayed as the oldest and most professional Klan. For the Knights, only certain "responsible and disciplined" skinheads are acceptable (*White Patriot* 1989). In addition to accentuating the quality of their leadership, the *White Patriot* (n.d.c:8) stresses the quality of the membership: "We emphasize ONE requirement for every member of The Knights, and that is that they conduct themselves with Christian character. We want our members to live their lives as honorable, decent, dignified WHITE people. If you act like a nigger or white trash then you don't belong with The Knights!"

Some movement groups have expressed their discontent with Robb's KKKK, and they suggest the Klan should be a much more militant and aggressive organization. *The Oklahoma WAR* (1992:1–2), edited by Dennis Mahon, criticized Robb's public rallies:

> If these "Klansmen' [*sic*] want to look like martyrs walking to the burning stake, it's their right. But please don't bring the honorable Klan's name into it. The Klan's name was to inflict terror and fear into our enemie's [*sic*] minds, not contempt and derision. The Klan's strength was always in its invisibility and nighttime raids of retribution on the traitors of our race.

The White KKKK, whose international office is in "Klansas City, MO," called Robb Robbstien the Grand Sensor and the Kosher Konservative

Klown (White KKKK n.d.a:2; n.d.b:8) and criticized him for attacking other Klan organizations, for his authoritarian leadership style, and for his unwillingness to take part in rallies sponsored by other Klan groups (White KKKK n.d.c:5). Richard Bondira, editor of the *Kourier,* which was designed to be an open forum for all the KKK organizations, published several of the "complaints about Thom Robb and his un-Klanish behavior, his broken promises, and his ignoring their just grievances" (*Kourier* 1993:n.p.). From what we have observed, both ideological differences, including those related to strategy, and personality differences create divisions in this movement as in other movements. Ideology and strategies related to protest and to more conventional tactics will be explored further in the next three chapters.

Conclusion

The movement has changed considerably over time, beginning first with the KKK, which was an indigenous organization started in the southern United States. The 1920s Klan was quite popular, attracted many members, and shared many values with the mainstream culture, but historical circumstances have changed, so that being a Klan member is now a stigmatized status. Once one organization, the Klan now has many different groups and leaders, some of whom don't get along with each other. The National Socialist philosophy and its identification with Adolf Hitler and the swastika have never been well-received in America. At times Klan and neo-Nazi groups have shared interests and rallies, and other times the leaders of these groups are also hostile to each other. Some of the significant figures in the movement were once part of Klan organizations but now have become involved in other associations to express their racial concerns.

Skinheads and Christian Identity supporters have provided more recent infusions of new life to the movement. Although the historical origins of both have been rooted in Britain, their forms have been modified in the United States. American skinheads tend to have more middle-class origins than the British, but white power music remains a critical component of the skinhead subculture and an important link to skinheads in other parts of the world. In the United States, skinheads have been mentored by various other groups in the movement, but they also have the capacity to be relatively autonomous. Christian Identity originated with British-Israelism, which provided a different interpretation of the Bible and of history than did most Christian churches. While Identity accepted much of British-Israelism, it did not support the political status quo as had the middle-class intellectuals of British-Israelism; rather it saw the American political institution as corrupt and caught in a Zionist conspiracy (Barkun 1994:243–47).

Our simple classification of Klan, National Socialist or neo-Nazi, Christian Identity, and skinhead only partially allows us to cover the diversity of groups in the movement. Kaplan (1993:33–42) divided the movement groups into seven categories; the first three (Klan, explicitly neo-Nazi, and Christian Identity) are similar to ours, and another, referred to as "hope seeking a means to fulfillment," included the skinheads. His other categories were "reconstructed traditions," "idiosyncratic sectarians," and "single-issue constituencies and lone unguided missiles." The reconstructed traditions sometimes involve attempts to build on religious traditions of the past and link them with racial concerns. This will be covered more thoroughly in the next chapter on ideology as part of our discussion of religion. One of the idiosyncratic sectarian groups, COTC, will also be discussed there. Single-issue constituencies, such as Holocaust revisionists, will be considered briefly as their beliefs are related to the overall ideology in the movement. Even though there are various classification schemes, it is especially important to recognize that individual movement members and even groups may very well belong to more than one of our categories.

Currently the overall size of the movement is not particularly great. In our interview, George Eric Hawthorne of Resistance Record Company contrasted the size of the movement with the media attention it has received:

> I always find it quite—I'm trying to look for the right word—perhaps perplexing that a movement that is really so relatively small—so relatively insignificant in comparison to the power structure—can get so much media attention. And I really ask myself the question—why? And I haven't really been able to come up with the clear-cut answer as to why. But one thing I can basically say is that the media has in more cases than not—has created a Frankenstein monster out of many different things . . . and I think that this movement is one of the things that they are doing it with. This movement is relatively insignificant at this stage and time. It's tremendously significant philosophically—but because of its low numbers of people involved—it is very insignificant. So, the media by basically doing stories on this type of thing are really serving to pro-

> mote it. No matter how much they think they are slandering it, they are still promoting it. Because it grows every time there's media attention on it.

He went on to stress that at least for the part of the movement with which he identified, the people were very ideologically and philosophically motivated and could have a very significant impact on history in the future. Kacy Lane, the daughter of David and Katja Lane, supported this view, stating: "We stand for what many people just feel they can't speak about. . . . The movement now is becoming younger and younger. People who are even younger than I have their ideals set and they know what they want. . . . I just think that great things are going to happen to this movement." "Der Kampfhund," a director of Northern Hammer Skinheads, commented to us about the wide variety of people in the movement, "The movement is full of many diverse, often conflicting viewpoints and has more than its fair share of hangers-ons, wannabes, and outright human trash. On the other hand there are many very good men and women involved who have some powerful and revolutionary ideas." In the course of our research, we have had contact with a number of articulate people, several of them quite young, who could enhance the development of the movement if they remain ideologically committed.

From the movement perspective, the hopeful point of view regarding the movement is also partially captured by Thorz Hammer in his response to our survey. He pointed out some indicators of growth in the movement—including the opposition to affirmative action and immigration, " 'conservative' talk radio," "pro-white music and religious groups" becoming "more obvious," and more people buying his book *WHAM!: Confessions of a White American Man!*. He concluded: "We will continue to repair our tribal culture, and we could see the establishment of the first White tribal nations since the dark ages."

Mike Streicher of the Hammerskin Nation believed the movement was growing, too, but recognized what might accompany the growth: "It will snowball into a much bigger movement until either the government gets so paranoid of us and takes action or more than likely what will happen is something (someone) will trigger a guerilla war and then a full-scale war reminiscent of the war in Ireland (IRA)."

One possible response to impending conflict with the government is for more of the movement members to go underground. According to an anonymous National Socialist:

I think the government/ZOG [Zionist Occupation Government] is going to 'crack down' on the militias and put stricter controls on guns. There are already agents infiltrating them and our White Racialist Groups. I think you will see a shift in the actual memberships in these organizations (a DECLINE in "official" membership—but not in beliefs). A lot of people will go "UNDERGROUND" and not join anything else *or* drop out of the groups their [*sic*] in. Some will continue to receive Literature/Newsletters from Racist groups—others will cancel their subscriptions and not have any mail like that come to the house or P.O.Box. I'm *not* predicting a decline in supporters of "our" cause, *only* a personal change in some people. Because of ZOG, some might want to drop out of site [*sic*]—but still be a warrior/comrade willing to fight when the time is right.

There may also be a process in which those who are not steadfastly committed to the movement will withdraw from it completely. Nathan Pett of the Battle Axe Skinheads and *Hail Victory* told us:

Eventually there's going to be a weeding-out where—when the government puts so much pressure on you and people find out how tough it really is . . . a lot of people drop out. And I think that's good though, because then the people that are worth your time are left and the people that are just there to waste your time are gone.

This would fit with what several in the movement have identified as the need for quality over quantity in order to bring about significant change.

Drawing on the past, we see that the U.S. government has infiltrated and tried to repress this movement and/or those who might be associated with it. Severe repression could destroy much of the movement and drive others underground. On the other hand, it is possible that repression could provide a means to unify the movement and attract additional support for it. The future development of the movement will depend on a number of historical circumstances, some that the movement can help shape and some that the movement may well not be able to control.

Chapter Three

Ideology

Regardless of how many tattoos I have on my shaved head, it must be stated clearly that I am not your stereotypical Skinhead. The fact of the matter is that there is a budding Pan-Aryan intelligentsia which includes several Skinheads. . . . Please note that this does not mean that I am a quiet little guy behind a desk, we still go out bashing baldies and other scum. The difference is that I know that our future, the future of our children, and the continuance of our genetic heritage depend on our actions today. "We must secure the existence of our Race and a future for White children."—David Lane's '14 words.' (John C. Sigler III also known as (aka) "Duck," Confederate Hammer Skinheads[1])

Although there are numerous meanings of ideology, Seliger (1976:14) has pointed out two fundamentally different ways ideology has been used. In the former, one labels something ideological because it is perceived as radical right or left rather than moderate or in the mainstream. This use limits the applicability of the concept to only certain extremist belief systems and often has a negative connotation. The other, which we follow, refers to a set of ideas that describe, explain, and justify the ends and means of political action. This use is more inclusive and views ideologies as integrated belief systems. According to Schwartz (1990:50), political ideology is "a set of more or less coherent and durable ideas and beliefs that can be drawn upon for understanding and explaining political events." However, it is important to recognize that ideology is subject to change, and movements struggle over how ideas and meanings are produced and developed. According to Snow and Benford (1997:458), movement organizations and actors are viewed as "actively engaged in the production and maintenance of meaning for constituents, antagonists, and bystanders or observers." Social movements are involved in "the politics of reality," trying to use evidence to define the way things are and should be (Goode and Ben-Yehuda 1994:119). A movement tries to legitimate its view of reality and rarely examines both sides of an issue in a scholarly manner.

Ideologies can either support the status quo or advocate changing the current political system. Typically when ideologies advocate change, they are attached to social movements, which can be defined as "organized efforts to promote or resist change in society that rely, at least in part, on noninstitutionalized forms of political action" (Marx and McAdam 1994:73). Heberle (1951:23–24) points out the crucial link between social movements and ideology:

> The first step towards an understanding of a social movement suggests itself by common sense: we want to know what it is all about. We want to know the end or goal, the objectives of the movement. . . .
>
> . . . we want to know the entire complex of ideas, theories, doctrines, values, and strategic and tactical principles that is characteristic of the movement. We call this complex the *ideology* of the movement, using the term in a broad, nontechnical sense.

The beliefs in the white separatist movement tend to be complex and intertwined, and knowing this movement's ideology is fundamental to understanding the movement. We explore ideology related to racism, separatism, anti-Semitism, religion, class inequality and capitalism, the U.S. government, and the New World Order.[2] We conclude by looking at the relationships between language and ideology as the use of language helps frame the ideology.

Racism and Racialism

A conventional sociological definition of racism identifies it as an ideology structured around three significant beliefs: "1. Humans are divided naturally into different physical types. 2. Such physical traits as they display are intrinsically related to their culture, personality, and intelligence. 3. On the basis of their genetic inheritance, some groups are innately superior to others" (Marger 1991:2). Somewhat similarly,

Davis (1978:91) identifies three key beliefs of racism as an ideology: Some races are physically superior and mentally superior to others; race causes culture and determines temperament; race mixing decreases biological quality (Davis 1978:94).

Gordon and Klug (1985:13) have distinguished the new racism from traditional racism. The traditional version is more a form of crude bigotry centered around a belief system that maintained the racial superiority of whites. In the new form, the argument rests more upon the idea of recognizing differences among peoples and wanting to maintain those differences. It is viewed as "natural" for people of one kind to group together and also natural for them to be cautious and perhaps antagonistic to those who are not the same as they are.

The sociological literature (Hraba, Brinkman, and Gray-Ray 1995; Kluegel 1990; Kluegel and Smith 1986; McClendon 1985; Sniderman and Piazza 1993) has identified a new or symbolic racism perspective in which many white Americans express a subtler form of prejudice than whites tended to do in the past. In general, the expression of biological or traditional prejudice has declined, but there has been increasing hostility toward programs favoring equality and integration (McConahay and Hough 1976; Kluegel and Bobo 1993; Schuman, Steeh, and Bobo 1985; Hraba et al. 1995). The traditional prejudice often included the belief in the innate inferiority of blacks such as in intelligence and/or the desire to maintain segregation or social distance. In the new racism whites are critical of government policies that seem to favor minorities, for example, affirmative action. McConahay and Hough (1976:23) defined symbolic racism as "the expression by . . . whites in terms of abstract ideological symbols and symbolic behaviors of the feeling that blacks are violating cherished values and making illegitimate demands for changes in the racial status quo." They suggested socialization played a key role in the development of symbolic racism. Kinder and Sears (1981) did not find direct racial threats to whites' private lives to have much influence on symbolic racism or antiblack voting behavior, but symbolic racism did influence voting. Bobo (1983) considered whether the subjective perception of out-group members posing a threat would influence one's views on busing and found that the opposition of whites to busing reflected group conflict motives rather than a new measure of prejudice such as symbolic racism. Kluegel and Smith (1983) found direct and indirect competitive self-interest to be predictors of opposition to affirmative action programs, and Kluegel and Bobo (1993) found that group self-interest and perceived discrimination were important influences on white opposition to race-targeted policy. The relationship between symbolic racism and traditional prejudice is not clear; they may well overlap (Kluegel and Smith 1983; Katz, Wackenhut, and Hass 1986). According to Kluegel and Smith (1986:192), "It appears that many Americans simply have added discrimination to motivation or innate ability differences in constructing their explanations of race differences in socioeconomic status."

The term *racism* is used in conflicting and sometimes contradictory ways (Wellman 1993:2). Smith (1995:1) acknowledges that "social science knowledge has not developed to the point that any consensus has emerged on how to define and give operational meaning to racism and its various modes or types." Although a rather simplistic distinction, some define racism using only biological distinctions while others use broader criteria. For example, Yeboah (1988) clearly distinguishes between whether the social and individual differences between races are due to biological differences caused by hereditary factors versus those caused by cultural differences. For him, only the former is racism, whereas the latter involves ethnocentrism. Langmuir (1990:311) also uses a relatively restrictive definition of racism, indicating it "proclaimed that humans were divided into clearly distinguishable races and that the intellectual, moral, and social conduct and potential of the members of these races were biologically determined." He further suggests that racism may be "too misleading and restrictive in its connotations" (Langmuir 1990:316).

There are, on the other hand, very broad definitions of racism. Williams, Lavizzo-Mourey, and Warren (1994:26) believe that the term *race* is a socially meaningful concept but of limited biological significance. Racism includes negative attitudes about other groups, prejudice, and discrimination. At its core, racism is an ideology that classifies and ranks human groups (Williams et al. 1994:29). Wellman (1993:4) suggests racism should be studied as "culturally acceptable beliefs that defend social advantages that are based on race." He (1993:57–58) points out that the definition of white racism has three faces: personal prejudice, institutional discrimination, and an ideological face using both cultural and biological reasons to justify the superior position of whites. The ways racism is exhibited are so "intertwined, so much a part of each other, that they are often inseparable"

(Wellman 1993:58). If one follows Williams et al.'s (1994) idea that race is socially constructed, racism could include cultural and biological explanations. Billig (1978a), in his research on the National Front, an openly racist party in Great Britain, believed his interviewees confused culture and race (as a biological concept) in their discussions of their belief systems. If indeed it is confusion, this may reflect the way social scientists and the media have defined, redefined, and used the term. Billig (1978b:274) found in his interviews that "the fusion of the inherited and the acquired allows a sense of moral superiority" and "the laws of genetics are inextricably bound up with spirit or will." Further he suggested that this fusion also exists in the Nazi beliefs about race.

Billig (1978a:164) pointed out that the sociopsychological view of racism "has in fact ignored the most central feature of racialism, namely the meaning of race to the racialist." Although *Webster's Third New International Dictionary* (Gove 1967:1870) equates racialism with racial prejudice and racism, many in the movement tend to define the term *racialist* as one who expresses love of their race. One of our respondents, Jack Wikoff, editor and publisher of *Remarks,* answered our inquiry about the meaning of racialist by stating, "A 'racialist' recognizes the reality of race and genetic heritage, but also acknowledges the effects of social environment," illustrating the fusion that Billig also found.

Many people in the movement are critical of the media that label them as "racists" and "haters." For example, the *David Duke Report* (1993a:4) offered a rather interesting reply to the accusation that Duke is a racist.

> As for the charge that my views are "racist," I'm at a loss to say whether or not I'll agree or disagree with that assessment. If a "racist" is one who seeks to oppress another race or deny its validity or the right of its members to pursue liberty, happiness, or justice, then I do take strong issue with that term being used to describe my point of view.
>
> However, if one defines the term, "racist" as does Johns Hopkins University's Professor Robert Gordon, namely that "a racist is someone who entertains the possibility of there being a non-trivial difference, perhaps genetic in origin, between racial groups on some dimension of important," then I'll not take issue, but rather will agree with that characterization.

This answer also helps illustrate the various meanings attached to the label racist.

Molly Gill (1993:77–78), a movement person who edits *Rational Feminist,* contended in her letter to *Anarchy* that

> "racism" is not a bad word. It is a word brainwashed into the American public's mind by the ethnic media masters of the nation as a pejorative word. Anybody with a brain in their head is a racist: He loves his/her own race and wishes to live among his/her own race rather than in a mixed jungle of "integrated" cultures which all hate each other but won't admit it.
>
> Look around the world today and see what enforced integration of cultures, as well as races, has done to the world. This bullshit about pretending that we are all equal is unhistoric, stupid as hell and hypocritical. The white race, or the European culture is the one which conquered the world and dominated it for centuries and is now being given a guilt trip about it and saying it isn't nice.

Several of our other respondents in the movement also tended to define racialist in positive ways. For example, Nocmar, a young man who belongs to a movement group called Clan Rook, wrote: "It in no way means hate for any other race, it simply means a love for my own race. Also that I am conscious of my race and proud of it, as should anyone about their race," and a National Socialist not wishing to be identified indicated: "Loving your own race—our Aryan Race—and putting the survival and self preservation of our 'folk' above all else. The White Race First!" In addition to the love aspect, there is a behavioral component, a willingness to act on behalf of the race to maintain racial purity. Harry Bertram of the Populist Party explained that a racialist was "Someone who loves his or her race and is willing to do something to preserve it," and Bobby Norton of AN declared: "I believe that our race is being destroyed systematically and if we don't take a stand—if we don't work to try to save our race the time is coming when there will no longer be a white man on the face of the earth. So being racialist to me is someone who has a great deal—probably more than an average amount of love for their own."

Although physical traits and intelligence are clearly associated in the racist literature, the relationship of race and intelligence has indeed been a controversial one in the social science literature. Marger (1991:22) has pointed out that most social scientists of today accept that the environment rather than racial inheritance is the major factor influencing intelligence, but occasionally research has challenged this view, including Arthur Jensen's work that maintained heredity was the major cause in explaining IQ differences between blacks and whites. The white racialist paper *The Truth at Last* (#371 n.d.:1) maintained that Jensen's 1969 work "found that two-thirds to three-fourths of the I.Q. difference is the result of genetics and not the environment." Kühl (1994:3–11) discussed a number of scientists who support the "new" scientific racist work, such as J. Philippe Rushton who maintained that whites and Asians were typically more family-oriented and intelligent than blacks and anthropologist Roger Pearson who advanced the idea that the white race is threatened by inferior genetic stock.[3] Simpson and Yinger (1972:55–56) have identified numerous concerns that social scientists have regarding the relationship of race and intelligence (IQ), including that, although average test scores of blacks may be lower, the scores are related more to factors subject to change than to racial differences. Also, a number of blacks score higher than the average white, and IQ tests have questionable reliability and validity. Simpson and Yinger suggest that one should not assume distinctive genetic or racial homogeneity of the different groups.

The 1994 publication of *The Bell Curve* by Richard Herrnstein and Charles Murray has been cited by movement people to support the racist view of the link between race and IQ. The movement paper *The Truth at Last* (#378:1) carried an article, "Book Threatens Liberal's Line on Racial Equality," that stated: "The book cites many sources proving that Negroes, on average, have an I.Q. 15 points lower than that of Whites. . . . Most importantly the book proves that I.Q. is *inherited* from ones [*sic*] parents and is *not* a product of environment."[4]

For Metzger (n.d.[5]), the ideology of racism is rooted in a biologically deterministic model. Racism is "one of the most powerful forces known to man. . . . Natural selection, racism and territorialism are as natural as the rising sun, and these forces cannot be defeated anymore than humans could stand in the path of a tornado." He maintains that the more antiracism is promoted, the more racism grows, thus suggesting this natural quality will not die but will flourish more when some try to extinguish it. This also seems to suggest the importance of environmental impact. A WAR cartoon by A. Wyatt Mann (n.d.) illustrates the racist conception of the black man's brain, including the influence of culture on the mind.

American Front (n.d.a.) has published a brochure entitled "Some Facts about Blacks" that illustrates their belief in a strong connection of physical traits with culture and intelligence. Traditionally liberal questions like "But haven't blacks been victims of oppression? Isn't this why most blacks are living in such poor economic and social conditions today?" are answered in such a way to suggest that it's not the

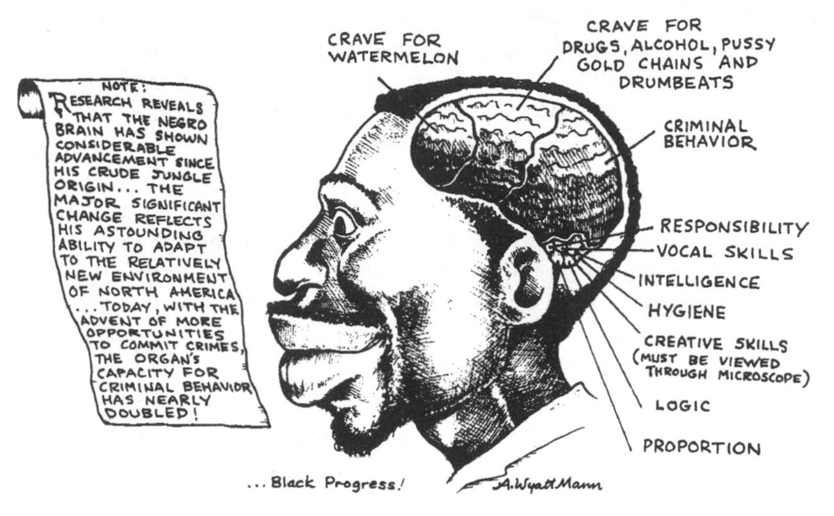

Figure 3. WAR cartoon of "What's on a Nigger's Mind" by A. Wyatt Mann (n.d.).

social conditions but the natural inferiority of blacks that makes them different. For example, the brochure suggests that although various immigrant groups have been oppressed, they have advanced more rapidly than blacks. Also, blacks did not create any of the "great civilizations of antiquity," and they score 15 to 20 points less than whites on IQ tests. In addition, American Front points out that William Shockley, who shared a Nobel Prize in physics, has maintained that the more conceptually difficult the questions on the IQ test, the greater the difference in scores between blacks and whites.

The Torch contained an editorial "Is the Negro to Blame?" by Pastor Thom Robb (1990:3). While trying to answer this question, Robb pictures Negroes like wild animals but cautions that people can't fault them for doing what is natural:

The Negro blames the White man and his power structure for the ill he must suffer. It is not, his fault, so they tell us, that they are forced to lash out in violence in order to gain the political reform they seek. They tell us that we are to blame because we have not dealt fairly with them. But should we actually blame the Negro for acting in a way that is ***natural*** to him? Do we blame an animal of the forest for acting in the manner which is his instinct? Of course not! Then can we really blame the Negro for acting in the savage manner which is his instinct?

Movement sources discuss numerous cases where perceived biological characteristics or cultural factors are noted to explain differences between the races. Next we consider how the concept of race has played a major role in shaping the movement's desire for separatism.

White Separatism

Many social scientists have viewed the white supremacist movement as a reactionary movement that wants to re-create a past social order. Somewhat similarly, the movement has been viewed as a countermovement to defeat or destroy the already existing civil rights movement. However, we believe that much of today's movement is separatist in orientation, wanting to remove its supporters from an integrated society. According to Barker (1993:xii–xiii), a former law enforcement officer who wrote a book describing the recent movement especially in the Northwest, "Although it cannot be denied that racist and supremacist beliefs are embraced by many in the movement, the term separatist probably goes further in defining their position than does supremacist. To them, the issue of racial separation is inherently more important than the desire for racial dominance or control."

Mrs. David (Katja) Lane of Wotansvolk—14 Word Press suggested that white separatism was key, whereas white supremacy wasn't significant:

Most white people that I know inside and outside the movement don't want to run anybody else's life, do not want to dominate other people, other nations. . . . I know personally in my heart I don't want to own or run China, or Africa, or Latin America or any other race or continent. And I don't think most people in the white power movement do. We just need to find our own place on this planet and we have come to recognize that it's an absolute requirement if we're going to survive, and we're denied our own nation, our own schools, neighborhoods, organizations, everything necessary for racial survival. To talk about whether one race is supreme is really irrelevant.

She also believed that the label *supremacist* could be used to demonize those in the movement.

The closeness of the 1995 vote over a secessionist referendum in Quebec Canada and the events in the former Yugoslavia are only two cases that illustrate the significance of the separatist agenda. According to sociologist James Davis (1978:145), "separatism reflects the belief that the only possible and acceptable route open to the group is total withdrawal from the dominant community." In the United States it was probably whites who first suggested separatist solutions to white and black relations in the eighteenth century (Davis 1978; Feagin 1971).

Shibutani and Kwan (1965) considered separatism as part of the struggle for cultural pluralism and indicated that separatists tend to do the following:

1. "Conceive of themselves as a group apart, a separate entity, not as a part of a larger population" (Shibutani and Kwan 1965:518).
2. Believe that their values are the only ones of real significance. They are not apologetic about their beliefs or customs.
3. Criticize others who do not support them, using terms such as deserters.
4. Emphasize the significance of ancestry or biological lineage, thus condemning intermarriage.
5. Reinforce their in-group feelings through rituals and celebrations of days of ideological significance.
6. Display their symbols with great pride, although many in society see them as marks of shame. Instead of feeling humiliation, they resent society for their condemnations.
7. Stress the glorious past.

In addition, Shibutani and Kwan (1965) noted that some may be "ardent racists" (p. 523) and their ideology may be supported by the complementary sentiments of love of the in-group and hatred toward the out-group.

Since separatism involves withdrawal from contact with the dominant community (Davis 1978:141), one may wonder why some whites would be advocating separatism for themselves when they are considered part of the dominant group. However, most whites in this movement do not see themselves as part of the dominant group and indeed feel betrayed by other whites who characterize them as racists and troublemakers. The music band Blue Eyed Devils makes this clear in the chorus of their song "Walk in Shame":

> Nigger lover, race traitor Walk in shame and hide your face
> Nigger lover, race traitor For false pride you sold out your race
> So now it's a civil war, white against white
> You against me, and I'll take your life

The predicted future race war will not likely be strictly black against white.

Barkun (1994:233) discusses territorial separation in the movement and points out that while the white separatists may disagree on certain parts, "all agree that short of overthrowing ZOG, the best path for the racialist right lies in somehow carving out a separate state." Mostly the area conceived of for the homeland is the Pacific Northwest within the borders of Washington, Oregon, Idaho, Montana, and Wyoming; this has been referred to as the Northwest Imperative. However, when Richard Butler of AN originally discussed a homeland as early as 1980, he seems to have envisioned something like John Harrell's "Golden Triangle." Christian-Patriots Defense League's Harrell had extolled people to withdraw to the center of the continent (the Midwest) to wait out evil Communism (Barkun 1994:107). Barkun believes the original suggestion of the Pacific Northwest probably came from Bob Miles in 1982. Aho (1990:57–58) suggests that Donald Clerkin of the Euro-American Alliance may have first advanced the idea of an "Europolis" as an armed encampment to be established in rough terrain, hard to access for those unwelcomed. Butler then reissued Clerkin's call. According to Major Clerkin in his March 13, 1996, letter to us, the late Pastor Bob Miles first told him about territorial separation of Aryans in North America. Since Clerkin is a Europeanist, he used the name "Europolis" for the proposed Aryan homeland.

In an undated publication entitled *The Birth of a Nation: A Declaration of the Existence of a Racial Nation Within Confines of a Hostile Political State,* Miles (n.d.b.) argued that the white race was at a crucial juncture because the political state was trying to destroy all racial differences:

> The course of the political state departs from the original beliefs of our fathers and the founders of this national State. **It is not the racial Nation which secedes from the political State. It is the political State which has seceded from the beliefs and the principles of our originally combined State and Nation. They have left us!**

Miles was thus putting the responsibility on the federal government for possible secession. He rejected armed rebellion and implored the political state to leave white separatists like himself alone:

If we are the modern "Neanderthals", then leave us in peace! Let us, our families, and our children be free of your modernistic garbage, your cookie-mold laws designed to compress everyone into a mud-colored nothingness! Let us go in peace! Let us be considered a Racial Nation of Aryans, living within the man-made boundaries of a political State. Let us be recognized as a Folk who have different beliefs, values, and different life-styles than those which comprise your "loyal" citizenry. Accept us as an element which is dolefully indigestible to you. You cannot consume us. You cannot absorb us. We are a strain that you cannot eliminate.

Miles (n.d.b.:back inside cover) included a map that was entitled "The Re-ethnization of North America," which illustrates the "alien invasion of North America" depicting territories of "mainly White Aryan occupation," "expanding alien, non-white occupation," and "heavy concentration of non-whites forces." The white areas were mainly in the five northwest states but included parts of Nevada, Utah, and Colorado.

According to *WAR* (1986:1) Miles indicated at the 1986 AN Congress that the Northwest Territorial Imperative would be achieved:

by White racialists moving to the area, buying land together or adjacent to each other and having families consisting of five and ten children. These children would be raised and educated in the tradition and fighting heritage of our own White people. We will win the Northwest by out-breeding our opponents and keeping our children away from the insane and destructive values of the Establishment.

Miles used religious justifications for the Aryan state by maintaining that Aryan spirituality should be free from contamination (Barkun 1994).

AN blends the concepts of race, religion, and politics/nation together to provide a form of unity in which race and religion neatly coincide under one national boundary. "Aryan Nations Theopolitical Platform" (n.d.b.) calls "for the re-establishment of White Aryan sovereignty over the lands of Aryan settlement and occupation" and "our Race is our Nation on earth." Further, according to the "Platform for the Aryan National State" (n.d.c.), only Aryans are allowed citizenship in this

THE RE-ETHNIZATION OF NORTH AMERICA

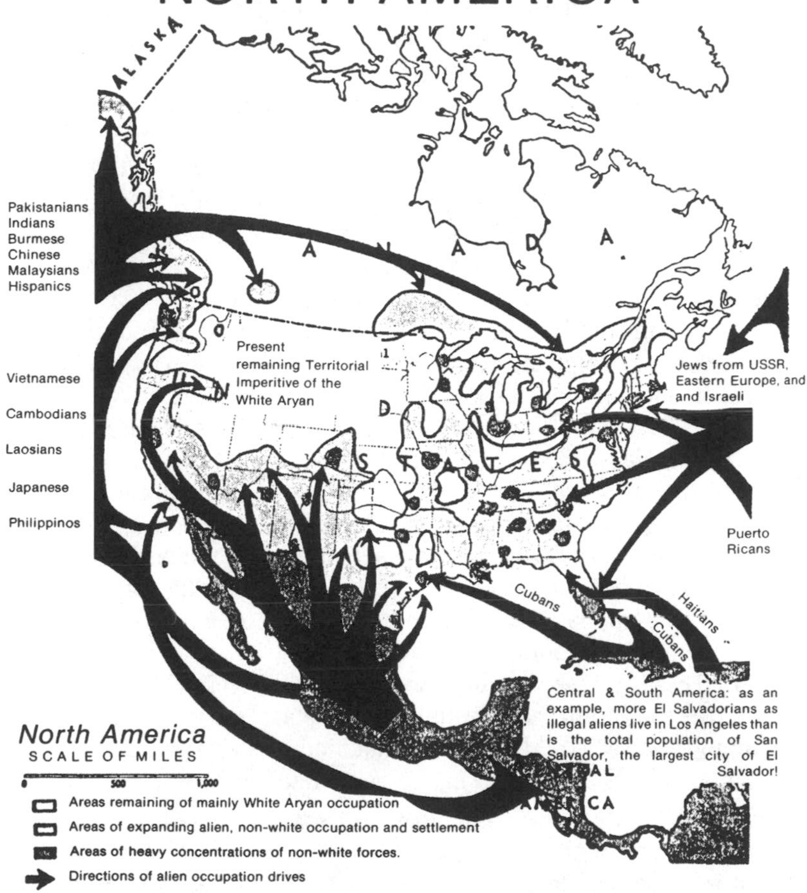

Alien Invasion of North America

In all the world's history never has a strong, productive, advanced Racial Nation of people, occupying a geographical territory, separated in the main by great oceans from the earth's diverse, primitive peoples, been invaded and occupied by these regressive alien hords with such impunity!

Aryan technology (Fulton's steamboat, Wright brother's airplane) plus Aryan treason made possible what was impossible for these mongrel peoples to accomplish. They, who have never dreamed of steam or jet power, land on our shores daily. Skilled Aryan captains, piloting Aryan-conceived craft, bring the alien hords to our shores in 747 luxury beyond the wildest imagination of ancient kings.

Map 1. The Re-ethnization of North America and the Territorial Imperative of Aryans in *The Birth of a Nation* by Robert E. Miles, n.d.b., back cover.

nation state, including voting rights, owning property, serving in the military or in law enforcement, holding political office, and so on. (Article I). True positive Christianity is encouraged, and other religious practices such as Talmudism (Judaism) and devil and heathen religions should be stopped (Article IV). Jews would be repatriated and their wealth redistributed. All members of the media would have to be citizens; publishing and circulating material not in the national welfare would be forbidden.

Many others connect the racial state with racial survival. A prominent movement figure, Louis Beam (1983:48), argued: "We must now separate ourselves from the mongrel nation that envelopes us. If our race is to have a future then a nation for ourselves, of ourselves, and by ourselves must be born on this continent!" David Lane, in "White Genocide Manifesto" (n.d.a:9), demanded "exclusive White homelands" in both Europe and North America because "the highest law is the preservation of one's kind." The *NSV Report,* a quarterly journal of the National Socialist Vanguard (1993:1–8), published "Brief History of the White Nationalist Movement," which described the movement as supporting a territorial imperative for a white nation and complete geographic separation of the world's races. The article suggested Klan groups did not press for geographic separation after World War II but over time have become more favorably disposed to this kind of separatism[6]; the National Socialist and Christian Identity groups have always been white nationalist in orientation.

In his essay "The Coming Aryan Republic" (1989:1–6), Clerkin argued that the "multi-racial/multi-cultural Staat" of "Washington criminal mongrelizers" could not be maintained. Instead of drawing very much on the U.S. Constitution, he recommended a system like the Roman Republic:

> All that is salvageable from that document [the Constitution] is certain elements of the Bill of Rights. The Constitution is therefore a tainted form, especially in the idea that *equality* should be the cornerstone of a government that serves the Aryan people. WE therefore totally reject the concept of not only racial equality, but also the false notion of individual equality. We have seen how unequally endowed individuals are in this world. Friedrich Nietzsche rightly stated that equality in nature is a fiction held by ideological fools and dangerous social tinkerers.
>
> What we have designed to govern us is removed to the period of the Roman Republic. The period of Roman Republicanism, which lasted four hun-

dred years (circa 450 B.C. to 50 B.C.), is the most perfect example of an aristocratic governance, one that reflected the innate inequality of individuals. Face it, most U.S. citizens do not vote; they don't care how they are governed. Media tell them what to think on a day-to-day basis. . . .

The Roman Republic was based upon the solidarity of the family as the prime unit in society. . . .

. . . we Aryans must reject the concept of equality—absolutely, as we construct our new Republic. This is not to say that the Aryan Republic will mistreat its people. Were it to descend to that level of misconduct, it would not be tolerated. But there is a natural "pecking order" in human affairs, just as there is amongst the lower orders of mammals. We cannot ignore this rank structure and succeed. Again, those who cannot stomach the idea that all men are definitely NOT created equal; they must resign themselves to the old, corrupt system operated by the Washington criminals. Our Aryan Republic will not tolerate liberalism. . . .

This Aryan Republic will be representative in operation. . . . Each person in the Aryan Republic will know his place—and be respected for serving in his place.

Mason in *Siege* (1992:89–91) advocated Hitler's National Socialism for the "state-to-be" once the system was destroyed. Rather than supporting authority at the county level, as Posse Comitatus had done, or at the state level, as NSRP had done, Mason argued for a strong centralized dictatorship:

In our view, the function of government is as the leader of its people, not merely caretaker or arbiter. Hitler said that the leading forces make the society and nation what it is and what it will become. This means taking the youth firmly in hand raising them up in the manner that our ideology commands so as to achieve the ever-more-perfect Race and State in the shortest possible time. Only a centralized government can accomplish this. So-called "rights" and "freedom" all take distant back seats to this highest goal. The task must be accomplished without petty interference from any quarter. . . . The word that will sooner or later pop up is dictatorship. We favor dictatorship: our own.

Mason is clear about what he perceives to be the best form of indoctrination and socialization in the separatist state.

"W.A.R. Position Paper *America First or Race First*" (WAR n.d.a.) suggests that WAR and Tom Metzger may have been the first to actually name the "ideological struggle, as White Separatism." Metzger (1996c:183) does not object to the Northwest Imperative but argues that the idea would not be "practical until after some kind of confrontation with the system. The system would never let you peacefully amass in one center of the country to promote ideas with which they do not agree." Other concerns of his revolve around economic issues and the amount of commitment to separatism:

> There is not an abundance of work in the Pacific Northwest. You have to have capital. You have to have people to come in and run the companies in which your people will work. You can do it, but it has to be based on somewhat of a fanatical zeal, and in the meetings I have been to on this, I just have not heard or see [sic] that zeal. I have heard talk. (Metzger 1996c:184)

In our interview, Metzger touched on his conception of the Aryan nation-state, which was quite Social Darwinist. In the spirit of Robert Michels's (1959) "iron law of oligarchy,"[7] Metzger indicated: "We believe that there is an aristocracy, a natural aristocracy that will rise to the top of any society, . . . an honest and good aristocracy . . . looking after the best interest of the culture and the race." He also indicated there shouldn't be any class barriers so that through competition whites from various social classes could become leaders. The emphasis would be on "the blood and the brains," suggesting that one's racial heritage and intelligence would be important in determining who would be the leaders. WAR (n.d.a.) also recommends applying white separatism internationally, pointing out the arbitrariness of national borders, and advocates smaller racial states that would be less likely to be drawn into the arms race and would be more aware of limited amounts of resources.

Somewhat similar to Metzger's view is Wilmot Robertson's (1992:9) conception of the "ethnostate" that would be created through "separation and reduction into small-scale political units, not accelerated coagulation into ever larger nations, empires and spheres of interest." The foreword to his book *The Ethnostate* (Robertson 1992:ix) identifies the significance of race to this new formulation:

> What is called for is a new form of government that would transform socially destructive into socially constructive forces. Race, now actively tearing countries apart, might be helpful in putting them back together, but this time in the form of autonomous, relatively self-sufficient collectivities that the author has chosen to designate as ethnostates.

Robertson (1992:16) stresses that the "basic *sine qua non* of an ethnostate, the prop on which it succeeds or fails, is racial and cultural homogeneity" but that being small in terms of both territory and population is essential as well. The ethnostate offers a sense of identity for its citizens and "is perhaps the only peaceful and sensible means of assuring white survival in an increasingly antiwhite, nonwhite world" (Robertson 1992:224).

The National Office of the National Alliance (1993) in its pamphlet *What Is the National Alliance?* called for white living space and an Aryan society that would be "racially clean." It includes an international design in which the white world would be rooted in Aryan values and harmonious with Aryan nature. This world would not necessarily be homogeneous, for there could be different societies such as Germanic, Slavic, Celtic, and so on.

Separatism rather than *segregation* is used by most movement people to describe their position. The International Separatist Front (ISF) (n.d.) defines the two concepts as:

SEGREGATION: Socially enforced isolation of a race, class, or ethnic group backed by a system of law. Always results in discrimination and lack of redress and opportunity for the oppressed group. Segregation eventually leads to rebellion by the segregated group.

SEPARATION: The maintenance of very separate and distinct cultures by divisions drawn primarily along racial and geographical lines. The desire and opportunity for self-determination. Free choice to remain with one's own kind in a setting free from unwanted intrusion by other racial groups, their influences, their political, and their religious systems. Freedom from oppressive genocidal governments. Racial sovereignty.

In our interview with him, Dennis Mahon, who is affiliated with WAR, expressed his dissatisfaction with segregation as "having the Blacks live on one side of the tracks and at night they go back there but during the day they're mowing your lawn—that's segregation. No, that's hypocritical as hell. . . . We got to do our own dirty work." James Dillavou of AN did not advocate segregation as a final goal of the movement, but he did see it as an acceptable short-term possibility before the beginning of separation in the United States. "If it was law and legal to do—have a white school and a black school—fine. I'd have no problem with it. . . . As the end desired thing—no, we would not want a segregationist society. But today's society. . . . it's a first basic step. . . . It depends on the situation."

Matt Hale, leader of National Socialist White Americans Party when interviewed and now leader of the World COTC, suggested crucial distinctions between the views of the past and the present:

We are separatists. We are—we don't consider ourselves supremacists in a sense because we are not out to rule anyone. We do believe the white race is a superior race, but we're not looking for the old, white supremacy where the white man's on top, the black man's on bottom and the black man is working for the white man, etc. We'd like to have a total geographical separation where no race is oppressing the other.

Jeff Schoep, a young man of the National Socialist American Workers Freedom Movement, also indicated to us his support of this view:

Well, we believe that the white people should have their own territorial imperative, their own nation. As in all the other races. National self-determination for all people. We agree with that so the blacks and everyone else deserves their own country also. We're not by any means out for the extermination of any race. We believe that everyone deserves their own country.

John C. Sigler III, aka "Duck," of Confederate Hammer Skinheads points out the applicability of separatism to the movement's goals:

To me, the term white separatism is simply a statement of our objectives. Any rational person must accept the fact that other races and cultures are not going to simply disappear, therefore, in order to continue our own cultural and perhaps genetic evolution, separatism represents the best interests of our people.

While most of our respondents view separatism positively, Molly Gill, who publishes *The Radical Feminist,* felt white separatism "means we whites will congregate in some living area such as the Northwest but it is a cop-out and sell-out since we Aryans founded and developed this USA as it was before the rot of the sixties was promoted by the Jews." She quite clearly sees the Northwest Imperative as an overly restrictive solution.

Not everyone in the movement makes clear-cut distinctions between separatism and segregation though. For example, in our interview with Rodney Stubbs, the Imperial Wizard of the American KKKK in Indiana, he felt the meaning of white separatism was similar to segregation and commented:

I believe segregation—the blacks should stay with the blacks, the whites with the whites. . . . Like the forced integration of schools and busing—I'm totally against that—you know. Working—at the workplace—ah, I see no problem with whites being able to work with blacks at a steel mill or wherever—but when they go home at night, the white goes home to his white family and the black should go home to his black or the gook or whoever we're talking about.

Even within the social science literature, the distinction may not always be clear between segregation and separatism. Pettigrew (1971), in his book *Racially Separate or Together,* did not seem to distinguish between segregation and separatism. He identified three key ideological assumptions of white separatists[8] that have parallels for black separatists:

1. "Whites and Negroes are more comfortable apart than together."
2. "Negroes are inherently inferior to whites, and this is the underlying reality of all racial problems."
3. "Since contact can never be mutually beneficial, it will inevitably lead to racial conflict" (Pettigrew 1971:301–2).

Pettigrew included the belief in white superiority in his assumptions of white separatism, but, as we have seen, movement members would not necessarily agree with this.

Many in the mainstream may find the Eastern Hammer Skinheads ("Definitions Every White Man Should Know" n.d.) white separatist definition of the Nation of Islam surprising. It is "the greatest ally of the White Separatist movement, who work for the logical end to an age of quarrel." Since the Nation of Islam and white separatists both favor the separation of the races, some in the movement advocate working together to achieve this goal. In a few cases the belief in separatism has actually prompted leaders of certain groups to work with blacks who favor separatism. Tom Metzger, for example, met with Black Panthers and even made a donation to Farrakhan. He told us that although Farrakhan was a fantastic speaker, he was concerned about separatists who use religious appeals. He commented: "I don't trust preachers and it seems like every time I try to deal with somebody who's a minister or preacher, I end up having problems. After working for over 10 years at building some kind of consensus and negotiations with blacks, we've come to the conclusion that we don't think it's going to happen." He felt that the black leaders weren't able to develop an infrastructure that would result in serious regional discussions.

According to *The Klansman* article "Unlikely Alliance Black Activists and Klan Unite against the System" (Baxter n.d.: 1, 13), members of The Invisible Empire, KKKK of Florida had joint demonstrations with black national activists who belonged to the Pan-African Inter-National Movement (PAIN) led by Chief Elder Osiris Akkebala. At one particular meeting, Akkebala maintained that racism involves the power to oppress, but the Klan today doesn't have such power and therefore is not a racist organization. John Baumgardner, then Grand Dragon of the Florida Klan, told the crowd that he favored repatriations and a reparation proposal made by PAIN. Having these joint meetings evidently led to some dissent among members of the national Klan, which may have been one of the reasons Baumgardner left that Klan. According to our interview with him:

We held a number of joint demonstrations here in Florida in the year before I left the Klan, which initially met with a lot of support from Klan leadership because I guess they thought that was an idea that could be exploited. We didn't look at it that way. We had developed a relationship with these people over a period of about six years and worked closer and closer with them behind the scenes and finally decided that we needed to take it out into the public's view and show them that maybe some of their ideas about the Klan weren't exactly correct. That we were able and willing to work with other races on issues that we shared a viewpoint in common. And, while it was popular at first with the national leadership, I think that overall the Klan membership around the country did not support the idea and put a lot of pressure on the national leadership to reject that and that's eventually what they did. They rejected the program. So, that's where the ISF was born.

The June 1996 edition of the *Florida Interklan Report* (1996a:2) edited by Baumgardner reported that he and a fellow Klansman had recently attended a Pan-African gathering in Orlando in which Minister Khalid Abdul Muhammed of the Nation of Islam identified the white man as "the Devil." Another part of that *Florida Interklan Report* (1996b:3) explained why it is important to work with other racial separatists:

Separation is the only answer for our problems—everything else has been tried. . . . Some militant blacks talk about how many crackers they are going to kill. I say kill all the crackers you want but leave white separatists alone or we will kill you. We know how to do that too. What we are trying to do by working with other racial separatists is prevent wholesale bloodshed. Some blood will obviously have to be spilled to get the government off our backs and to get the die-hard ignorant reactionaries out of the way but until that happens nothing substantial is going to change for the better.

Although certainly not typical, these are examples where parts of the movement have been willing to work with others of a different race who share the same strategy of racial separation. For movement members, racial separation should ideally lead to the movement achieving the preservation of the race.

The Major Goal of the In-group: Preservation and Advancement of the White Race The primary emphasis of this movement is on the preservation or the uplifting of the white race. The 14 Words of David Lane, a member of the Silent Brotherhood who is imprisoned, characterize the sentiment of the movement: "We Must Secure the Existence of Our People and a Future for White Children" (Lane, n.d.b:1). Similarly "Information for Prospective Members of the National Alliance" (National Alliance n.d.:1) makes the primacy of race clear: "Our ultimate goal is to build a better world and a better race." "White Aryan Resistance Positions" (WAR 1995a:11) also states it succinctly: "The great White Aryan race must be advanced and protected at all costs and above all other issues." In the Klan literature, the first item to explain what the Klan stands for (KKKK, n.d.b Harrison AR; Invisible Empire KKKK, n.d., S. Vineland NJ; Federation of Klans, n.d. Chicago, IL) is "The White Race: The irreplaceable hub of our Nation, our Christian faith, and the high levels of western culture and technology." The only way whites and the "Negro race . . . can develop their full potential and culture is through racial separation." The Klan is viewed as the savior of the white south and thus the preserver of the white race for all of America. Members are expected to "pledge themselves to the protection, preservation, and advancement of the White race." Only white non-Jewish American citizens can join the Klan. A well-known Klan slogan is "Racial Purity Is America's Security."

Skinheads also indicate the centrality of the white race in their lives. One who asked to be unidentified wrote: "My role is to live for my race and better myself so that ultimately I can better my race. Also, to be there for the movement when needed, ex. Rallies, marches, etc. . . ." To him *white separatism* meant "that our race should be separate from any other race, so that we can grow and prosper and better our race and ourselves."

Blood and Honor (USA), a skinzine (skinhead publication), identifies "THE WHITE RACE" as its cause (n.d.) and often publishes interviews of members of white power bands. Some of the names of white power bands illustrate their focus on race, including RAHOWA (Racial Holy War) "which is being waged right now for the survival of our kind on this planet" (*Blood and Honor* 1994a:4). The band name New Minority refers to "the White race and especially to the White male who is indeed becoming a minority on the continent which he himself pioneered" (*Blood and Honor* 1994b:9).

The lyrics often make it clear how significant the white race is in the lives of the band members and their supporters. For example, in Nordic Thunder's "My Honor, My Pride" part of one verse states:

> I think of the White children, so innocent and pure
> For they are the reason I am fighting in this war
> If I were the last man left I would carry on the fight
> To save my racial heritage and keep it pure and White
> I've sworn to protect my people, for that I am crucified
> I live for my Race and for my Race I will die

The tremendous commitment to the cause and membership in the elite group is also illustrated in Bound for Glory's song "Still Standing Here:"

> Some call me a Nazi, Some call me a man of hate
> Because I choose to speak my mind makes one irate
> Because I'm a man of honor, my actions speak louder than words
> for I prefer being a wolf than a sheep in your herd
> I have broken all the vices that have been placed in front of me
> My will is stronger than their chains, my strength has set me free
> I've seen so many before me fall giving that ultimate sacrifice
> That my well of tears have run dry, now I'm a man cold as ice
>
> [Chorus:]
> I don't ask others to follow the path I take
> I'm headed in only one direction, so make no mistake
> Reality is no joke, that's why so many live in fear
> Somedays I'm still surprised that I'm still standing here

The idea of standing up or standing tall for one's race is an important theme in the skinhead music that attracts young people to the movement or encourages them to share their beliefs. According to Joe of Nordic Thunder:[9] "One of our major aims is to release new material so that we can get our message across to White kids and keep the fire burning" (*Blood and Honor* 1994c:9).

The Folk (Volk) in National Socialism

The "folk" in National Socialism is an excellent example of the in-group. National Socialism has been considered a particular form of fascism by some social scientists. For example, Billig (1978b:6–8) identifies four key elements of fascist ideology: (1) nationalism and/or racism, which espouse a belief in the unity of a nation or race; (2) anti-Marxism and anti-communism because these belief systems would divide the race or nation on the basis of class differences; (3) statism, a strong belief in the role of the state to protect the race or nation and the capitalist system; and (4) the first three features are advanced in such a way to threaten democracy and individual freedom. According to this view, Nazism is a subset of fascism with its particular racial ideology and anti-Semitism that was advanced by Hitler. Rejai (1984:37), who considered fascism and Nazism[10] together in his analysis of various ideologies, identified nationalism, racism, and expansionism as key concepts. The " 'folkish (völkisch) state' . . . is an organic whole protecting, preserving, enhancing, and glorifying the quintessential traits of the Aryans" (Rejai 1984:39).

The Eastern Hammer Skinheads' "Definitions Every White Man Should Know" (n.d.) gives the *American Heritage* definition of National Socialism as "the ideology and practices of Nazis; especially the practice of state control of the economy, racist nationalism, and national expansion"; the white separatist version is "a form of government based on the ideology of Adolf Hitler in which unemployment is non-existent, medicine and transportation is socialized and racial separation is dominate [*sic*]. see Beneficial." Other movement literature such as the *NSV Report* of the National Socialist Vanguard (1989a) point out love of country and love of race are core to National Socialism as the German NSDAP used it. For some in the movement, National Socialism provides the means to implement the goal of preserving and advancing the Aryan race.

According to Matt Koehl and Official Program, NSWPP (1980), the folk is limited to those Aryans[11] who prove themselves worthy of it. The New Order (*White Power* 1983a:1) made its objective clear: "It is the goal of the New Order to attack the spiritual syphilis which is eating away at the soul of our Race in a bold and uncompromising manner, and to destroy the infection by massive doses of the proper antidote—the pure, undiluted medicine of the National Socialist world view as conceived by Adolf Hitler." The NSWPP platform states, "Our people must be turned away from the present path of materialism, cynicism, and egoism and become inspired by racial idealism and a rebirth of traditional Aryan spiritual values" (Official Program, NSWPP, Koehl, 1980:n.p.[8]). Jordan (n.d.:4–5) notes that "National Socialism stands relentlessly opposed to every manifestation of ill health, ugliness, and degeneracy in the cultural and spiritual, no less than in the political and economic spheres. . . . It evaluates good and bad, right and wrong, as that which benefits or harms the folk." This particularly illustrates how the determination of what is moral is strongly tied to the sense of the community, what is good for one's race. Race, history, and culture are essential ingredients for the folk and are embodied in the same blood, soil, language, and customs. "Folk is a community of descent and fate" (*SS Race Theory and Mate Selection Guidelines* translated by Karl Hammer 1990:9).

In the "enlightened community . . . anything which interferes with the smooth and harmonious functioning of society must be ruthlessly suppressed" (Official Program, NSWPP, Koehl, 1980:n.p.[3]). Thus the community takes precedence over individual desires. "National Socialism's belief in the folk as the basic value, and its totality of outlook, result, figuratively speaking, in thinking with the blood on all questions . . . It upholds the dictum, 'All for the folk and the folk for all' " (Jordan n.d.:6,8). The folk ideal and sense of community are quite hierarchical and elitist in National Socialism. Within the folk there are "hereditary differences of capacity to serve the community. Accordingly for the maximum good of all, the superior must lead the inferior. The natural leaders must be selected, established as a hierarchical elite under a supreme leader, and empowered to fulfill their functions" (Jordan n.d.:7).

The NSDAP/AO wants to re-create a National Socialist–led, reunified German Reich and "ultimately, a New Order in Europe and throughout the White world conducive to the survival, health, happiness and further development of our Race" (Lauck 1991). The first tenet of the New Order's (n.d.a) brochure "Principles of National Socialism" identifies the upward struggle of our race and the fight for

Figure 4. Aryan Warrior Carving the 14 Words of David Lane Designed by Ron McVan of Wotansvolk—14 Word Press.

the common good of our peoples. Clan Rook, an organization with National Socialist and Odinist leanings, is "dedicated to the Aryan Volk's evolution toward a higher species" (Clan Rook n.d.). To achieve their goal they engage in numerous educational activities including the following:

EXPOSING HISTORICAL LIES, MEDIA MANIPULATION AND THE BRAINWASHING OF OUR PEOPLE BY THE SO-CALLED EDUCATIONAL SYSTEM.

EDUCATING THE WHITE PEOPLES IN THEIR TRUE ARYAN HISTORY, TRUE ARYAN SPIRITUALITY, TRUE ARYAN HERITAGE AND CULTURE, TRUE ARYAN VALUES, AND WHAT MUST BE DONE TO MAINTAIN THESE.

The important role that the media and education could play in shaping Aryan beliefs is recognized.

Perceived Threat from the Out-Group Major racial concerns of the white separatists include the perceived threats from intermarriage,[12] minority population growth, growing minority crime rate, increasing immigration, and the loss of jobs to minorities. Some of the social science literature already mentioned has noted that self-interest and perceived threat may be key in helping understand symbolic racism. From the movement point of view, intermarriage or miscegenation destroys the "Aryan race." One article on actress Sally Struthers and her unhappy love life with three Jewish men is entitled "White Renegade Learns Too Late That Race-Mixing Is Forever" (*White Power* 1983b:2). She has a half-Jewish daughter and thus, according to the article, has committed an act of unforgivable racial pollution: "The air, the waters and the land can all be cleansed if they become befouled, but racial pollution destroys the purity of Nature for all time." A leaflet from New Order (n.d.b) entitled "Help Save This Endangered Species" shows a white woman and her white daughter, thus suggesting a similar line of thought. It claims that whites will become a minority in the United States by 2030.

An additional leaflet (NSLF Headquarters, n.d.) quotes George Lincoln Rockwell as saying, "The lowest forms of humanity are breeding so fantastically fast that we will soon suffer the worst plague in history . . . THE BLACK PLAGUE." Hispanics as well as blacks and Jews are criticized for the decline in the Aryan race. Storm (1983:2) believes both blacks and Hispanics are destroying the white race: "These friendly folk from the South (Hispanics) are breeding at an even earlier age than the niggers, which was long viewed to be impossible. . . . Spics intermarry at an even higher rate than niggers. Many foolish whites consider the taco bender as one of their own since they are not black." Whites will be extinguished according to Storm, if this pattern is not stopped.

Another common fear played on in the literature is that whites are losing their jobs to minority group members, especially to immigrants. Asian nations particularly are cited as having taken jobs away from American workers (*The Thunderbolt* 1983a:1). There is fear of the "Yellow Peril" as well as the "Black Plague." *The Truth at Last* (n.d. #364:1) declared "Anheuser-Busch Dumps Whites Gives Jobs to Non-Whites" and *The Truth at Last* asked "Future White Minority?" and noted how America's standard of living is declining:

> Immigrants are flooding into our nation willing to work for the minimum wage (or less). Super-rich corporate executives are flying all over the world in search of cheaper and cheaper labor so that they can "lay off" their American employees. . . .
>
> . . . many young White families have no future! They are not going to receive any appreciable wage increases due to job competition from immigrants—**meaning both legal and illegal immigrants!** (n.d. #355:10)

Movement publications suggest that not only are the number of minorities increasing through their high birth rates and immigration, but crime has greatly risen. One issue of *The Truth at Last* (n.d. #350:10) headlined "Negro Crime Wave Sweeps America" and another (n.d. #374a:1) echoed "Negro Crime Out of Control." According to the latter:

> Black crime is clearly out of control in America. This 12% of the population is committing 64% of all the violent crime nation-wide. This figure reaches 90% or more in many major cities. Liberals understand this grave threat, but refuse to admit to the fact that it is a *racial problem*. (*The Truth at Last* n.d. #374a:1)

WAR's cartoons, especially those by A. Wyatt Mann, are well known in the movement and are one of the reasons *WAR* has been described as having "some of the most outspoken and vehement racist and anti-Jewish rhetoric in the neo-Nazi movement" (George and Wilcox 1992:375). One cartoon (*WAR* n.d. vol. 11, #1a:20) of the Aryan and "the biggest blackest nigger" on the beach shows the black man kicking sand in the face of a young white man and woman. The black man

Figure 5. Cartoon of the Aryan and the Biggest Blackest Nigger Designed by A. Wyatt Mann, in *WAR* Vol. 11, #1, p. 20.

tells the white one he would beat him up but he needs his strength to rape white women. The young white man gets sick and tired of being a "liberal democrat," decides to subscribe to the WAR newspaper and gets a *real* body. Then he becomes the "Nazi of the Beach" telling the black man "Fuck you, you dope-dealing ghetto ape." The cartoon portrays the black harassing the white woman and dealing drugs and the white man eventually learning to stand up for his beliefs.

Movement leaders used the Los Angeles riots of 1992 to reinforce their beliefs about blacks. *WAR* (n.d. vol. 11, #2a:3) has a cartoon of a black man grinning, wearing an X T-shirt, and carrying a TV set with its price tag still attached. There is a broken window of TV City behind him. According to the caption, the L. A. Riots made blacks happy. In addition to portraying the looting, another cartoon (*WAR* vol. 11, #2b:2) depicts the violence showing a large black man just having thrown a white man against a truck. The caption suggests Reginald Denny was paying for being white but queried the readers about how much sacrifice they would make.

In their song "Race Riot," which is part of their album *Declaration of WAR,* RAHOWA also picks up on the image of the race riot and applies it in a more general sense to the racial strife and the threat to the white race.

> *Race Riot* (Hawthorne/Armstrong/Latvis)
> Bloody riots on the streets, the niggers run amok,
> Tremble in fear, White man, the reaper's in the shadowland,
> Save your children, lock your doors,
> You can't come out here no more,
> On this eve blood shall be shed,
> The streets and rivers run deep red.
>
> [Chorus:]
> Don't you know we're fighting a Race Riot! Race Riot!
> Don't you know we're fighting a Race Riot! Race Riot!
> Don't you, Don't you know?
> Don't you, Don't you know? White man!
>
> Violence, anger released full-force,
> Racial tensions explode their course,
> You could've made all so well,
> Now your land's a living hell.

One response of whites to race riots and violence in general is to arm themselves. An American Front (n.d.b) flier headlines "Whites Must Arm! IT'S A JUNGLE OUT THERE" because of antiwhite hate crimes in Los Angeles and other metropolitan areas. Here again the 1992 riots in Los Angeles seem to have helped intensify the racial stereotypes. Robb's *White Patriot* (n.d.b #89:1) shows a picture of three black men, at least one of which is kicking a white man on the ground. Part of the caption

Figure 6. L. A. Riot Cartoon with Looting Designed by A. Wyatt Mann in *WAR* Vol. 11, #2, p. 3.

Figure 7. L. A. Riot Cartoon of Trucker Paying "Luxury Tax" Designed by A. Wyatt Mann, in *WAR*, Vol. 11, #2, p. 2.

reads " 'Get the white man' was the howl coming from this pack of Negroes as they began to kick this White man, caught with the wrong color of skin in the wrong neighborhood." Underneath in red it states "This is your brother/your father/your son!" Further below is the statement "The recent riots that occurred throughout the nation resulted from the acquittal of the four policemen on trial for the alleged beating of Rodney King sends a powerful message to White America. . . . To us the message is crystal clear, 'If you think you have trouble with minorities now—wait until they become the majority.' " The perceived threat of the victimization of whites by savage blacks is emphasized.

Rubin (1994) examined the attitudes of the white working class and lower middle class in the United States in her book *Families on the Fault Line: America's Working Class Speaks about the Family, the Economy, Race, and Ethnicity.* These whites did indeed feel threatened from such things as immigration, intermarriage, and affirmative action policies. Rubin (1994:186) explained it this way:

> It's this confluence of forces—the racial and cultural diversity of our new immigrant population; the claims on the resources of the nation now being made by those minorities who, for generations, have called America their home; the failure of some of our basic institutions to serve the needs of our people; the contracting economy, which threatens the mobility aspirations of working-class families—all these have come together to leave white workers feeling as if everyone else is getting a piece of the action while they get nothing.

She points out that being white no longer automatically means dominance in politics and argues that although it might well seem ridiculous to many, especially minorities, that white men are victims, "Yet it's not wholly unreal, at least not for the men in this study who have so little control over their fate and who so often feel unheard and invisible, like little more than shadows shouting into the wind" (Rubin 1994:245). Rubin's ideas seem applicable to many white separatists who feel their concerns are not being heard and therefore they want to form a new society.

Intolerance toward the out-group of minorities is frequently exhibited, but whites who lack interest or disagree with the goals of the movement are also criticized. At rallies, whites in the crowd are often asked to join the marches. Whites who aren't involved in the movement are sometimes referred to as "sheeple" (people who act like sheep being led to the slaughter). Clerkin (1996:1–2), concerned by the power of ZOG, the implications of the passage of the Anti-Terrorism Bill, the "invasion by racial aliens, the incorporation of America into the World Village, and the absolute dissolution by fiat of natural rights of the Aryan-American Staatsvolk" (p.1), clearly holds the average white person accountable: "I place the blame on Boobus americani, the lamebrains, the BLANKOS, who still make up a voting majority. The overthrow of the White race on this continent was made possible by their own apathy and cowardice" (pp. 1–2).

WAR (1995b:1) reflects on the implications of the defeat of Germany in World War II and the misguided attitudes of many whites who have been willing to fight against other whites in various countries:

> On the heels of the great Anglo-Jew celebration of the defeat of Germany, one must ponder the following. In reality, white sheeple celebrate the destruction of white civilization. Placing blame is useless. The facts are that none of the white nations involved have returned to their racial greatness of before the Great Aryan Slaughter.
>
> Positive Eugenics, racial separation and a host of other pro-Aryan advances were destroyed in the process. . . . Never follow the Washington Criminals into economic war or war against another white nation. Your war is right here at home and it's a war for the race.

The cry for white America to wake up and develop racial consciousness is illustrated in RAHOWA's song:

> *White People Awake* (Hawthorne/Latvis/Armstrong)
> White People Awake, Save Our Great Race
> White People Awake, Save Our Great Race
> You know our system's run by the secret societies,
> They're doing what they need to bring the White Race to its knees,
> We gotta rise up now, White man, take a stand!
> If we all bond together we can take back our homeland!
> White People Awake, Save Our Great Race.

NSDAP/AO (1994b:1) makes a similar plea: "Whiteman! [*sic*] Don't roll over and play dead stand up and fight for an all-White America!" Pete Peters of Scriptures for America casts the issue in religious overtones. He wrote *America the Conquered* (1991:vii) stressing America had been conquered unaware and that "It's time we wake up!," citing Isaiah 52:1,2 "Awake, awake . . . Shake yourself from the dust, rise up, O captive Jerusalem: loose yourself from the chains around your necks." As suggested by these examples, whites who are not part of the movement are blamed sometimes as much as minorities or even more for the current situation and need to have their racial consciousness raised.

White Power

The term *white power* is frequently used to suggest the movement's desire for white power to control the threat from the out-group. According to an anonymous skinhead, white power is "being able to live in a truly homogenous state . . . where you don't have to support, cope, or cater to a person of color or of a semitic persuasion. A system run by whites for whites. To be able to show our pride and live as a proud volk without having 'multi-culturism' shoved down our throats." Angelena Summers, who has been associated with SS Action Group and Adolf Hitler Free Corps, wrote white power meant to her that "white people can have their own life free from niggers, their crime, and jewish control of our government." Rook Prime of Clan Rook viewed white power as "the power needed for white sovereignty in white lands, the power to control white destinies in white manner in whatever direction that might take us, the power to heal our souls and our material existence as a people, the power to repair the environment that the greedy damaged and the complacent ignored."

"White power" is also a common chant heard at rallies as well as a potential label for the movement. As John C. Sigler III, aka "Duck," of the Confederate Hammer Skinheads noted: "In my opinion 'white power' is simply a generic term denoting a pro-white position. Being one who enjoys the use of coordinated system of semantics, I generally reserve 'White Power' for drunken barroom conflicts and rallies and marches."

At times, movement people question whether the use of the term *white power* is appropriate. Among them are Richard Ford of the Fraternal White Knights of the KKK, John Standring of the Christian Guard, and Tom Metzger of WAR, all who have pointed out that whites are currently in powerful government positions but they do not represent the views of the movement. Standring, in his interview, told us:

> The majority of the Congress is white. And that's white power. And the majority of the Senate is white and that's white power. And the White House is white supposedly and if that's the kind of white power you have reference to—I'm opposed to it. I'm not for that kind of white power because they've taken our taxes and given them away to foreign countries and they put the widows and orphans on the street.

These are two related views of white power—one that it is desired by the movement to help achieve their goals and the other that recognizes that currently the whites in power do not represent the movement's concerns. The separatists' view of the illustrious past, though, seems to provide another example of white power.

Glorifying the Past White Civilization During the time of the European colonial powers in the nineteenth and early twentieth centuries, many writers emphasized the contributions of white civilization to the development of the world. This can be seen in the writings of people like Count Arthur de Gobineau and Houston Stewart Chamberlain in Europe and Madison Grant and Lothrop Stoddard in the U.S. (Marger 1991:33). According to de Gobineau (ca. 1853–55): "History shows us that all civilizations derive from the white race, that none can exist without its help, and that a society is great and brilliant only so far as it preserves the blood of the noble group that created it" (quotation taken from ADL n.d.b:34). Ideas like these were later espoused by Adolf Hitler in *Mein Kampf*:

> All the human culture, all the results of art, science, and technology that we see before us today, are almost exclusively the creative product of the Aryan. . . . If we were to divide mankind into three groups, the founders of culture, the bearers of culture, the destroyers of culture, only the Aryan could be considered as the representative of the first group. From him originate the foundations and walls of all human creation, and only the outward form and color are determined by the changing traits of character of the various peoples. (quotation taken from ADL n.d.b:39)

Various groups in the current movement indicate strong beliefs in the contributions of whites to civilization. *The Truth at Last* (n.d. #371:1) notes how civilization can be saved only if the intelligent white race is preserved: "Civilization is upheld by the superior White genetic pool."

Christian Identity also stresses how the Anglo-Saxon-Scandinavian and Germanic peoples fit God's description of His chosen people (Comparet n.d.a:12–14). "They are a great nation and a company of nations, all of the same race" (p. 12), "they are very numerous" (p. 12), "they are a maritime people" (p. 12), "they are the greatest military powers" (p. 13), "they have expanded in colonies in all directions" (p. 14) and "they have maintained the continuity of the throne of David" (p. 15). On this last point, Comparet suggests that "the lineage is clearly traced in the histories of Ireland, Scotland, and England, unbroken down to the present British Queen Elizabeth" (p. 15).

The KKKK introductory issue "This is the Klan" (*White Patriot* n.d.a:2), asks: "Why do you think white people are superior to black people?" The response is:

The question facing our people is "Do we have a right to exist?" You see, even if white people were nothing more than a race of cave men that roamed the forests, half-naked and spoke in grunts, we **still** have a right to maintain our culture and our racial identity. . . .

But we know that we are more than simple *cave men*. From our race, a mere minority of the world's population, have come the literary classics of a William Shakespeare, the creative genius of a Thomas Edison, the military genius of a Hannibal, the political vision of a Thomas Jefferson, the art of a Michelangelo, the scientific insight of a Galileo, the pioneer spirit of a Davy Crocket and the compassion of a Florence Nightingale.

Our people have explored the frontier, have conquered diseases, have tamed the wilderness, have looked deep into the heavens, have left our footprints upon the surface of the moon, have researched the depths of the mind, have brought warmth where it was cold. . . .

Our people have given much to the advancement of civilization and what a pity it would be if our people should cease to exist.

This statement notes the greatness of the white race without explicitly maintaining its superiority over other races.

Our decision to call the contemporary movement *separatist* should not be construed to mean that we don't believe that most, if not all, whites in this movement feel they are superior to blacks. Part of their belief is rooted in perceived biological differences between the races and in the case of Christian Identity in their interpretation of the Bible as whites being God's "chosen people." Some movement members also frame their beliefs as *white supremacist,* although others avoid using that term. Pastor August B. Kries III of Posse Comitatus told us: "I wear the label white supremacist with no problem. I don't try to hide it. . . . Like—anybody that calls themselves Identity, Racial Identity, or Christian Identity—is nothing but a white supremacist." Pastor Kries III did indicate that he believed "that there's those out there that call themselves white separatist that truly are just separatist. They just believe in living separate from the other races and then there's those out there like I that believe that we are supreme over all the other races."

Steve Bowers of the National Socialist group Adolf Hitler Free Corps told us: "I guess I am a white separatist in the fact that I don't want them in my country, but I'm more of a white supremacist than a separatist." When asked to explain what he meant by white supremacist he told us:

I believe that the Aryan race was ordained by nature or providence or God or whatever you—whatever term you prefer—I believe that it was ordained to be

> the master of the planet earth. And history seems to point in that direction and only in the latter half of the. . . . 20th century have we retreated from that. And I think it's just because our people have grown soft and weak due to endless liberal propaganda and the control of the media and things like that. So, by supremacy . . . I definitely believe that . . . we are masters and we've got to regain our position of authority in this world.

Bowers expressed concern about how some basic beliefs in the movement have been framed, including the use of terms like *racialist* and *separatist.* He referred to himself as a racist rather than a racialist and told us:

> What we have in this movement today is a bunch of guilt-ridden, little men. They're not convinced that they're right. They allow television to convince them that they're wrong and so they try to sugar-coat, hide their little guilt feelings by terms like *separatism* and *racialist* and things that sound nice, but don't mean anything in the long run. In other words, if you're going to be a Nazi or you're going to be a Klansman—by God—be one.

Bowers recognized some in the movement were concerned by how they had been labeled, but he did not want to make the movement's views more palatable. Rather he called for the movement to be "much more militant and much more fanatical and quit allowing these little ideological differences to get in the way."

Most people in the movement indicate preference for some form of separatism to preserve the white race and avoid race-mixing. The Klan especially stresses the historical contributions of the white race and the fraternal aspects of their organization, while neo-Nazis draw on National Socialist Aryan ideals propagated initially by Adolf Hitler. Christian Identity supporters, which include many Klan members, stress the link of the lost tribes of Israel to the Aryan race, and skinheads use racialist music to attract youth to the movement and express their separatist beliefs and dedication to the cause.

In the last 15 years or so, *separatism* has become a key term in the discourse of the current movement. The ideology of the movement is not constant and nonproblematic; rather, movement groups and their leaders and supporters have been actively involved in formulating ideas and meaning for those in the movement. The ideology has been and continues to be subject to modification in response to both the internal changes in the movement and the external social, economic, and political developments.

Anti-Semitism

Sniderman and Piazza (1993:53) found that people's acceptance of black stereotypes was closely related to their acceptance of Jewish stereotypes. There is a long history of anti-Semitism in Western societies. Lerner (cited in Sifry 1993:92) defines anti-Semitism as "the systematic discrimination against, denigration, or oppression of Jews, Judaism, and the cultural, intellectual, and religious heritage of the Jewish people." Quinley and Glock (1979) identified several key negative stereotypes of Jews, including being monied and dishonest, clannish and conceited, and pushy and power hungry. The key characterization of Jews over time seems to be that "of the Jew as a cheap, miserly manipulator of money, forever preoccupied with materialism, and consequently possessing virtually unlimited economic power" (Glock and Stark 1966:109). Sifry (1993:93) noted a November 1992 ADL survey that found about one-fifth of U.S. adults showed anti-Semitic views. Favoring social distance from Jews or stereotyping them as dishonest or greedy seems to be on the decline, but the images that Jews have too much power or that they support Israel more than the United States have actually increased (Sifry 1993). Marger (1991:207) points out that at times the attributions of Jewish power appear contradictory. For example, Jews have been pictured as both leaders of the world capitalist conspiracy and of the world communist one.

Langmuir (1990:351–2) questions the standard definition of anti-Semitism, stating "we as social scientists should free 'antisemitism' from its racist, ethnocentric, or religious implications and use it only for what can be distinguished empirically as an unusual kind of human hostility directed at Jews." To him, Jews face hostility that is similar to what other groups face on the basis of their group membership, but they also experience situations where actual Jewish existence is seriously threatened as "the Jews" irrationally become some kind of symbol that justifies they can be eliminated from the world.

Anti-Semitism is viewed very differently from the movement's perspective. According to *Webster's Third New International Dictionary* (Gove 1967:2065), the definition of *Semite* is:

> 1: a member of one of the peoples listed in the Scriptures as descended from Shem, a son of Noah 2: a member of one of a group of peoples of southwestern Asia speaking Semitic languages and chiefly represented now by the Jews and Arabs but in ancient times also by the Babylonians, Assyrians, Aramaeans, Canaanites, and Phoenicians.

Christian Identity maintains that the majority of the white race are the descendants of Noah's son Shem and thus are predominantly Semitic. To them the Jews have little if any Semitic ties:

> Since the majority of people in modern Palestine and the world who call themselves "Jews" are descendants from a "Turko-Mongolian tribal people" known as Khazars, and have "little or no trace of Semitic blood in them," but are rather descendants of Ashkenaz who was one of the sons of Gomer, who was a son of Japheth, then anyone who would be critical or oppose these people cannot be anti-Semitic. Anti-impostors, anti-liars, anti-deceivers, anti-con artists, anti-Christ haters, yes. But anti-Semitic, no. (Rick Savage, compiler of "Frequently Asked Questions and Answers on Israel-Identity," transmitted on the Internet Feb. 27, 1995)

When we asked John Standring of the Christian Guard how he would respond to the media labeling the movement anti-Semitic, he said: "Well to begin with you have to define the word *semite.* The Arabs are semites and I'm not anti-Arab. Therefore, I would not be anti-semitic. We believe that we're the descendants of the lost sheep of the house of Israel which makes us semitic. And I'm certainly not opposed to myself and my family." As we pointed out before, according to Christian Identity beliefs, the white race is predominantly Semitic. Therefore, from their point of view, white people should not be accused of being anti-Semitic because that would mean they are against themselves, which would not make sense. From their perspective, anti-Jewishness may characterize the movement but not anti-Semitism.

Several of the stereotypes of Jews are shown in one of A. Wyatt Mann's cartoons (*WAR* vol. 11, #1b:21) showing a Jewish man with a long nose pictured in his underwear holding stacks of dollar bills in unknown denominations in his hands. He is shrewd and scheming, living off of others, and lying about the Holocaust. This image of Jews as portrayed by white racialists is quite different from that of their views of other minorities. Jews are seen as more powerful and a much more formidable opponent; indeed they are the main force shaping events that are harming the white race.

In 1973 J. B. Stoner made it very clear that the Jews are the principal force needing to be overcome:

> It is necessary for every White racist to recognize the fact that the White Race does have enemies.... In their natural state, White people would not interbreed with negroes. However, in the captivity of Jew propaganda and of the

Figure 8. Cartoon on the Jewish Parasite Designed by A. Wyatt Mann in *WAR,* Vol. 11, #1, p. 21.

Jew news media and Jewish control of education, innocent White people are duped into mating with negroes even though it is unnatural . . .

The negro is a violent enemy and he is a biological enemy because negro blood destroys White blood when the two are mixed together. However, the negro is not the enemy. The Jew is THE enemy of our White Race and the Jew is using the negro in an effort to destroy the White Race that he so passionately hates.

Simply observe Jew Propaganda on radio, television, in Hollywood, in the schools, in the newspapers, in the churches, in community life and in politics and you will see that the Jews are the driving force behind the mixing of the races. (Quotation taken from *ADL* n.d.b:40–41 excerpted from *The Thunderbolt,* October 1973)

According to the movement perspective, the minds of white people are being poisoned to accept things like homosexuality, race-mixing, and negative feelings about one's own race.

The Jew-controlled entertainment media have taken the lead in persuading a whole generation that homosexuality is a normal and acceptable way of life; that there is nothing at all wrong with White women dating or marrying Black men, or with White men marrying Asiatic women; that all races are inherently equal in ability and character—except that the character of the White race is suspect because of a history of oppressing other races; and that any effort by Whites at racial self-preservation is reprehensible. (National Vanguard Books 1991:20)

The movement supporters use the acronym ZOG (Zionist Occupational Government) to illustrate just how strong they believe Jews are in the United States. A flier that was distributed by the Christian Guard lists "Politicians Who Are Owned by 'The Jewish Lobby' " (n.d.). *The Truth at Last* published a number of articles critical of Clinton's political appointees headlining such things as "Jewish Influence Is Awesome Makes Up 56% of Clinton Appointees" (n.d. #368:1), "Clinton Names Two Jews to Federal Reserve Board—Discriminates Against Christians" (#373a:1), and "Media Suppresses News That Second Court Nominee Is a Jew. *Clinton—First President in History to Nominate* * Two Jews to the U.S. Supreme Court—and ** Two Jews to the Federal Reserve Bank Board" (#373b:1). Even after the November 1994 election results hurt Clinton's Democratic Party, *The CDL Report* (The New Christian Crusade Church 1994:1) headlined "DESPITE MID-TERM ELECTION RESULTS U.S. CONGRESS AND PRESIDENT STILL SUBSERVIENT TO ISRAEL." Another *CDL Report* (The New Christian Crusade Church n.d.:7) maintained that "As White society is mesmerized by the theatrics of enraged Blacks, Zionists slip a few hundred thousand more Orientals and Hispanics in, slip a few billion dollars more to Israel, etc." An American Front (n.d.c) flier boldly states "CAPITALISM IS JEWISH!! AND THE TRUTH IS. . . . 'ANTI-SEMITIC.' " Three pigs are lying on bags of money with dollar bills floating in the air. One of the pigs has a Star of David on its forehead. The movement's perception is that Jews not only control the government but also the media and international banking and have been the driving force behind communism.

The reinterpretation of the Holocaust, sometimes referred to as the "Holohoax" by movement people, has generated a great deal of controversy. Most white separatists support certain tenets of Holocaust Revisionism, but revisionist historians may not necessarily support white separatist ideology. According to Bradley R. Smith (n.d.), Committee for Open Debate on the Holocaust, revisionists agree with the conventional interpretation that Germany under Hitler and National Socialism did designate the Jews for special and cruel treatment. The Jews were perceived to play a significant role in international communism and to be especially dangerous to the war effort. Smith parallels how the Jews were viewed in Germany with how the Japanese were perceived in the United States at the time of World War II. The revisionists, however, do not accept the conventional view that the policy of the German state was to exterminate Jews by either placing them in gas chambers or letting them die due to abuse or neglect. They also challenge the statistic of 6 million Jews dying. Further, they say there were no execution gas chambers in any European camp controlled by Germans; rather, they were fumigation gas chambers to delouse clothing and other material. Mark Weber (n.d.n.p.) of the Institute for Holocaust Review contends that "the Holocaust extermination story is breaking down as suppressed evidence becomes better known, and as more people become aware of the facts about what is certainly the most hyped and politicized chapter of modern history."

The white separatist literature tends to agree with the revisionist interpretation. For example, an article entitled "No 'Gas Chambers' Were Ever Found" (*The Thunderbolt* #289, 1983b:4) provided "documented evidence" that "no extermination camps" existed in Germany. Instead, Communist Poland housed the "death camps and we must take the Red's word for it that such events occurred." Germany only maintained detention centers, and "there was never any planned extermination of Jews." *The Truth at Last* (n.d. #376a:1) claimed "Holocaust Story Used to Exploit Taxpayers" in the form of billions in foreign aid to Israel and special refugee status for Russian Jews (p. 1). In addition "*Schindler's List* Suppresses Fact That Germans Prosecuted Camp Head" (#376b:4) and "Jews Admit 1.8 Million, Yet Tell World 6 Million!" (#376c:5).[13]

The U.S. Holocaust Museum opening in Washington D.C. in 1993 also generated considerable controversy, in part because of the topic and in part because the building is on government land although actually built with private money (e.g., "Holocaust Museum Is Biggest Fraud in History—Already Cost Taxpayers 33 Million" by *The Truth at Last,* n.d. #365:8–10 and also "The Holocaust Museum, An Album of Agony [Headline from the *Washington Post*]" by Hans Schmidt [1993:1–6] of German American National Political Action Committee [GANPAC]). Schmidt (1993:3) maintains that the museum does not have any proof about either the existence of gas chambers or the planned extermination of Jews; nor does it provide convincing statistics on the death of 6 million. He contends that "when all is said and done, I am convinced that this museum is one of the best propaganda ventures *for Adolf Hitler* I've seen so far" (Schmidt 1993:1).

White racialists strongly challenge that the Holocaust took place and see it used as propaganda to control others. One interpretation of this manipulation suggests the propaganda helped lead to the creation of the Israeli state:

> We assert that the 'Holocaust' lie was perpetrated by Zionist-Jewry's stunning propaganda machine for the purpose of filling the minds of Gentile people the world over with such guilt feelings about the Jews that they would utter no protest when the Zionists robbed the Palestinians of their homeland with the utmost savagery.
>
> Israel could not have been created in 1948, nor could it have survived since then, without the ability of Zionist agencies to exert financial, political and moral blackmail against the Gentile world as a result of never-ending 'Holocaust' propaganda. (*'Holocaust' News* n.d.:1)

From the movement perspective the Jews have shrewdly managed to obtain economic, political, and ethical power.

In this movement, issues related to race and Jewishness are central. The movement's interpretation of the trial involving the charges against O. J. Simpson for the murders of Nicole Brown Simpson and Ron Goldman helps illustrate the preeminence of these concerns in interpreting events. Some have suggested that Simpson may have done society a favor by killing a race mixer and a Jew. *The Truth at Last* (n.d. #374b:1) headlined "Nicole Simpson Would Be Alive Today Had She Married a White Man! *Simpson Case Proves That Interracial Marriage Violates the Laws of Nature.*" *Jew Watch* (n.d. #45:1) noted "Race-

Mixing Proved Fatal Again for Another White Woman." In its caption below a picture of Ron Goldman, *Jew Watch* asked "Were the people on the L.A. freeway cheering for O. J. because he had killed the Jew Ron Goldman?" and a caption below a picture of O. J. Simpson commented, "His jealousy of not being able to hold on to a White wife, led to the 'hate-crime' killings." The images of the violent criminal black man, the race traitor white woman, and the hated Jew are intertwined in this white racialist worldview.

Religion within the Movement

Shared religious beliefs could help unite people in the movement, but differing religious views are potential divisive forces. Many of the movement members espouse the religious beliefs of Christian Identity including about 40 percent of our sample. Kaplan (1993:42–43) identifies certain key ideological variables that characterize Christian Identity in particular and the "White Supremacist constellation" in general. They include the following: "(1) a Golden Age Myth; (2) the perception of a 'Theft of Culture'; (3) scripturalism; (4) a Manichaean world view; (5) a conspiratorial view of history; (6) an unyielding self-image of the adherent as a member of a much persecuted elect or 'Righteous Remnant'; and (7) a millenarian view which centres either on the imminence of apocalypse or on some form of chiliasm." Kaplan (1993:43) argues that the outside observer may view these beliefs as either naive or lunatic but they "result from a certain strain of logic common to millennialist movements throughout their long history." These characteristics are somewhat similar to the characteristics of separatism with its in-group versus out-group vision and its emphasis on the glorious past.

Traditionally millenarianism referred to a 1,000-year period of ideal Christian society. Believers in Christian Identity are actually premillennialists, believing that Jesus will return prior to the start of the thousand-year period. Barkun (1994:103) points out that Christian Identity's millenarian vision includes powerful racist and anti-Semitic ingredients. The current meaning of millennialism has broadened to include "a pronounced chiliasm, positing the ultimate goal of an utopian society of such perfection as to make its realization impossible within the conventional framework of history" (Kaplan 1993:32). In his study of the Church of Israel, Kaplan (1993:31) found that the members' millenarian view included a desire "to withdraw to the greatest possible degree from a society seen as inherently contaminating." It may be that for some the vision of a white separatist state fits with the millenarian view that Kaplan has suggested.

Specifying the relationship of Christian Identity to Protestantism and especially to fundamentalism[14] is complex. Bock (1995:36) indicated Christian Identity supporters comprised a small proportion of fundamentalists and an even smaller part of Christianity; however, the National Council of Churches has adopted a resolution that basically suggested Christian Identity wasn't a legitimate means to express Christian beliefs. MacLean (1994:93) stated that in the 1920s "Through Protestant fundamentalism, the Klan consolidated middling men against the impious classes beneath and above them." During the last 20 years or so, some Klan have become ardent supporters of Christian Identity. For example, Thom Robb, director of the KKKK, is a Christian Identity pastor as well. His Klan literature stresses the Klan's strong link to Christianity since the Knights promote the ideals of Western Christian Civilization and are composed of White Christian men and women who are united because of the bond of shared blood and faith. Donnie A. Carr, Ohio Grand Dragon of the KKKK led by Imperial Wizard Neumann, told us, "For the Klan religion is the lynchpin (no pun intended) of our organization. Without the help of Yahweh, all is futile."

Drawing on Dan Gayman's writings, Barkun (1994:105) suggests that fundamentalists may provide a very good source of recruitment to the movement. Aho (1990:175–77) found that among the Identity Christians in his general sample of Idaho Christian Patriots, 59.6 percent (110 of 185) were from conservative or fundamentalist Protestant backgrounds. Also 18.2 percent (29 of 159) of the Christian Constitutionalists in his survey were from fundamentalist or conservative Protestant background. While Aho (1990:53) maintains that fundamentalism is an element in all Identity doctrines, Barkun suggests that although Christian Identity and fundamentalism are millennial with an apocalyptic view of history, each one's millennialism is quite different. He characterizes Identity millennialists as "an eccentric mixture, simultaneously fundamentalist and anti-fundamentalist, optimistic and pessimistic, Christian and occult" (Barkun 1990:132) and also argues that "Far from constituting an offshoot of Fundamentalism, as is often supposed, Christian Identity rejects the futurist orientation of most Fundamentalists" (1994:104). Identity does not accept the typical fundamentalist view of the rapture, which is that those who are saved will not have to experience a period of Tribulation including wars and other dangers; rather, Identity looks forward to fighting the forces of evil during the Tribulation. At present, whites in the movement see themselves as struggling against the current government's policies related to civil rights and affirmative action. The government is committing racial treason, but racial redemption will follow. Instead of the traditional view of Armageddon, what may be occurring is a prolonged confrontation between the Aryans and both the Jews and non-whites (Barkun, 1990); in the conspiratorial web, Jews are seen as the major force controlling the government, banking, and the Federal Reserve System.[15]

Key to understanding the ideology of Identity is its interpretation of the Bible and biblical history. According to "This Is Aryan Nations" (n.d.d): "The Bible is the family history of the White Race, the children of Yahweh placed here through the seedline of Adam." The Adamites (descendants of Adam) are the Aryans while Pre-Adamites are creatures (possibly the beasts of the field) that came into existence before Adam and are not Aryan people. People of color are pre-Adamic, suggesting a lower form of species. Drawing on the interpretation of Jarah Crawford, an Assembly of God minister, Aho (1990:97) points out that for Christian Identity there may even be two creations of man—Genesis 1:26–27 based on pre-Adamic man and Genesis 2, when a male was created in the early part of the chapter and later a woman was created from Adam's rib (Aho 1990:97). "Adam," or Aw-Dam, means "to show blood in the face, flush or turn rosy," according to Strong's Exhaustive Concordance to the Holy Bible (Aho 1990:97). Only Aryans can blush, so they must be the descendants of Adam while Cain is believed to be the offspring of Eve and the devil. According to Comparet in *The Cain-Satanic Seed Line* (n.d.b:32), there is both biblical and archaeological evidence to suggest the existence of the seed line of God's own children and the separate existence of the satanic seed line. Jews are regarded as the children of Satan because the liaison between Eve and the devil gave birth to the Jewish race. Not all Christian Identity people support this idea of dual seed lines however.

According to Mark Thomas[16] (1993), a Christian Identity pastor who was ordained by Richard Butler and supports the dual seed lines, other ideological differences within Identity include whether Christmas should be observed, what day the Sabbath is, the dietary regulations, the definition of marriage, and whether the group should join together with nonbelievers to achieve their goals. Probably the most significant division within Identity is that between the more passive and the "militantly aggressive" (Seymour 1991:399). Kaplan (1993:34) supports such a distinction, arguing that all of Identity proclaims a revolutionary ideology because "the very act of proclaiming the truth as they know it is the ultimate revolutionary act." However, in one faction the revolution is an internal one characterized by "political quietism" and withdrawal while in the other it is militant and forceful, including resorting to the use of weapons.

From the Identity perspective, other Christian churches have been corrupted into believing that Jews are God's chosen people. Dispatch 76 of the Christian Guard, a movement association, explains how the lost tribes of Israel got to Europe. It contends that Israel (the Northern Kingdom) and Judah (in the South) were at war:

> In 2ND Kings 17:6 and 18:13 we find that Israel and most of Judah have been taken into captivity by the Assyrians. Many claim that this was the end of the ten tribes of Israel who had separated from Judah, but in Hosea 12:1 we find that the Israelites were alive and well, and had entered into a covenant with the Assyrians. They were to follow the east wind which would take them through the Caucasus mountains and into western Europe, where they would become known as Caucasian people, fulfilling the prophecy of Nathan to David in 2ND Samuel 7:10 that God would take Israel out of Palestine and plant them in a place of their own. There Israelite-Caucasians founded the western nations of Germany, France, England, Ireland, Scotland, Wales and Scandinavia, and were later converted to Christianity, for Jesus told his disciples in Matthew 10:5–6, "Go not into the way of the Gentiles, but go rather to the lost sheep of the house of Israel." They did, and the White Caucasian Israelite countries became known as the Christian nations of Europe and kindred peoples. (Christian Guard n.d.)

Thus, according to the Identity interpretation, there is a key linking of religion and race. In personal correspondence (1996), Dr. Richard Dixon (Th.D) also tied his belief in Israel Identity, which "teaches that the Anglo-Saxon White race is the true Israel of old," to race and separatism:

> We are called to be separate. . . . We believe that miscegenation, for instance, is sin, and we know that it is preached and taught in every pseudo-Christian church. This is not hate, it being totally separated to do the will of our Master, Holy Yahweh. One other aspect is that we do *not* worship the fellow that the

pseudo-Christian church calls "Jesus." We don't even call Him by that name, simply because that name (Jesus) was not the name given to Him. There is no place in scripture that tells us to worship the Messiah, so therefore we do worship His Father, Yahweh. This is a point that separates us from all other religions, because we are the only Christian Faith that adheres to this doctrine. Lastly, we do not refer to our Faith as a religion because a religion is made by man for man and is a crutch to be dominated with, whereas our Faith was made by Yahweh for Israel, and that is us.

Dr. Dixon thus sees Christian Identity as quite distinct from other forms of Christianity, which he considers to be false.

According to CDR (1992:42–43), Christian Identity helps bind the white supremacist movement in the United States: "Instead of *Mein Kampf,* Identity uses the Bible as the source of its ideology." This is readily apparent in Identity Pastor Pete Peters's (n.d.a) brochure "The Bible—Handbook for Survivalists, Racists, Tax Protestors, Militants and Right-Wing Extremists." Identity provides religious unity for various racialist organizations and exposes people with such religious orientations to the racialist aspects of the movement.

In addition to Christian Identity, two other religious belief systems are playing significant roles in the movement. The COTC, founded by Ben Klassen in 1973 with his first book *Nature's Eternal Religion,* is dedicated to the survival, expansion, and advancement of the white race. COTC calls its religion Creativity, which Kaplan (1993:38) considers "an odd blend of rewritten Christianity, health faddism, and histrionic racism." It sees the laws of nature governing the universe, and nature does not approve of miscegenation or mongrelization of the races. Jews are believed to be the most dangerous enemy followed by "niggers" (Klassen 1973:273). The Bible was written by Jewish scriptwriters, and accepting Christianity is a "cowardly flight from reality" (Klassen 1973:283). With his book *The White Man's Bible,* Klassen (1992:1) stressed four dimensions of his all-inclusive religion: "A Sound Mind in a Sound Body in a Sound Society in a Sound Environment." Creativity encouraged "**the finer specimen of our race to have more children . . . the poorer specimen to have fewer or none**" and is designed to provide a "**powerful Racial Religion**" (Klassen 1992:121).

Klassen evidently committed suicide in 1993, but before his death he encountered problems trying to find a successor to run the organization and publish *Racial Loyalty.* ADL (1993c) issued a research report entitled "The Church of the Creator: Creed of Hate," which noted that some of COTC supporters were associated with violent activity and that COTC seemed to have ties with WAR, National Alliance, and several skinhead groups, including RAHOWA, but was feuding with Thom Robb's KKKK and Harold Covington. In 1995 Matt Hale (1995a) changed his organization from the National Socialist White Americans' Party to the New COTC and altered his focus from a political solution to a religious one. Then in 1996 he became Pontifex Maximus of the World COTC (Hale 1996a). SPLC (1997b) reported that COTC had 14 active chapters in different states in 1996.

Hale (n.d.), in his White Struggle audiotape #28 "Creativity Not Nazism," identified several key differences between Creativity and Hitler's National Socialism: (1) Creators are concerned about the identity of the entire white race, whereas the Nazis focused on the German people; (2) the Nazi movement was a political one, whereas the Creativity movement is based on racial faith. A racial faith eliminates split loyalties; (3) Creativity denounces Christianity, but Hitler didn't really speak to the concern of Jewish Christianity; (4) rather than seeing "the Jewish problem" as mainly a political one, as the Nazis did, Creativity realizes it intrudes into all aspects of life; (5) the Nazi movement was hostile to their "white racial neighbors," but Creativity recognizes the importance of white solidarity rather than nationalism; (6) Hitler allied with the Japanese, but Creativity would not be partners with any enemy of the white race; and (7) the Nazi mythos embodying the stormtrooper etc. is different from the American cowboy era and other attributes involved in the building of the United States:

> Creativity is rooted in American soil and in the pioneering of early Americana. . . . No salvation will come out of Germany or anywhere else out of tired, confused, and strife-torn Europe. . . . Only America still has the white power that can still smash the Jewish monster. I repeat. It will either happen here or nowhere. Just as the Klan did a great job in the South during the 1870s and the 1880s, so the Nazi movement under Hitler did a tremendous job in Germany during the 1920s and the 1930s. But those eras are past and gone. And neither of these ideologies any longer fit America. (Hale n.d.)

Not only does Creativity challenge Christianity; another religion variously referred to as Wotanism, Odinism, or Ásatrú does as well. Social scientists consider Odinism to be a form of neopaganism that is trying to reconstruct ancient European pre-Christian religions (Adler

1986:233). More specifically, Adler (1986) and York (1995) examined Odinism under Norse or Nordic paganism. In contrast to most neopagans, most supporters of Odinism do not believe in universal religions and seem to be politically conservative[17] and may not be comfortable with feminism, diversity in sexuality and lifestyle, or anarchism (Adler 1986:277). York (1995:126) maintains that Odinists, unlike most other neopagans, support neotribalism and emphasize racial purity and the family unit. Kaplan (1993:36) characterizes Odinist ideology as "explicitly anti-Christian, . . . often anti-Jewish, and exclusivist in terms of racial minority groups" but recognizes there are differences in thought and practice among Odinists, with a key distinction being between racialists and nonracialists. Sometimes, though, the line between the two groups is blurred because of the difficulty of "separating ethnic pride from racial mysticism" (Kaplan 1993:36). Further, Kaplan (1994–1995:11) points out that "the emphasis on racial mysticism and, in its most extreme manifestation, pronounced neo-Nazi sympathies" is not easily demarcated.[18]

Alice Rhoades, an editor of a journal of Northern European Paganism, believed: "There's been a general assumption that the Norse religion is connected with the Nazis because the Nazis used Norse symbols. And neo-Nazis sometimes get attracted to Odinism, because the trappings are the same" (cited in Adler 1986:274). Flowers (1981:280) analyzed selected neopagan Ásatrú groups and tried to distinguish them from "more political, often primarily racially motivated groups with their philosophical roots in the Romantic, sometimes pseudo-Germanic, religious revival in 19th century Germany." Although some Odinic groups in both the United States and Britain have tried to disassociate themselves from right-wing or National Socialist ideologies, Flowers felt individuals with such ideologies existed on the periphery, creating dissension within the religion.

Certainly not all Odinists belong to the movement we are analyzing, but some do. Indeed, about 20 percent of our interviewees indicated some identification with Odinism. Believers in Wotanism, Ásatrú, or Odinism have been variously criticized for being racist and hateful. According to the Odinist Fellowship,[19] it does not promote religious or racial hatred: "We believe that every racial group and subgroup, every folk, is a unique, non-repeatable biological historical phenomenon that should be preserved" (cited in York 1995:125 based on the Odinist Fellowship's newsletter *The Odinist,* no. 122, 1989:1f) and

"Although every race and ethnic group is threatened by cosmopolitanism and homogenization, our chief concern must be for our own Folk, an endangered minority. We support the awakening of racial consciousness for all peoples as a bulwark against assimilation" (*The Odinist,* no.123, 1989:4 taken from York 1995:126). Stephen McNallen (1994:4) of Ásatrú Folk Assembly (AFA) has expressed his concern about being labeled racist:

> To my mind, the sort of ideas we've been airing here have no relationship with what *Newsweek* and CBS call racism. An honest statement that we have inherently different religious needs and expressions doesn't even imply *dislike,* much less hatred. Is it racism to love my people? Is it racism to prefer my people over others? Is it racism to want my people to survive and thrive for a thousand millennia hence? I don't think so. I think these things are natural and good—for us, and for others.

McNallen, like others, stresses his view about how "natural" it is to want to be separate.

Crawford et al. (1994:1.13) discussed Ásatrú Alliance in their documentation of a decade of hate. The Ásatrú Alliance, a free association of independent kindreds, evidently drew up bylaws trying to avoid conflict on the "racism" issue. While its first bylaw declared "ASATRÚ IS THE ETHNIC RELIGION OF THE INDIGENOUS NORTHERN EUROPEAN PEOPLES," the fourth one indicated "THE ALLIANCE IS APOLITICAL; IT IS NOT A FORUM FOR, NOR SHALL IT PROMOTE ANY POLITICAL VIEWS OF THE 'LEFT' OR 'RIGHT' (*Vor Trú* 1993:37). The racism issue seems to be framed in the debate over whether Ásatrú is universalistic (new age Ásatrúar) or an ethnic or tribal religion (traditional Ásatrúar). The secretary-treasurer of the Alliance, Valgard Murray, stated he was acting as an individual rather than a representative of the group when he signed a declaration that has generated some controversy. It included the point that "the Asatrú Religion is open to everyone, and welcomes anyone who wants to join it" as well as the statement that "any local group in the alliance is free to decide who its members will be" (Murray 1995a:42). Murray (1995b) indicated that his acceptance of the statement of the openness of the Ásatrú religion was only an admission of fact since some kindreds are open. He personally believes Universalist Ásatrú "denies the existence of the Folk Soul and also the rights of ethnic Europeans to self-determination" (Murray 1995b:34).

Eric Lowe of Second Mountain Kindred indicated to us that his Odinist group is religious but not political and not really part of the movement, although its parent organization, the White House Network, is. According to him, Second Mountain Kindred "is concerned with religion and promoting the concept of faith, folk, and heritage." Its goals include "cultural and religious education and promotion of way of life (i.e. Odinism and idea of folk)." It has a jointly published newsletter VÁR HAMARR (Our Hammer) that "details progress of projects on behalf of religious rights, civil rights for Odinist inmates."

In our interview, Ron McVan of Wotansvolk—14 Word Press stressed the importance of educating people so that they would know about their own heritage:

> The white youth today are being taught a whole new curriculum in the schools. . . . The generation we grew up—we got a lot about Rome and Greece . . . but even back then in the 50s there was little talk of the ancient Celts . . . that whole segment of northern Europe which is very important because that's the seed-bed from which we all have come. . . . We try to cover that part of ancestral history. . . . What we want to do is inspire people to feel good about themselves as white people, as Aryans.

He also pointed out their literature doesn't dwell on society's problems because people are already aware of them. Wotansvolk—14 Word Press wants to be innovative and "grow with the youth too."

Although its origins may not be clear, Odinism could have drawn some of its recent inspiration from the crisis Germany faced during the Weimar Republic. Some National Socialist party leaders in Germany became interested in the revival of pre-Christian forms of religion (Kaplan 1994–1995). In 1936 C. G. Jung wrote an essay entitled "Wotan" that, according to Billig (1978b:14), sketched a psychological picture of National Socialism or "nazism as the embodiment of pre-Christian mystical striving, in this case the spirit of the ancient war god Wotan." Jung (1947:8) characterized Wotan as:

> A fundamental characteristic of the German soul, an irrational, psychic factor, which acts like a cyclone on the high pressure of civilization and blows it away. . . . Apparently every one had forgotten that Wotan represents a primeval Germanic factor and that he is the most accurate expression and inimitable personification of a basic human quality which is peculiarly characteristic of the German.

Ron McVan and Mrs. David Lane (Katja), both with 14 Word Press and Wotansvolk, display the art and symbols of Wotanism. Picture taken at Aryan Nations, April 20, 1996.

But Wotan has more than one side as noted by Jung's (1947:11) discussion of another author's work on Wotan: "It shows that Wotan is not only the god of rage and frenzy, incorporating the instinctive and emotional side of the unconscious. Its intuitive and inspiring side also manifests itself in him, for he understands the runes and can interpret fate."

The fall 1995 issue of *Runestone* and the pamphlet "Why Ásatrú," obtained from Stephen McNallen of AFA indicate that Odinism is the original religion of northwestern Europe. The customs of the Germanic tribes (currently English, Germans, Scandinavians, and Dutch) are closely related to the practices of the Celts (currently Irish, Welsh, and Scottish). Ásatrú has a number of gods and goddesses (spelled with capitalized G's). Among them are Odin, the father of the gods who is known for wisdom, ecstasy, and magic; Thor, renowned for his strength and might; Frigga, mother of the gods and also known for her wisdom and concern with family and children; Frey, a god of fertility, love, and joy; and Freya, the goddess of fertility and love who also has a warrior part as well. The gods are not masters of a universe dominating humans but rather models or personifications of forces of nature for a particular folk ("Why Ásatrú" n.d.). Flowers (1981:289), drawing on Jung's ideas, noted that the gods weren't perceived "as independent transcendental beings, but rather as exemplary models of consciousness, or archetypes, which serve as patterns for human development." Unlike Judeo-Christianity, these gods are not the objects of worship.

According to *Wotanism in Today's World* by Wotansvolk (1995), the acronym W.O.T.A.N. is used to stand for "Will of the Aryan Nation." From its beginnings in Northern Europe about 300 B.C.E., Wotanism evolved among the Teutons and was especially popular during the Viking Age (800–1100 C.E.). It was forced underground by Judeo-Christianity and later gained status among the Germanic peoples late in the nineteenth century and during the two World Wars. Wotanism is a nature-based religion that values human freedom and individuality and "set for itself a final goal of bringing into being a noble race" (Wotansvolk 1995:4). The connection between race and religion is significant, but race has priority: "Any form of religion or belief system that does not spring naturally from the soul of the race, that is not born of the blood, will ultimately destroy the threads which link men with nature and kinsmen with kinsmen. A race without a mythos and belief of the blood drifts aimlessly throughout history" (Wotansvolk 1995:4).

The mythos provides meaning and value, often through symbols and rituals, to a people's historic experiences. The Wotansvolk (n.d.) flag is the banner for Aryan unity, displaying red and white stripes; red indicates the blood of the martyrs who are in Valhalla and white stands for the nobility of the Aryan race. The solar wheel in the center represents Allfather Wotan or Wotan's eye that he sacrificed for wisdom. Also Huginn and Muninn, Wotan's ravens, appear on the flag signifying thought and memory. A number of rituals and celebrations are associated with Wotanism, including seasonal ones related to equinoxes and solstices. The "14 Codes of the Aryan Ethic" and the *Havamal* (*The Words of the High One*) provide guidance to the Aryan. *The Poetic or Elder Edda,* a collection of poems probably first written down in the thirteenth century based on oral traditions, stresses pride, modesty, moderation, immortality, courage, wisdom, friendship, caution, hospitality, love, and self-reliance (*Wisdom from the Edda,* 1996).

At times there is conflict between Christians and non-Christians within the movement. John Murphy of the Bedford Forrest Brigade, an independent Florida–based Klan, described the Christian ties of the Klan:

> We are Christians of virtually all denominations. We tend to be fundamentalist. There is some dissatisfaction lately with "Judeo-Christianity." The politically correct trend seen in some churches, as endorsement of homosexuality and relative moralism, has renewed interest in Odinism and similar religions as the true religion of the European people. Christianity provides us with the moral framework of our groups, as well as, the spiritual outlet.

Frank DeSilva, a public figure and member of Die Bruder Schweigen (Silent Brotherhood), believes there is a transition from Christianity to neopaganism occurring in the movement:

> Religion is for the race-culture that created it. In consequence to this, the movement is becoming predominately non-christian. Catholicism becoming increasingly more non-white, as the Vatican reinforces its ranks with non-europeans, it is increasingly becoming more familiar to hear about one or another group forming on the lines of the 'new paganism'. I prefer to call it Natural Law, as an 'idea', but as religion, it may take many names.

Matt Hale (1995b:5), now Pontifex Maximus of COTC, directs his condemnation of Christianity toward movement organizations: "We need to convince the Klan, Aryan Nations, and other Christian organizations that Christianity hasn't saved the White Race yet and nor will it." *The Struggle,* the publication of the World COTC, has contained articles critical of Christian Identity and Odinism. Hayhow (1996:2) criticized Identity supporters for putting " 'God' (or 'Yahweh') before Race," and Walsh (1996:3) maintained Odinism also placed its gods above race and was not now racially sound: Although Odinism " 'once' proved conducive to racial adhesiveness, its outmoded and ridiculous superstitions and penchant for placing the attributes of an array of 'gods' above those of our Race is nothing but a detriment to our progression and an insult to our intellect."

David Lane, who Kaplan (1993:36) describes as a political activist and extreme racialist, believes the Aryan race was doing well before the advance of biblical religion, which was incompatible with racial survival and nature's laws (Lane, n.d.c). Judeo-Christianity preaches racial mixing and thus racial genocide (Lane, n.d.d:19,20). "The White race cannot share Gods or religion with other races" in part because of the need to survive and avoid potential destruction of its uniqueness (Lane, 1994a:36). Lane (n.d.e:2) stresses the need for both white separatist states and religion: "What we must understand today if we are to survive as a race is that we must have geographic nations and a religion which are exclusively ours." Lane is critical of Christianity, but he doesn't endorse the atheistic COTC, even though he thinks some of its ideas are useful. Rather, he considers himself a deist who believes there is "an intelligence motivating force throughout the universe and behind Nature's Laws" (Lane n.d.c:1). Lane (1994a:33) identifies several "Mystery religions," including Odinism, that "used different mythologies and/or different names in different languages for the Gods and Goddesses. . . . The mythologies were used both to represent the powers of the Creator evidenced in nature and personified as the Gods and Goddesses, as well as to instill the folkish attributes considered necessary at a particular era of history." The mythologies have various levels of meaning and intellectual interpretation far beyond their literal one. Lane (1994a:36) believes that "the best religion for our folk today is almost certainly Odinism. Odin . . . is the best representation of All-Father, the Creator for the White race today."

WAR has criticized the link of religion, especially Christianity, with the racial movement; in the "History of WAR" videotape (part III), Tom Metzger states: "We have no particular religion; your religion is your own business. But we believe that if there is a religion in our movement it's your race, and my race is my religion and my skin is my uniform." WAR's (n.d.b) "Position Paper on Religion" is even more critical of religion, saying it's based on faith and has been destructive to the white race. Both Christianity and Judaism are perceived to be occult control mechanisms over the people. According to the position paper, "You cannot serve two masters; one being the Judeo-Christian myth, and the other being in favor of the White eugenics idea. For yet a little while, we must have patience with those among us that have been unable or unwilling to throw off the subversive middle eastern cult religions. However, time is running out, and the albatross of Christianity will surely destroy our reformation, if not subdued" (WAR n.d.b).

In his June 16, 1996, WAR phone hot line message, Metzger commented specifically on Israel Identity, including his past association with it, and then mentioned Odinism:

> This religious belief [Identity] has made significant inroads into the right-wing racial movement. I know. I was there. I cannot belittle the honest work of those who do believe by faith in this idea, but I must say the concept is totally without real historical merit. There is no way an Aryan can be a Hebrew or vice versa. It is time to get our minds out of the midst of the Middle East and into research on the ancient history of European culture—white culture which has been deliberately hidden in lieu of worshipping the national history and figures of alien semitic Jews. . . . Some have said that Tom Metzger is an Odinist. Tom Metzger is not an Odinist and some have said that the Odinists believe that Thor and all these people or gods or whatever—the Vikings are still flying around in the sky. I have never met an Odinist who did believe that. But to set the record straight, Tom Metzger if he has a religion—it is the race. Period. And that's it.

Again Metzger stresses that the crucial issue is race.

Christian Identity minister Thomas (1993), who published *The Watchman* of the Pennsylvania Christian Posse Comitatus before his arrest, argued that Christian Identity is opposed to the ideas of mainstream Christianity. A key division between Christian Identity and neo-paganism is that while Christian Identity draws on the Bible to support their view that the white race is the descendant of Adam, Odinists and other pagans follow the more conventional belief that Jesus was Jewish and the Jews are Israel.

In his autobiography, Lane (1994b:30) indicated he hoped to heal some of the divisions between Christian Identity believers and Odinists by showing they may have similar roots. At the April 1996 Aryan Youth Assembly at AN, Mrs. David Lane (Katja) gave her imprisoned husband's speech that called for unity:

> No longer can we afford to divide our energies or diffuse our focus with religious dissension or peripheral issues. . . . For the sake of unity we must find and embrace a common denominator. That denominator is the self-evident truth that nature and nature's laws are the work of the Creator, no matter what name we use for God or what our perceptions of God may be. Even those who reject the idea of a creative intelligence called God must acknowledge that we are subject to nature's laws. In the Declaration of Independence of the American colonies of July 4, 1776, we find the term "Nature and Nature's God." The creators (COTC) among us use a book titled "Nature's Eternal Religion." The Wotansvolk have the second of the 14 Codes of the Aryan Ethic, which says, "Nature's laws evidence the divine plan, as the Natural world is the work of Allfather." And for the Identity folk among us, I'd like to quote three verses verbatim from the oldest book of the bible, Job chapter 12. "But ask now the beasts and they shall teach thee, and the fowls of the air and they shall tell thee, or speak to the earth and it shall teach thee, and the fishes of the sea shall declare unto thee. Who knoweth not in all these the hand of the Lord hath wrought this." Again we see confirmation that nature's laws evidence the divine plan.
>
> Friendly debates about the names for God, about religious symbols or rituals, or parables and allegories used in religious teachings are understandable and acceptable. But the moment such debate detracts from nature's highest law, which is the preservation of our own kind, then the debate violates divine law. Nature's laws are a holy book written by nature's God, a book not subject to translation, editing or distortion. Let nature's laws mediate any dispute. If that does not work, then put the dispute aside until we have accomplished the 14 WORDS. Does anyone really care what name the colored races use for God after we are extinct? (David Lane n.d.f:1–2)

The importance of nature for all three religions could serve as a bridge to link the three religions.

Although Barkun (1989:418) has suggested that "if any belief may be taken to be both central to and characteristic of contemporary 'white supremacism', it is 'Identity' theology," it is important to recognize it is not the only religious belief professed by members of the movement. The extent of the centrality of "Identity" beliefs to this movement needs to be examined further. While Identity is certainly key to many, it may not be to those believing in other forms of Christianity, National Socialism, Odinism, and/or to those whom religion is not of importance and/or to those who believe religion is a matter of individual preference.

In our research we asked about the role religion plays in the movement. Most of the people we surveyed believed that religion was very important. In response to the open-ended question of why it was important, about one-third expressed the belief that religion could help unite people in the movement. Others, though, indicated how problematic the role of religion is within the movement. One independent, Eric Hagen Watts, noted that most National Socialists were likely to be agnostic or atheist. An anonymous National Socialist who said his religion was Odinism indicated that religion was only somewhat important in the movement and "only to the extent that a lot of 'Identity' people support our Aryan cause." "Aryan Man" commented that he thought religion was a very important issue for the movement:

> because it's screwing a lot of our chances up. Because people put too much emphasis on it. . . . Whether you call God Odin or Wotan or Yahweh or Jesus—I don't think it makes a lot of difference cause I think all those names . . . they're the same. It's just people trying to interpret it. Different ways of arguing about it and it's a tool. I think it's another tool of ZOG. I think the hierarchy sits back and laughs at our squabbles about religion.

William J. Murray, a state leader of SS Action Group, also saw religion as divisive: "I feel that religion should be a private matter, and should not act as a basis for our decisions. . . . Because of the diversity of religious beliefs in this Movement, there has been a great deal of infighting. I believe we should all agree on one thing, and that is that our Race is our religion!" "Nocmar" of Clan Rook felt religious differences could be considered later so as not to disrupt the movement now: "Religion remains to be a major obstacle to total unity, unfortunately. . . . To some groups religion is very important and therefore must be respected by other groups. The main emphasis is on the fact that we are all fighting for the white race and we should not single out our one difference and dwell on it. There will be time for that after we have won." Such statements illustrate religion may not necessarily be a unifying force. While the Klan, Identity, Creators, and Odinists are likely to advocate linking race and religion, their religious views vary. It is racial beliefs that define the entire movement.

The Economic and Political Systems

American Capitalism and Class Inequality A common thread running through parts of the movement literature is how big business and major capitalists are perceived as detriments to the advancement of the white worker. Metzger's WAR and the American Front (Portland, OR) are strong advocates of "The Third Position,"[20] which emphasizes the importance of the white worker while criticizing capitalists and government officials. In American Front's brochures, the "right" and the "left" are briefly examined as "opposite ends to the same stick of materialism" (American Front n.d.d). According to "White Workers Who's on Your Side?" (American Front n.d.e), on the right "the conservatives have mutated the tenets of democracy in favor of the wealthy. The power in our country lies not with the people, but with the rich and elite." The left is viewed as "thoroughly opposed to racial nationalism for whites, yet admittedly defend it for other races." There is "*unfair* ultra-abused protection for minorities at the expense of the white worker." Both the views of the right and left are thus rejected resulting in "The Third Position" supporting "revolutionary racial nationalism" against the "twin evils of Capitalism and Communism." Mahon (n.d.:5) explains the potential conflict between capitalist elites and racial concerns: "The modern capitalist care not one iota for workers welfare or . . . Racial or cultural issues. The number one emphasis must be, that the profit motive must be subordinated to what is in the best interest of the Race."

Johnnie Pipes, the regional coordinator and Grand Titan for Robb's KKKK in Florida, argued that big business was more supremacist than the Klan:

> We've been called supremacist. Well, a supremacist is somebody who wants to take and rule over another people . . . we do not want to rule over anybody. . . . You look at the big businesses that are down there taking advantage of cheap, Mexican labor. . . . Those are the supremacists. . . . One of the worst things I ever thought could have happened was this NAFTA deal that took away so many American jobs.

While Robb's KKKK mention the plight of the white worker losing jobs, they reject "The Third Position." Members of the Knights come from *all* walks of life and from all parts of the country (*White Patriot,* n.d.a:2). *The White Patriot* (1989:8) made the KKKK position perfectly clear in its "NOTE!":

The Knights of the Ku Klux Klan rejects the so-called *Third Position* and its Marxist dogma of "class struggle" as well as all other Jew infested political and social teachings that would put schism between our racial brothers, such as Democrat vs. Republican, North vs. South, Catholic vs. Protestant, rich vs. poor, workers vs. bosses ad nauseam.

Other groups from the KKK have supported "private property and ownership of business, but an end to high-finance exploitation" (Empire Publishing n.d.).

The agenda of the National Socialist Front (1992:2) calls for "an end to the exploitive uncontrolled capitalist system" and "a true form of free enterprise without the threat of financial exploitation hanging over the heads of the Aryan Working class." Social programs will help the old, sick, and disabled, but there will not be a welfare state. Hitler's ideology would provide the "guiding force" for America. "The Official Program of the NSWPP" (Koehl 1980) and "What We Stand For . . . Goals and Objectives of the Nazi Party of the New Order" (n.d.) both called for an "honest economy" to serve the needs of the people rather than big bankers or multinational corporate profiteers. "We must put an end to both economic freeloading and economic exploitation in America" ("What We Stand For . . . Goals and Objectives of the Nazi Party of the New Order," n.d.). The official program asked for full employment, price stability, public control of all banking and credit institutions, and all utilities and all monopolies. It also sought the confiscation of all conglomerate holdings, cancellation of usurious debts, and interest-free loans for families, farmers, and small businesspeople.

Jordan (n.d.:7) describes the socialist element in National Socialism as involving regulation of private enterprise in which there would be equitable division of the benefits of society. It is neither Marxist socialism where the state owns the means of production and there is "economic over-government of the ant heap" nor is it the "predatory individualism of the capitalist system, which is the economic under-government, or anarchy, of the jungle." Somewhat similarly, Robertson (1992:144), in his work *The Ethnostate,* calls for self-sufficiency and urges overhauling of both capitalism with its inflation, booms, and busts and socialism with its "petrified centralization." The National

Office of the National Alliance (1993) distinguishes between Marxism and laissez-faire capitalism, finding weaknesses in both. Marxism fails to recognize the inequality of human beings and their need to compete and advance themselves, and capitalism gives strong incentives to individuals without any goals for the society. Too much motivation simply for personal gain results in the rich dominating the society because of their control of capital. Rather, the economic system must be committed to "the long range welfare and progress of the race" (National Office of the National Alliance 1993:4).

In general the movement rejects both the exploitation that exists in the American capitalist system and the state control of the economy in communism. Not only is the economic system in need of fundamental changes but so is the U.S. government.

The U.S. Government The movement criticizes the U.S. government for a number of its policies, including affirmative action that denies jobs to white men, gun control legislation that takes away one's ability and right to protect oneself, the allowance of illegal immigrants to enter and stay in the United States, the legalization of abortion for white women, and the placement of federal guards at abortion clinics where white genocide is being practiced, and so on. The policy of multiculturism is viewed as having betrayed the white race. Ed Reynolds's newsletter (January 11, 1995) of SS Action provides a comprehensive statement of many government policies the movement condemns: "We have to understand the real problem . . . ZOG . . . THE FEDERAL GOVERNMENT . . . They are the ones who have twisted around all the laws, are taking our guns away, set-up White Patriots, send billions of dollars to Isreal every year, feed every nigger in Africa, Haiti and the so-called United States, along with every gook, spic and wetback who crosses the border . . . I SPIT MY CONTEMPT AT THE SYSTEM." (Ellipsis points are inserted by Reynolds, material is not missing; the spelling "Isreal" is intended.)

Although both the movement and the resistance criticize the U.S. government, Mahon (1994:6) of Oklahoma WAR points out the differences between the two in their attitudes toward the U.S. and their interpretation of history:

> There is a definite line of demarcation in the thinking and ideology of right-wing conservatism and Revolutionary Aryan Resistance. "Movement" people believe that the United States' Federal government is basically historically

benevolent, that evil or deceived politicians have temporarily taken control of power, and if we can just awaken the masses, we can get our country back. The CRAP have been saying this for 30 years. Aryan Resistance fighters believe the Federal rats usurped its authority and declared total war against the white race and its self-determinism in 1860, when it devastated the South in the war for Southern independence. The Federal government, from then on, continued its planned genocide of our European homeland in this century with two fratricidal world wars.

After the April 19, 1995, bombing of the Alfred P. Murrah Federal Building in Oklahoma City, militia groups received a great deal of attention, including discussions of possible links between militias and "white supremacist" groups. SPLC (1995e:1) named 224 militias and their support groups and identified 45 of them as having ties to neo-Nazi and other white supremacist groups.[21] It (SPLC 1996c:38) also claimed that "white supremacists like Beam and Pierce provided Patriots with their ideological under-pinnings." In the fervor generated by the bombing, Peter Applebome (1995:13) wrote in the *New York Times* that "a virulent hatred of the Federal Government and issues like gun control have replaced race as the issues that bind the movement." Although not completely clear, it appears the movement he is referring to is "the loosely knit movement" of the "radical right." Both radical right and left as well as some in the mainstream have antigovernment attitudes, including concerns about the suppression of various groups and negative perceptions on how the government handled Waco and the Ruby Ridge siege.

The white separatist movement focuses on race and is up-front about many of its concerns about the survival of the white race. Although it shares facets of antigovernment attitudes with many militia, it is difficult to conceive of one unified aboveground movement being forged with militias that publicly deny racial issues, as did many of those who testified before the Senate Subcommittee on Terrorism June 15, 1995. Some in the white separatist movement join militias and vice versa. Chip Berlet, analyst at PRA, and Mathew N. Lyons (1995:24), a freelance writer, suggest that "pre-existing elements of racist, anti-Semitic, or neo-Nazi movements, such as Posse Comitatus, Christian Identity, or Christian Patriots" are *one* of *eight* streams feeding into the militia movement, but that does not mean all militia members are "racists and anti-Semites."

George and Wilcox (1996:249) stress that the "ideological roots of the militias are somewhat obscured by the highly individualistic nature of their adherents." Further, they question how strong the link is between racist groups and the militias:

> Although fund-raising letters by antiracist groups state otherwise, the alleged "links" between the modern civilian militias and the neo-Nazi and other racist para-military groups seem few and far between. These mostly consist of charges that some militia members had attended racist meetings or had spoken with KKK or neo-Nazi representatives.
>
> Unable to demonstrate rampant racism and anti-Semitism in the militias, the Anti-Defamation League and Southern Poverty Law Center have claimed that the KKK and neo-Nazi groups have "infiltrated" the militias, but these claims are based on only a few incidents. Another claim is that the conspiracy theories espoused by militias parallel those of racist groups on several points. This is often true, but as we shall see, they occasionally parallel those of the far left as well. (George and Wilcox 1996:250)

There is currently no consensus about the relationship between racist groups and militias, but the social science literature tends to be more cautious than the mass media in their discussion of the linkages.

Some white racialists are joining militias, but other groups are issuing warnings about the militia. For example:

> First we wish to cover the 'Militia connection'. . . . Let's get something straight right off the bat—While most of these militias may have 'white supremacists' in them they are equally or more made up of race traitor scum and they have given us no reason to support them in any way except for our shared hatred of the Federal dog. And to me that just isn't enough. (We Are the Law #4:n.p.)

Furthermore, Tom Metzger (1995:2) in a *WAR* editorial noted:

> The Oklahoma City bomb suspects are still being referred to as racists. That's strange since McVeigh's best friend in Kingman, Arizona, runs with Indians and Nichols has a mail order Filipino wife. The press should blame race mixers, not racial separatists.

Antigovernment attitudes characterize much of this movement, but they also describe numerous other movements as well.

The New World Order The movement's perceptions of the global links between the political and economic systems are illustrated in discussions of "the new world order." National Vanguard (1994) argues that the American elite is becoming part of the international elite of financiers, controllers of the mass media, and multinational corpora-

Figure 9. Army of Israel Smash the New World Order pamphlet cover (with permission from David Dalby).

tion executives while American and European workers are having their standard of living lowered to that of workers in the Third World. As immigrants flood the United States and Europe, a nonwhite majority will be created and "national boundaries will for all practical purposes cease to exist" (National Vanguard 1994:3). According to

Mahon (n.d.:5), "The Capitalist NEW WORLD ORDER has the 'odor' of a World Wide Plantation where slaves of all races toil for the elite taskmasters."

National Vanguard (1994:3) believes that the "Jew World Order" might be the best name for the future political and economic arrangements since "The New World Order . . . can be traced . . . back to the beginning of this century . . . when Jewish leaders from a number of countries held a series of Zionist Congresses . . . to map a strategy for taking advantage of the tensions then developing among the major European powers." According to the *CDL Report* (New Christian Crusade Church 1992a:1–2), one wing of the one-world government movement wants the world to be controlled by Jews.

The United States is sometimes viewed as under the control of the Zionist United Nations/One World Government, serving as enforcers for the new world order (Mehus 1992). According to Army of Israel's (n.d.) Identity skinhead publication "Smash The New World Order": "There is an international conspiracy to have every nation under the authority of a One World Government. This government is the New World Order. It is controlled by the United Nations. The goal global communism." Treaties such as the North American Free Trade Agreement (NAFTA) are perceived as harming the American worker and promoting alliances between different nations and races. NAFTA facilitates the development of the one-world government, which benefits wealthy elites but not the American people (New Christian Crusade Church 1992b:1–4).

White racialists have historically tended to perceive an interlocking of Communists, Jews, certain American politicians, international bankers, and capitalists, which are now resulting in the New World Order. The constitution and bylaws of the old NSRP illustrated this: "Communism is Jewish. Communism is one of the Jew plans, along with the United Nations organization and other world government schemes, to destroy us and conquer the world. . . . Our party proposes for the Government to expel all communists from this Nation. Without the Jews, there would be NO communism!" (taken from George and Wilcox 1992:364).

WAR (May 1994:12) points out the threat of an overarching state structure: "The rise of the super state based on economics is a direct threat to racial integrity. The super state must be viewed as an enemy that is easily infiltrated by alien semites to destroy the Aryan culture for power and profit." The movement typically believes the images of global government, international economy, and multiculturalism all work against the development of a racial state and therefore must be struggled against. The movement's positions on politics and economy will be explored further in the last chapter on political economy.

Ideology and Language

People's belief systems are closely intertwined with their views of reality. White separatists see themselves as distinct from the larger population that includes both minorities and other whites and often have ideas quite different from those expressed by many in mainstream society. Because other whites stigmatize racialists in part through the use of the dominant language, white separatists have reframed certain words in the English language to show their point of view. As already noted, racialism and anti-Semitism are defined differently by many in the movement than by those in the mainstream; those opposed to the movement tend to refer to it as the "white supremacist" movement, whereas movement members more often call it a "white power," "racialist," or "white separatist" movement. According to many movement people, crosses are "lit" in their ceremonies rather than burned, nonwhites are called "mud(d)" races, and civil rights activists are "white-race haters." Movements in general typically try to reframe issues and change the symbolic meanings of key items, and this movement certainly follows that strategy.

Reinterpretation of History Klandermans (1991:9) argues that social reality is so complex that there may be completely different interpretations of what is happening and "one situation can produce a variety of definitions, sponsored by competing actors." Social movements "frame, or assign meaning to and interpret, relevant events and conditions" (Snow and Benford 1988:198). White separatists use language to provide their versions of history and contemporary events that tend to be at odds with the more mainstream or conventional ones. For example, according to the mainstream conventional interpretation of history, blacks were brought to the United States as slaves, and this history of slavery has certainly helped shape the pattern of racial inequality in contemporary America. On the other hand, an article in *The Thunderbolt* (1983c:1) maintains that black slaves were indeed fortunate persons: "The black slaves had their lives saved because the tribal leaders who enslaved them in the first place would have either tortured them to death or eaten them—thus blacks brought to America were lucky—WE SAVED THEIR LIVES!" Not only was their physical existence threatened in their "native land," but blacks were suffering from spiritual neglect. "They never would have heard of God; never would have heard of Christian virtues, Christian lives, Christian heaven, nor Christian hell" (Watson, n.d.:11). Another example is the article "Kennedy Attacked Mississippi Not Cuba" (*The Thunderbolt* 1983d:14), which portrayed James Meredith's admission to the University of Mississippi as an invasion in which "Kennedy felt pleased in forcing integration upon prostrate, oppressed people, using an occupation army."

The leaders of the movement portray themselves as revolutionary patriots similar to those of the American Revolution. An AN catalog contains in large letters Thomas Jefferson's statement: "Rebellion to Tyrants Is . . . Obedience to God." The conclusion to the *Official Program of the NSWPP* (NSWPP, Koehl 1980:9) echoes the Declaration of Independence, stating that they are proud to declare themselves revolutionaries who are building a new order, and concludes with "For the fulfillment of this program . . . we pledge our lives, our fortunes, and our sacred honor."

In-group Love versus Out-group Hate Perhaps the best example of the use of language illustrating ideology is how the movement's members have responded to the mainstream's labeling them a hate group. Part of their strategy is to use a language stressing their "love" of their race as the core value rather than hate. Parts of the movement have tried to redefine their public image so they would be perceived as working for the best interests of white civilization. A typical call for unity is made on the basis of love for one's race: "The highest motivation for our fraternity is love: love of our people's unique heritage and character, love of freedom, and love for a new era for our people. If we are to restore the unity and brotherhood of our people, we must first restore it within our own hearts and ranks" (*White Patriot* n.d.d:6). Such emphasis provides a positive in-group feeling.

Movement people also label their opposition, rather than themselves, as the real hate group(s). In the racialist view of reality, the tables are turned so that selected minorities and protest groups against

CHRISTIAN SOLDIER

ACCURATE REPRESENTATION OF CHRISTIAN WHO IS PATRIOTIC AND BELIEVES THAT THE ANGLO-SAXON, GERMANIC, SCANDANAVIAN & KINDRED PEOPLE ARE THE ISRAEL PEOPLE OF SCRIPTURE AND NOT THE JEWS OF TODAY.

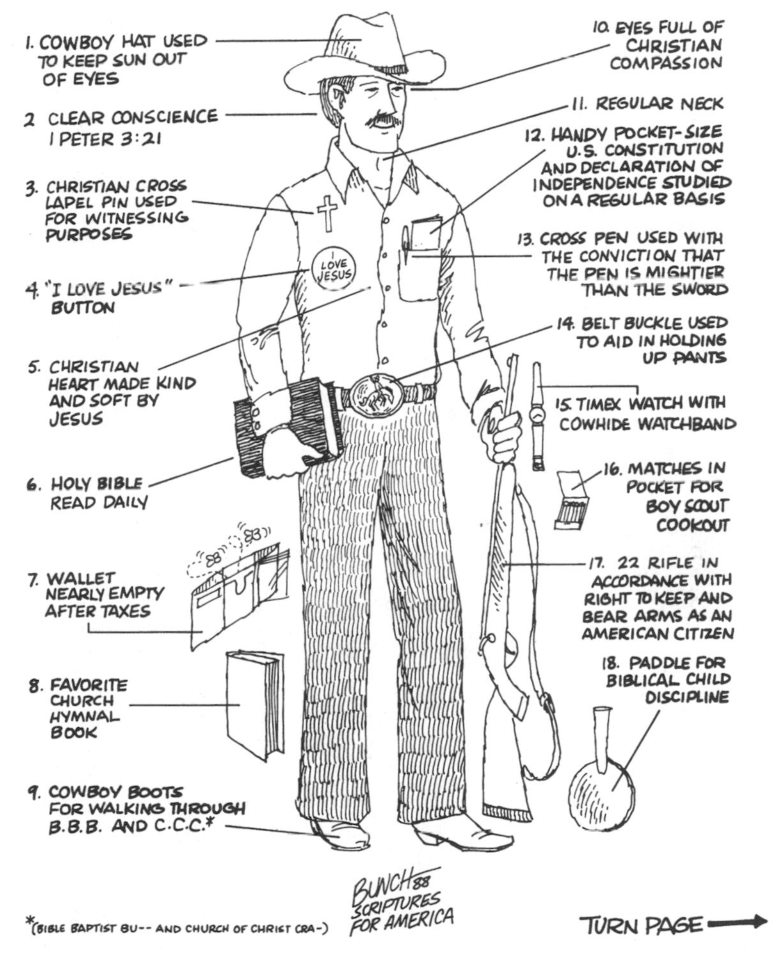

Figure 10. Scriptures for America on Christian Soldier and Villain from *The Real Hate Group* by Pastor Pete Peters, n.d.b, pp. 19–20.

CHRISTIAN VILLAIN

SAME CHRISTIAN SOLDIER AS DESCRIBED AND DEPICTED BY JEWISH ORGANIZATIONS IN THEIR HATE GROUP REPORTS, AND IN THE JEWISH-CONTROLLED MEDIA. THIS REPRESENTATION FREQUENTLY DISPERSED TO VARIOUS LAW ENFORCEMENT AGENCIES & MAJOR TV NETWORKS.

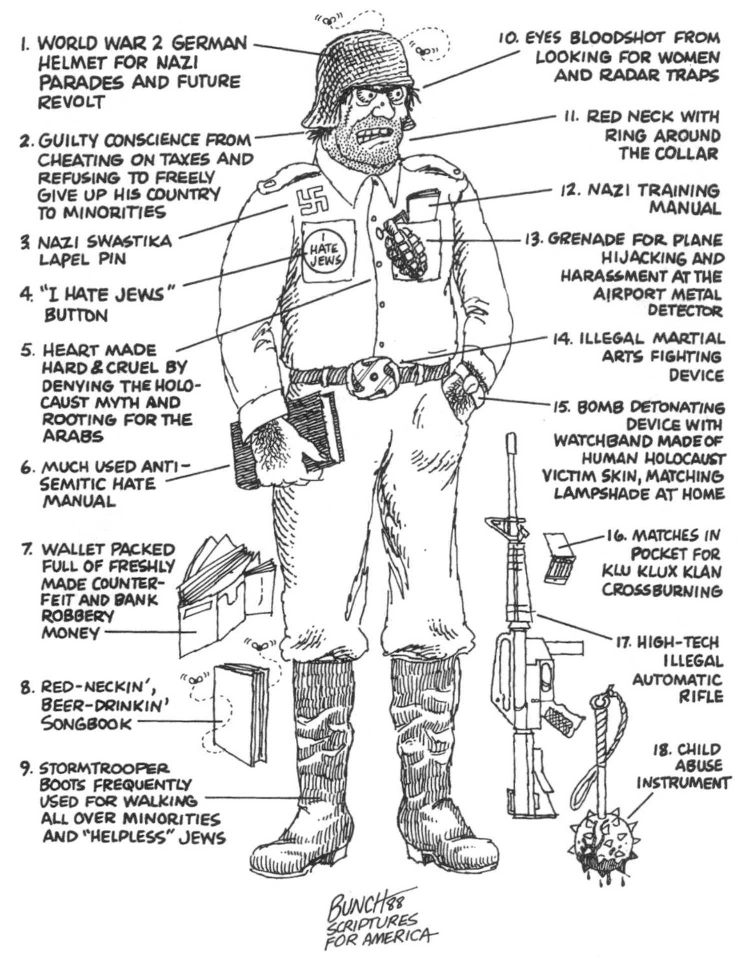

Figure 10 (*continued*)

the Klan and neo-Nazis become the hate groups. In Dubuque, Iowa, and Janesville, Wisconsin, Thom Robb of the KKKK and Ken Petersen[22] formerly of the National Knights told their audiences that the real hate group is out there, referring to the anti-Klan demonstrators. With the chanting anti-Klan people in the background on the "Geraldo" program (aired September 16, 1992), Ken Petersen declares, "We're not looking for a violent confrontation, but you can see who the animals are and who's inciting to riot. We're here for a peaceful rally and a program of white unity between different organizations." When Geraldo points out that the Klan supporters are armed with bats, tire irons, and so on, one movement supporter replies that "police told us we have to protect ourselves . . . [we're] protecting the white race."

Identity minister Pete Peters (n.d.b:19–20) described a Christian soldier and villain (shown in figure 10). The "Christian Soldier" "believes that the Anglo-Saxon, Germanic, Scandinavian and kindred people are the Israel people of scripture and not the Jews of today" and carries a Bible in one hand and in the other a .22-caliber rifle "in accordance with right to keep and bear arms as an American citizen." The inaccurate "Christian Villain" is described by Jewish organizations and the Jew-controlled media and has a much used anti-Semitic hate manual, a red-neckin', beer-drinkin' songbook, and a high-tech illegal automatic rifle.

In its response to the question "Do you believe in hatred?" the American Front stated that their ideals were rooted in love for their own people rather than hatred. It felt that critics and the mass media labeled them as being hateful because the American Front has pointed out that the "non-white mass that is overtaking us is harmful to our existence" (American Front n.d.d).

Metzger and WAR, however, openly advocate use of hatred and love and accept the label of *racist*:

> Are you designing hate material for your community? Yes, I said hate. WAR seems to be the only group around that honestly embraces hate as well as love. Our enemies hate us and we hate them. WAR hates any individual, group or institution that fights racism. Yes racism. I am a full blown racist and I believe in race—and specifically my own race. Anyone that stands in the way of the best interests of my race must be hated with a perfect hatred. At the same time love for ourselves, our families, and our racially conscious associ-

ates should be boundless. Reserve love for those that benefit your cause—reserve hatred for those that would sidetrack your mission. Properly thought out forms and focused hatred is a great revolutionary ally. If hatred is not your ally, it is an enemy to be feared. (Metzger 1993b)

The *Florida Interklan Report* (1995a:1) also stressed the need for a "pure hatred" against the "system that each day inches forward like a mighty genocidal steam roller towards the destruction of your own kind" rather than blind hatred against people of a different race. It suggests the movement needs to be revolutionary rather than reactionary, recognizing that "The enemy is the system—the system of international world dominance." Justin Cook, who at one time was a youth leader of AN, also noted a role for hatred in the movement: "Spreading the white word, making our people proud of themselves, not going out and promoting just hate. Everybody says there's no hate in our movement—it's not a hate movement, but you can't have hate without love." Thus, although some in the movement attempt to counteract the hate label, others recognize that hatred can be a powerful force against one's enemy.

Conclusion

In formulating ideology, movements face a number of decisions related to their goals and strategy. Ash (1972:230) pointed out that three key choices exist: (1) between single-issue demands and multiple demands, (2) between radical concerns and ones that do not question the present system of wealth and power, and (3) between attempts to influence those who hold power and efforts to replace them. She generalized: "The broader the goals of a social movement, the more central its focus, and the greater its threat to class structure, the less likely it will be to succeed (Ash 1972:12). In his study Gamson (1975) found that groups that wanted to displace their target (e.g., elites) do *not* do well, and this seems crucial to the success rate. Of the 53 groups he studied, two-thirds of those groups with limited goals were able to achieve new advantages as were two-thirds of the others if they were not trying to replace or destroy an antagonist.

Advocating separatism in order to maintain the white race is a radical strategy that surely challenges the current power structure and will be extremely difficult to achieve. Even though movement members may disagree with each other on the appropriateness of labels like *racist* and *supremacist,* most consider themselves separatists, and they are definitely proud of their race and its achievements. David Lane's 14 Words "We Must Secure the Existence of Our People and a Future for White Children" provide a focused and well-known ideological summary of the movement's goals. These words are at the core of the movement, but a number of other ideological concerns exist about the power of Jews, the U.S. government, capitalism, communism, and the Holocaust. Although these issues tend to complement each other in their support of the white race, they could also distract the movement from advancing its main goal of separatism and the survival of white children. Issues related to religion, class inequality, and loyalty/patriotism for America potentially divide the movement. Christian Identity has assumed some prominence in the movement, especially within certain Klans, but fundamentalist and other Protestant beliefs should not be ignored. The historic roots of Odinism or Wotanism in Europe may facilitate its acceptance within the movement, especially by National Socialists. Skinheads have variously been attracted to Christian Identity, Odinism, and COTC as well as to WAR's message.

Bell (1973:126) argues that the chances of American Nazism gaining success are limited because the movement has not developed basic attainable goals and because "probably no individual in the twentieth century has been so despised by Americans as Adolf Hitler." He notes how Hitler was venerated by Germans everywhere for his high ideals and for restoring Germany to great power status, but that when "in the 1930's powerful and articulate models of public opinion . . . held Hitler responsible for turning Germany into a ruthless police state. . . . he became a symbol of evil" (Bell 1973:126). In our phone conversation with a movement person using the name "G. Raubal,"[23] she noted the extreme reactions movement people like herself encounter even today at the mention of Hitler's name.

One of the strategies used by part of the movement is to modify the language of the dominant group to fit the movement's conceptions of reality. Certain words take on meanings shared by movement supporters and help unify the movement. The "movement" and the "resistance" factions debate the use of other techniques such as whether to use political campaigns or more militant methods, whether to have organized rallies and marches or avoid such public displays, and whether to have formal organizations or develop leaderless resistance based on informal limited group associations. Indeed, ideology is not stagnant but is being produced and shaped. In the next chapter we will examine protest activities that often help call attention to their ideology.

Chapter Four

Protest and Violence

And as far as my organization, the Battle Axe Skinheads is concerned . . . it's pretty much an underground group where . . . we believe in . . . leaderless resistance—small groups of people all over the country who are connected, but we don't wear uniforms, we don't believe in marching publicly, we don't have membership cards, we keep it underground and secret. Kind of like the Invisible Empire of the 1800s in the South, but more modernized and I think better modified. I think that the old way of like marching and the David Duke route of trying to run for office—that's ridiculous. I think we need to find better tactics to achieve our goals. (Nathan Pett, Battle Axe Skinheads and *Hail Victory* publication)

Social movements engage in political activity of various forms. Sometimes it takes the form of attempting linkages to more mainstream or conventional routes to power, and sometimes it involves less conventional or what some refer to as extraordinary means to gain influence (Marger 1987:275). Because of the large amounts of material on this topic, this chapter will consider the less conventional activities while the next chapter will focus on the movement's connections to the mainstream routes for influence. We wish to emphasize that all the aspects discussed are needed to understand the politics of this movement. Some movement groups may be engaging in activities that are covered in both chapters.

The concept of protest has been used in various ways (Lofton 1985:1). For example, *protest* can refer to the "unconventional and often collective action—taken to show disapproval of, and the need for change in, some policy or condition" (Frank et al. 1986:228). In this sense protest can be legal or illegal, peaceful or violent. Others view protest as one of the three major classes of action. According to this tripartite conceptualization, "Protest struggle stands between polite and violent struggle, a kind of 'middle force' . . . protest eschews or at least avoids the extensive physical damage to property and humans found in violent struggle on the one side and the restraint and decorum of staid politics on the other" (Lofton 1985:261). Eisinger (1973:13) distinguishes between a generic definition of protest as "any form of verbal or active objection or remonstrance" and the more technical one referring to a conceptually distinct set of behaviors. In the latter, protest refers to a number of types of collective action that are "disruptive in nature, designed to provide 'relatively powerless people' with bargaining leverage in the political process." In protest, actors are trying to maximize their resources while minimizing the costs. Protest thus can be distinguished from political violence by this attempt to minimize costs. Those engaging in violence could experience major costs such as death, serious injury, or loss of freedom. Protesters use the implicit threat of violence, whereas those using violence are explicit in their intention to harm.

Gamson's (1975) *The Strategy of Social Protest* seems to consider violence as a form of protest. The objective of social protest activities is to gain support for a movement's cause (Gamson 1975:140). Protest is typically engaged in to achieve certain kinds of resources for the movement, such as attracting new members, reinforcing solidarity of current members, obtaining material rewards such as money or equipment, or gaining attention for a particular ideological position. At times protest activities hinder those opposed to the movement, for example, by making the opposition look bad (which can make the movement look good), destroying their resources, or eliminating key figures through political assassination.

As Gamson (1975:140) points out: "The form that protest takes is viewed as the result of an interaction." Movement groups or individuals in the movement could engage in a show of strength that may or may not be challenged by other groups, including law enforcement. Symbolic acts may be designed to challenge the power of another group or governmental authority (Tilly 1970 cited in Gamson 1975). For example, we saw the ZOG flag burned at a protest rally in Pulaski, Tennessee, to challenge governmental authority. Protest demonstrations, which include sit-ins, rallies, marches, and pickets, are the most frequent form of publicly accessible movement activity. A *demonstration* can be defined as "an organized, noninstitutionalized, extraordinary form of political expression; a gathering of people (or a person if sponsored by or acting as a representative of an organized group) engaged in the act of making known by visible or tangible means a public display of group feeling" (Everett 1992:961).

At times social protest activities may result in violence. In fact, violent activities of movements are a common form of political participation. Gurr (1989a:13) identifies four significant changes in how group violence has been studied. First, most social scientists have come to recognize that group violence is typically a result of "real grievances over underlying social, economic, and political issues" rather than pathological acts of misfits in society. Second, choices are being made by the groups, their rivals, and authorities that *all* influence the likelihood and the type of violence. Third, "authorities have substantial responsibility for violence, either by their own action or through inaction in the face of private violence" (Gurr 1989a:13). Last, violence is often an effective tactic in gaining recognition and concessions, particularly if it is the result of a prolonged social movement. Gamson's (1975:81) analysis of 53 challenging groups supported this finding, although he cautioned that the relationship between violence and successful outcomes is not simple. Violence needs to be studied as an instrumental activity designed to advance the goals of the movement group. Participants use violence because they believe it will promote their cause. Similarly Tilly's (1978) resource mobilization approach maintains that movement participants select their methods on the basis of what resources are available at a particular time; collective violence should be viewed as a normal activity in a struggle for power. Political violence can also be viewed as "the result of reasoned, instrumental behavior" (Crenshaw 1992:7). In general, those who are discontent or involved in some protest "are no more nor less rational than other political actors" (Gamson 1975:137).

Because of space limitations we will examine only certain key examples of protest and violent activities in the movement. We will first look at the strategy of public rallies and marches as a form of social protest followed by an examination of the very different strategy of leaderless resistance. We will then consider violence associated with the movement, including three case studies of violent confrontations that illustrate the diverse paths to violence that movement activity may take. Violence is not always initiated by the movement groups or members.

It is the interaction of movement and nonmovement people that is key to understanding the forms of protest and violence.

Rallies and Marches

Rallies and marches have been a typical form of political expression by many groups in the movement. In opposition to the civil rights movement of the 1960s, more neo-Nazi symbols and anti-Semitic rhetoric appeared at Klan rallies, including the use of statements that argued that integration was a Communist-Jewish conspiracy (Chalmers 1981:352). By the mid-1960s "the Klan could not halt the much more extensive revolution that was taking place in civil rights" (Chalmers 1981:386).

Later, near the end of 1970s, there was a dramatic increase in rallies, marches, cross burnings, confrontations, and shootings in various communities. Chalmers (1981) describes how advocates of civil rights would raise issues about police violence or the quality of justice for blacks. This likely would be followed by a march and maybe a boycott of racist merchants. A Klan organization would then respond, promoting white resistance and trying to recruit new members. Demonstrators from both sides might encounter each other on the streets although law enforcement tried to keep the struggling groups and their marches separate. The Justice Department helped local governments formulate rules for marches and public meetings and write laws against carrying weapons by marchers or spectators. There would be some arrests, many suspended sentences, some convictions, and eventually an "uneasy peace" (Chalmers 1981:407).

Many of today's movement groups are engaging in rallies and related activities. These functions often involve speeches and cross lightings; some are more public than others. SPLC (1994b:1) reported 243 demonstrations in 1992 and 1993 by "hate groups" in this country. The pattern in the 1990s is quite different from that of earlier years when Klan and related groups were seen as the aggressor clashing with the civil rights marchers. At current rallies violence is more likely to be initiated from the counterdemonstrators who protest the movement's events. Although some may be from the local community, many counterdemonstrators travel from cities possibly hundreds of miles from the rally in order to denounce the demonstrators. One of our respondents, Bill Werner of the Templar KKKK, reported: "What I see at rallies and marches is that the protesters are ALOT more aggressive and violent towards us. We do what we do peacefully. We don't want

The police presence facing the anti-Klan crowd at Thom Robb's Knights of the Ku Klux Klan public rally in Janesville, Wisconsin, May 30, 1992. When the snow fences were pushed down, the police sprayed the crowd with water from fire hoses and threatened the use of tear gas.

trouble. None of us want to be in jail for something stupid. We have jobs and families also." John Murphy of the Bedford Forrest Brigade provided us with a list of rules his organization follows at rallies: no weapons, no alcohol, and no offensive, abusive, or threatening language or gestures. All lawful orders of police and fire departments are to be followed and appropriate force in self-defense is to be used only as a last resort. A spokesperson is assigned to speak to both the police and press.

Often the main purpose of the rally is to recruit new persons, although attracting media attention is important as well. Communities experiencing racial unrest or bad economic times are good potential sites for rallies. For example, in Dubuque, Iowa, the proposed Constructive Integration Plan had been met with considerable resistance within the community. Some residents feared that "recruitment" of minorities to this almost all-white city would take away their jobs or potential jobs of their children. Both Richard Barrett of the Nationalist Movement and Thom Robb of the KKKK engaged in public activities in Dubuque. We attended Robb's 1992 rally in a small park downtown.

Police allowed only media and supporters inside the area while law enforcement kept counterdemonstrators behind fences, but not far from the Klan. When speeches were given, someone threw an egg at the Klan. Robb then used the situation to his advantage, explaining that the real haters are "out there" rather than inside with the Klan. A major problem occurred after the rally when some of those who supported the Klan tried to leave the area and at least one was attacked. Robb evidently kept contact with Dubuque because in May 1995 he informed us that the Council for Diversity, which had replaced the Constructive Integration Plan, had collapsed.[1]

Klan rallies are frequently held in Pulaski, Tennessee,[2] the birthplace of the original Klan. Originally the rallies may have evoked tension, especially the 1989 AN rally that featured Louis Beam and Richard Butler. Pulaski's citizens were named "The Persons of the Week" by ABC's "World News Tonight" when only a few townspeople turned out for this rally and many of the businesses closed. The rallies we attended in 1993 and 1994 were relatively peaceful, probably in large part because few outside demonstrators were present and the town may have grown accustomed to the rallies. Some of the law enforcement officers stayed inside the courthouse while Klan leaders and others spoke outside on the steps. On one occasion black faces appeared in the courthouse window behind where the Klan spoke, evoking the chant "Nigger Nigger out out out" from movement supporters, but no one came out.

Our experience in Rockford, Illinois, is in sharp contrast to Dubuque and Pulaski where police had allowed us to talk with rally participants. We formally asked Rockford police to admit us to the June 11, 1994, rally of the KKKK and to treat us like they would the media. As requested, we provided letters from both our sociology departments and the names of police we had contacted at other rallies. In spite of our efforts, the police department denied us access without any explanation. Box 1 gives Dobratz's first-person description of the rally and events leading up to it.

The Rockford community did many of the things *Klanwatch*'s special report "Ten Ways to Fight Hate" (SPLC 1994f) recommended. For example, community leaders advised people to stay away from the rally, they planned an alternative activity, they didn't try to stop the rally, and the police responded quickly to trouble. Some in Rockford also found a unique way to show opposition by having a physical and spiritual cleansing of the courthouse steps the day after the rally (*Rockford Register Star* 1994:5A). The idea of the Klan's presence needing to

Box 1.
Dobratz's Rockford, Illinois, Experience

On the morning of June 11, 1994, I was standing at the junction of a state highway and an interstate near Rockford. So many thoughts raced through my mind, not the least of which was what was I doing here waiting for the Klan. My mind played back the conversation with an internal affairs law enforcement officer on June 9. I had asked why my colleague Stephanie and I couldn't be treated like the press at the rally. Both Stephanie and I had current Georgia press credentials, which we had obtained by making a special trip to Georgia to have our pictures taken. He told me we had been denied, and I replied I knew that but I wondered why. He said the Chief of Police said no, but I told him that wasn't a reason. He countered that it was and informed me I'd never get into the rally. He probably did not know I had already talked with Thom Robb's KKKK national office and Dennis McGiffen[3] who was organizing this particular rally. When the internal affairs officer had asked if I wanted a copy of the criteria for press credentials, I said yes and waited. Eventually he returned and said the criteria would not be available until Saturday, the day of the rally. I had left the public safety building without saying how amazing this all was to me. There *were* criteria but no one could see them until the rally.

For a June day it was very hot on the road. I recalled my conversations with an ACLU representative who had said I had the right of association with the Klan even if I was not a member. My thoughts rushed back to my conversations with McGiffen and Robb just the night before. When McGiffen had informed the police I was accompanying the Klan, they had told him no, I couldn't come. When Robb heard this, he talked to the police, who evidently told him how I had been all over the city creating trouble. I told Robb that I had talked with a city attorney, the mayor's office, the mayor, a county official, and the major newspaper as well as the ACLU. After being turned down by all these, I planned to exercise my right of association with the Klan, and he was willing to have me do so. Law enforcement relented when they talked with Robb, perhaps out of fear that Thom Robb would deliver on his promise to have another rally shortly if they didn't let me in, or perhaps it was the realization that they could be sued for violating my rights of association.

(continued)

All these thoughts continually swirled through my mind as I noticed a few cars with Klan members pull off the interstate and stop near my car. McGiffen and I talked briefly, and then I followed the other cars to the designated rendezvous with law enforcement. A couple of other cars with Klan supporters were already there as well as the police. While waiting I began an interview with McGiffen. Eventually the police had all the cars follow them to another location. Once there we got into vans and were taken to the rally site but not where the counter-demonstrators could see us. More waiting. Then we were allowed to go to the courthouse steps that all the Klan ascended. I stood off to the side below the steps. The rally started about a half hour later than scheduled. The press were allowed to approach the Klan and ask questions, but a fence separated the Klan from the media. The "spectators" were kept about half a block away behind other fences. The newspapers reported 22 Klan, a crowd of 750, and more than 300 officers. For a short time, the Klan played previously taped music, and then several speeches were given. After the rally, the Klan and I left the area and eventually were driven in the vans to where our cars were located. I then finished my interview with McGiffen. I had told the Rockford mayor that the most dangerous place to be would be with the crowd, and indeed violence had erupted in the crowd when three people evidently unfurled a Confederate flag. Seven people were arrested, only one from Rockford. The *Rock River Times* headlined "A+ for police, F- for protestors." Schier (1994:8) reported how hatred came out of the mouths of protesters as well as Klan: "Death, death, death to the Klan. . . . Racist Klan go to hell, F— the Klan! Death to pigs! Kill them. F—ing Nazi bastards!"

be washed away illustrates the stigma associated with the Klan. When all was said and done, the city spent $83,424. Some residents were upset with the high cost, but there seems to be few alternatives. The U.S. Supreme Court ruled in 1992 that a local ordinance giving administrators the ability to adjust the fee for a parade permit on the basis of the cost of providing security was invalid (SPLC 1992c). Klan and related groups have First Amendment rights to free speech.

On May 11, 1996, the American KKKK had a rally in Portage, Indiana, which we attended. As per our request, the police department allowed us the same access to the rally as the members of the press.

Unlike Rockford, they had two separate areas for the public—one for those supportive of the Klan and one for those protesting the Klan. The two areas were about 100 feet apart so that only verbal confrontations were possible. Before entering either of the areas people were searched for weapons and objects that could possibly be thrown. After the rally the protesters against the Klan were allowed to exit first and return to their cars. Then the supporters of the Klan left and went to their cars, which were parked in a different location. Similar to the Rockford rally, the Klan themselves were bused in and back out to an unknown area. It seems to us that when there are crowds, keeping the pro- and antigroups separate facilitates crowd control and results in fewer arrests.

Many of the groups who engage in public rallies and marches also have their own private gatherings. Some groups reject the public functions, in part because participants in them can be easily recognized by law enforcement and groups opposed to the movement. Some of those who do not support public gatherings have turned to leaderless resistance.

Leaderless Resistance

The philosophy of some of the more militant in the movement has shifted toward "leaderless resistance," which uses but modifies the Communist cell model where a leader directs the activities of several cells, but people within each cell do not know participants in other cells. Beam (1992:1–7) strongly advocates leaderless resistance where individuals and groups operate independently and do not even report to a central leader. The "Sons of Liberty" of Boston Tea Party fame and the Committees of Correspondence during the American Revolution are examples of how this concept works. Leaderless resistance participants should react similarly to a variety of events because they share the same ideology. Those who are not truly committed to the movement are likely to be weeded out. Beam (1992:5) acknowledges that such a strategy has its problems but is "a child of necessity." Tom Metzger of WAR also strongly supports this philosophy, and like Beam he feels it is necessary at this particular point in time. WAR (1993a:5) suggests that leaderless resistance "tactics automatically improve damage control immensely" and "very loose networks and isolated individuals make a very poor informant strategy."

The discussion about the use of leaderless resistance in the movement has developed at least partially as a result of legal cases involving prominent people in the movement. Since the 1980s a number of legal cases and private lawsuits, often initiated by SPLC, ADL, or CDR, have been effective in harming movement organizations because of the participation of their members or possibly supporters in violent activity. Examples include the following (Hoffman 1989; SPLC 1989; SPLC 1991; SPLC 1995f:4):

1. A $7 million award against the United Klans of America (UKA), who turned over their national headquarters to the mother of Michael Donald who had been lynched by UKA members. The UKA seems to have split apart as a result.
2. A suit against the Invisible Empire, Southern White Knights and its leader Dave Holland led to an award of nearly $1 million damages to civil rights marchers who were attacked in Forsyth County, Georgia, in 1987.
3. Court orders against Klan paramilitary camps in Texas (associated with Louis Beam) and North Carolina (associated with Frazier Glenn Miller). A federal indictment claimed that Miller and others conspired to train and equip a paramilitary group; charges included that they received weapons stolen from a federal armory. In 1986 Frazier Glenn Miller was convicted of contempt of court because of violating an earlier agreement prohibiting paramilitary training. Miller eventually testified for the government in trials against movement members.
4. A $12.5 million judgment against Tom and John Metzger, WAR, and others in the murder of an Ethiopian in Oregon.
5. A suit filed against William Pierce of National Alliance resulted in his being ordered to pay $85,000 because he received and resold property fraudulently transferred to him by COTC leader Ben Klassen.

Although some leaders of the movement advocate the cell structure and leaderless resistance, *Evil Harvest* (Colvin 1992) chronicled a case that signals its potential for grave danger. Mike Ryan joined a local Posse Comitatus after hearing lectures by James Wickstrom, national head of the organization. He was more attracted to the Christian Identity message than other Posse members who focused especially on concerns over taxes and farm foreclosures. Ryan broke away to form his own "cell" when Wickstrom suggested that it was time for Ryan to gather his own flock. Ryan was convinced that Armageddon would take place in Kansas (Colvin 1992:84) and that he "embodied the spirit of the archangel Michiel, the warring angel of God" (Colvin 1992:110). As they prepared for the impending war, his group participated in a series of robberies to acquire money and the equipment they needed to build the bunker for the battle of Armageddon. The "cult" situation intensified as Ryan had the group break away from the Posse and take control of a farm near Rulo, Nebraska, that was considered the perfect site for a paramilitary camp. Ryan engaged in polygyny, extreme domestic violence, child abuse, blackmail, extortion, and eventually the brutal torture and murders of two people, insisting the deaths were "Yahweh's will" (Colvin 1992:348–49).

Wickstrom did not have contact with Ryan during this period, but the survivalist training he and other group members had received and Wickstrom's Posse message were used to justify extremely violent behavior, even against other whites who claimed to believe in Yahweh. Mike Ryan was sentenced to death and his son Dennis received life in prison. The cell structure may shield national leadership from implication in violent incidents such as the Ryan case, but these situations possibly threaten the continued existence of groups who spawn these circumstances, with increased dangers to members and possible legal implication in situations that escalate out of control.

Certainly not everyone in the movement agrees with the idea of leaderless resistance,[4] and even Beam recognizes some may wish to retain their positions as leaders of organizations. Many still favor organizational hierarchy with leaders directing activity to accomplish movement goals. The National Office of National Alliance (1993:6) recognizes the need to build a "revolutionary infrastructure" that would include a "structured collection of people and other resources organized for . . . generation and dissemination of propaganda, recruiting, fund raising, self-defense and internal discipline, intelligence gathering and evaluation, planning and guidance." Dr. Pierce (1993:4) himself believes that "Americans no longer have the guts and self-discipline to engage in solitary guerrilla warfare. . . . Virtually none of the individuals who fantasize about such activity—or talk about it with friends until the secret police swoop down and arrest them all on conspiracy charges—are really capable of action." He concludes that "we always will need organization and strong, centralized leadership, for action as well as for propaganda."

In our interview at AN, Tim Bishop criticized resistance without leaders:

> I've got the evidence inside why this resistance won't work. It's called prison mail. . . . basically, you get 50 different people going 50 different ways and

whatever happens to enter their minds at the moment. Lots of them are gonna end up in prison. If you have a leader there that says—this is the rules and regulations you're gonna follow—we're gonna channel all our efforts in this area right here—we're all gonna pull on the same rope—we're all gonna basically work for a common cause and keep our efforts channeled in positive areas for our people—then you have something that will win.

Bishop believes that, without leaders, movement supporters could lack direction and some might be imprisoned for illegal activities. Arthur Jones (1993:5) also pointed out that "the young people we need to build a true national movement for achieving power are left to fend for themselves and end up in jail or in prison far more than is necessary." In addition, he noted that the youth would not be able to benefit from the knowledge or experience of the veteran activists. John McLaughlin, in his interview with us and in his writings (1993:6), pointed out that for some, leaderless resistance is a "cop-out" for avoiding organizational activities and commitment. He also suggested that since the movement has had problems finding competent leadership, leaderless resistance has sounded attractive to some. On the other hand, McLaughlin (1993:6) suggested that "for certain quality individuals because of their job, or circumstances, or geographical location, leaderless resistance is the proper and best form of action." "Der Kampfhund," a director of Northern Hammer Skinheads, tended to agree with McLaughlin and noted the advantage of a large organized force at another period of time:

Leaderless resistance is great for the intelligent, resourceful person with a certain amount of military training. The masses, even of our race, will always need some type of structure and no one can deny that groups like the Sturm Abteilung (SA) had a very powerful psychological and social influence which helped to catapult the NSDAP into victory.

The debate about the use of "leaderless resistance" as a major strategy or as one of several to be employed in the movement is likely to continue for some time.

An Overview of Violence and the Movement

In his book *The Racist Mind: Portraits of American Neo-Nazis and Klansmen,* Ezekiel (1995:xxix) maintains that "the movement would disappear if it did not periodically re-earn its reputation for violence." Violence provides a "hidden subtext . . . the almost unspoken possibility" that cannot be disregarded (Ezekiel 1995:xxx). Ezekiel distinguished four different kinds of movement people based on self-control and amount of involvement. The first type is the national leader and those in other leadership positions who display long-term commitment to the movement. Louis R. Beam Jr. (1983:55), a longtime movement figure, has been critical of many movement leaders who do not recognize the link between violence and a successful movement: "First owing to the timidity, faintheartedness, and irresolution of all but a handful of leaders, . . . few have instructed their members in the theory and philosophy of what we all know must be eventually done if we are to save ourselves—kill the bastards."

Ezekiel's typology also includes the typical members who are not fanatical and do not want to harm nonwhites. They desire to belong to a "serious" group, and the possibility of violence suggests to them that this is a serious organization. The third type is the loose cannon, unpredictable and ready to explode. If he does erupt, he is likely to be imprisoned but the movement gains from the notoriety: "His action is indispensable, as it keeps alive the aura: This movement *can* be violent" (Ezekiel 1995:xxx–xxxi). The final type is the potential terrorist who adheres firmly to the movement's ideology and wants to act on behalf of the ideology. According to Ezekiel (1995:xxxi), "his spirit needs the comradeship of the tight terrorist cell." The image of cells suggests small groups of people who operate in secrecy, planning and engaging in violence to further their cause. However, how really "secret" these cells are is a question that needs further examination. According to the 1989 *Terrorism, Violence and Insurgency Report,* there has recently been more "ideologically motivated terrorism including acts by white supremacists" (Hoffman 1989:5) and "extremist, white supremacist paramilitary groups oriented toward 'survivalism,' outdoor skills, guerrilla training, and outright sedition are a new phenomenon" (Hoffman 1989:6).

Lutz and Zeskind's (1987) study of hate violence suggested that the principal cause of the violence is *not* organized white supremacist actions but underlying social tensions; the movement, though, could be seen as providing a "language" of racism. Part of the movement has "become more deliberate and ideological in its choice of targets and techniques" (Lutz and Zeskind 1987:17). For example, Beam (1983: n.p.) developed a point system so that one could "intelligently judge the effectiveness of proposed acts against the enemy." An entire point is needed for one to become an Aryan Warrior; an act directed at the control center for policy formulation and decision making would be rewarded with one point, an act against the opinion makers would result in 1/3 point, and so on. The lowest point value was 1/1,000 if actions were simply directed toward the recipients of civil rights policy, including blacks, Hispanics, and other minorities.

An additional study also questions how directly involved movement members are in individual acts of hate violence. Levin and McDevitt (1995:7) distinguished three types of motivation for actual hate crimes: (1) thrill or excitement; (2) defensive, such as protecting one's neighborhood; and (3) mission hate crimes that are carried out by people dedicated to bigotry, frequently Klan, National Socialist, or skinhead members. Interestingly, in their study of the Boston Police Department reports, only one of 169 hate crimes could be classified as a "mission" offense. It seems that a number of careful studies are needed to examine the linkages of the movement groups, members, and supporters to issues of hate violence and hate crimes. With this in mind, we will now briefly consider violent activities that have been associated with the Klan, National Socialists, skinheads, and Christian Identity.

Ku Klux Klan and National Socialists

The Klan after the Civil War used violence and the threat of violence to challenge the policies of Reconstruction, to gain control over blacks, and to force out the "carpetbaggers" from the North. According to Gurr (1989b:206), the first Klan "probably was the greatest perpetrator of private violence in American history" and its resistance ultimately was quite successful, resulting in the "reestablishment of southern white hegemony" (Gurr 1989a:20). On the other hand, MacLean (1994:xi) argues that the second KKK, the one of the 1920s, was "the most powerful movement of the far right that America has yet produced." The Klan embodied many characteristics that on the surface appear contradictory or incompatible, such as being both "mainstream and extreme . . . anti-elitist and hateful of blacks and immigrants, pro–law and order and prone to extralegal violence" (MacLean 1994:xiii). While Brown (1989:41) suggests blacks were only a "secondary target," MacLean argues that probably about half the victims were white and half were black. Whites were much more likely than blacks to be flogged for moral offenses such as adultery, failure to support one's family, abuse of their spouses, and neglect of children. Toy (1989:134) believes the Klan of the 1920s was "more unified and less overtly violent than its Reconstruction-era predecessor and civil rights period successors," often substituting intimidation for organized violence.

The 1954 Supreme Court case against the segregation of public schools may have sparked the growth of the third Klan and its use of violence. Violence accompanied the civil rights sit-ins, freedom rides, and demonstrations in the early 1960s.[5] For example, four black girls were killed in the September 1963 bombing of a Baptist Church in Birmingham, Alabama; two men with Klan affiliations were arrested. The murders of civil rights activists James Chaney, Andrew Goodman, and Michael Schwerner in June 1964 in Mississippi eventually led to convictions of Sam Bowers, leader of the White Knights of the KKK, and six others. In March 1965 Viola Liuzzo, who had been helping transport people to and from a civil rights march in Alabama, was murdered. One of the Klansmen in the car from which the fatal shots were fired was an FBI informant. President Johnson appeared on national television and stated: "We will not be intimidated by the terrorists of the Ku Klux Klan" (Wade 1987:351).

In June 1963 civil rights leader Medgar Evers was murdered in Mississippi. Byron De La Beckwith was tried twice in 1964, but both juries deadlocked, failing to reach verdicts. Beckwith was found guilty in a third trial in 1994, *30 years* after his first trial. Key witnesses included two KKK members turned FBI informers who testified they heard Beckwith suggest he was involved (Harrison 1994:A26). One of them was Delmar Dennis, a famous Klan informer in the case involving the three aforementioned civil rights workers. Dennis testified that Beckwith spoke at a closed 1965 Klan meeting, suggesting, but not confessing, that he had killed Evers (Booth 1994a:A2). Booth (1994b:A1, A21), a *Washington Post* staff writer, pointed out that many legal experts felt Beckwith had a strong case for appeal. His lawyers repeatedly argued "Beckwith's constitutional rights to a speedy trial and due process were violated" (Booth 1994b:A1, A21). It was not possible to reinterview dead witnesses or even examine crucial evidence that had been lost, including the bullet that had killed Evers. Although some testimony from the 1964 trial was read into the record, the judge refused to let Beckwith's 1964 testimony be read. Beckwith's attorneys did not let the 73-year-old Beckwith testify at this trial because he evidently did not remember much of what had happened 30 years earlier. Much of the evidence was circumstantial, including his rifle with a fingerprint being found at the scene and a car similar to his being seen nearby. Beckwith has maintained the rifle was stolen and he was 90 miles away in Greenwood at the time of the death. Witnesses described Beckwith's racist beliefs, which included how he believed blacks were "beasts of the field." Booth (1994b:A21) claimed Beckwith's "racist ideology was a liability this time. His defense attorneys . . . pleaded with jurors not to focus on Beckwith's sensational beliefs but on the alibi testimony of former Greenwood police officer James Holley, who said he and his partner saw Beckwith in Greenwood some 90 miles away from Jackson on the night Evers was murdered." Clearly, changing social and political conditions had worked against Beckwith this time.

Early in 1979 in North Carolina the neo-Nazis and Klan seemed to be gathering strength, and anti-Klan groups were willing to challenge them. A "Death to the Klan" march was organized in Greensboro by the Communist Workers Party (CWP) on November 3, 1979. Klan, with ties to neo-Nazis, evidently fired on the protesters, killing five members of the CWP and wounding others. Twice juries found the participants in the shootings not guilty. Virgil Griffin of the Klan celebrated: "I feel like I died and went to heaven. . . . No matter what the communists may say the KKK is here to stay" (Wheaton 1987:280). Survivors and widows filed a $48 million civil suit against 65 defendants, including Klan and Nazi members, agents from the BATF and the FBI, and the Greensboro Police Department. The jury ruled no conspiracy and rejected any punitive damages, but they did hold 8 defendants liable for injuries to 3 of the 16 plaintiffs. Evidence from the Greensboro trials illustrated how an informant's activities may have helped precipitate the violence (Toy 1989:144). Wheaton (1987:286) points out that utilizing undercover agents and informants is especially problematic, and there needs to be clear differences between monitoring groups for possible criminal activity and encouraging the activity.

Ridgeway (1990:79) dramatically described the Greensboro killings as

> the best-known in a series of escalating outbursts of racial violence by what was coming to be known as the "white resistance." This resistance movement was different from any that had come before, representing a coming together of previously independent, often quarrelsome groups on the far right. . . . For the first time, it was possible to see the outlines of a new phase in the far-right movement, which would come to be known as the Fifth Era.

Bob Miles, an insider in the movement, wrote *33/5,* which stands for The Order in the Fifth Era of the Klan that Ridgeway noted. According to Miles, the first three Klan eras roughly correspond to the Klans of the post–Civil War, the 1920s, and the civil rights era. The Fourth Era was the television era of the "excellent super salesman. It knew its product and it sold it like a carnival huckster. Unfortunately, it was not able to deliver the product which it so competently sold" (Miles 1983:4). It seems likely Miles was talking about David Duke and others using the media to gain attention. The Fifth Era Order returns to its original emphasis on secrecy, noting that "secrecy breeds fear" and "respect begins with fear" (Miles 1983:5). This Order should be an invisible one perceived to be operating in "wartime": "It is the hour of struggle for the very existence of our Folk on this earth, and in this land" (Miles 1983:7). Currently the Florida Black KKKK (n.d., received 1995) members reject the idea of popularizing the Klan and use the Reconstruction Era Klan as their model. They assert: "We are always there, in the shadows, ever vigil, always watching."

Skinheads

During the late 1980s and early 1990s, skinhead violence received a great deal of notoriety. Two books, *Skinheads Shaved for Battle: A Cultural History of American Skinheads* (Moore 1993) and *American Skinheads: The Criminology and Control of Hate Crime* (Hamm 1993), illustrate the violence in the movement. Moore (1993) entitles his first chapter "Obsessed with Violence: The Skinhead Decade." On the first page of chapter 1, Hamm (1993:3) mentions one source that indicates that during the 1980s "skinhead violence included 121 murders of blacks and gays in urban areas across the nation, 302 racial assaults, and 301 cross burnings." Some difficulties in using statistics like this are that one does not know how "skinhead" was determined and by whom, if these skinheads are part of the movement, and whether a few skinheads created numerous acts of violence.

In Hamm's (1993:106–7) study, there were 22 terrorist skinheads and 14 nonterrorists. To have been considered a terrorist, at least half of a person's violent activities needed to be against people of another race and the person had to have indicated that he became a skinhead because he was fighting for the survival of his race. Hamm found that violence was pervasive in the skinhead subculture, although seven in his sample had not engaged in any fights. An ADL Report (1993a) considers skinheads the most violent of the current movement groups and details 22 deaths in the three-year period from July 1990 through June 1993. Many of the deaths were minorities, but there were also incidents like one skinhead killing another over one's boots or the death of a homeless person that suggest the violence isn't only directed at racial and ethnic minorities. The 1995 ADL report noted an additional 9 homicides, totaling at least 37 from December 1987 to that time. SPLC (1995a, b) indicated a sharp decline in organized neo-Nazi skinheads in 1995 but modest growth in 1996 (SPLC 1997c). Also SPLC (1997c:14) claimed that there was an upsurge in skinhead-related violence in 1996 that reversed the recent trend. They had identified only 29 crimes attributed to skinheads in 1995, but this increased to 51 in 1996.

Interestingly, Moore (1993:72) points out how influential the "watchdog" organizations have been in shaping the analysis of skinheads in the United States:

> When their racism became known, it was attacked by a variety of organizations, particularly the Anti-Defamation League, the Southern Poverty Law Center, and the Center for Democratic Renewal, all of whom shared the role of social guardians attacking racism and hostility to minorities, manifested by individuals or groups. Skinhead behavior was labeled unacceptable and deviant, but generally unaccompanied or unmitigated by the concept that appeared so often in treatments of the skinhead phenomenon presented by academics in England that "deviance was a social creation, a result of the power of some to label others." (Hall and Jefferson, 5)

Occasionally an American article might note that the deteriorating economic position of young white males played a role in shaping their behavior.

The song "Boot Party" by Max Resist illustrates the central role of violence in the skinhead subculture:

Bootparty
We like to party in a violent way
I guess it's just a symptom
of the youth of today
We get drunk on the violence we cause
With total contempt
and disgust for the law

Bootparty, Bootparty, Bootparty
It's you we invite to our
Bootparty, Bootparty
You'll feel the heat of our boots
tonight.

A song that illustrates the potential for violence or intellect ("sword or pen") in struggling for the cause is "The Hammer Falls Again (Ragnarok)" by Bound for Glory. Ragnarok refers to the destruction of the universe.

The Hammer Falls Again (Ragnarok)
There's an oncoming fight, wrong against right
The final battle is in sight

Columns of power in the final hour
It's will versus evil, there's no place for cowards
Politicians to Pope, there'll be no hope
There is no escaping the day of the rope
Will darkness descend? Will this be the end?
Can you tell me what lies around the bend?

It's a fight to the end, be it sword or pen
The people say when at the fall of the hammer
Like a wolf to his den, ready to defend
Boys become men at the fall of the hammer.

. . . .

Some live a lie, some prefer to die
Some stand up and dare to defy
Strength in the mind shows us the sign
We can't be separated from our own kind

Some skinheads believe that violence is hurting themselves and the movement. Brogan (1995:4), himself a skinhead, noted how some skinheads have ended up in prison due to drunken brawls and gang fights and recommended skinheads should be an army in waiting: "Just because we are not at war with guns in our hands at this time, by no means allows us to have any less courage, honor, or nobility." *Resistance Magazine* (1994b:17) carried a small segment entitled "A Word on Violence" that pointed out that, although violence plays a major role in political struggle, right now it is more important to invest in ideas rather than chasing after fantasies of terrorism. Metzger (1996b) also showed his concern with skinhead violence and drinking in his WAR Hotline of June 9, 1996. He pointed out that three skinheads had died in San Diego county that week—one who was involved in a fight with another skinhead and two who had died in a car accident in which the car had reached speeds of 100 miles per hour:

At this rate, the skins will do themselves in. Jews and others need not apply or even fire a shot. Most problems we have with young skinheads occur due to excess drinking of alcohol instead of sticking to the racial struggle (i.e., educating friends, distributing pro-Aryan literature, promoting racial t.v., writing articles and programs and other positive programs). The emphasis is on endless partying and in most cases, excess drinking which leads to avoidable confrontations, accidents, and even killing each other. We feel very badly for the families of these skins and some of them were very good skins, we understand. But, to waste their life is to go AWOL from the real racial struggle.

These are examples of skinheads or others recognizing the violence within their group and realizing it needs to be changed to help promote their cause.

Christian Identity

Hoffman (1989:6) argues that the "unifying thread" in the ideology of right-wing terrorism is the "so-called Christian Identity movement." Similarly, Smith and Morgan (1994:44–45) maintain that "most right-wing terrorists are ideologically bound by religious beliefs. The Christian Identity Movement provides the link that has tied rightist groups in America together." White (1989) too supports this argument, suggesting that several principles derived from Identity justify violence and right-wing revolution. They include the promise of a militant second coming coupled with the development of Christ's Kingdom on earth, the hate for the anti-Christ tied to love for one's own people, the idea that religious salvation can be achieved only through individual struggle, and the belief in conspiracy theory. Christian Identity members see themselves as being part of a Holy War with ZOG; terrorism would be an excellent means for a small group to gain the attention of the government.

Kaplan (1993), however, questions the strength of association of Christian Identity with terrorist tactics by arguing that Identity supporters have rarely turned to revolutionary violence; rather, the typical pattern is partial withdrawal from society with rare and quite short violent outbursts. In the "quietist" mode, adherents acquiesce to the state in spite of denouncing the government. The "activists," on the other hand, advocate using force to bring about revolutionary change. Kaplan maintains that only the organization of the Silent Brotherhood has really put the rhetoric into a plan of real action.

Opinions on Violence from Movement People We asked movement people, "Do you think there are times when violence is justified in the movement?" and "If yes, under what circumstances?" Their replies ranged from violence in self-defense to much more aggressive alternatives. This reflects the movement itself, in which some advocate only aboveground demonstrations and others, revolutionary underground action. The typical response was that violence is justified in self-defense. Major Donald V. Clerkin, B.S., L.L.B. of the Euro-American Alliance Inc., elaborated on the self-defense issue "as a last resort in most cases, but always in self-defense. We oppose gratuitous violence—violence for its own sake, violence in order to terrify or intimidate. We don't allow members who merely want to inflict pain on someone else." Richard Barrett of the Nationalist Movement had an interesting view of self-defensive acts: "We would encourage people to seek solutions that are peaceful but yet are self-defensive. So, be self-defensive. Be confrontational. Don't back down. Don't surrender your rights. But be aggressive only up to the point that you are still within the law." He also commented that there was "desperation in American society. . . . There is violence as a desperate act of desperate men."

Harry Schmidt, state chairman of the Populist Party in the state of Washington, explained his party's approach, which includes "challenging the existing system in a peaceful nonviolent manner." In more detail he explained:

> The nationalist rights are being violated into an international world order. But by participating in a nationalist, political party at this time. . . . They can experience the system. . . . Be aware of how we're losing . . . how laws are enacted and how they're used against us and the political process in general so that after a disaster, after a revolution, a coup, probably not by any of our people—probably by a military or probably by one greedy faction against another or a natural disaster or whatever—whatever the means—there will be the pieces to be picked up. And I think that if we . . . educate and familiarize ourselves with the mistakes that are made in the legal process, then we can have a framework to rebuild. And I think it's important that we have a solution instead of just look forward to a revolution or a death and destruction or changing of the guard.

It was important to Schmidt that one understand the system and be able to offer possible alternatives to improve the society.

Tina Higgins, who is associated with WAR and Central New York White Pride, linked peace and war as two sides of the same coin: "The Goddess of Peace must walk hand in hand with the God of War" and violence might be justified "when this government has become an enemy of the people. Unfortunately that day has come. (It has been here for a long time.)" Mrs. David (Katja) Lane of Wotansvolk—14 Word Press commented on the relationship between nature and violence, telling us: "I'll repeat that nature demands everything that we do and are. Nature is perpetually violent. Nature is as much life as it is death. . . . Nature is as much being predatory as being prey. Let me quote Richard Scutari . . . 'rifles and bayonets turn the real pages of history and rifles and bayonets are the only thing that will save our race.' " Joseph Janette of AN also believed there was no alternative to violence if one is to achieve the white separatist state:

When it comes down to the second American Revolution—most people call it a race war . . . we just learned today some other people call it the Armageddon—it's going to have to come down to violence. They're not going to give us our national state no matter how many people we get.

Barry Peterbuilt, a skinhead from Missouri, noted the diversity of opinion on the issue while giving his own perspective:

It really depends on who you speak to and what their goals are. Right now we are in a transition period as I stated earlier and it is unclear as to whether or not violence will be necessary. Personally, I feel that violence is a very good motivation for governments and institutions to take any group seriously. The PLO, ANC, IRA and too many other groups throughout history to count have pressured, through violent means, their governments to take their demands or wanted reforms seriously. Currently, I look at the IRA/ Sinn Fein collective as the prime example of what a modern revolution must look like. The people that would support you must know that at some point the political rhetoric stops and that action will begin when you are laughed from the bargaining table. In the USA, though, at this time we do not have a truly organized and well funded underground but only "lone wolves" who carry out most of the politically violent acts.

Violence will totally be necessary when our "Constitutional rights" are abolished whether by law or by harassment from the law enforcement of our country. They have done much to stifle our "rights" already but we are by no means in a worse situation than the other countries in the world. As long as we can promote our message through speech and print and music etc. . . . I feel that we should use these to our utmost potential. [Ellipsis points were used by respondent]

Like Barry Peterbuilt, John C. Sigler III, aka "Duck," of the Confederate Hammer Skinheads identified a variety of international revolutionary examples and the government's attempts to restrict the movement. He argued that violence was both an effective strategy and inevitable:

Violence works, contrary to the nonsense of popular society, when the oppressed take up arms, the oppressor is forced to recognize and appease him. In the last few years, this country has taken Europe's lead in attempting to suppress our movement's ability to communicate to the people. By God, if they will not hear our voices, they will hear our bullets. The movement has become more militant the world over, war is coming and there is no stopping it. We are not like the old men of the movement who are waiting for some great catastrophy to start the war. We are going to start it and the world will take us seriously again. This is inevitable.

"Valkyrie" felt that "the era of an above ground monolithic movement" has ended. "The future Revolution will be carried out by small loosely affiliated groups using principles of Guerrilla warfare." "Lone wolves" (people acting on their own) may characterize the underground at this point, and there may be potential for groups to act coordinated by leaders and/or small cells to be driven by shared ideology. On the other hand, in an article for *The WAR Eagle,* Jost (1993:6) of NS Kindred pointed out:

We all know that the White racial movement is adorned with a dismally large number of kooks, screwballs, sociopaths and government informers. But it is less known that there are a growing number who live in a fantasy world of revolution and guerrilla warfare. . . . At this time, revolution or guerrilla warfare is strictly for losers. The call to arms and revolution is completely irresponsible, very dangerous, and it plays right into the hands of our enemies.

He argued that Aryans need to change themselves and be more "disciplined" and "solution oriented" to "lead humankind out of degeneracy and chaos, toward the golden-age envisioned by our great Aryan preceptor." Whether the movement should engage in violent activities or when will be the appropriate time to act militantly are other issues of contention within the movement. We will now examine three cases of violent action frequently discussed in the movement.

Violent Confrontations and the Construction of Martyrs

The interaction between those believed to be movement supporters and law enforcement can prove deadly. Although there are several examples of this occurring in the movement, we illustrate it in the shoot-outs of law enforcement with Gordon Kahl and the Silent Brotherhood (Brüder Schweigen), especially Bob Mathews, and the siege of the Weavers at Ruby Ridge. Gordon Kahl was a tax protester who had belonged to some movement-related groups, while Randy Weaver considered himself a white separatist but not a "joiner" of any groups. Bob Mathews, on the other hand, led an organization that challenged the government. Events surrounding these three people have taken on great symbolic importance for the movement as heroes and martyrs are created and provide a standard against which others can measure themselves.[6] George Eric Hawthorne (n.d.:2–3) of Resistance Records makes it clear how significant the Brüder Schweigen were and are for him and others like him:

> As a Racial activist, as a man who has to endure many hardships to remain active (as all public heretics must), I have the sacrifices of men like Robert Mathews, David Lane, Richard Scutari, and the rest of The Brüder Schweigen to remind myself that if they can give all they have given (and in the case of all, but Mathews, still are giving), I can certainly make my comparably meager sacrifices without complaining. . . .
>
> Success is contagious and so is courage and sacrifice. When those around you are marching fast, you push yourself to go harder. . . .
>
> So, when we are down, when our hearts are weary, when we have begun to tire of the battle that rages on, we think of The Brüder Schweigen, and we are reinvigorated to fight harder for the epic task which lays before us.

The creation of martyrs contributes to the ongoing life of the movement.

Gordon Kahl

For the story of Gordon Kahl, we draw extensively on *Bitter Harvest* (1990) by James Corcoran, whose reporting on Gordon Kahl was nominated for a Pulitzer Prize, and *There Was a Man* by Capstan Turner with A. Jay Lowery, the authorized biography told through the voice of Kahl's granddaughter. There is much agreement with the general facts, but some differences are expressed in the interpretation of events. Some details are chronicled in *There Was a Man* that are not mentioned in *Bitter Harvest*. We also draw on legal documents filed for Yorie Von Kahl by Attorney John W. DeCamp[7] (1996a, b, c) for the U.S. District Court for North Dakota in the case *United States of America vs. Yorie Von Kahl,* which was received by the court on April 16, 1996.

During the farm crisis of the early 1980s, Gordon Kahl, a highly decorated World War II veteran, struggled like many others to keep his land in North Dakota. With family income rarely exceeding $10,000 per year (Corcoran 1990:62, 71), his $33-a-month disability pension at times fed his family (Turner and Lowery 1985:xiii). Kahl, at one time a

Congregationalist, Mormon, and John Birch Society member, joined the Constitutionalist Party that wanted to abolish federal income tax and viewed the Federal Reserve System as a "private corporation controlled by Jewish owners of eight international banks" who wanted "to destroy Christianity and establish a one-world government run by communists and socialists" (Corcoran 1990:51). In 1967 Kahl wrote to the Internal Revenue Service (IRS) refusing to "pay tithes to the Synagogue of Satan" (Corcoran 1990:51–52). By 1973 Kahl was attracted to the Posse Comitatus, which blended Christian Identity beliefs with the planks of the Constitutional Party; he became the Texas coordinator for the Posse in 1974. Kahl gained considerable visibility in 1976 when he and five other Posse members appeared on television urging people to stop paying income taxes. After this Kahl was charged for failure to file income taxes in 1973 and 1974. His lawyer argued that he was being tried because of the television appearance in 1974 rather than for simple tax evasion, since Kahl had quit paying income taxes in 1969. The IRS did not deny that accusation. Gordon was given one year in jail with five years probation. A psychological evaluation found him to be "fanatically religious, with schizophrenic characteristics, but not psychotic" (Corcoran, 1990:53–55). Turner and Lowery (1985:xii) maintain that Kahl could be considered "paranoid about government agents," except that "his fears and predictions about what was to happen to himself and his property became actual events."

Upon his release, Kahl did not violate his probation or commit a crime until he refused to file income taxes in April 1980. Since he felt the government was "harassing" him over income taxes, he stopped returning his monthly probation reports. In November the IRS filed a lien against 80 acres of his land, since he owed almost $35,000 in back taxes. In early 1981 the IRS put his land up for auction, and a warrant was issued to arrest Kahl for probation violations (Corcoran 1990:56–57). DeCamp (1996a:6–7) suggests that the warrant was for an "alleged" misdemeanor probation violation and was faulty for three reasons. First, Gordon Kahl had been given an illegal five-year felony probation; second, if he had been given a legal probation it would have already expired; and, third, the supporting grounds for issuing the warrant were defective. Also, U.S. Marshal Muir had been instructed not to serve the warrant by higher authorities.

During the fall and winter of 1982, Kahl continued his political activities at farm rallies across the Great Plains. Despite the popular press reports and images created by officials, Turner and Lowery (1985:xi) suggested that by this time Kahl was no longer a member of the Posse Comitatus or any other organization. Kahl had never even met Wickstrom, the Posse leader (Corcoran, 1990:145). Kahl had, however, made it clear that he would not make it easy for officers to arrest him. According to Corcoran (1990:63), "Despite the rough talk, Kahl didn't seem anxious to confront the authorities."

U.S. Marshal Muir decided to try to arrest Kahl February 13, 1983, although there was internal disagreement on this decision and on how the roadblock was set up. A shoot-out developed at the roadblock that left Muir and a deputy marshal dead, the deputy county sheriff critically wounded, another deputy marshal and Yorie, the son of Gordon Kahl, injured. After making sure Yorie got to a doctor, Gordon and his friend Scott Faul escaped. A manhunt followed with Scott Faul turning himself in late the next day along with a statement from Gordon Kahl that maintained he acted in self-defense as he felt they were going to be "slaughtered." He also said that he did not fire the first shot. It was not certain who fired first and some of the ballistics information was unclear. The debate seemed to focus on whether Marshal Muir or Yorie Kahl shot initially. Corcoran (1990:144) pointed out that there were unresolved questions about the marshals' actions: "Why and where the marshals tried to do what they did would be questions that would haunt the government throughout the search for Gordon Kahl, through the trial and months and years beyond. . . . And they were questions to which the government had no answers."

The FBI surrounded the Kahl house on Monday, and then on Tuesday they shot a Labrador dog on the property. When no one responded to the order to surrender, they threw 26 gas canisters in the house and fired hundreds of rounds for over an hour. Gordon Kahl was not there, and the manhunt continued. The trial of the people who were with Gordon Kahl at the roadblock was held very quickly. Joan Kahl, Gordon's wife, was acquitted of conspiracy and harboring charges, but Yorie Kahl and Scott Faul were convicted of murder May 28, 1983. On June 24 they received two life sentences plus 15 years. A friend was sentenced to 10 years. In a 1989 letter to Senator Burdick, Yorie Kahl (1989:18) maintained: "I am no criminal—this you well know." Also he wrote:

> And it is equally true, is it not, "when treason doth prosper, none dare call it treason"! But I dare, and I do.
>
> Even with the heel of this Jew/Masonic hydro on my throat, I remain adamantly loyal to my people and nation! (Kahl 1989:19)

Joan Kahl Britton remains committed to helping Yorie Kahl in the judicial appeal process. Attorney DeCamp (1996a) has identified a number of reasons why Yorie Kahl was not given a fair trial. For example, Judge Benson knew Marshal Muir quite well and was his Masonic brother and sponsor. Benson was well known for his lack of sympathy for those who were involved in confrontations with government agents as shown in his handling of the Leonard Peltier case.[8] The wounded Yorie Kahl had been denied counsel and was held incommunicado for 10 days, although he was interrogated by law enforcement. Further, he did not receive effective assistance from his court-appointed counsel. Government officials hindered or prevented potential witnesses testifying for the defense and did not share information about informants and undercover agents that was relevant to the case.

While on the run Kahl sent his version of the shoot-out to friends, supporters, and journalists, indicating Yorie was the first person shot and accepting full responsibility for the deaths and injuries to law enforcement. In Arkansas, Leonard and Norma Ginter and others befriended Kahl, but eventually the FBI found his location. On June 3, 1983, while Agent Blasingame was showing the search warrant to the Ginters outside their home, shots were fired. Rather than following the directive asking Kahl to surrender, Matthews, the county sheriff, had entered the house. According to Corcoran (1990:244–245), Matthews and Kahl may have shot each other simultaneously. Matthews may also have been hit by a shotgun blast fired through a front window by another officer. Matthews fell into U.S. Marshal Hall's arms and said, "I think I killed him." He died later that day from loss of blood. Much later, the *Arkansas Democrat* newspaper in Little Rock maintained it was unlikely that Kahl and Matthews killed each other because the autopsy results revealed that both Kahl and Matthews were shot to death from behind. Authorities never found any spent shell casings from Kahl's rifle (Corcoran 1990:249). DeCamp (1996b:25), drawing on statements from the Ginters and former FBI agent Dero Downing, claims that Matthews came out of the house and was shot in the crossfire of government agents. After Matthews was out of the house, Corcoran (1990:245) indicated a dozen officers and two SWAT teams "laid down a withering barrage of gunfire and tear gas canisters that shattered the windows and left the concrete front of the building pockmarked." Using diesel fuel, they intentionally burned down the house, although their initial public statement said the tear gas accidentally started the fire. Drawing on the thoughts of the FBI agent who was not present on the scene but was in charge of the manhunt for Kahl, Corcoran (1990:248) wrote: "The truth would come out, and when it did, the lawmen would appear to be liars as well as vigilantes gone amok." Setting the house on fire badly mutilated Kahl's body and destroyed evidence. DeCamp (1996b:21) maintains that Kahl was intentionally killed to prevent him from testifying at a future trial. The government had helped make Gordon Kahl a martyr for the movement, "a symbol that time for talk had run out. It was now time for action" (Corcoran 1990:148).

The Silent Brotherhood

Atkins (1992:5) points out that the only American white separatist group to have been involved in widespread terrorism was "Brüder Schweigen," or the Silent Brotherhood (sometimes also called the Order or the White American Bastion). *Terrorism* is defined as "the systematic use of murder, injury and destruction, or the threat of same, to create a climate of terror, to publicize a cause, and to intimidate a wider target into conceding to the terrorists' aims" (Wilkinson 1986:208). Political terrorists use moral ideological justification to explain their actions (Atkins 1992:4). One typology of terrorism includes the following: factional terrorists who may be "extreme" nationalists and separatists wanting self-determination or autonomy; ideological terrorists desiring fundamental changes in the political, economic and social system; and issue group terrorists trying to change or block the change of certain policies rather than reorder the system itself (Wilkinson 1986:209). Those advocating white separatism and engaging in terrorism would seem to fit the factional terrorist type best. Determining who is a "terrorist" is a fascinating illustration of the labeling process. As Goldstick (1991) points out, we praise the freedom fighter and condemn the terrorist. The rules are made by the victors, not the defeated, reminiscent of an epigram: "Treason doth never prosper: what's the reason? For if it prosper, none dare call it treason" (taken from Goldstick 1991:262). David Lane (1995 interview with Meredith Vieira) of the Silent Brotherhood stated that the only difference between a patriot and a terrorist is control of the press.

The Silent Brotherhood, or Brüder Schweigen, saw themselves as revolutionaries and heroes fighting against a society trying to destroy the white race. The name *Brüder Schweigen* refers to a fighting elite in the German National Socialist movement and was selected by the Silent Brotherhood's leader, Robert Jay Mathews, the most renowned hero and martyr for the more militant part of the contemporary movement. Mathews was especially critical of the major role he saw Jews playing in the American government. Mathews, at one time involved in the John Birch Society and the Sons of Liberty, supported National Alliance and spoke at one of their national meetings. He attempted to create a white-only homeland in the Pacific Northwest, but only one couple actually came because of his relocation service. Mathews had not been raised in a racist household. Flynn and Gerhardt (1995) suggest that the Brüder Schweigen members had often sacrificed their careers and families to participate in the group. Most members of the Silent Brotherhood had been law-abiding people who had become frustrated with the direction America was taking and wanted to do something about it, rather than just talk as they felt AN was doing. Members of the Silent Brotherhood were probably younger than the general memberships of the groups from which they came. Their educational levels were somewhat typical, including both high school dropouts and college graduates. Neighbors described some of them as "likable" and "good workers" (Aho 1990:66). They do not fit the image of deranged men on a spree of violence.

Bob Mathews gained some of his recruits by placing ads in movement or patriot newsletters looking for people down on their luck, including Vietnam veterans. Aho (1990:185–86) believes that one of Mathews's tactics was to put the potential recruits in his debt by loaning or giving them money and inviting them to stay on his land near Metaline Falls, Washington. Further, Aho (1990:185–86) argues that the typical path of recruitment for all the Christian patriots he studied is similar to the way most people join movements, a "multi-step" process of mobilization in which work relationships and one's associations including religious membership, family, and friends play key roles in encouraging people to join a movement.

Brüder Schweigen ultimately had their own counterfeiting press, safe houses, and arms caches in Idaho, Montana, Oregon, and Washington and may have been "complicit" in five deaths (Aho 1990:7). Some (Coates 1987; Aho 1990:62–63) suggest Mathews followed ideas from *The Turner Diaries* by Andrew Macdonald (pseudonym for Dr. William Pierce, leader of National Alliance). SPLC (1991) has referred to this book as a "blueprint for a white revolution" (p. 57) and "a revolutionary manual" (p. 43) for the Order. In late September 1983, Bob Mathews formally created the Silent Brotherhood, composed of National Alliance supporters Richard Kemp and Bill Soderquist; Dan

Bauer, Denver Parmenter, Randy Duey, and Bruce Carroll Pierce who had been involved in AN; David Lane, originally a Klansman and AN representative; and Ken Loff, a farmer described by Flynn and Gerhardt (1995:xii) as Mathews's closest friend. With Loff's six-week-old child in the center of the circle, the men repeated an oath of loyalty stating, "I, as an Aryan warrior, swear myself to complete secrecy to the Order and total loyalty to my comrades. . . . We are in a full state of war and will not lay down our weapons until we have driven the enemy into the sea and reclaimed the land which was promised to our fathers of old" (Flynn and Gerhardt 1995:126). The child was a symbol of the concern about the future generations of white children. Secrecy actually was not always followed and sometimes in retrospect poor judgment was used in deciding who one could trust. An agenda was adopted that included raising of funds, for example, from robberies; recruiting of new members; dispersing donations to other groups; assassinating enemies of the white race; and creating a guerilla operation engaging in sabotage.

A partial list of the crimes that some of the Silent Brotherhood engaged in include: counterfeiting; bank robberies of $25,000 in Seattle and $3,600 in Spokane; armored car heists of Continental Armored Transport Company for $40,000 and in Seattle's Northgate shopping mall for $500,000; the bombing of the largest synagogue in Idaho; the disappearance of Walter Edward West of AN who may have talked too much; the murder of Alan Berg, an abrasive Jewish radio talk-show host, on June 18, 1984; and a Brinks armored car robbery of $3.6 million near Ukiah, California (ADL 1985a:3–6). Reports suggest that the Silent Brotherhood developed a hit list, and Alan Berg was its first victim. The inner circle of Bruders were evidently split on whether there should be assassinations. Morris Dees of the SPLC was allegedly at the top of the list because of the civil suits against movement leaders and organizations. Norman Lear, the TV producer of "All in the Family" featuring Archie Bunker, "Sanford and Son," and "The Jeffersons," was number two, followed by Berg who had been quite obnoxious in his dealings with movement supporters, including Lane, who had debated with Berg on his radio program. After Berg's death some came to believe Berg was not the best target because he was so offensive on the radio that he probably helped promote the negative image of the pushy aggressive Jew (Flynn and Gerhardt 1995:297).

During the Ukiah robbery, Mathews dropped the gun of another Bruder member; this provided authorities with a major clue linking the robbery with the Order. After that robbery, the inner circle argued about strategy and delegating authority; finally it was decided that Mathews would continue to coordinate, plan, and recruit, while Pierce would take part of the group to another area. Organizations and people reportedly designated to receive money included Richard Butler of AN; William Pierce of National Alliance; Frazier Glenn Miller of North Carolina KKKK; Louis Beam, former Klan leader; Tom Metzger of WAR; and Bob Miles of the Mountain Church (Flynn and Gerhardt 1995). Mathews "wanted to cement the fragmented right wing, with stolen money as mortar" (Flynn and Gerhardt 1995:22) and went on a trip to the East where he likely distributed part of the money and met with Tom Martinez, who he was trying to recruit and who had helped distribute counterfeit money. Later Martinez betrayed Mathews by helping FBI agents locate Mathews and Gary Yarbrough at a motel in Portland. Mathews escaped but was wounded in the hand. Yarbrough was arrested; previously his home had been searched by FBI agents who had found various weapons, including the submachine gun that had been used to kill Alan Berg.

The wounded Mathews ended up on Whidbey Island off Washington's northwestern coast with some other Order members. He drafted what many call a Declaration of War on ZOG: "being of sound mind and under no duress . . . we declare ourselves to be in full and unrelenting state of war with those forces seeking and consciously promoting the destruction of our faith and race" (Flynn and Gerhardt 1995:419). Those present signed it, a few not using their real names. It appears that an unknown person tipped off the authorities about their location. On December 7, 1984, the FBI's hostage and terrorism commando SWAT team closed in on Mathews, Duey, and the Merkis located in different houses; many of the Bruders had already left. Duey rushed out of one house carrying an Uzi machine gun but surrendered, shocked to find he was surrounded by white men rather than minorities. The Merkis eventually surrendered after burning considerable but not all the evidence in the house. Mathews refused to come out, but he allowed someone with him to leave. In the negotiations Mathews was asked what he wanted, and he replied parts of eastern Washington, Idaho, and Montana for an Aryan homeland. While Flynn and Gerhardt (1995:442) comment, "It was not an auspicious start to negotiations," it clearly reflected the ideology of Mathews. Eventually agents entered the home but, encountering heavy gunfire from Mathews on the second floor, they retreated. Agents decided to fire illumination flares into the house, knowing it was likely the flares would set the house ablaze because of the ammunition there (Flynn and Gerhardt 1995:446). Even with the fire Mathews refused to come out and died inside on December 8, 1984. His badly burned body was later found with his Brüder Schweigen medallion embedded in his chest.

The "Ode to Bob Mathews" by fellow Bruder David Lane (n.d.g:10–11) indicates how many movement people revere Bob Mathews as the premier Aryan warrior.

Ode to Bob Mathews (David Lane)
It was the eighth day of December
In nineteen eighty-four.
A full moon witnessed to the deed
On the nation's western shore.
Bob Mathews made his final stand,
He vowed he'd run no more.
He loaded his gun and spit in the eye
Of the jews and their federal whore.

. . . .

So, they rounded up an army
Of maggots and faggots and reds.
Race traitors and cowards and jackals.
And other kinds of feds.
The jews had given the orders.
Race traitors would obey.
By the hundreds they came to murder
The greatest White man of his day.

They brought helicopter gunships.
And their army did deploy.
They thought they'd break the spirit
Of this fearless rebel boy.
But even as they poured their fire
Through barricaded doors.
His bullets whistled by the heads
Of treasonous federal whores.

. . . .

They knew they'd met their match.
So they set the house on fire.

And soon the flames touched the sky.
A Viking funeral pyre.
White brother, how I miss you.
Who can take your place.
As the leader of the army
That fights to save our race?

As you march through fair Valhalla.
Asgard's mighty hall.
Number one among the Vikings.
I can hear you call:
"Arise, you Aryan Warriors.
I've shown you how to fight!
You owe it to my children
To battle for the right."

In National Alliance's tape of Bob Mathews speech "A Call to Arms," Dr. William Pierce (1991) stressed the symbolic importance of what Mathews had done. Mathews stood for courage, strength, and the willingness to sacrifice it all for the white race. Pierce believed that although Mathews may have been premature, he identified the need for action and recognized that the enemies of the white race would have to be killed.

Numerous skinhead bands have dedicated songs to Bob Mathews. For example, the song "R.J.M." (Robert Jay Mathews) by Max Resist stresses how he was a hero who wouldn't surrender or compromise his beliefs:

R.J.M.
Robert Jay Mathews,
he formed the Order
he swore to fight
The injustice and tyranny,
That we have lived in all our lives
When The Order struck the system
They took ZOG on for our rights
Until a traitor named Martinez
Turned him in to save his hide

RJM We salute you
RJM Your spirit won't die
RJM A Martyred hero
RJM Oi Oi Oi Oi

Not all movement groups have been supportive of the violence of the Silent Brotherhood. For example, Christian Identity Reverend Dan Gayman returned money he was given and testified against some of the Silent Brotherhood (Flynn and Gerhardt 1995). Thom Robb of the KKKK has upset fellow Klansmen by being critical of Mathews. WAR (1993b:6) points out that Ed Fields of *The Truth at Last* accused Mathews of being a CIA agent. Thus it is important to realize there is not complete consensus in the movement on either who is a hero or on the role of violence in the movement.

After Mathews's death, other Silent Brotherhood members were eventually captured. On April 12, 1985, 24 members of the Order were indicted on racketeering and conspiracy charges. Many of the Order turned and helped the federal government and/or pleaded guilty. Ten refused and were convicted after a 16-week trial. Sentences generally were 40 years, but Bruce Carroll Pierce received 100 years. In April 1987 Pierce, Lane, Scutari, and Jean Craig were indicted in federal court in Denver *for violating Alan Berg's civil rights*. The state of Colorado evidently did not believe it had enough evidence to try the people for murder as it never filed charges. Pierce, alleged to be the triggerman, was found guilty and sentenced to another 150 years consecutively, and Lane, alleged to be the driver of the getaway car, was given another 150 years consecutively without parole until the first 50 years are served. Lane has contended that he was not in Denver at the time of the shooting, but the woman he was going to visit had been killed by a truck and the building that may have had his bus receipts had burned. Scutari and Craig were found not guilty of this offense.

On the ABC "Turning Point" program on the Silent Brotherhood (October 5, 1995), Bruce Carroll Pierce said the movement would eventually win because time is on its side. Although imprisoned, David Lane publishes *Focus Fourteen,* the official newsletter of 14 Word Press, with his wife, Katja, and friend Ron McVan. Lane has tried to appeal his case on the grounds of double jeopardy since it appears he and Pierce may have been convicted for the homicide of Alan Berg both in Seattle and Denver federal district courts. The government claims that the Seattle RICO (Racketeer-Influenced and Corrupt Organizations) prosecution needed proof of a patterning of racketeering activity and the homicide while the Denver civil rights case involved the homicide, racial motivation, and employment issues. Yet the homicide seems key to both cases.[9]

Richard Scutari (1995:1) also remains steadfast in his beliefs, stating in *Focus Fourteen* that it may not have been worth it personally, but he would do it again:

I truly believe that our culture and the survival of our Race are in jeopardy. As a man who holds the virtues of honor, loyalty and duty at the core of my soul, I was duty bound to do no less. In fact, I am amazed that others have not picked up where we left off.

The survival of our Race is on the line. If it takes the imprisonment of one-third of our men and the death of another third in order to win this war, then that is a cheap price to pay. The alternative would be far worse. Would it be worth it to those who die or suffer in prison? Hell no!! But, it will be worth it to future generations of White children. That is what this struggle is supposed to be all about. Those with a White Soul understand this. Those without a White Soul make up excuses of why they cannot or should not fight.

14 WORDS,
Richard Scutari
Brüder Schweigen, POW

Figure 11. Aryan Warrior Ready to Fight for His Cause Designed by Ron McVan of Wotansvolk—14 Word Press.

Scutari's use of POW, like that of other Silent Brotherhood members, indicates that the imprisoned Bruders see themselves as "Prisoners of War" and do not believe the U.S. government is their government. His description of costs and benefits to his actions provides support for the general social scientific finding that "terrorists do what they do because they are relatively rational human beings and not because they are crazy or something is psychologically wrong with them" (Ross 1994:177).

In addition, Frank L. DeSilva (1996), one of the Silent Brotherhood POWs who served 11 years and was released in 1995, suggests that the story of the Brüder Schweigen is not yet over:

> In the early 80's, there were certain men, a tribe actually, who called themselves die Brüder Schweigen, or Silent Brothers, and developed a concept roughly this: there were traitors, men of deceit, bad character, and greedy for power, which had destroyed a once great People, as well as their nation. These men thought that silently, they would change things, events, and history, for it was their Nation and People that had been destroyed. Well, as stories tell, these brave and gallant men failed in their attempt to change events but no story is ever really over, and no final chapter is planned any time soon. For even though these silent brothers are now fading in jungles of concrete and steel, their spirits remain ignited with the same passion for those Folk they sacrificed all to defend. They live, in part, because people like you believe in them, what they stand for, what they have died for.

Christian Identity has been linked with terrorism at least in part because of what the Silent Brotherhood did. Yet the connection needs to be explored further. Mathews's own beliefs tend to suggest how problematic this link may be. Flynn and Gerhardt (1995:108–109) point out that in 1982 Mathews had his son baptized at AN but then comment: "Mathews returned only a few times to Aryan Nations, more for the fellowship than for the religious doctrine. Mathews believed in God, but he assembled his own teleology by borrowing selected tenets from a menu of faiths and from Odinism" (Flynn and Gerhardt 1995:109). Barkun (1994:230) sums up his view of Mathews by saying, "All that one can conclude is that Mathews had some familiarity with Identity, and sometimes represented himself as a believer, without evincing any continuing interest in either its doctrines or its churches." Some tensions may have existed in the organization between Identity supporters led by Bruce Carroll Pierce and others. According to Aho (1990:65), the Brüder Schweigen initially consisted of disenchanted members of AN, Klansmen, and one survivalist; they were joined by born-again Covenant, the Sword, and the Arm of the Lord (CSA) Christian knights, Identity churchgoers from Colorado, some members of National Alliance and the John Birch Society, and a few Christian Constitutionalists. The Silent Brotherhood and the movement in general are diverse in organizational ties and religious beliefs, making it difficult to generalize about their specific views.

There have been offshoots of the Brüder Schweigen. Eldon "Bud" Cutler, a security chief at AN, attempted to contract the killing of Tom Martinez and was sentenced to 12 years. Brüder Schweigen II was a group charged with the September 1986 bombings of three buildings in Coeur d'Alene, including a federal building and the home of Reverend Bill Wassmuth, an activist critical of AN.

Perhaps the most far-reaching indictments against some of the Silent Brotherhood were presented in the sedition trial at Fort Smith, Arkansas, in 1988. In addition to Lane, McBrearty, Pierce, Scutari, and Barnhill, three of the major leaders of the movement, Butler, Miles, and Beam were charged with seditious conspiracy or plotting to overthrow the government. Barnhill reportedly asked that he not be convicted of the same robberies he had already been convicted of. Two of the government's witnesses were Frazier Glenn Miller and Jim Ellison, who had been in charge of his own survivalist compound as part of the CSA. The government's case was strikingly full of witnesses who had much to gain if there were convictions. Many of the witnesses, including Ellison, were "trading testimony for favors" (Ezekiel 1995:26), and some may have had sentences reduced or charges dropped. The Justice Department wanted the jury to believe that a group had plotted to overthrow the government in front of people they did not know very well and in spite of their knowing that paid informants and hidden FBI agents often attended the AN Congresses. Ezekiel (1995) argues "it is not plausible" (p. 29) and "the government's case violates common sense" (p. 36). All the defendants were acquitted, and Beam reportedly marched outside and saluted the Confederate Memorial.

The Tragedy of Ruby Ridge, Idaho

Jess Walter's (1995) book *Every Knee Shall Bow* recounts what happened to the Weaver family on Ruby Ridge. This is a very tragic story[10] that tells much about how the movement is perceived and how the various levels of government and their agencies act. It also should help readers understand why movement supporters so deeply mistrust the government. In August 1992 there was an 11-day standoff at the Weaver cabin on Ruby Ridge, a location accessible mainly by four-wheel drive vehicles. Deputy U.S. Marshal William Degan, Samuel Weaver, the 14-year-old son of Randy and Vicki Weaver, and Vicki Weaver, Randy's wife, were all killed before the siege ended.

The profound impact of the Silent Brotherhood on law enforcement in the Northwest can be seen in how authorities came to view this white separatist family with religious beliefs similar to Christian Identity. Randy Weaver and his wife, Vicki, had attended some gatherings at AN but had not joined. According to a description of the conversation Randy Weaver had with Kenneth Fadeley, the government informant:

> At the end of the meeting, they talked about the Aryan Nations. "What do you hear from down south a little ways?" Fadeley asked.
>
> "I haven't heard anything from them," Randy said.
>
> "I've never felt comfortable with them," Fadeley said.
>
> "I don't like them," Randy said. They were back to the same conversation they'd started two years before, when they . . . agreed that "the movement" needed new leadership. (Walter 1995:102)

Although Weaver was not a joiner, he evidently had opinions about the direction the movement needed to go.

In late 1990 federal agents requested Randy Weaver to spy on AN, indicating that his assistance might result in authorities being more lenient on a firearms case that the government was preparing against him. Weaver does not deny selling sawed-off guns to Fadeley because of his need for money, but stories differ on whether he was entrapped by the government informant to sell the weapons. What is clear is that he was found not guilty of the charge.

After Weaver refused to spy on AN, he was indicted in December 1990 on federal charges of making and possessing illegal firearms. In January 1991 he was arrested while coming off the ridge by the county sheriff and three ATF agents who had tricked him in order to charge him. The magistrate then *erroneously* informed him that if he were convicted, he would likely be expected to reimburse the government for costs, and if he forfeited his bond, Weaver's land, the only real asset he had, could be sold to make up for the $10,000 bond (Walter 1995:123). After leaving the court, the Weavers prayed about what to do and decided to stay on the mountain. Randy Weaver received a letter that indicated his court appearance was to be March 20 rather than the February 19 he had been previously told; yet on February 20, a failure-to-appear warrant went out and the U.S. Marshal Service became involved.

To illustrate how quickly Randy Weaver was "demonized," the chief deputy marshal wrote that the Weaver case could be like the Bob Mathews case and his cabin was compared with Whidbey Island (Walter 1995:126). Vicki Weaver sent a letter dated February 3, 1991, to Maurice Ellsworth, the U.S. attorney for Idaho, that stated, "Whether we live or die we will not bow to your evil commandments." Her attachment contained a quote from Bob Mathews that read in part: "War is upon the land. The tyrant's blood will flow" (Walter 1995:125). Deputy U.S. Marshal Dave Hunt visited northern Idaho and developed a picture of Randy Weaver that included he was, at least in practice, paranoid; Vicki, not Randy, was in control; and there was cause for concern because of the Weavers' racial, antigovernment, and religious beliefs. The Weavers came to fear that Randy would be convicted, they'd lose their property, and then their children could be taken away. They told a reporter from a small weekly paper that the issue was more about their religious beliefs than shotguns (Walter 1995). Aho (1994) points out that the Weavers were defined as neo-Nazis and their behavior was interpreted in that light. Not only were the Weavers stigmatized, but they also stigmatized the federal government, believing "they were sworn agents of the Zionist Occupational Government or servants of the Queen of Babylon—that is to say, they were evil incarnate" (Bock 1995:266). While "the Weavers were becoming demonized in the public mind . . . the family was complicitous in its own victimization; in this case by emphasizing the religious significance of their stance" (Aho 1994:57).

On August 21, 1992, a surveillance mission was "bungled" (Miller 1992:A6). Two teams had been on and around the Weaver property on August 21. One of their dogs, Striker, appeared to have picked up a scent; Randy, his 14-year-old son, Sammy, and Kevin Harris, a family friend who was staying with them, followed the dog, probably hoping the dog was tracking a wild animal. All three were armed as they often were, Kevin with a 30.06 hunting rifle and Sammy with a lightweight .223 assault-type rifle. Sammy and Kevin went one path while Randy went the other, knowing both paths would join in a Y formation. The big yellow lab gained on the three U.S. marshals, Degan, Cooper, and Roderick, who were now backing off from their surveillance. The dog caught up with Roderick. The sequence of shots that followed is controversial. Cooper and Roderick testified at the trial that Degan told the boys to freeze and identified himself as a U.S. marshal. Then Harris supposedly shot Degan. Cooper returned fire thinking he hit Harris. After that, Roderick shot the dog. No one admitted shooting Sammy Weaver in the back. However, Kevin Harris claimed Degan did not identify himself. First, according to Harris, a camouflaged man (Roderick) shot the dog; then Sammy cursed and fired, followed by a shot nearly ripping off Sammy's right arm. Kevin shot to defend Sammy, possibly killing Degan. Sammy retreated but was shot in the back; Kevin ran to Sammy's body, found no pulse, and ran back to the house. Randy Weaver, on the other fork, had realized "ZOG" forces were there, fired some shots in the air, shouted to the boys to get home, and ran back up. After the shooting, Randy and Vicki Weaver retrieved Sammy's body from the road and placed it in their birthing shed.

After the body of Degan was taken off the mountainside, FBI investigators found seven bullets missing from his gun, although Cooper maintained that Degan had not fired a shot. Norris, one of the other marshals some distance away, testified that the first shot was a "distinctive sound of a two-twenty-three" which could *not* have come from Kevin Harris's gun. Ballistics experts indicated it was a bullet from a weapon like Cooper's 9-mm machine gun with silencer that killed Sammy Weaver. During the trial, the defense attorneys questioned Cooper's story and wondered why Roderick would have shot the dog *in the back after Degan was killed* (Walter 1995).

With the death of Degan, the FBI took over the case, first sending more than 100 state and federal officers with helicopters and armored personnel carriers, including all 50 Hostage and Rescue Team (HRT) members. More agents would come later. Rules of engagement were formulated and reformulated in a complex process still unclear.[11] The deadly force policy, typically used in standoffs, suggests: "Agents are not to use deadly force against any person except as necessary in self-defense or the defense of another" (Walter 1995:190). Yet, at Ruby Ridge, the FBI seemed to believe the rules of engagement were that they could and quite possibly should shoot any adult male who came out of the cabin with a gun. In his book *Ambush at Ruby Ridge,* Bock (1995:14) included excerpts from the 542-page Department of Justice task force report (which has been selectively released to news media). Part of one of those excerpts discussed the rules in the operation plan that were submitted to the FBI headquarters for review:

If any adult in the compound is observed with a weapon after the surrender announcement is made, deadly force can and should be used to neutralize this individual. If any adult male is observed with a weapon prior to the announcement, deadly force can and should be employed, if the shot can be taken without endangering any children.

Before 6 P.M. on August 22, the HRT, including Lon Horiuchi, was in place around the Weaver cabin. Sara, the oldest Weaver daughter, Randy, and Kevin came out of the cabin. Randy checked the north perimeter and then decided to see his son's body in the shed. When he reached up to unlock the shed, Horiuchi shot Randy Weaver, whom he supposedly thought was Kevin Harris. Horiuchi claimed he feared the person was going to shoot at a helicopter somewhere above. Vicki Weaver opened the cabin door and yelled for all three of them to come back in. Randy, followed by Sara and Kevin, entered the doorway as Horiuchi fired a second shot that went through the door, killing Vicki Weaver, who was holding her 10-month-old baby, and severely wounding Kevin Harris. In the trial Horiuchi claimed he was aiming for Harris to prevent him from shooting from the house and harming someone else or the helicopter. Much debate has ensued about whether Horiuchi had followed the militant rules of engagement *or* the deadly force policy. Members of the Senate Subcommittee on Terrorism have expressed concern about whether a *retreating* person could be shot in accordance with the deadly force policy. FBI director Freeh argued that it was a hard call to make, but he believed that Horiuchi's second shot followed the standard deadly force policy. On the face of it, it is difficult to comprehend how Horiuchi was firing in self-defense or defending another person or even defending the helicopter when the people were retreating to a house. No shots were ever fired from the house at someone or at a helicopter during the siege. Two government reports did not find fault with the "second shot," but the Department of Justice Task Force evidently concluded that the shot that killed Vicki Weaver and wounded Kevin Harris was unconstitutional. The Subcommittee on Terrorism, Technology and Government Information of the Senate Committee on the Judiciary (n.d:88) found that the second shot was indeed unconstitutional and inconsistent with the FBI's standard deadly force policy and even the special Rules of Engagement (with Senator Feinstein dissenting).

August 21 and 22, 1992, ended supposedly without law enforcement knowing that Sammy and Vicki Weaver were dead. Also remarkably, the Weavers and Harris had not been asked to surrender on August 22. On August 23 FBI agents discovered Sammy Weaver's body in the shed. Sara and Randy Weaver believed the government already knew Vicki was dead and found it extremely upsetting each time the negotiator used her name. While listening to the radio Randy Weaver became upset because the government was calling them white supremacists and AN members, when in fact they were separatists who did not belong to any group (Walter 1995:222).

During the siege, a robot brought a phone close to the cabin, and the negotiator repeatedly asked Randy to take the phone. Later, it was revealed that the robot not only had a phone but a rifle pointed at whoever would pick up the phone. During the attempts to negotiate, Randy Weaver yelled out that he would talk with Bo Gritz, Special Forces Vietnam War hero and Populist Party candidate for president of the United States. Pastor Dave Barley of America's Promise Ministries played an important role in bringing Gritz to the scene. On August 28 Weaver told Gritz that Vicki was dead and Kevin was severely wounded. On August 30 Vicki's body was removed and Kevin Harris was evacuated to a hospital; on August 31 Weaver surrendered, believing that Bo Gritz had arranged for the famous Gerry Spence[12] to be his lawyer. While Spence had been contacted, he had not formally agreed to take the case but eventually did. Spence (1993:11) did not support Weaver's religious or racial views but believed that if rights are taken away from those he opposes, they could be taken from others as well: "for the ultimate enemy of any people is not the angry hate groups that fester within, but a government itself that has lost its respect for the individual." Spence contended that government agencies had demonized Randy Weaver for his beliefs.

Assistant U.S. attorney Ron Howen, who had been cocounsel in the Brüder Schweigen case, felt Weaver's religious beliefs were the driving force that led to the violent confrontation (Walter 1995:268–69). Howen developed a complex indictment that outlined an alleged conspiracy involving Randy and Vicki Weaver and Kevin Harris as well as other unnamed members of the Weaver family. Leaving Iowa and predicting a violent confrontation, buying the property and building the cabin, writing statements and sending letters were all part of the conspiracy according to the indictment (Bock 1995:125–26). In July 1993, after the longest jury deliberations in Idaho federal courts, Randy Weaver was found guilty only of failure to appear in court and having committed a crime while on pretrial release. Kevin Harris was not convicted of anything.

In August 1995 the U.S. government settled a civil suit out of court with the Weaver family. The proper caveat is that such a settlement does not indicate the government accepted any responsibility for the deaths at Ruby Ridge. However, the award of $3.1 million ($1 million to each of the surviving Weaver children and $100,000 to Randy Weaver) may well speak louder than the caveat. *Newsweek* reported that the Justice Department averted an "expensive humiliation" (Morgenthau et al. 1995:26).

According to Aho (1994:51), "The standoff on Ruby Ridge was an attempt by society in the person of the state to choke down a monster of its own making." It fed the movement's already deep-seated concern about the government. A few months after the Ruby Ridge siege, a meeting was called by Scriptures for America Pastor Pete Peters to discuss what had happened and plan for the future. Between 150 and 175 men from the right wing, including white separatists, attended (Cooper 1995; Ross 1995a; SPLC 1995g). One of the reports resulting from the meeting was a modified version of Louis Beam's essay on leaderless resistance. The United Citizens for Justice was formed as a Weaver support group led by Louis Beam, Chris Temple, and John Trochmann (Cooper 1995:716). Figure 12 illustrates Scriptures for America's view of Ruby Ridge, placed in historical perspective.

In their album *The Fight Goes On*, Bound for Glory sang about the Ruby Ridge tragedy:

> *Judgment Day*
> 400 men surrounding a cabin
> In the land of the free tell me how can this happen?
> Murdering women and children in the name of humanity
> Tell me who's the true masters of hate
> A separatist family or a police state?
>
> Tell me who would you brand the public enemy?
> They took your son, they took your wife
> Without ever giving them a chance . . .
> This means war, you federal whore
> I'll make you wish you never lived
> Your morals are weak, your standards, they reek
> You always take but you never give

Figure 12. Scriptures for America Portrayal of the Government Involvement in the Ruby Ridge Tragedy in Pastor Pete Peters, n.d.c, p. 3.

I'll hunt you, I'll stalk you, kill you one-by-one
The tide will turn the other way
Hunter becomes the hunted, sentence will be passed
When it comes—Judgment Day!

The song not only condemns the activities of the federal government but suggests they will be avenged.

In our July 1995 interview at the AN World Congress, John Bangerter, an Army of Israel skinhead who had corresponded with the Weavers and had been one of the many Weaver supporters on the perimeter of the Ruby Ridge siege, told us his involvement in the movement changed from "a social club" to a very "serious" endeavor. He indicated:

> I didn't understand really until then the kind of fight we were up against—the kind of people we were dealing with and how true it really was that our government was corrupt to the point of no return. That changed my life completely. And that changed the whole movement. That changed the whole movement when Gordon Kahl got murdered and Robert Mathews. But see, those were men that got killed. That's expected. That's, you know, that's how it goes. But when a woman and child got killed, that changed everybody's way of thinking. I know it did.

In addition, he expressed deep regret about what had happened at Waco, especially to the children during the government siege of the Branch Davidians that ended with a conflagration killing about 80 Davidians in 1993. Both Ruby Ridge and Waco events are frequently noted in movement publications as examples of federal "tyranny."

Conclusion

To understand protest and violence, one must always consider the interactions among movement participants, antimovement people, and law enforcement. This movement, like others, is protesting perceived grievances and injustices, especially by the federal government. The perceptions of participants may not typically correspond to the mainstream's interpretations, but deep-seated inequalities and injustices exist in American society, and movement people are not immune from experiencing them. Having and expressing racist beliefs may result in their being stereotyped and stigmatized, which in turn could influence how movement participants are treated by law enforcement, lawyers, and the judicial system and in everyday life. One of the skinhead publications, *Right as Reina,* (1995) reported that a white separatist family had been persecuted by the media and others for their beliefs. Warriorbreed skinheads had evidently placed fliers entitled "Guns Don't Kill People, Black People Kill People" under car windshields at a march by a group unsympathetic to them. The post office box of the skinhead group was on the literature, and the post office box holder was fined $25 for violating a law against windshield distribution. Much worse, according to the skinhead article, the media used the family name and showed their house on television and in the newspaper. The article identified the effects of this: "The family was terrified of being shot by Blacks, unable to walk through the neighborhood, forced to flee, the wage earner in danger of losing his job and ultimately forced to move out of their home" (*Right as Reina* 1995:1). The Weavers' experience at Ruby Ridge documents just how far demonization could go. Aho (1994:50) discusses "a sociology of the enemy" and points out that the standoff on Ruby Ridge is an excellent example in mutual construction of enemies. Each side demonized the other using basically the same techniques.

Those who belong to the movement develop and carry out strategies that within the context of the various facets of the movement's ideology make sense. Some engage in public rallies and marches, some favor more private functions, and others do both. Those who participate in rallies do so to recruit new members and gain attention for their cause; they may face potential violence from counterdemonstrators. Leaderless resistance is a recently developed movement strategy, partly in response to the lawsuits and government actions against movement leaders and/or their organizations.

Different forms of protest may have different likelihoods of violence, but challenging the federal government certainly has a relatively high potential for trouble. To struggle against the government that was perceived as destroying the white race, the Silent Brotherhood engaged in terrorism and developed an assassination list that included political figures opposed to the movement. Some of the money the Silent Brotherhood robbed was allegedly given to aboveground organizations or groups, but much was never found. Gordon Kahl refused to pay his taxes and also showed his disdain for the federal government in other ways while Randy Weaver refused to come down off the mountain for his court case.

Although we are not advocating the use of violence, one must recognize violence has the potential for both positive and negative effects for the movement, including gaining attention for the movement and encouraging some to participate or join and discouraging others. Violence has marked this movement because many movement people believe violence can be an effective strategy and because of government response to this movement. Movement heroes and martyrs have been created to demonstrate the importance of sacrifice for the future of the white race. Human beings "need to know that their existence is somehow significant in the cosmos, that they are justified" (Aho 1994:23).

Gibson (1994), in his book *Warrior Dreams,* discussed the emergence of a paramilitary culture in the post-Vietnam era in the United States. This "New War culture" was only occasionally attached to the conventional military or law enforcement units. It developed in part in response to America's failure to win the Vietnam War. In addition, other social transformations and economic changes played a role, including the decline of U.S. manufacturing strength and worsening economic situations for many. "Also, during the 1970s and 1980s, the United States experienced massive waves of immigration from Mexico, Central America, Vietnam, Cambodia, Korea, and Taiwan. Whites, no longer secure in their power abroad, also lost their unquestionable dominance at home" (Gibson 1994:11). American men dreamed about war and warrior images, including the idea of using force to return "illegal aliens in the U.S. and the hordes of non-whites in the Third World . . . to their proper place" (Gibson 1994:12). Gibson (chapter 10) identified various racist groups and individuals that became involved in the paramilitary culture, including the Silent Brotherhood; the National Alliance, which published William Pierce's novel *The Turner Diaries;* Louis Beam's Texas Emergency Reserve; Gordon Kahl; Bill Wilkinson; and Glen Miller Jr. There was also a "paramilitarism as state policy in the Reagan-Bush era" (chapter 12) that included counterterrorist units like the SWAT teams. Even with the Clinton administration, "warrior myths continued to influence public policy" (Gibson 1994:302).

Senator Grassley, in his opening remarks to the Senate Subcommittee on Terrorism, Technology and Government hearings of September 6, 1995, on Ruby Ridge, addressed the culture of law enforcement with special elites trained to kill first, not only on the international front but the domestic one. "At Ruby Ridge, this culture led to a military buildup that would have impressed Saddam Hussein. . . . There is no room for this culture in law enforcement." Senator Craig, in the hearings, described the law enforcement culture as filled with arrogance and lacking accountability. Yorie Kahl's attorney, DeCamp (1996a:26), compared the Kahl events with those at Ruby Ridge, arguing that the "mind set" of the U.S. Marshals Service was responsible for the shoot-out in Medina and the death of Gordon Kahl.

It is likely this culture encouraged the FBI promotion of Larry Potts, who had been officially in charge of Ruby Ridge. FBI director Freeh testified to the subcommittee that he used poor judgment in promoting Potts but indicated he had at the time talked to many people about Potts's qualifications. Perhaps his circle of confidants is more restricted than that of movement people, who have been criticized for limiting their associations to those who reinforce their conspiratorial worldview. It is also likely that this culture continues as evidenced in the failure of the U.S. government to fully disclose what happened at Ruby Ridge and how the debacle was covered up. A final assessment of responsibility and imposition of sanctions has not been forthcoming.[13]

The reaction of law enforcement when they feel threatened from an impending rally, a death of one of their own, or a bombing needs further study as does the competition between federal, state, and local law enforcement. The role of FBI infiltrators and other informants in the everyday life of the movement needs to be examined to see if and how they influence and possibly accelerate movement violence. The reliability of the testimony of such people and of movement people who have defected needs to be evaluated, not only in the Ft. Smith sedition trial but in other trials as well, including that of the Silent Brotherhood.

Results of survey research[14] suggest that Americans trust their government only some of the time, they often don't believe that public officials care what they think, and many whites are concerned about "preferential treatment" for minorities. Sniderman and Piazza (1993:112) argue that "preferential treatment excites resentment and anger that other issues of race do not." It should not be particularly surprising that some people engage in protest and join movements as a means of expressing their dissatisfaction and their desire for change. Although few Americans actually participate in the white separatist movement currently, the failures of government, citizens' lack of trust of government, and their concerns about perceived "preferential treatment" for minorities could encourage the growth of various movements, including this one.

Chapter Five

Political Mainstreaming: An Alternative to Protest and Violence

It would be easier to bring down this decaying system from the inside, everybody knows that. I am in your colleges, your military, and soon your police force. We are deeply embedded. It is important to voice our opinion in government. Perhaps the cleansing of this system can occur through peaceful political means. It is when this approach fails that we need to take up arms. This country was built on revolution. It will go down on revolution if need be. (Nocmar of Clan Rook)

Although we have defined social movements so that they include the use of noninstitutionalized means of politics, movements also employ institutionalized means. When movements use conventional strategies to gain influence in the political system, they typically involve what Lofton (1985:257) refers to as "polite," "ordinary," or "diplomatic" action. He points out that there are "manifestly protest/movement organizations doing a great deal of prosaically diplomatic and lobbying action along with the centerpiece of protest action that they are also carrying on" (Lofton 1985:257). Such movement activities involve working within the established political order trying to get politicians and individual citizens to accept their ideas as one of the possible interpretations of reality and then perhaps as part of the prevailing political ideology. In our society many do not consider the pursuit of "normal" political activities by people with ties to the white separatist movement as "polite" or "ordinary" because of the stigma attached to the movement and its beliefs. However, those engaging in this mainstreaming activity may be trying to reduce the stigma of the "racist white supremacist" label. According to Schur (1980b:150):

> What stigma-protest groups aim for is such a politicization or "normalization" of the perceived deviation that it will gain full acceptance as falling within a range of acceptable variation. Defining the situation as involving a "variation" presumably carries no connotation of disvalue or discredit, even if it continues to imply something slightly out of the ordinary. At a theoretical extreme, the latter implication might also be removed, so that the behavior or condition could be treated as but one of many, equally ordinary patterns.

To be perceived as "ordinary" would indicate very successful mainstreaming for white separatists. In addition to perceptions, social movements have the power "to reshape mainstream institutions" (Marx and McAdam 1994:121). Here we focus especially upon mainstreaming through electoral politics although other connections are discussed as well.

As expressed by Nocmar in the quotation at the beginning of the chapter, white separatists are of mixed opinion about the efficacy of attempts to mainstream their values and beliefs. A large segment of the movement favors running for political office as a route to "legitimate" power and as a positive propaganda tool. Others are pessimistic about utilizing the ballot box, realizing the potential for cooptation into the system they oppose. The opinions of people in the movement concerning institutionalized political parties, the electoral process, and conservative populist candidates will be explored after an examination of the concept of populism has been applied to the racialist movement. Then we examine the electoral paths to influence used by George Wallace and David Duke, followed by a discussion of right-wing divisions related to racial politics. This should provide the reader with a sense of the significance of neopopulist conservative candidacies and the linkages of nonmovement politicians to white separatism.

Populism

There are various definitions of populism,[1] some tied to specific historical periods and countries. According to Klee (1989:140), *populism* embodies a "democratic suspicion of central power" and the belief "that too few people have control over capital and decision-making." It stresses the "simple people," the "underdog," and the "working man." Worsley (1993:731) suggests that the populist ideal is that "of a society run in the interests of the common people by a party and government that will eliminate inequitable social divisions." Populism often blends "economically radical" views with "socially reactionary and exclusionary" ideas (Klee 1989:141). It can be nativist, stressing the values of a narrowly defined "American" community against various outsiders. This is reminiscent of the in-group versus out-group distinction made in our earlier discussion of separatism. Populism can degenerate into xenophobia and racism (Klee 1989:141).

In the United States, rural movements have often been the wellspring for progressive, or left-wing, populist sentiment during periods of economic downturn. The "Farmer's Alliances" of 1873 gave birth to the People's Party, which changed its name to the Populist Party in the early 1890s (Hicks 1961:238). The Populists attracted broad-based support in the Great Plains states along with Texas and Oregon (Piven and Cloward 1989:42–43). Populists advocated "welfare state protection" from the big capitalists who were promoting economic modernization; they mistrusted major politicians, bankers, and large entrepreneurs and wanted a return to "a less differentiated society," the uniting of "social structure and religiously-inspired morality" (Dubiel 1986:81). Populists seemed to believe that government in the hands of the people was positive, whereas government in the hands of remote professional politicians controlled by monopoly capitalists was not beneficial (Klee 1989:140). Although populism attacked the problems of industrialism and argued that the welfare of people was a responsibility of the federal government, its character also resembled the "cranky pseudo-conservatism" of the 1950s, which included nativism, provincialism, and anti-Semitism (Hofstadter 1955:19). Saposs (cited in Saloutos 1968:114) suggested that fascist tendencies were expressed by some members of the Populist tradition.

Initially, the Populists of the late 1800s attempted to bridge the interests of poor blacks and whites who "wanted business and the wealthy to pay their share, the corporations regulated, and aid given to the poor farmers" (Chalmers 1981:23). The Populist Party was eventually destroyed due, in part, to the racial divisions created by political elites to destroy the black-white coalitions. "Race baiting" followed Populist candidate Bryan's defeat in the 1896 presidential election as elites appealed to poor whites for support (Piven and Cloward 1989:82). Since many poor rural whites expressed nativist sympathies embedded in early populism, fanning the fires of racism was not difficult. Poll tax laws and literacy tests were introduced as a "white supremacy measure" which, ironically, resulted in the political disenfranchisement of both poor blacks and whites (Piven and Cloward 1989:82–83). Political elites successfully converted the potential for class war into racial division. Fishman (1981:171) contended that Populist leaders of the late 1800s coopted the "revolt of poor whites," distorting populism into the ideological justification for the development of white supremacy.

From his study of the Indiana Klan of the 1920s, Moore (1991:11) concluded that it was a "populist organization . . . promoting the ability of average citizens to influence the workings of society and government." While they were united by the ethnic nationalism of the period, "the Klan's ideology stood as a particularly important example of white Protestant attitudes, not a deviant exception to mainstream thinking" (Moore 1991:31). Their concerns about prohibition, crime, and corruption should be placed in the context of "industrial growth and economic concentration," which had "eroded established patterns in community life, undermined traditional, commonly held values, and diminished the ability of the average citizen to exert strong influence in public affairs" (Moore 1991:11). Moore (1990:342) reviewed the literature on the Klan in different communities and concluded that the KKK was more populist than nativist and "represented mainstream social and political concerns, not those of a disaffected fringe group."

Scholars and activists studying and confronting white supremacy have linked the contemporary movement to fascism as expressed in Germany and Italy in the 1930s and 1940s (e.g., Rosenthal 1994). Dutt (1934) analyzed the rise of European fascism and concluded that the middle class was significant in its rise as well as the lumpen proletariat and the working class. During periods of economic crisis, the bourgeoisie is capable of creating a reactionary mass movement to serve the interests of finance capital (Dutt 1934:89). Although the social and economic conditions that led to the rise of fascism in Germany as discussed by Dutt (1934) are somewhat similar to current conditions that have led to the resurgence of the far right[2] in contemporary American society (Rosenthal 1994:22–25), we suggest that fascist ideologies in the United States are blended with populist sentiment as an expression of the political, economic, and cultural organization of American society.[3]

As noted in chapter 2, some organizations in the movement are sympathetic to variations of Hitler's National Socialism while other groups and representatives reject that model, its philosophy, and symbols.

Since Americans fought fascism in Europe, anti-Nazi sentiments are still prominent on our cultural landscape and among factions in the white power movement, particularly traditional Klansmen, who oppose identification with Nazism. Despite this rejection, many of their philosophical underpinnings, such as xenophobia and anti-immigration stances, are compatible with fascism. However, our society as a whole is part of the international capitalist economy, which is not compatible with the nationalistic models of German or Italian fascism. When ultra-conservative or fascist philosophies are framed in our society, they fit more closely into certain aspects of the history of American populism.

Griffin (1995:4) argues that fascism is actually a form of "populist ultra-nationalism" that is concerned with a "decaying" nation. The nation is conceptualized as an

> organism with its own life-cycle, collective psyche, and communal destiny, embracing in principle the whole people (not just ruling elites), and in practice all those who ethnically or culturally are 'natural' members of it, and are not contaminated by forces hostile to nationhood. (Griffin 1995:3)

Although fascist movements seek to destroy democratic political institutions as they stand in opposition to both liberalism and conservatism, these movements may use democratic electoral tactics as a route to power. To acquire the power to create their vision of "social renewal," fascist movements are forced to mask open hostilities and coalesce with conservative factions sharing common "enemies" and priorities (Griffin 1995:4). According to Lyons (1995:245), fascism can be both populist and elitist. It is populist because it tries to mobilize "the people" against perceived enemies, but elitist because "it treats the people's will as embodied in a select group, or often one supreme leader." Ethnic scapegoating and conspiracy theories are frequently used in fascism. Although it is critical of other ideologies like conservatism, Marxism, and liberalism, it uses some of their concepts and practices.

Wasserman (1979:248) suggested that a populist movement should only be defined as one "that either has direct linkage with the original Populist Party, and/or is concerned with the unequal distribution of income and wealth in a society and attempts to mobilize all the population through the electoral process to change this situation." He argued that considering social movements to be populist, even if they share some qualities, is too generic to be meaningful. However, we believe that it is meaningful to view the white separatist movement as an expression of populism. This is because of its ideology as well as the historical linkages to populism at the turn of the century. There are varieties of populism with roots in both the right and left. Left and right populist movements

> share an anti-statist, decentralizing vision with deep roots in U.S. history. Both legitimate their goals through appeals to democracy, the community, self-help, and the everyday concerns of the common person, and both envision gradual but militant struggles to restore civic participation against the encroachment of powerful interests. Further both offer solutions to the present crisis that contain a strong moral as well as economic and political thrust. (Boggs 1986:129)

Dubiel (1986) argues that now two different perspectives have emerged discussing populism in the United States—the left identifying right-wing populism (p. 84) and the right describing left-wing populism (p. 83). In both situations the label "populist" is always used negatively (p. 86). He further distinguishes three strategies for mobilizing the "populist potential" (p. 91). The one that is most related to the way the term is considered here is the "regressive or reactionary" strategy that uses "feelings of injured pride rooted in ethnocentric, sexist, racist, and authoritarian interpretive models" to secure or enhance one's power (p. 91).

Contemporary Right-Wing Populism Contemporary populism in the United States has clear historical linkages to the late 1800s, but the progressive reformism of that era seems to have been abandoned by the current Populist Party. An ADL report entitled "The Populist Party: The Politics of Right-Wing Extremism" (1985b) found similarities between contemporary populism and its nineteenth-century ancestor. First, anti-Semitism has been embedded in some populist conspiracy theories that finger " 'the Jew' as an usurer and financial oppressor" with international networks. Second, nativism was expressed in the nineteenth century as opposition to immigration, which is reflected in the contemporary "America First" anti-immigration policies to protect America's "cultural heritage" (pp. 8–9). Phillips (1993:237–38) noted similarities between the development of racial quotas as a salient political issue in the 1990s and the "fear among Northern Protestants in the mid-1890s of job preferences going to Catholics with the help of big-city political machines." Racial tensions were used to "defeat populist challenges" and present "black-white populist coalitions" in the south during that period.

Diamond (1995:258) suggested that the contemporary racist right was split between two approaches to social change in the early 1980s: "bullets" or "ballots." She argued that, ultimately, neither approach served to broaden support for the "racist right." Zeskind (1984:23) agreed that "night-riding, terrorism, military training and vociferous hate-mongering" were not attractive to people outside of the movement. Betz (1994:37) claimed that

> a majority of citizens in most Western democracies no longer trust political institutions that they consider to be largely self-centered and self-serving, unresponsive to the ideas and wishes of the average person and incapable of adopting viable solutions for society's most pressing problems.

In European countries, people are either "turning their backs on politics altogether or use the ballot as a means of protest" (Betz 1994:37).

Phillips (1994:213–14) characterized the growing political discontent as "middle class radicalism" signaled by the "surprise 1991–92 election showings of angry outsider candidates" like David Duke and Pat Buchanan who spoke to "racial and international apprehensions" (Phillips 1993:237). He warned that

> the frustration among Americans that has built up since the late 1980s is real and valid, and apparent revivals of national confidence will only be temporary without changes in the political, governmental, and interest-group system. (Phillips 1994:231)

However, addressing the concerns of the "radical middle," such as the declining high-wage sector and increased concentrations of wealth, would require working outside of America's two-party system. Their strategies and goals would run counter to "the country's most powerful interests" who have benefited from "the fruits of polarization" and would oppose "middle class populist economics" (Phillips 1994:85).[4]

Diamond (1995:140–41) argued that right-wing populism became a "euphemism" for the Americanist movement in the 1960s. Americanists sought to define what it meant to be American and what America's relationship should be to the rest of the world. The John Birch Society and Liberty Lobby were self-proclaimed Americanists battling communism and the civil rights movement. The Liberty Lobby borrowed the populist label, which had been attractive to the "proto-leftist" American farmer's movement in the late 1800s. The new Americanist populism appealed to disenfranchised farmers during the 1980s farm crisis, calling for a renewed "patriotism, support of racial and other forms of social inequality, and the promotion of policies to benefit a strong middle class" (Diamond 1995:141).

Willis Carto, an admirer of Adolf Hitler dating back to his 1950s involvement in the "Joint Council for Repatriation to Deport Blacks to Africa" to prevent "the niggerfication of America" (ADL 1985b:1; Zeskind 1984:3, 17–18), was the architect of the Liberty Lobby. It was first announced in 1957 as "a new pressure group for patriotism in the nation's capital" and received support from well-known ultraconservative John Birchers such as Taylor Caldwell (Mintz 1985:66, 70). After a long history with the Liberty Lobby and the Americanist Movement (Diamond 1995:152), Carto wrote a series of articles in *The Spotlight* that led to the publication of his book entitled *Profiles in Populism.* He redefined populism to broaden the far right's circle of influence (ADL 1985b:1; Zeskind 1984:3, 17–18).

The Populist Party was reconstituted in 1984 through the efforts of Carto's Liberty Lobby, which publishes *The Spotlight.* In the beginning, the party was even housed in Carto's headquarters in Washington, D.C. The ADL claimed that Carto designed the Populist Party as a "Trojan Horse" to bridge the far right with mainstream politics (ADL 1985b:1). Some of the members and organizers in the party had ties to the 1968 campaign of George Wallace, while others have clear ties to white supremacy, such as Ralph Forbes (Sword of Christ), Jerry Pope (NSRP), Van Loman (former Grand Dragon of the Ohio KKKK), Keith Shive (leader of the Farmer's Liberation Army), Joseph Birkenstock (member of the Posse Comitatus), Robert H. Weems Jr. (spokesman at events for the NSRP, KKKK, and Christian Patriots Defense League), Retired Colonel Jack Mohr (leader of the Citizens Emergency Defense System, a paramilitary wing of the Christian Patriots Defense League), R. C. Morgan (leader of the America Alert Program, distributor of *The Spotlight*), A. J. Barker (NAAWP), and Hal Beck (Liberty Lobby board member who said that the Populist Party had values similar to the Klan and made a commitment to work with them) (ADL 1985b:2–3; Zeskind 1984:7–11). Weems, the first chairman of the Populist Party, had a long history in the KKK and had even used a pseudonym in an attempt to cover some of his Klan activities. The biography of Weems that was printed in *The Spotlight* did not mention his Klan past (Zeskind 1984:15).

In *Profiles in Populism,* which was published in 1982, Carto pictured populism as a blending of political and economic nationalism with a commitment to "free enterprise" and the middle class. Anti-Semitic conspiracy theories were used to justify racial prejudice (cited in Diamond 1995:261). Diamond (1995:261) argued that Liberty Lobby used "populist" as a euphemism for people and movements termed "neo-Nazi" or "fascist" (e.g., David Duke). A new edition of *Profiles in Populism* was advertised in *The Spotlight* in an article entitled "America's True Beliefs" by Vince Ryan (1995a:11) who wrote:

> We have also contended that the positions of Liberty Lobby are the true beliefs and convictions of the American people. That the people are ready to take up the cry of populism manifested itself clearly in the congressional and state elections of 1994. It was certainly not a Republican victory *per se,* but a demand by the people that their lawmakers stop destroying the greatest country in the world and return to the Constitution.

Ryan summarized an editorial by Richard N. Goodwin, adviser to Presidents Kennedy and Johnson, and praised Goodwin for promoting the "genuine populist tradition" despite his "liberal" shortcomings.

The front-page story of that issue of *The Spotlight* was "Populism Sweeping America: Democrats Jump Ship" by James P. Tucker Jr. (1995:1), who felt encouraged by "America's political earthquake," which was jolting "the internationalist, world-government Establishment with politicians everywhere fleeing their stigma." Tucker said that some Democrats have turned to the Republican Party, others have left politics completely, and some are considering third-party candidacies in states like Mississippi where people "cannot forgive Republicans for the harshness of reconstruction." Tucker attributed the "defections" of Democrats to the "rising tide of patriotism, populism and a desire to put America first." *The Spotlight* (1995a:6) promoted an audiotape series entitled "School of Politics," sponsored by the Populist Action Committee, which prepares populist candidates for successful campaigns. Carto (1996), along with the Liberty Lobby staff, edited a recent book entitled *Populism vs. Plutocracy,* which claims that "populism is the only social, economic and political system which withstands the degenerative effects of modern, industrial society on the family, nation, race and culture" (p. xiii).

Bob Richards, known as an Olympic decathlete and media representative for Wheaties cereal, won 66,000 votes when he ran as the Populist Party presidential candidate in 1984 (ADL 1985b:1). Although he disavowed anti-Semitism and denied knowing the ties of other populist candidates to the "racist right," he ran on a platform with ideas that are compatible with the ideology of some groups related to the white power movement, such as the Posse Comitatus. He wanted "America First" and advocated ending income tax and free trade, abolishing the federal reserve, developing "tariff barriers," and curtailing " 'low-wage labor' immigration" (Zeskind 1984:1–2).

As discussed more thoroughly later in this chapter, David Duke ran as the Populist Party candidate for president in 1988. Then in 1992 Colonel James "Bo" Gritz, the man who negotiated with Randy Weaver to help end the Ruby Ridge tragedy, was the candidate. *The Populist Observer* (Richert 1993:1) proudly headlined that Gritz and the Populist Party had convincingly defeated all the other third parties. Gritz received 98,775 votes from 18 states plus write-ins. Factionalism has hurt the Populist Party, though, including the fact that the electoral front for Carto's Liberty Lobby did not support Gritz's presidential campaign (Diamond 1995:265). Although we noted apparent rifts in the Populist Party at the national convention we attended in 1993 (Chicago, Illinois), articles in recent issues of *The Spotlight* and other Liberty Lobby publications suggest that Carto appears to be reasserting his power in the populist arena.

"The Populist Party of America: A Platform for the 1990s" (Populist Party n.d.:n.p.) wanted to "protect the family farm," "end the destruction of America's economy," and "re-vitalize the free enterprise system." While the party maintained that it supported "an end to all forms of racism," it claimed that it "will not allow any racial minority to divide or dominate the society-nation in which the minority lives." It wanted an end to affirmative action, proclaiming: "A vengeful civil rights industry, together with the media and government, has institutionalized 'affirmative action,' quotas, racial preferences in educational admissions and job promotions, and other racist programs." The Populist Party has opposed "feminism, women's equality, civil rights for homosexuals, and racial equality" (Zeskind 1984:1–2). Although the Populist Party is right wing, its antistatist and nativist positions fall outside the pale of traditional conservatism.

Movement Views of Mainstreaming Political Participation and White Racialist Candidates

In this factionalized movement, our research participants expressed mixed support for the mainstream political process. Almost one-fifth of the people we interviewed reported that they had personally run for a political office, and almost two-thirds told us that members of their organizations should run for political office. In addition, about half of those interviewed felt that running for political office was very important. Of those who felt that running for office was acceptable, less than half believed they should run on the Republican and/or Democratic parties. About 15 percent identified with the Populist Party. In keeping with the revolutionary resistance position, about a quarter said that members should not enter the mainstream political arena. Others indicated it depended on the situation.

White racialists have run campaigns with mixed success. Harold Covington, a U.S. Nazi Party leader, lost in a 1980 general election but did win more than 40 percent of the votes in the Republican primary for North Carolina attorney general. Gerald Carlson, former Nazi party member, won the Republican primary in the suburban 15th District of Michigan and attracted a large percentage of votes in a 1980 general election (Phillips 1993:235). In addition, Tom Metzger, then a KKK leader, won the Democratic Party nomination for Congress in the suburban 43rd Congressional District of California in 1980. In our interview, Metzger said that it was the largest congressional district in California, until he won the primary and the district was split. Barry Black of the Keystone KKKK has served as constable in Pennsylvania.

Movement people pointed to difficulties stemming from their attempts to obtain a political office. J. B. Stoner, a former attorney, said that he ran for offices in Georgia and Tennessee several times as a candidate for lieutenant governor and a state congressional seat. Stoner said that the percentage of voters casting a ballot for him continued to grow. He suggested that "the Jews figured they'd better silence me, so they sent me over to Alabama prison where they rehabilitated me." Despite his inability to win an election, Stoner said that it was very important to run for political office: "If we could get some of our people elected to office why that could possibly be used as a base for making more progress on winning national power." White racialist candidates have at times been shut out of the Republican Party, so the current political party structure in the United States has been considered a large part of the problem. As reported in the *White Patriot* (n.d.e:9), Thom Robb tried to run as "a Republican candidate for the 39th District for the Arkansas State Assembly," but "the Republican Party refused to certify Mr. Robb's candidacy and Mr. Robb failed to win a court battle to be placed on the ballot for the general election." In our interview, Robb described the situation as he saw it:

Three weeks before the election, the Republican Party refused to certify me as a candidate. We took them to court. Our lawyer read to the judge the Arkansas state statutes verbatim out of the Arkansas law books that the party has two weeks to challenge the candidacy of a candidate. If they do not challenge within the two weeks, they have got to accept the candidate. The Republican Party in Arkansas waited three months. The judge said, "Well that may be what the law says, but I don't see it that way."

Others have also failed to gain acceptance by the Republican Party. According to the ADL (1988b:92), Ralph Forbes won a school board election in 1985 for Pulaski County, Arkansas, but he "unsuccessfully sought the Republican Party nomination for Lt. Governor" in 1986. In our interview, Forbes said that he had encountered difficulties similar to those experienced by Robb, so he initiated a suit in federal court. The movement has generated a few of its own parties, including the NSRP and, more recently, the America First Party with which Ed Fields has been involved.

Despite the difficulties encountered by white power candidates, Stanley McCollum, former Imperial Wizard of the KKKK, argued that running for political office was still very important even though both parties had sold them out. He said:

Whether or not you win or lose or draw, it gives you a vehicle to get your message out to max your numbers. That's the name of the game. You've got to reach the people with a message before they're going to understand what you're about.

Matt Hale, Pontifex Maximus of the COTC, ran for the East Peoria, Illinois City Council in 1995 but lost the election, winning 14 percent of the vote. He said:

When I run again for City Council, I will be running as much as anything to spread the word of Creativity and the white racial cause. Whether I win or not, is not even really all that important. We will win just by spreading the message through the political process to our race. (Hale 1996b)

However, he expressed dismay over the political process, which creates the illusion of voter choice. Hale (1996c:1) wrote:

The reality, though, is there *isn't* a choice in any meaningful sense, for in order to become a Republican or Democratic candidate for president, the person must have already sacrificed the interests of his people for the interests of the Jews. This is hardly a "choice" for which White people should feel guilty for not exercising. It's like choosing between being shot by firing squad or being hanged—neither is particularly "pleasing" and nor should a person confronted with these options think he has much "choice" in the matter.

Best, the state director of the KKKK in Florida, said that running for office was "the only way that our ideas and beliefs are going to become political. The only way to become a political movement is to do it from the inside."

Sean Haines, of AN and Blood and Honor, felt that the movement should not rule out any possibilities "to try to save a future for the race." Although he felt that both the Republican and Democratic parties are being used against the interest of whites, he said that "if we start eliminating possibilities and start limiting ourselves, you know, if we're not careful it could steer us into a dead-end alley and we'll screw ourselves." He suggested that he could support any party, even "a new Buddhist Party" if it was doing something for the white race and the "end means are good for us." Stormi of the Templar KKKK said that running for political office was a way "to better fight the government's laws that are enacted against our race." John Murphy of the Nathan Bedford Forrest Brigade of the KKK agreed that entering the mainstream political arena was favorable "as a means for change" even though the movement is divided on the issue.

As a result of failed attempts to run for office, some white separatists realize the need to develop alternative strategies. Andrew Jones of the New Jersey Chapter of the Invisible Empire of the KKKK suggested the need for concealment. He said, "I don't suggest it to anybody as far as, you know, being public about your Klan affiliation and running for any kind of office." Joseph Ross, Imperial Wizard of an Independent Klan organization in Indiana, said that running for political office was not a top priority. However, he proposed a strategy by suggesting that prospective candidates find out from the clerk's office which seats remain vacant, so that it would be possible to run unopposed. Ross said:

A lot of these little offices can't even get good people to run. They don't even have anyone there. They're unoccupied all of the time. We sent a person to the Republican Committee. He got to know the chairman and the next thing you know the chairman said, "Well, we'd love to have someone."

Ross seems to be suggesting a strategy similar to Pat Robertson's Christian Coalition, which has been successful in adopting a grassroots strategy targeting local areas first.

Although most people in the movement we interviewed favor running for political office, a considerable proportion did not see it as useful. For example, Richard Butler of the Church of Jesus Christ Christian, said:

> If they try to join the system, why then they become part of the system. So, running for political office is not the way we feel to do it. We have run for the separation of our race. Once we've got one people brought together and we become a separate people, then we will establish our nation and the territorial imperative that our nation has to live on.

Tina Higgins of WAR and Central New York White Pride expressed her frustrations with the political system when she wrote us that

> under this present system we can make no significant changes. Do you think blacks would vote to end affirmative action, or that blacks, mexicans, asians, etc. would vote to repatriate themselves to their countries of origin?

Jack Wikoff, the editor and publisher of *Remarks,* sounded a familiar theme when he told us that "the electoral process is rigged. Voting allows the ruling elite to monitor how well their behavior modification (the media) is working. White revolution is the only solution." John Bangerter of the Army of Israel agreed, stating "I just don't believe that the system's going to work anymore right now. It's not even working. The voting process doesn't work anymore. We're in the war stage right now." Molly Gill, editor of the *Rational Feminist,* "cut to the chase" when she commented, "Politicians are not warriors; they are crap artists. They will sell out their mothers for power and wealth." Bill Albers, Imperial Wizard of the American KKKK said that "you can't beat a crooked card game. And that's what you've got in this country. You got a crooked government, so how can you run for political office and straighten things out? The only thing we see is that there's a revolution coming and that's a solution." David Lane (n.d.h) of 14 Word Press and member of the Order wrote:

> The "leader" who speaks of *voting* a White nation is a lying whore-deceiver. If he pretends our race can survive without exclusive White Nations, he ignores the lessons of India, Persia, Carthage, Egypt, etc., and is a lying whore-

deceiver. If he leads people to rely on the constitution to preserve us, he is a lying whore-deceiver. If his issues are taxes, money and the Federal Reserve while the race dies, he is a lying whore-deceiver.

Katja Lane, also of 14 Word Press, expressed similar sentiment to us in our interview noting that "America is the murderer of the white race, so to become part of the system is to become a murderer of the white race. When we have our own nation, that would be different." These dissenting statements are associated with the resistance approach in the movement rather than cooperation with ZOG.

Whereas the media and many scholars consider the white racialist movement to be ultraconservative, a number of people in the movement argue that their political values and strategies are revolutionary. From the disagreement expressed by our research subjects, the diversity of movement philosophies and strategies clearly leads to a variety of opinions about the efficacy and role of institutionalized politics. We will now turn to two political candidates who exemplify the use of racial politics and consider their ties to the movement.

Two Case Studies of Mainstreaming through the Electoral Process

Far-right populist appeals have been successful in electing a number of politicians across the country, and some scholars suggest that the white power movement has ideological and concrete linkages to populism. Over two decades of political life, George Wallace drew together a broad base of right-wing populist support that led to the "southernization of American politics" (Egerton 1994). Through a number of presidential campaigns, George Wallace attracted the attention of Republicans, such as President Nixon, who "coopted the domestic issues—law and order, school desegregation, and increasingly conservative position on court appointments—that had" made Wallace's candidacies so appealing. Wallace's racial politics was attractive to southerners and made inroads among northern voters as he "kindled the deep discontents of an embittered national political minority" (Carter 1995:369–70). Wallace stood at the threshold anticipating "the conservative groundswell that transformed American politics in the 1980s" by giving "voice to a growing national white backlash in the 1960s" (Carter 1995:466). The "southern strategy" drove a wedge in the Democratic

Party "converting Wallace Democrats into Nixon, Reagan and Bush Democrats." Racial resentments were used "to make 'liberal elites' and big government, rather than big business, the new target for populist ire" (Powell 1992:16). Although he drew support from a general electorate, Wallace's racial politics attracted leadership from the Klan and other movement organizations. We will also examine the politcal career of David Duke. His 1989 election to the Louisiana House of Representatives provides one of the most dramatic contemporary examples of a person with close ties to white power organizations who has reframed the message to facilitate political mainstreaming.

George Wallace and the Southernization of American Politics
The racial and economic strife of the late 1800s has persisted into this century and led to the popularity of conservatives utilizing populist antiestablishment rhetoric. In response to the resurgence of the Klan in the 1920s, the Democratic National Convention in 1924 attempted to pass a resolution to condemn the KKK by name. However, the resolution failed with the delegates divided nearly in half (Kazin 1995:104). As mentioned in chapter 2, even Harry Truman expressed "a willingness under pressure to sacrifice principle for ambition" as he sensed the influence of the Klan in Missouri's local elections (McCullough 1992:159, 164–65). Southern populist leaders such as Huey Long of Louisiana in the 1920s and 1930s, Theodore Bilbo during the New Deal era, and James E. (Big Jim) Folsom, governor of Alabama in 1946 and 1954, paved the way for George Wallace. With the rise of the civil rights movement in the 1950s, the antiestablishment rhetoric began incorporating direct appeals to white racial fears. Politicians, like Folsom, experienced pressures from the White Citizens' Council[5] to maintain a segregationist position.

George Wallace provides an excellent example of a conservative politician surviving the transition into the civil rights era, blending populism with racism. He rode into political life on the tails of "Big Jim" Folsom, beginning his first term in the state legislature in 1947 as Folsom entered the Alabama governor's mansion. Like Folsom, Wallace resisted an antiblack stance and even requested that the governor appoint him to the Board of Trustees at the famed Tuskegee Institute. Although Wallace opposed the 1948 civil rights plank passed at the Democratic National Convention, he did not walk out with the other Alabama delegates or endorse the Dixiecrats in the presidential election that year (Kazin 1995:227–30).

During the rising tide of racial antagonism, Wallace learned to flow with the racial sentiments of his constituency. He was elected to the Alabama circuit court in 1952 and became known as the "fighting judge" defending the southern tradition of segregation. Wallace stopped the removal of segregation signs from railroad stations, threatened to have FBI agents arrested if they attempted to investigate the "racial makeup of Southern grand juries," and refused to wear judicial robes, which would "symbolically separate him from his constituents." In 1956 Wallace cut ties with Folsom, calling him "soft on the nigger question" (Kazin 1995:230), because Wallace had learned that it was the "kiss of death" to be considered soft on racial issues in Alabama political contests.

In 1958 Wallace lost the gubernatorial election to Patterson, the state attorney general, who was seen as a "foe of integration" (Carter 1995:92). After losing that election, Wallace told his aides, "Well, boys, no other son-of-a-bitch will ever out nigger me again." He later denied making that statement, but his campaign rhetoric and political associations through many elections at the state and national levels revealed his success in using racial segregation to win. In 1962 Wallace hired Asa Carter as his speechwriter. Carter[6] was an organizer of the White Citizens Council and founded his own KKK, which brought him into association with Robert Shelton, the Imperial Wizard of the United Klans of America. Although Carter was not directly implicated, his followers were linked to the stoning of Autherine Lucy on the University of Alabama campus,[7] the assault of Nat King Cole, the random beating and castration of a 33-year-old "mentally retarded" black, and assaults on civil rights activists. Asa Carter is known to have shot two of his own Klan members when questioned about the organization's finances (Carter 1995:106–7).

Wallace appealed to rural and small-town voters to win the gubernatorial race in 1962. In his inaugural address, he spoke to supporters:

> Today I have stood, where once Jefferson Davis stood, and took an oath to my people. It is very appropriate then that from this Cradle of the Confederacy, this very Heart of the Great Anglo-Saxon Southland . . . we sound the drum for freedom. . . . In the name of the greatest people that have ever trod this earth, I draw the line in the dust and toss the gauntlet before the feet of tyranny . . . and I say . . . segregation now . . . segregation tomorrow . . . segregation forever. (Carter 1995:108)

When Wallace was asked about his shift toward the "politics of race," he said: "I started off talking about schools and highways and prisons and taxes—and I couldn't make them listen. Then I began talking about niggers and they stomped the floor" (Carter 1995:108). Asa Carter provided Wallace with racist campaign propaganda as well as the Klan voting constituency.

Wallace did not personally have a "coherent racist philosophy," and he considered the anti-Semites and conspiracy racialists to be "nut cases." However, Wallace did associate with racialists such as Ed Fields of the NSRP (Carter 1995:139) and Willis Carto of the Liberty Lobby. Goldwater had won the Republican Party nomination in 1964 on a states' rights platform, so Wallace ran as an American Independent Party candidate in 1968 with the help of Carto and Asa Carter.[8] They wrote a pamphlet entitled "Stand Up for America: The Story of George Wallace," which depicted him as the only "candidate willing to confront 'Blacky' and the liberal-Communist conspiracy which had seized control of the federal government" (Carter 1995:297). When people wrote to Wallace about his political beliefs and requested membership information on the KKK, he distributed that pamphlet.

Initially, Wallace decided not to run a racial campaign in the 1968 presidential election that occurred in the wake of the 1964 Civil Rights Act and the 1965 Voting Rights Act (Diamond 1995:13). A. B. Chandler, the former governor of Kentucky who brought Jackie Robinson into professional baseball, was going to be Wallace's running mate to attract the "border states." Trammel, an adviser to Wallace, said, "We have all of the Ku Klux Klan, we have the Birch Society. We have the Citizens' Council." It was hoped that Chandler would appeal to "some decent people—you [Wallace] working one side of the street and he working on the other" (Carter 1995:356). But pressure from big donors, like Bunker Hunt who opposed Chandler as an integrationist, resulted in the selection of Curtis Lemay, former chief of staff of the Strategic Air Forces in the Pacific who presided over the bombing of Japan. Wallace got only 58 electoral votes, winning the Deep South plus Arkansas. Nixon had successfully coopted Wallace's social issues by focusing on law and order, school desegregation, and the need for conservative court appointments (Carter 1995:367, 369).

Richard Nixon feared the resurgence of Wallace in the 1972 election and attempted to defeat Wallace as early as 1970 when he made a $100,000 cash contribution to Brewer's campaign, Wallace's gubernatorial opponent. Brewer was first in the primary election but failed to win a majority. Nixon put an additional $300,000 in cash contributions to Brewer's runoff campaign, so Wallace "pulled out the stops." Gerald Wallace said "We'll just throw the niggers around his [Brewer's] neck." After a strategy session, an aide said, "Promise them the moon and holler 'nigger.' " Wallace went on to win the election using Klan-style propaganda, such as "Wake up Alabama! Blacks vow to take over Alabama" (Carter 1995:388–95).

Gearing up for the 1972 election, Pat Buchanan, "Nixon's right-wing conscience," who said that Wallace had found popular social issues, advised Nixon to take a hard conservative position to win Wallace voters. Following Buchanan's advice, Nixon admitted his administration's mistake in "carrying out school desegregation plans" and said that "he was opposed to forced integration in housing and education" (Carter 1995:396, 423). During this period, Nixon's "Alabama Project" was investigating the corruption in Wallace's state political machine.[9] Although numerous instances of graft and corruption were uncovered, including the involvement of Wallace's brother Gerald, none were linked directly to Wallace himself, who would be able to claim that he was "the piano player at the whorehouse." The investigation of Gerald was dropped in 1972 (Carter 1995:400–406).

After Bremer's attempted assassination of George Wallace left him a paraplegic, Nixon's attention shifted to George McGovern, resulting in the infamous Watergate incident. Documents indicate that Colson, after a conversation with Nixon in the Oval Office, asked E. Howard Hunt to plant left-wing propaganda in Bremer's apartment (Carter 1995:441). However, the apartment had already been searched and cataloged by media observers, prohibiting that "plant" which would have linked Bremer to McGovern. Of course, Nixon won that election but later left the office in disgrace.

George Wallace attempted to run for the presidency again in 1976, but his ill health prevailed, and after his loss in the North Carolina primary, he supported Jimmy Carter. Wallace remained in the Alabama governor's mansion until 1986 when he left politics due to the continued deterioration of his health and personal problems. In his later political years, Wallace's views moderated as he equated his "suffering to the suffering of black people and asked for their forgiveness" (Carter 1995:461). Did Wallace really change after the assassination attempt? His former adviser, John Kohn, said:

If George had parachuted into the Albanian countryside in the spring of 1962, he would have been the head of a collective farm by the fall, a member of the Communist Party by mid-winter, on his way to the district party meeting as a delegate by the following year, and a member of the Comintern in two or three years. (Carter 1995:15)

Although Wallace moderated his views as he was retiring from political life, the far-reaching effects of his "southernization of America" remained (Egerton 1994). Carter (1995:468) said:

George Wallace had recognized the political capital to be made in a society shaken by social upheaval and economic uncertainty. As the conservative movement reached high tide, it was no accident that the groups singled out for the relentless abuse and condemnation were welfare mothers and aliens, groups that are both powerless and, by virtue of color and nationality, outsiders. The politics of rage had moved from the fringes of our society to center stage.

Impressed by Wallace's successful electoral appeal, the Republican Party emphasized the development of a "southern strategy" focusing on racial divisiveness in "its drive to dominate the south for the next two decades" from Nixon to Reagan (Diamond 1995:13). George Wallace arose out of "national (and especially southern) racial and cultural frustration" from 1964 to 1972. However, the recession of 1973 was the beginning of America's long economic downturn. Economic concerns joined cultural and racial fears, paving the way for a new wave of populist candidates like David Duke (Phillips 1993:233, 235).

David Duke: Klansman, Neo-Nazi, and/or State Representative?
David Duke has been the subject of much attention from the media and scholars as a candidate who demonstrates the possibility of white separatists entering the mainstream political arena relying on Wallacite populist electoral coalitions. One of the big questions has been "Who is the real David Duke?" (Turque et al. 1991:24–28). Although Duke disavowed Nazism publicly, Hill (1992:94) examined the ideological currents in Duke's speeches and concluded that Duke, like Hitler, successfully "adapted Nazism to the fears, aspirations, prejudices, and political culture of the nation, thus representing himself as part of the national political tradition" (Hill 1992:95). Bridges (1994:71) also suggested that "Duke saw the Klan as only a means to an end: smashing the power of Jews and asserting white supremacy." Duke left orga-

nized National Socialism to avoid American anti-Nazi sentiment and turned to the Klan, which would be seen more positively by the general public. He was "convinced that Americans would never tolerate an open identification with Nazism." However, Shelton and other more traditional Klan leaders were critical of Duke's move away from Klan Kraft (Bridges 1994:71).

Biographies of David Duke show that his ideas originate from Nazism, the Klan, and more mainstream philosophies typical of the White Citizens' Council. Despite Duke's claim that his Nazism was simply a teenage transit, he has been heavily influenced by National Socialism and blended those early ideas into his "new Klan." Duke's interest in white separatism began at the age of 14 as an outgrowth of a high school research paper and involvement with the White Citizens' Council. Duke read the works of right-wing scholars like Carlton Coon and William Shockley and decided that racial integration was the cause of a variety of social ills such as crime. He became a regular at the White Citizens' Council and saw Barry Goldwater[10] as his first "political hero" (Zatarain 1990:79–81). Duke's activism continued through high school, and he joined the KKK in 1967 at the age of 17 (Zatarain 1990:86, 96–101).

"The Nazi of Louisiana State University"

After graduating from high school, Duke attended Louisiana State University (LSU). He had become disenchanted with the White Citizens' Council and the "ordinary racism" of the KKK. He maintained Klan contacts but became more intrigued with "The Jewish Question" through a Catholic priest from the Citizens' Council who felt that the Jews were destroying Christianity (Zatarain 1990:110–11). In his sophomore year at LSU, Duke discovered the NSLF, which was a neo-Nazi group supported by the ANP. He was impressed with *White Power* by George Lincoln Rockwell and formed a corps of "five or so members" known as "Dukies." Duke appeared at Free Speech Alley, which had been the vehicle for student expression, particularly concerning the Vietnam War (Zatarain 1990:116–22). Although he thought that his ideas were moderate, he met stern opposition, which led to several dramatic incidents at Free Speech Alley. For example, an African American student confronted Duke's ideas by challenging Duke to explain the difference between their hands. Not receiving a satisfactory answer, he acquired a knife from a spectator in the audience and cut his hand, asking Duke to do the same. While Duke declined the challenge, another white student took the blade. Duke said:

> It [doesn't] mean a thing. I could walk across the street to the science lab and get a big, hairy rat and his blood would be just as red. Any good blood pathologist could instantly tell the difference between white and black blood. (Zatarain 1990:123–24)

A picture of the two bleeding hands appeared on the front page of LSU's student paper, *The Reveille.*

Despite the opposition to his views, Duke wore a Nazi uniform to protest William Kunstler, an antiwar activist and lawyer, who spoke at Tulane. Duke carried signs that read "Gas the Chicago 7" and "Kunstler is a communist Jew." The public exposure brought his father's disapproval, leading Duke to express remorse over his association with National Socialism. However, he did not denounce white racialism and the belief that "racial survival was the most important objective." Duke quit the NSLF but joined the White Student Alliance (WSA), which was the youth arm of the NSLF (Zatarain 1990:129, 131). With the help of some right-wing groups, he published *The Racialist,* which mirrored his earlier thoughts on National Socialism and contained numerous populist beliefs (Zatarain 1990:137). He later formally broke with the WSA in a letter denouncing Hitler as "the greatest disaster to ever befall the white race."

The Rise of a New and Modern Klan and Early Campaigning

Duke rejoined Jim Lindsay, his Klan mentor and surrogate father. First they created the White Youth Alliance (WYA) in 1971 and later formed the National Party, which was intended to be the political activist youth organization for the KKK (Bridges 1994; Zatarain 1990). Businesspeople with far-right values from across the country funded this new organization, which claimed to have 600 members within one month, and began publishing *The Nationalist* (Zatarain 1990:174–75). Duke delivered a speech protesting the murder of a 17-year-old white woman, saying:

> We're gonna keep on going 'till we win political power in this country. You can boil down the problems (of the country) into two words: Jews and Niggers. Every great institution and American tradition is being attacked and is being befouled by these people who are determined to destroy this country. (Bridges 1994:31–32)

Despite Duke's expressed desire to distance himself from his Nazi past, the same rhetoric remained and *The Nationalist* advertised videotaped speeches of George Lincoln Rockwell (Bridges 1994:31–32). Duke became the Grand Dragon and national information officer of the KKKK in 1973 and published *The Crusader*. Although its early editions focused on more middle-class issues such as busing, some of the content and materials advertised for sale were the same as in his earlier neo-Nazi newspapers (Zatarain 1990:187–92).

Duke's national visibility as a "media star" began on Tom Snyder's "Tomorrow" television show, where he used the media to his advantage by deflecting questions away from talking about racism toward discussions of America's "dispossessed majority." Although he was trying to represent the "new Klan" as a mainstream political organization, two of his statements ran counter to the new image he was attempting to create. First, Duke condoned "lynching a black man who he said had recently raped and murdered two white women in Baton Rouge but had gotten off on a technicality." Second, he revealed that the Klan was stockpiling weapons and food in rural areas to prepare for the revolution, since "the white people in this country are going to have to fight if we want to maintain our society." Despite those statements, Snyder was struck by Duke's appearance as "intelligent, articulate, and charming" (Bridges 1994:45–47).

After completing a history degree in 1974, Duke utilized his role as "national information director to supersede everyone else in the movement" (Zatarain 1990:199–203). He became the Grand Wizard in 1975 after Lindsay was murdered (Bridges 1994:55). Duke attracted a number of key figures, such as Don Black, William Grimstad, James K. Warner, Louis Beam, and Tom Metzger, to the movement in the early 1970s (Bridges 1994:40–41, 59). During this period, Duke was ambivalent publicly about violence. He was supportive of Klansmen who had been convicted of violent acts, but he also wanted to distance himself from those in the movement who engaged in violence. Although those near Duke had legal problems, he was not known to have participated in "typical Klan acts" (Bridges 1994:53).

With Tom Metzger as his campaign manager, he ran for the state senate in Baton Rouge as a Democrat in the fall of 1975. Duke's message blended conservatism and white rights, but he lost his first election, receiving only 33 percent of the votes (Bridges 1994:55–57). He said:

> Over 11,000 people went to the polls and voted for my ideals. The movement has just started. We've just begun. This is not the ignorant redneck from the hills voting for me. The voters are just about ready for us. (Bridges 1994:57)

Bill Wilkinson, Duke's rival in the Klan, emphasized violence and made appeals to constituencies that Duke was trying to avoid. When Wilkinson broke away from Duke's Klan in 1975, he got a copy of Duke's "secret" membership lists and other literature (Bridges 1994:68).

During the late 1970s, Duke channeled his energies into becoming "the undisputed Klan leader." He drew media attention by announcing events that he predicted would be heavily attended. For example, Duke and Metzger, who was serving as the California Grand Dragon at that time, claimed that the Klan would control the U.S.-Mexico border from San Diego to Brownsville, Texas, with 500 to 1,000 Klansmen. The "Klan Border Patrol" attracted extensive media attention even though it consisted of only "seven Klansmen in three old sedans that featured hand-painted 'Klan Border Watch' signs taped to the doors" (Bridges 1994:67).

Under pseudonyms Duke wrote two controversial "moneymaking" books. *African Atto* was a "seventy-page manual that purported to teach street-fighting techniques to blacks in preparation for the race war." *Finders-Keepers* utilized sexually explicit language and advised women how to increase their physical attractiveness. Several leaders, including Tom Metzger, left Duke in the late 1970s, in part as a response to Duke's "egomania" and "womanizing" (Bridges 1994:74–80).

Despite the waning support of some key leaders, Duke ran as a conservative Democrat for the Louisiana Senate in Metairie in 1979. He defined himself as a "white-rights advocate" focusing on a "Program of Courage" that was antiwelfare, antitaxes, and antibusing, as well as opposed to "reverse discrimination" and the "forced integration of public schools." After a "door to door" campaign, Duke lost the primary, winning 26 percent of the votes (Bridges 1994:80–81). Following on the heels of that loss, Duke ran for president in 1980, declaring that he "planned to 'take up where Wallace left off.' " At age 28, he campaigned in only a few states and was not able to attract news coverage. Duke canceled the campaign in March, claiming that "minimum entry age laws" were "specifically designed to keep me off of the ballot" (Bridges 1994:82–83).

Duke's appeal in the Klan was also dwindling by the late 1970s. "Wilkinson's gun-toting, tough guy image" was more attractive to a growing number of Klansmen, and it made Duke's "non-violent ballot-box approach" (Bridges 1994:84) less believable to the public. Duke incorporated the NAAWP in 1979 and tried to gain money for it by selling his Klan membership list for $35,000 to Wilkinson. However, Wilkinson contacted the media and Duke's attempt to sell the list was videotaped. David Duke quit the Klan three days later saying:

> I'm resigning because I don't think the Klan can succeed at this point, because of its violent image and because of people like Bill Wilkinson. He's low and dishonorable. And people see Wilkinson and believe all Klansmen are like that—bad and violent. All the good in the world I have done and could do doesn't make any difference because most people don't differentiate between Klans. They think we're all like that, and that's disgusting. (Bridges 1994:87)

Later on, it was revealed that Wilkinson served as an FBI informant from 1974 to 1981 (Bridges 1994:84–88).

Mainstreaming "Civil Rights for Whites"

Duke's NAAWP attracted some Klan members to the new white rights organization. Duke reframed his racialist message to redefine his concerns. In an early article entitled " 'Love' and 'Hate' " (NAAWP News n.d.a:1), he wrote:

> Often, I am accused by liberals, Jews, and blacks as being full of hate. While I recognize the fact that there is far more hatred among non-whites toward whites than vice versa, I must admit that some racialists give the impression of being full of hate.
>
> Some really are. They have grown to hate the culture distorters and destroyers so much that they have become consumed by it and thus lost their perspective. They have grown to hate evil so much they have lost their ability to love the good.

The article went on to redefine love:

> "Love" the integrationists say will save us. What "love" has forced integration brought? . . . It's "love" they say, to finance and promote black birth rates and encourage massive non-white immigration to America, while encouraging white people to practice birth control, be sterilized and intermarry with blacks. To attempt to limit black or Jewish birthrates is "hate" filled "genocide" they say, but to wipe away the unique beauty and spirit of the white race

is "love." Is it really? Let us not be afraid of either word, love or hate. So my friends, let us hate those who want to destroy us, but let us not be consumed with it. Let us love the beauty that is still with this planet and our people, yet still not close our eyes to the plight of our people.

He reframed the core of his "racialist" message from his Nazi-Klan past as "equal rights for whites" (NAAWP 1980:2) demanding

an immediate end to racial discrimination and quotas against white people in employment, promotions, scholarships, and in union and college admittance. We want American government, military, education and business to make excellence the sole criterion for advancement.

He argued that the NAAWP was the white answer to the NAACP, which "promotes an atmosphere of resentment and hatred toward whites. The NAAWP seeks greater racial understanding and goodwill by showing that when all things are considered blacks have enjoyed far more benefits from their association with whites than they have endured deprivation" (NAAWP 1992b:6). Duke said that racialists needed to define themselves instead of allowing a society and its media, "dominated by those who want to destroy our people," to label racialists:

The media is constantly characterizing "white racists" as unfeeling, hate-filled, unfair and ignorant, and too often white racialists have acted out the part in real life better than Archie Bunker does on television. That kind of behavior on the part of people who are supposed to be on our side, only reinforces the Hollywood stereotype. . . . As for those who want to use the term "nigger" on the media and speak of violence and suppression, I suggest that they are not needed, for they can be found before the public almost every night of the week on Big Brother's idiot box in the living room. . . . Our first task is to promote our beliefs in such a way as not to distort them while at the same time in a fashion that the average American can understand and identify with. . . . The second task is taking the above approach and reaching the public with it. (NAAWP n.d.b:3)

Duke realized the difficulties that would be encountered trying to mainstream the message and change "Hollywood-type racist stereotypes." Despite his attempts to mainstream the organization, interest in the NAAWP declined to a membership of 1,000 by the mid-1980s (Bridges 1994:105).

More Adventures in Electoral Politics

Duke's participation in anti-integration demonstrations gained him much-needed national media attention in January 1987. This encouraged him to run for the presidency again in 1988. He ran as a Democrat, but the party shut him out of the debates. Duke explained the shunning by the Democratic Party:

> The Democratic candidates . . . know that there are too many American people out there who would agree with my position. I do not favor abortion, but I feel that birth control must play a role in resolving the welfare dilemma. The people using birth control measures are more productive, hard-working tax payers. (NAAWP n.d.c:1)

Despite his campaign rhetoric, which predicted that he would give Jesse Jackson a "run for the money," Duke won only 3.8 percent of the votes in the Louisiana primary and did not win any delegates. Duke became the nominee of the Populist Party with Ralph Forbes, a former ANP member under George Lincoln Rockwell and the Arkansas Populist Party chairman, as his campaign manager. He was not excited about a third-party candidacy, realizing that the campaign would be ignored. The Populist ticket qualified in only 12 ballots, and the party had to rent a mailing list from the Liberty Lobby to solicit funding (Bridges 1994:136–37).

On the heels of that loss, Duke received a third of the vote in a special election for a vacated seat in the Louisiana state legislature. Then in the runoff election, Duke won the legislative seat with 50.7 percent of the votes in Jefferson Parrish, which was 96.7 percent white. Local racial tensions were high, and Duke altered his campaign rhetoric to exclude the anti-Semitic attacks used during the presidential campaign (Bridges 1994:139–41).

Numerous political analysts have examined the constituencies that supported Duke along with the socioeconomic environment that made his candidacy appealing to white voters. Although Duke's appearance had been altered through cosmetic surgery, Powell (1992:12–13) suggested that his victory was really a consequence of changing structural conditions:

> The conjunction of declining income, growing political cynicism, and intensifying racial polarization inclined those voters to embrace an insurgent alternative to politics-as-usual. Duke became the preferred protest candidate because

> of his ability to convince angry whites that blacks were the source of their problems, which enabled him to deflect old-fashioned Longism into channels of reactionary populism.

Powell (1992:15) believed that "racial attitudes hardened during the Reagan-Bush years" due to Republicans "bottom fishing for Wallace votes" and argued that "conservatives exploited racial resentments to make 'liberal elites' and government, rather than big business, the new target for right-leaning populist ire." Guillory (1992:8) agreed, suggesting that the Republican Party was strengthened in the South "by willingly serving as a vehicle for white resistance and disaffection." Nationally, Bush was linking race to crime, at that time, with Willie Horton ads.

Although not much was known about Duke prior to his victory in the state legislative race, opposition claimed that his Nazi-Klan past would convince whites not to vote for him. However, Duke's campaign manager argued that his roots in the Klan would "tell white and black voters alike" that he means business (Powell 1992:18). Some analysts suggest that Duke won with the Wallace constituency of low-status blue- and white-collar workers pulling in Republicans and southern Democratic populists. When the GOP endorsed Duke's opponent, his antielite populist constituents did not identify with the party. As one homemade yard sign put it, "No one tells District 81 how to vote!" (Powell 1992:26–30). Duke's message

> addressed white working-class economic grievances, gave vent to resentments against "special interests" (read: blacks), and legitimized the furies of white backlash by wrapping it in the shibboleth of "equal rights" for all, special preferences for none. (Powell 1992:32)

Howell and Warren (1992:81, 85, 90–91) argued that Duke's Nazi-Klan past prevented him from getting potential support for his views, but his issues were popular among whites across the country. Their research found that one-third of whites held very intense racial feelings and that nationally whites' views were just less intense than the Louisiana voters who supported Duke. Whites tended to support symbolic racism expressed by general antiblack feelings and a belief that blacks "fall short of the American ideals of individualism and the work ethic." Electoral support for David Duke was "related to intense racial attitudes more than simple racial conservatism" (Howell and Warren 1992:89).

Thornton, Whitman, and Friedman (1992:41) suggested that "white prejudices are now evolving a bit like a virus. While the most virulent forms have been stamped out, new and more persistent strains continue to emerge." The old right's biological inferiority argument has been replaced by "the modern day cultural version, a lack of ambition and laziness." A *Washington Post* (Gladwell 1995:7–10) survey found that whites hold misperceptions about blacks that feed symbolic racism. For example, 65 percent of whites believed that there was "little difference between the social and economic conditions of blacks and whites." Those respondents also "opposed additional federal spending to help low income minorities." In political contests, Duke benefits from those holding such attitudes.

After his legislative victory, Duke wanted to distance himself from the Populist Party. However, he attended its meeting in Chicago because several Populists were longtime friends and supporters. Duke told them that he would always be a "Populist Republican." En route to a press conference, he was photographed shaking hands with Art Jones, the vice chairman of the ANP. At the conference a reporter asked Duke why he was associating with a Nazi. Jones yelled, "You creep" (Bridges 1994:154–56). Rickey (1992) used this incident along with other information on Duke's links to Nazism in a failed attempt to prevent Duke from being seated in the Louisiana state legislature. Although Lee Atwater and the Republican National Committee (RNC) censured Duke with a unanimous vote, the Louisiana Republican Committee did not agree.

There are differing opinions on the effects that Duke had on the state legislature. Some argued that he was just another vote in the house, whereas others saw a far-reaching impact. He did not pass any bills through the legislature, despite numerous attempts. His campaign chairman for the senate race, Howard Farrell, claimed that Duke absorbed all the animosity for Republican legislators who voted for bills like "workfare" (McMahon 1992:130). For example, 17 of the 18 Republicans in the Louisiana House supported Duke's anti–affirmative action bill. Duke said: "I hope to see a lot of mainstream candidates who privately think these things [who will] start vocalizing these ideas in political races . . . I think I represent the change" (McMahon 1992:131). State Senator Dennis Bagneris, a black from New Orleans, agreed with Farrell's assessment to some extent:

> Duke did have an impact, but it's not the impact portrayed in the media. He set up comfort zones for those already in the House who already voted the

way he votes. They didn't switch the way they vote, but they feel more comfortable with his taking the lead. (McMahon 1992:129)

Apparently, Duke vocalized sentiments that were already held by some conservative senators, but his values were not far-reaching enough to affect legislation (McMahon 1992:126).

Next, Duke ran for the United States Senate in 1990 against a three-term Democrat, J. Bennett Johnson. He lost that election with 44 percent of the overall vote, but received 57 percent of the white vote. Rose (1992:157, 175, 184, 191) found that Duke had populist appeal among people who felt that they personally lost income due to the government. Duke was not viewed as "wishy washy," since he was more extreme on issues than his supporters. Once again, symbolic racism played a crucial role, since Duke supporters agreed that "whites are superior to blacks" and denied the existence of "racial discrimination against blacks." Duke's strongest showing was among white males with strong support from white Democrats. Half of white Republicans voted for him (Rose 1992:191). The study also suggested that, unlike George Wallace, Duke would not have national appeal.

Just weeks after Duke lost the senate race, he entered the Louisiana gubernatorial contest. Although Duke captured only 32 percent of the vote in the primary, analysts argued that the results signaled an increased support for him, since he ran against Roemer, the incumbent governor, and Edwards, a former three-term governor (Rose and Esolen 1992:217). As the Republican candidate, Duke garnered 43 percent of the white vote, 54 to 57 percent of white Democrats, and virtually no blacks or Republicans. Duke's strongest base of support was in Jefferson Parish, his home district, where he received 69 percent of the votes. Those most likely to vote for him were "whites not registered as Democrats or Republicans." As in the 1990 race for the U.S. Senate, his supporters tended to be "less hostile to the KKK, less drawn to the New Orleans metropolitan area, and less well educated" (Rose and Esolen 1992:220–21). To justify their vote for Duke, angry white supporters used moral outrage against affirmative action and the welfare system to rationalize their choice. David Duke claimed that he was being treated unfairly, and his supporters saw him as a symbol of "how they themselves, individually and as a group, were treated unfairly and picked on" (Rose and Esolen 1992:214).

During the runoff, a growing opposition to Duke developed, and fear brought voters to the polls. Duke was running against Edwards, who at the end of his third term as a Democratic governor, faced "a recession, a huge deficit, indictments, unpopular proposals, and a publicly known gambling problem." Anti-Duke people, aware of Edwards's political baggage, used bumper stickers like "Vote for the Crook! It's important." The business community warned that Louisiana would lose business and jobs if Duke were elected governor. Blacks also feared his racial views. The black turnout "exceeded white turnout rates for the first time in a statewide election for office." Organizations in the black community rallied to get out the vote. "Though blacks constituted only 28% of registered voters, they represented 31% of runoff voters and 49% of voters for the winner." Edwards also attracted white votes with family incomes over $50,000 and with some college education (Rose and Esolen 1992:226–27). While Edwards won the election, Duke received 55 percent of the white vote (Rose and Esolen 1992:213).

From 1989 until 1992, Duke was constantly campaigning in an election. Paul Allen (n.d.), the former treasurer, announced his new direction for NAAWP when he replaced Duke as the president of the organization in 1992. Two weeks after David Duke lost the gubernatorial race, he declared his candidacy for president again in 1992 as a Republican (Bridges 1994:238). However, he was quickly undercut by Pat Buchanan, who entered the 1992 presidential race six days after Duke announced his candidacy. Buchanan's press secretary said that he entered the race to prevent Duke from being the only challenger to Bush from the right. Pat Buchanan was a more mainstream political figure who was able to draw greater support as a protest candidate than David Duke, who did not fare well in the Republican primaries, receiving only 7 percent of South Carolina, 9 percent of Louisiana, 11 percent of Mississippi, and 5 percent on Super Tuesday. By comparison, Buchanan won 27 percent and Bush took 62 percent of Louisiana, Duke's home base.[11] Duke quit April 22, but the effects of his candidacy remained. He brought "welfare reform," affirmative action, and quotas into the national political arena. In addition, Bush felt pressured to distance himself from Duke, so he signed the Civil Rights Bill and did not campaign actively against quotas. Those decisions cost Bush support from the more conservative electorate (Bridges 1994:248–49). Duke asked, "Where are all these conservative heroes when we've needed them? Where was George Bush when Ted Kennedy and his crowd were trying to shove another punitive Civil Wrongs Act down our throats? Why he was in his office, drafting up similar legislation" (*David Duke Report* 1993b:1).

Some analysts have attributed Duke's success to his media savvy. Duke did hone both his physical image through cosmetic surgery and the delivery of his message. He depicted himself as a "nice guy and reasonable fellow" who gets picked on by the media for extreme ideas from his youthful past because the media is afraid of his message (Esolen 1992:137–38, 146). The media news coverage of Duke's Nazi-Klan past was "too little too late." Esolen noted the media's structural problems such as the lack of adequate research staff to cover specific stories with an extended time line. When Duke was interviewed, he was able to dismiss journalists' inquiries since they did not have specific information (Esolen 1992:143, 153).

Other analysts have argued that Duke benefited from structural changes in the economy and political culture as he

> articulates a form of anti-establishment politics that basically ignores the establishment. He defends the little people by directing their anger toward the littler people, not toward the big people, with wealth and privilege, at the top. It is an odd kind of populism that divides the people rather than uniting them against the elites. (King 1992:250)

Although Duke's past campaigns did not replicate George Wallace's extensive electoral victories, he has continued his quest for the political mainstream by announcing his 1996 campaign in Louisiana for the U.S. Senate (Duke 1996). It remains to be seen whether or not future campaigns will enable him to proliferate his own political power; however, right-wing discourse and debate in the current political arena echoes the antiestablishment rhetoric and symbolic racism of Duke campaigns.

Movement Views on Duke

With the rise of David Duke, media images often portrayed the white separatist movement as a covert mainstreaming mechanism reaching subtly into every corner of society. However, David Duke is a controversial figure within the movement as well. Many people feel that Duke sold out, becoming a "kosher conservative" by publicly disavowing his past in National Socialism and the Ku Klux Klan. COTC's leader Matt Hale (1996b) commented about Duke on his hot line:

> We don't dis-support him. We are not against him, but we do not take a conscious effort to support his candidacy. David Duke, in our opinion, has gone

too far in his denunciation of his past and Adolph Hitler, who he's called a "madman" and things of this nature. He has also tried to appease the Jews which we, of course, find absolutely abhorrent. We will not win this war by compromising with our enemies and playing footsies with them. We must win by remaining true to our doctrines, true to our principles, and adamant that the Jewish parasite must be removed from North America and eventually the world.

The National Socialist Vanguard (1989b:1–3) expressed similar guarded sentiments about Duke's 1989 election to the Louisiana House of Representatives. "David Duke's victory signifies a turning point in the effectiveness of the Zionist Occupation Government's propaganda war against white people" and opened the door to the election of other white racialists across the country. However, they did not "endorse the character of David Duke because he has already sold out our race." Examples were given of Duke disavowing his ties to the movement and his traitorous behavior at the Populist Party meeting when "Snake Oil" Duke denounced an association with Art Jones of the America First Committee and another Klansman at a press conference. Other instances of Duke's white traitorous conduct were mentioned in another National Socialist Vanguard (1990:5) newsletter:

Duke's actions are those of a conservative and not The Great White Hope. Although we do not endorse Duke, we would still like to see him win just to prove our point again—that the White public will support a person with a Klan and/or Nazi background when the conditions are right regardless what he really is.

NS Bulletin, the official newsletter of the New Order (Milwaukee, WI), was critical of David Duke's denying his National Socialist past and feared that he was another George Wallace who would use his "born again Christian" experience to claim that "a religious experience" made him " 'more tolerant' and 'less bigoted' and showed him that Blacks and Whites could indeed live together in the same society." New Order (1992a:6) reported that "Critics . . . wonder whether he plans to become just another plastic politician trying to ride a wave of rising middle-class frustration for his own purposes." In another article entitled "No Compromise" New Order (1992b:7) discussed the dangers of falling for conservative sellouts:

A generation ago, there were those who looked to George Wallace as their great white hope, even though never once did he advocate a racial program.

> But by slyly using certain code words, he succeeded in duping thousands of eager racialists into thinking that he "is secretly one of us." The net result: sell-out, betrayal and disillusionment.

Tom Metzger (1996d) of WAR also does not support mainstream conservative politicians, in general. He said on his hot line:

> Forget the conservative right. They will never campaign for racial revolution. They deny, deny, deny racism all the way down the track. In fact, most are scared stiff of even being called racist. Deal only with those who are proud to be racist. Even your enemies have no respect for closet racists. There's nothing more sad than to listen to a conservative right winger on the air qualifying everything he says with "I'm not a racist. I'm not like those people." They are sickening and need to be destroyed.

The cartoon by A. W. Mann, a WAR associate, called "The David Duke Makeover" (see figure 13) is a graphic example of the anti-Duke sentiment expressed by many in the white separatist movement.

Others have offered support for Duke's candidacies. *Instauration* (1992) was critical of Buchanan for undercutting Duke's potential impact in the 1992 presidential campaign. Michael Storm (NSDAP/AO n.d.) wrote an article supportive of Duke's 1996 campaign for the U.S. Senate. Storm (1996:2) hoped that a Duke victory would "blow the lid off Gerhard's[12] illegal kidnapping and imprisonment!" Although "Aryan Man," one of our interviewees, didn't think movement members running for office would have "a huge impact," he felt "we have to make our presence known." He commented:

> I supported David Duke and a lot of people in the movement don't tend to support him that much because they think he's a sell-out. I think that's a bunch of garbage because he just can't run for office and say—OK you . . . [inaudible] fucking niggers out and this and that. . . . He's trying to be a politician. I think it would be great if he would get elected this year [1996] in the U.S. Senate.

The Spotlight (1996a:14–15) supported Duke's 1996 bid for the U.S. Senate as a populist campaign and solicited donations. Duke placed fourth of 15 candidates receiving more than 140,000 votes (11 percent of the electorate) in Louisiana's open primary system (ADL 1996:40). *The Truth at Last* (n.d #356a:8) praised Duke whose "most important contribution to the Patriotic movement was to move us into the 'mainstream.' " David Duke "launched the tide of White enlightenment

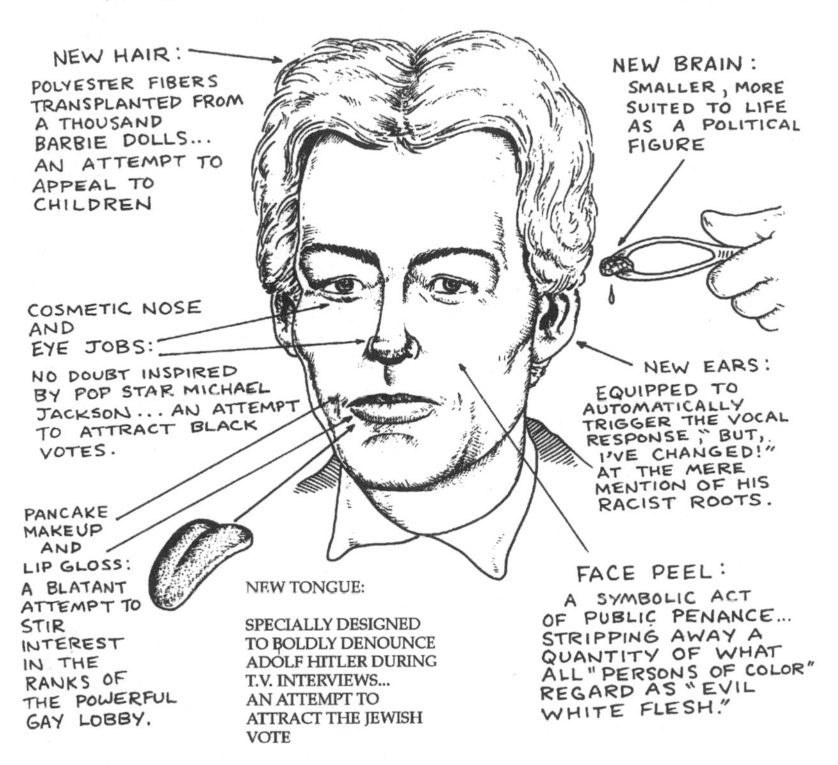

Figure 13. WAR Cartoon of David Duke Designed by A. Wyatt Mann (n.d.n.p.)

which is now sweeping the nation. White people are rising up and we are going to take back our nation."

David Duke's prominence in the mainstream has led to images that the movement as a whole is attempting to penetrate conventional social institutions as a route to power. However, as we have shown, there is mixed sentiment about entering the status quo political arena as a strategy for social change. In fact, David Duke arouses as much controversy within the white racialist movement as he does in mainstream discourse.

Splits and Schisms among Right-Wing Pundits: Linkages of Mainstream Politics to White Separatism

Some candidates without known personal ties to the white power movement, like Pat Buchanan, have adopted similar values and right-wing populist strategy, leading to successful political campaigns and winning endorsements from far-right organizations like the Liberty Lobby. America's racial divide has been utilized by other mainstream candidates, including President Bush's fanning the fear of blacks in his Willie Horton ads to win the 1988 election (Diamond 1995). Bush also panned affirmative action with antiquota rhetoric to feed white fears of job loss (Guillory 1992:8). Ross (1995b:171) suggested that white supremacy has also been able to expand its influence by converging with the "radical Christian Right, as represented by Pat Robertson, and nationalist ultra-conservatives as represented by Pat Buchanan." White separatists often share the beliefs of the antiabortion, antigay, and English-language-only movements.

In the late 1980s, major splits emerged in the Republican Party. Anti-communism had provided a rallying cry for solidarity among conservatives in the "free world." The supposed "end of communism" shook up the right wing, which had focused national priorities on cold war strategic defense initiatives. By the 1992 election, it was also difficult to blame the L.A. riots and other social ills on liberalism, which had been out of power too long (Phillips 1993:243). The New Right[13] conservatives would flirt with the organized racialist right but generally sought social distance from blatant racism and were more attracted to intermediaries such as Pat Buchanan.

Several right-wing factions came to the fore, which have been major forces shaping current sociopolitical American discourse. Diamond (1995:274–75) explored the neoconservative and paleoconservative debate that began in the late 1980s. She suggested that the conflict revolved around a number of key issues, such as the revival of "nativist anti-semitism versus Zionism, and competition over administrative appointments and foundation grants." Paleoconservatives tended to be more nativist and anti-Semitic and supportive of competition. Although the adherents in the debate were few, there were large numbers of conservatives who felt uncertain about Bush's politics when he broke with Reagan's agenda on the issues of taxes and civil rights. For example, Bush portrayed the Civil Rights Act of 1991 "as a Democratic attempt to enact racial quotas" and found a way to "override Democratic attempts to dabble in class warfare and economic populism" (Phillips 1993:241). However, Bush did not receive blanket support from Republicans, since upper-income moderates were not attracted to his "racial tactics," and right-wing voters were more likely to support Buchanan and Duke. Bush was not seen as sincere enough in his antiquota position; Buchanan and Duke charged that Bush betrayed low- and middle-income whites by signing the Civil Rights Act. Bush was unable to build a coalition in the 1992 election as he was torn between two irreconcilable constituencies (Phillips 1993:242). Ultimately, Duke's support of racial quotas led Bush to abandon that issue, making Duke, Buchanan, Brown, and Perot the heirs to "center extremism and middle American Radicalism" (Phillips 1993:243–44).

Neoconservatives supported the New World Order as America sought to spread its "democracy around the world" (Diamond 1995:275). Our immigrant history was viewed favorably by this constituency, which was disproportionately Jewish and Catholic and not particularly concerned with the changing American social landscape. However, neoconservatives were opposed to the political correctness movement and multiculturalism. They did not promote class and status group equality, but they did support state intervention to maintain a marginal level of "social welfare and tranquility."

In contrast, paleoconservatives opposed state subsidy of the poor and civil rights legislation supportive of minorities. They sought to strengthen the state's role in the production of a "domestic moral order dominated by native-born Christian white men." Paleoconservatives viewed the state's international role as protecting the interests of America's business class. The federal government should remain neutral in international affairs, unless war became necessary to protect American capitalist interests (Diamond 1995).

In the 1970s the Christian Right began developing its own base of political support, which became more clearly evangelical at the end of the cold war (Diamond 1995:228–56). Members of the Christian Right opposed abortion, gay rights, and public funding of the National Endowment for the Humanities. While Jerry Falwell's Moral Majority was disbanded in 1989, Pat Robertson, another evangelical televangelist, utilized his 1988 presidential campaign to organize the Christian Coalition. By 1992 the Republican Party had been penetrated by the Christian Coalition, which has continued to play a key role in the development of the party platform. It has also been relatively successful in local and state politics pushing for antigay initiatives, with a defeat in Oregon and a victory in Colorado.

Diamond (1995) suggested that the paleoconservative agenda was closely tied to the "racist right" through the presidential candidacy of Pat Buchanan and David Duke's successful campaign for the Louisiana House of Representatives. Paleoconservatives like Buchanan and Samuel Francis, editor of *Chronicles* magazine, argued that Duke's ideas had been dismissed too readily. They said that Americans had become dispossessed and realized the threat to future generations caused by the attack on "American civilization." Buchanan said that the press considered Duke's positions on affirmative action, welfare, crime and education as " 'code words' for racism." However, they were rallying cries for Louisianans who were suffering hard times and found Duke's "middle class, meritocratic, populist, and nationalist" positions appealing (cited in Diamond 1995:273). After Duke beat Roemer in the gubernatorial primary and moved into the runoff election against Edwards, Buchanan said:

> Both the GOP establishment and conservatives should study how and why white voters, who delivered Louisiana to Reagan and Bush three times, moved in such numbers to David Duke—and devise strategic plans to get them back. What to do? President Bush might take a hard look at illegal immigration, tell the U.S. Border Patrol to hire some of those vets being mustered out after Desert Storm, veto the Democrats' "quota bill," and issue an executive order rooting out any and all reverse discrimination in the U.S. government, beginning with the F.B.I. (Bridges 1994:244)

Buchanan and Duke's views are virtually indistinguishable. Buchanan campaigned for cuts in welfare, increasing patrol of the U.S.-Mexico border, lowering taxes, ending racial quotas, and an America First policy. Buchanan flirted even further with white separatist rhetoric when he said that Congress was an "Israeli Occupied Territory." He also held a private meeting with members of the Populist Party to obtain information about Carto and the party (Bridges 1994:244–45).

Did Buchanan simply imitate Duke? In a recent interview, Duke said, "I am happy with the way things are going. Imitation is the sincerest form of flattery . . . the country is moving in my direction . . . Senator Gramm and Mr. Buchanan and Jack Kemp are all sounding like David Duke" (CDR n.d.b). Duke said that "I think that Pat Buchanan sounds more like me every day," but Chapman (1992:3) and others have cited examples to suggest that Buchanan's values are rooted in his family history and have been cultivated throughout his political career. In an attempt to win "the segregationist vote," Buchanan flowered the graves of two Confederate ancestors—one was a slaveholder who was taken prisoner and the other died as a civil war soldier. "He vowed to avenge General Sherman's capture of his great grandfather" by running well in Georgia (Chapman 1992:3). In 1990 Buchanan's anti-immigration position led him to ask "whether 'Zulus' or 'Englishmen' would be easier to assimilate" (Bridges 1994:245; EXTRA 1992:12). While serving as a White House aide Buchanan wrote a private memo to Nixon citing an *Atlantic Magazine* article as evidence that "heredity may determine intelligence and noting that blacks consistently score lower on IQ tests than whites." From that study, Buchanan argued that integration would lead to friction rather than accommodation. In an interview on "Meet the Press," Buchanan claimed that he was simply summarizing that article ("Meet the Press" 1992:9). As mentioned earlier in this chapter, Buchanan did advise Nixon to take a hard conservative line to capture the segregationist Wallace votes, which makes Buchanan's claim that he was simply summarizing research in the Nixon memo unbelievable. Buchanan requested to be named the ambassador to South Africa due to his affinity for its "white racist government" (Chapman 1992:3). Despite criticism, Buchanan went on to receive 37 percent of the Republican vote in the 1992 New Hampshire primary (Diamond 1995:294).

Gentlemen's Quarterly (Judis 1995) included a lengthy article on Pat Buchanan that outlined his campaign issues in his bid for the 1996 Republican Party nomination. In addition to his anti-internationalist economic platform, Buchanan clearly supported many of the values of the far right, such as ending affirmative action's "race-based discrimination," controlling U.S. borders to prevent non-European immigration, ousting the UN, ending foreign aid, auditing the Federal Reserve and returning to the gold standard of hard currency, closing the Department of Education with its "secular humanist" slant biasing our educational system for children, supporting the Confederate flag, and favoring a "pro-life" orientation. Judis (1995:252) expressed concern about Buchanan's appeal to the Liberty Lobby, John Birch Society, and "the most intolerant parts of the Christian right."[14] He compared Buchanan with George Wallace and had a difficult time reconciling Buchanan's populist concerns with the "xenaphobe who summons up the dark intolerance, even fanaticism, of the old right" (Judis 1995:232, 252).[15]

A number of far-right and white power organizations have supported Buchanan's candidacy. *The Spotlight,* the Liberty Lobby publication, did not initially endorse Buchanan's current bid for the presidency in 1996. However, *The Spotlight* (1995b:6) ran an advertisement for "Rapid Press," which sells "Pat Buchanan for President '96" bumper stickers. Although that did not suggest an endorsement for Buchanan, the advertising policy states that "We will not knowingly publish ads which . . . are contrary to THE SPOTLIGHT'S interests" (1995c:15). The telephone number for his headquarters was also listed at the end of an article that saw a possible victory for Buchanan, since he was second place in New Hampshire and had won "46% of the vote on the first ballot" in the California Republican Assembly (CRA). The article reported that Buchanan did not win the CRA endorsement, because "Phil Gramm ordered all of the Gramm delegates to join forces with the Alan Keyes campaign to keep Buchanan from winning" (*The Spotlight* 1995d:2).

In *The Spotlight,* Ryan (1995b:14) said that the Liberty Lobby represents the populist values of the majority of Americans, which "is no longer an obscure 19th century political appellation but a living political faith espoused by those who truly believe in America First." Like David Duke, Pat Buchanan calls himself a "populist Republican" as he stands up against the "one worlders whose sole wish is to put the hardworking men and women of America on a Global Plantation where they will be at the mercy of the elitist overseers." In another article, Ryan (1996a:18) said that "populism as enunciated by Buchanan is hated and feared by plutocrats everywhere because it eliminates the class warfare they need to maintain and control." However, Ryan (1996a:18) was concerned with whether Buchanan would break away from his ties to the Republican party to join the growing populist movement or "remain with a corrupt political organization." Ryan (1996b:17) urged Buchanan to build "a new party that will quickly enlist the support of the populist, pro-American, hard working and God-fearing people in both the Republican and Democratic Parties." As the Republican primaries drew to a close, Blair (1996:5) said that Buchanan had lost the nomination due to the stacked political process. Ryan (1996c:18) blamed the

Democratic and Republican parties which call "anyone who truly stands for America and the Constitution and opposes plutocratic internationalism" a "fascist, Nazi, racist Jew-hater." Despite some reservations and concerns over Buchanan's Republican ties, *The Spotlight* formally endorsed Buchanan in the February 26 issue (Piper 1996).

Other white racialist publications also supported Buchanan's candidacy. For example, *The Truth at Last* (n.d. #356b:5) said that "America First is the battle cry of the Buchanan campaign. He is a man of integrity who refuses to compromise." Another article in *The Truth at Last* (n.d. #387:14) said that:

> Liberals are now blasting Buchanan as an "isolationist," an "economic nationalist," who, horror of horrors (to them) put America first. According to them, he is also "racist" for wanting to keep out all of those wonderful colored immigrants who aid the New World Order by keeping those "greedy American workers" wages down.

In a similar vein, Pierce (1996:1–5) of the National Alliance wrote a supportive article charging that the "controlled media are trying to convince the public that Buchanan's too extreme." He said that Buchanan is considered too extreme because he opposes illegal immigration, NAFTA, and foreign trade. Pierce was critical of the media and Republican Party for calling Buchanan an anti-Semite because he does not support the Jewish-Israel agenda. *All the Way* (1996:2) evaluated Buchanan's positions and concluded that he leaned toward Nationalist views by denouncing aid to Israel. "He has welcomed Nationalists on his various TV and radio shows over the years and is regarded by Eastern European freedom-fighter groups as a staunch anti-communist. He takes a strong stand against all abortions, however, which contradicts the Nationalist Eugenics Position." *The Jubilee* (1996b:6) also printed an article supportive of Buchanan's "pull no punches" campaign style. They were impressed with Pat Buchanan's willingness "to go toe to toe with the anti-Christ Israeli(e) lobby" and his antihomosexual and antiabortion positions.

The ideological linkages of the white power movement to paleoconservatives are obvious. Hardisty (1995:3) also noted "violent members of the anti-abortion movement, Christian Reconstructionists, David Duke and Pat Robertson" were bridges between the movement and paleoconservatives. Putting the antiabortion message into action,

Michael Griffin, a former Klansman turned born-again Christian, assassinated abortion doctor David Gunn. Antiabortion is a common white survivalist theme: "Life—The White Choice" (Army of Israel 1995a:1). J. B. Stoner's "Crusade Against Corruption" also espouses the antigay values of the Christian Right, which are expressed in his slogan "Thank God for AIDS."

The Christian Right distances itself from the blatant racism of white separatists and has been focusing on multiracial constituencies, but they do share many of the "moral" values of white separatists. Nineteen Duke supporters were elected to the Louisiana Republican central committee in November 1992 (Sifry 1993:92), and 60 "born-again" members of the Louisiana Republican central committee elected in 1988 voted as a bloc in 1989 to prevent the censure of Duke from the House of Representatives (Rickey 1992:76–78). The Reverend Billy McCormack, who served as the Christian Coalition's Louisiana state director, was a Duke supporter (Diamond 1995:292). Members of the Christian Coalition were "saddened" by Duke's loss in the gubernatorial runoff. For a time, it seemed that a "fusion" between evangelicals and the racist right was possible until Pat Buchanan's 1992 presidential primary campaign provided a more palatable alternative to Duke (Diamond 1995:292).

While public linkages between paleoconservatives, the Christian Right, and the white racialist movement are clear, connections with the neoconservative New Right are more covert. Bellant (1991a) documented linkages between the far right and the New Right in *The Coors Connection*. Bellant points to associations between the far right and the Coors family, which was a major financial contributor to Reagan's Contra effort in Central America. Members of the Coors family have served on the Council for National Policy, which is a "secretive group of the foremost right-wing activists and founders in the United States" (Bellant 1991a:36). Joining Oliver North on the confidential membership list were Richard Shoff, who was a former Indiana Klan Grand Kligrapp (state secretary), and Tom Ellis, who served as the director of the Pioneer Fund, a "foundation which finances efforts to prove that African Americans are genetically inferior to whites." The Pioneer Fund supports the Helms network and has granted funds to researchers such as the late William Shockley, Arthur Jensen, and Roger Pearson, who summarized his racialist views by writing: "If a nation with a more advanced, more specialized, or in any way superior set of genes mingles with, instead of exterminating an inferior, then it commits racial suicide" (Bellant 1991a:4). The Coors family was also instrumental in the creation of the Conservative Caucus in 1974 that was developed in the aftermath of the American Independent Party, which had ties to the Klan (Bellant 1991a:53–54).

Joe Coors founded the Heritage Foundation, a prominent New Right "think tank," in 1973 by donating the first year's budget of $250,000 (Bellant 1991a:1). The Heritage Foundation publishes *Policy Review,* and Pearson served on the editorial board until a *Washington Post* article revealed his political activities as chair from 1975 to 1980 of the American branch of the World Anti-Communist League, which had Nazi core members. Although he was dropped from *Policy Review,* "several Heritage leaders joined the editorial advisory board of Pearson's *Journal of Social and Economic Studies*" (Bellant 1991a:4–5). These examples highlight an organized network of interlocking directorates with New Rightists accepting membership from far-right organizations and donating their resources directly and indirectly to racialist causes.

In *Old Nazis, the New Right and the Republican Party,* Bellant (1991b:xviii–5, 20) revealed more direct pro-Nazi ties to the core of the New Right. Pat Buchanan was Reagan's press secretary when Reagan came under fire during his second administration for the trip he made to the cemetery in Bitburg, Germany. Reagan "characterized the Nazi Waffen SS as 'victims.' " Upon his return to the United States, Reagan held a luncheon to repay an election debt to the Republican Heritage Groups Council, which used anticommunism as a cover for their "emigre fascist network." Ethnicities "ranging from Albanians to Vietnamese" were represented, but Blacks and Jews were excluded. Delegates at the 1986 meeting expressed "no desire to have either community represented on the Council." During George Bush's 1988 presidential campaign, he assembled members of the network to form an ethnic outreach unit. Eventually eight members resigned as people were charged with "anti-Semitism, racist leanings, and Nazi collaboration."

This Republican network of emigres had roots in the RNC's Ethnic Division, which was formed in 1952 during the Eisenhower-Nixon campaign. The Displaced Persons Commission assisted immigration to the United States between 1948 and 1952. It allowed 400,000 to enter the United States after the war. In 1950 the Baltic Legion (Baltic Waffen SS) were allowed to enter. Prior to then they were considered hostile to the government as pro-Nazi and were barred from entry. Bellant

(1991b) suggested that the RNC Ethnic Division provided the core of the Republican Heritage Groups Council in 1969 that became "a standing ethnic council within the GOP" after Nixon's victory. Members of the council had strong ties to Hitler's pre–World War II networks in Europe. Bellant uncovered numerous examples of linkages between pro-Nazi organizations and the Republican Party through entities such as the American Security Council and the National Confederation of American Ethnic Groups.

Conclusion

McAdam (1988) has viewed social movements as "simply 'politics by other means,' often the *only* means open to relatively powerless challenging groups." However, in spite of the stigma associated with the white separatist movement and the mainstream political establishment denouncing white separatism publicly, it is clear that formal relationships as well as ideological similarities exist between the movement and the establishment. Some attribute part of the decline in Klan membership to the election of Ronald Reagan, who "advocated the same views as did nonviolent Klan members" (Bridges 1994:89). Rackleff (1989:C5) said that "the GOPs southern strategy led right to Duke's doorstep."

> David Duke's victory, in spite of national Republican opposition showed that a party cannot turn racist sentiments on and off at its convenience. You cannot strike a Faustian bargain with racism one day and walk away from it the next.

In 1980 Reagan made a campaign stop in Philadelphia, Mississippi, the site of the killing of three civil rights workers, and "spoke about states' rights," too. Reagan received an endorsement from the Klan, which he later rejected after Patricia Roberts Harris, the secretary of health and human services, mentioned the endorsement to a group of black professionals (Harris 1980:A30). Gilliam (1984) noted that the Klan supported Reagan again in 1984, and he was not quick to reject their endorsement. Bill Wilkinson, former Imperial Wizard of the Invisible Empire, KKKK, said of Ronald Reagan, "Anytime you have all the blacks and minorities in this country opposing, strongly, one man you know he has got to be doing something good for the white race." Did David Duke mainstream his ideas or has the mainstream shifted far enough to the right, setting the stage for him and others with a similar message? In reality, both changes have occurred. For two decades, the GOP has sought to southernize American politics. At the same time, David Duke shifted away from the overt racism of his Nazi-Klan past toward the "socially acceptable" realm of symbolic racism. Pat Buchanan, Newt Gingrich, and the "Republican Revolution" have openly brought the "white rights" agenda of David Duke and other mainstreaming white separatists "into the fold."

Chapter Six

Toward a Political Economy of White Supremacy

Economics is important to the welfare of the Aryan people. When economics threatens the existence of the race, then those economics and trade policies must be radically changed. The present Coca-Cola society is a direct threat to the race and the stability of the world. Economic determinism must be secondary to racial determinism. (WAR 1995c:11)

A political economy analysis of white supremacy will be useful toward examining the contemporary circumstances that have led to the development of the contemporary white separatist movement. The political economy perspective examines:

the interrelationships between the polity, economy, and society, or more specifically, the reciprocal influences among government . . . the economy, social classes, strata and status groups . . . [and] the manner in which the economy and polity interact in a relationship of reciprocal causation, affecting the distribution of social goods. (Walton 1979:1, 9)

Earlier chapters have noted the ideological currents within the movement and the way that those philosophies have created a variety of organizational structures and strategies. This chapter will examine the current social, political, and economic forces that have led to the resurgence[1] of the white racialist movement. Historically, white supremacy and Eurocentrism have dominated in the United States. However, the expressions of white supremacy have been shaped by the historic conditions of different eras. For instance, the economic system of slavery thrived on segregation while the institutionalized racism of our contemporary political economy has marginalized the individual expression of white separatism and led to the creation of the so-called "militant fringe." Left-wing social activism has been examined to determine the social conditions upon which progressive action rests (Blumberg 1984; Fisher 1984; Piven and Cloward 1979). However, the institutional conditions that have affected the white separatist movement have not been considered rigorously.

Social Movements, Political and Economic Forces

As political and economic conditions change, social movements either adapt to the changing social milieu or perish. Boggs (1986:21) noted that "movements typically flourish where there are mounting crises of legitimacy, where the old systems of social and authority relations are challenged by broad cultural ferment or social upheaval." Social movements have difficulty creating social change due to an unfavorable balance of sociopolitical conditions or as a consequence of an undeveloped ideological system and poor organizational structure, leadership, or strategies for action. As conflict arises out of the populace, success depends on "the capacity of diverse movements to form cohesive social blocs" as they confront the power of the "state, party systems, interest groups and corporate bureaucracies" (Boggs 1986:21). The use of the concept "institutionalization of conflict" arose in the early 1900s as part of the discussion of the pluralist model, which restricted political opposition to the "bourgeois public sphere" (Boggs 1986:22). The populist state sets the rules and boundaries for political conflict within a "stable interest-group framework." If conflict "spilled beyond those boundaries, potentially subversive opposition was generally contained within political limits." Though resistance does occur, the government is able to contain rebellion by drawing the conflict back into the state's own political arena (Boggs 1986:22). Despite the state's containment mechanisms, social conditions in the 1960s led to the development of broad-based movements that were rooted in the crisis of capitalism. Boggs argued that those movements were unlikely to disappear due to the persistent and increasing social decay endemic to late capitalism. Hence, the issues raised by contemporary movements "cannot be expected to disappear simply through the good intentions of political leaders" (Boggs 1986:23). Boggs (1986:129) also noted that the capitalist crises have produced similar "populist movements on both the right and left." As discussed in chapter 5, the white power movement has both ideological and organizational linkages to right-wing populism, with candidates utilizing populist platforms and, in some instances, running as populist party candidates.[2]

Rubenstein (1989:322) suggested that memories of the 1960s highlight the "inefficacy of older forms of group rebellion," which produced symbolic changes, like Acts of Congress, without real benefits. When the legitimacy of the government and preexisting forms of sociopolitical struggle are questioned during a period of growing disenfranchisement of the masses, there is a possibility of the development of new forms of revolt. He noted the current tendency of minority and white ethnic youth to engage in "communal violence" in the form of street fighting. After periods of "fruitless, relatively nonviolent struggle," groups are more likely to resort to mass violence. Identity groups define themselves culturally and tend "to move outside traditional legal and moral boundaries, either when their legitimate expectations are dashed, or when their very existence is threatened." These groups tend to view themselves as "nations within-the-nation, cultural entities struggling for some form of self-determination" rather than being part of a national or international movement (Rubenstein 1989:315). Although authorities attribute episodes of mass violence to "a few evil schemers," Rubenstein (1989:311) suggested that those periods are "directly related to the social, political, and economic objectives of domestic out-groups and to the maintenance of their identities."

Americans who are most likely to oppose violence "believe that their ethnic, economic, or occupational groups 'made it' . . . without resorting to violence." However, most groups in the United States have not acquired the "means for controlling capital and wielding significant political power" (Rubenstein 1989:311). Rubenstein (1989:312) argued that "American institutions" have facilitated "the assimilation of group leaders into existing political and economic structures," however, their "constituents" have not experienced significant benefits.

Racialism and Economic Determinism

The white separatist movement focuses primarily on a racial analysis, but leaders and rank-and-file members are clearly concerned about political and economic forces that they perceive as negatively affecting the white race. In "Right Woos Left," Berlet (1992) examined attempts by the far right to make "alliances with the left around anti-government and anti-interventionist policies" during this period of "financial and social turmoil" (Berlet, 1992:4, 6). Williams (1987:318) noted the following parallels between New Left and New Right ideologies:

> [a] call for the creation of genuine community [and] for an end to political and social alienation—although the basis on which this community is to be founded ranges from individuality and participation to religiosity and Americanism.

He also noted that both perspectives sense "a social order characterized by inequality, one dominated by a well-entrenched elite—although the identity of that class is in dispute." Williams (1987:326) suggested that the ideological parallels result from sociopolitical problems endemic to this economic period, which is characterized by "state intervention in the economy, an ideology of technical rationality producing a depoliticized public, and a class structure rooted in the development of postindustrialism." Thc populace is responding to the problems caused by bureaucratization, alienation and class inequality.

People in the white separatist movement blend economic issues with racial concerns. They argue that the economic system is set up to destroy the quality of life for the average American white family. Molly Gill, editor of *The Rational Feminist,* wrote:

> More in Europe, and the USA are waking up to the danger to the white race after years of media brainwashing. They are getting fed up with the USA overrun with Third Worlders who, even illegal aliens, demand to suck off the white middle class as always. More are getting sick of losing jobs to the third world and other races here in this country. An awakening has begun!

In our interview with Bobby Norton of AN, he predicted that

> the economy is going to get worse. I think there is going to be more violence in schools, and I think, with those things in mind, the job market is going to be thinner so I think it will drive more youth to our movement. . . . I think the economy is going to get really bad so that's also going to bring a lot of suffering on us but it is going to make our ranks swell.

About a third of the people we interviewed attributed increased movement membership to poor economic conditions, whereas others discussed political issues such as the Brady Bill, the Anti-Terrorism Bill, gays in the military, urban violence, and affirmative action.

Although the white racialist movement has continued to exist in periods of abundance and scarcity, we argue that rank-and-file members will be more attracted to the white separatist ideology during economic downturn as they experience the negative effects of declining opportunities. Beth Helen Reynolds of the SS Action Group responded:

> The movement will continue to grow and more people will begin to wake up to this jews-and-niggers-run country. As times become more desperate, people will become more extreme. History proves this. Since we are extremists, it's pretty obvious that we will grow.

Some people shared the economic problems and other social pressures they have experienced in their personal lives that led them to the movement. For example, a Klanslady from Mississippi had a manual inserting job at a newspaper company that she termed "dirty work." She told us in our interview that the movement was growing due to the lack of decent jobs at a livable wage, "violence in the streets . . . everything." When asked what caused those things, she did not know.

> What caused it? You know, lots of reasons. I think all that violence on T.V. You know we used to run a small grocery store, you know, and we kept, you know, black movies, those kinds of movies, they're really bad. They're violent, they're violent.

She thought about the answer that she had given thus far and said, "That ain't got a thing to do with jobs. . . . In a way it does. As far as jobs I . . . you're asking the wrong person." When pressed further she indicated to us that she felt "tripped up." The woman sensed a growing economic plight from her personal experiences, which led her to the movement to defend her economic rights as a white woman. However, racialism did not provide the conceptual tools for her to analyze changes in the social structure that led to the economic decline she experienced.

Leaders in the white separatist movement have often highlighted economic fears as a recruitment tactic. Aware of the downward mobility of the middle and working classes, some organizations incorporate left-wing concepts and strategies for recruitment. Some white power groups have also seen the need to reorient their strategies due to changing sociopolitical conditions, such as the number of legal cases against their groups and/or leaders and the passage of the Brady Bill and the Anti-Terrorism Act. While the movement assumed the anti-communist and nativist positions of the John Birch Society, it developed the ideology of racialism to distinguish itself from both the communists that movement members opposed and the John Birch Society,[3] which has been more mainstream and nonrevolutionary.

Tom Metzger (1996e) discussed the relationship between race, economics, and class on his WAR Hotline saying:

> Actually we're looking at three elements. One, economics. That triggers upheavals. Two, class triggers. And finally, race. Oh, it won't get super hot simply with race, but it will end up being very hot with race. The recent vote on welfare, if carried out, should hurry things along as large numbers of whites desperately try to find jobs that aren't there anymore. They're all gone. Can you imagine a few months or even one month in the ghetto or the barrio without welfare checks? Welfare has always been a bribe by the middle class to head off riots in the street by mainly nonwhites. So this could be a very good move in our direction.

Since the economy affects race relations, Metzger expressed concern that economic determinism could lead to the destruction of the white race, its culture, and its traditions. In our interview, he argued that racial determinism is essential for racial survival:

> Instead of just always blaming that on just the Jews or just the Blacks and things like that, our position is you have to look at your own race and we're in a racial civil war is what I see. I used the terms racial and cultural pluralism opposed to economic determinism so we naturally oppose monopoly capitalism and Marxism because we don't see economic theories as a panacea for the best interest of the people.

The racial war to which Metzger referred is a "war of whites against whites. If that war cannot be won by racial cultural determinists, nobody's gonna win." Why are the nonracial whites the enemy? He explained:

> It is logical to look to the leadership of the race which should be people in power who are white and if they failed to do everything they can to support their own people then no other race could trust them either and if they don't do anything to ensure the survival of their people and their children, then they are the enemy. It doesn't make a difference how blonde their hair is or how blue their eyes are.

Metzger rejected the label of "right conservative" and defined himself as a "racialist revolutionary." Wes, of the American Front, also promoted the revolutionary attitude when he wrote:

> The people are on the edge. The system knows this. They try and get us to fight and bicker uselessly amongst ourselves. The system is not stupid. They are very sly and cunning. The sly and cunning of pure evil. WE are too smart to fall hook line and sinker for their trickery. This time we WILL win. We WILL win in the end. (*Revolutionary Nationalist,* n.d.:12)

John Baumgardner, editor of the *Florida Interklan Report,* utilized similar imagery when he wrote "Always act, never react" (1995b:1) and "Be revolutionary not reactionary" (1995c:3). In "Quotes from Che," Baumgardner's *Florida Interklan Report* (1995d:3) warned Klansmen to remember that "partisan warfare is a valuable instrument of revolutionary struggle. Don't reject these ideas because they are labeled 'communist.' " He said that the "repressive nature" of the "capitalist state" is being "exposed and recognized." It is clear that some leaders are willing to use aspects of a left analysis in the creation of a revolutionary attitude.

Throckmorton (1993:10–11) defined the "third position" as hereditarianism, which suggests that the nature of social relationships is determined by "heredity, free will and environment, in that order." He argued that

> Intragroup and intergroup inequality will persist no matter who is in charge. True enough, the nature of the social system will affect who gets on top: business entrepreneurs under capitalism, political entrepreneurs under socialism, and a mix under our current combination of big government and managerial capitalism. Nevertheless, the degree of inequality will not change much. (p. 10)

Throckmorton reasoned that "the left-right division is not the size of government but the equalitarian doctrine." The left wing blames society with inter- and intragroup inequality, whereas the right wing blames individuals with free will "for their lack of discipline and effort." Outside of the traditional left-right analysis, hereditarians would not blame individuals or the society since inequality is considered a natural consequence of evolution.

As discussed earlier, WAR also articulates what it termed the "third position" as "neither right nor left. It is a racial separatist tribalism relying on the natural laws of evolution." WAR rejects the spirituality and mysticism typical of many white power organizations, to embrace a purely biological and racial vision of the future. Metzger argued that "the world is so screwed up with mythology and mysticism." As Metzger explained the "third position" to us, it was intriguing to see the interweaving of ideas that originate in disparate ideologies. In our interview, we explored the nature of the political continuum. He said, "I don't believe in right-left period." From dialogue with leftists in the early 1970s, he learned that "the problem is not the right and left. It's who's on top and who's on bottom. It's vertical, it's not horizontal." Metzger said that Germany has "a law that makes it illegal [for] the left and right to come together to get political power."

In light of his analysis, he elaborated on the relationship of the left to his "third position."

> We had to move towards a broader based movement and so we recruited from the left and we recruited atheists, agnostics and all kinds of people. I couldn't do that as a Klansman because of their rules and regulations so I had to break away to do the ideas I was interested in. I still maintain, you know, friendships with some Klan leaders, always encouraging them to be more progressive. Liberals always use that term a lot so I use it, too. Quit doing the things that you have done a million times before and didn't get you anywhere.

He said that he had tried talking to leftists, since he was using many of the same terms and yet they could not understand each other.

> We try to say, well your word for this is this and our word for the same thing is this but you are trained Pavlovian style and so are we that when you say this word, we 'Ahhh . . .' it's a leftist. We can't do what a leftist does. We have to do something different. We have to do the opposite. It's a conservative thing. Whatever the left does you have to be against. Whatever the right does you have to be against. See?

Despite frustrating dialogue with "the left," Metzger mentioned that he had leftist friends and found a useful working relationship with a journalist writing for *The Nation*. In general he expressed dissatisfaction with the media who are "really afraid to put out the whole picture of what I'm talking about cause they know we've been quite successful in recruiting from the left. The editor of my paper was an ex-Trotskyite." Metzger said that the political tensions between the left and right in the United States are in a "holding pattern." He suggested that many whites on the right and left are aware of what Perot termed "gridlock" and WAR is trying to bring them out and together. He said that "the conservative movement [is] in the Trojan Horse and the left wing's just as controlled, so you've got to break out of that death cell . . . or go fishing and enjoy yourself." In the end, "resistance . . . all runs into the same river and it's a lot more effective than a structured organization."

As an example of "progressive thinking," Metzger combines environmental and racial arguments. He said that it is logical to argue that if "we're going to save the whale why not save the white race? If your premise is everybody's the same, all people are just human, [then] it won't make a difference; but our argument is what if they're not, you can't replace it; it's gone." WAR's search of the literature turned up an article entitled "Eco-Facism: Environmentalism as Racism," which appeared in the antiracist newspaper *Turning the Tide,* published by People Against Racist Terror (1994:28–29). Metzger points to the Hitler Youth movement's involvement in the 1920s and 1930s outdoors and ecology movement in Germany as evidence that Hitler fathered the Green movement.

WAR has also taken some other positions that are partially compatible with a left analysis. On the WAR Hotline, Metzger[4] expressed support for Noam Chomsky's criticism of NAFTA, which would in all likelihood displace workers here in the United States. Rodney Stubbs, Imperial Wizard of the American KKKK, also expressed anger to us over NAFTA and the General Agreement on Tariffs and Trade (GATT) and concluded that America has been "sold down the tubes." Although the Klan is trying to "bring it back," it "is probably too late" to salvage America.

Other governmental policies that have been opposed by the left were also discussed in our interview with Metzger. He was critical of the CIA involvement in Central America and applauded the left wing for exposing the Contras. WAR associates were advised not to "get involved down there . . . because you're just supporting the very people that you're fighting here." As Metzger supports nationalism and separatism, he said, "I'm pragmatic . . . I want the Nicaraguans to run their own country, how they want to run it. I don't care what kind of government they want. I don't believe in outside intervention." Although Metzger's reasons differed from a left-wing analysis, he was in favor of the Puerto Rican Independence Movement. He said, "I don't want millions of Puerto Ricans coming here. Then why would I be against them having their own Puerto Rico? A lot of this is pragmatic. You know we're not becoming sweethearts. We're just talking politics here—racial politics." Metzger also talked about the genocide of Native Americans and suggested that "they should have killed every white man that came ashore. The Native Americans had a bad immigration policy."

In our interview with Michael Storm of the NSDAP/AO, he spoke against capitalist policies that export American jobs to third world countries. Storm said, "When you betray your people, you betray your race for profit. The perfect example is the United States of America. What's the number one export in America? Jobs." He was concerned that "our own people cannot be employed in our own country because some 'third worlder' will work for thirty-five cents an hour which is a bonanza to them and a devastation to our economy and our people here. Corporations don't give a damn about the people." The Army of Israel (1995b:2) was critical of U.S. financial aid to Mexico. In its article entitled "Price of Beans," they asked:

> How could we possibly have so much interest in Mexico to give them that much money when our national debt is soaring to outrageous heights? Is slave labor from Mexico really good for our economy when it puts Americans out of work and we have to give the Mexican government money just to keep it afloat? If we are going to keep sending our jobs South of the border, we might as well not even have a border. We might as well let them come over here and work for nothing and turn America into a third-world nation. But who will bail us out when we go bankrupt?

A skinhead in Raphael Ezekiel's *The Racist Mind* (1995) was critical of "rich whites" with their money, fame, mansions, and fancy cars "burning up all the gas we have to use to live with, to live on. We need that gas to get around. Drive our old clunker down to the store or something. They're burning it up left and right in their big limos." Many people in the movement make class distinctions among whites and are angered by the lack of racial concerns and support from rich and politically powerful whites.

Since white separatists share some class concerns with the left, we explored with Metzger the possibilities of building bridges with leftists to tackle issues related to poverty. We asked him if linkages to the left might be possible; he replied, "as long as it's not based on some idea of utopianism. We do not accept any kind of idea other than struggle as the natural way of life." He considered the left views and solutions to poverty as unrealistic. The oppressable will be oppressed. "That's where we run into problems with the pie in the sky left." An anonymous Klansman from Colorado expressed similar concerns. From his reading of Marx as an undergraduate student, he had difficulty "deciphering the difference between theory and practice. In theory, it sounds great, although their practices are failures."

David Mehus of the Confederate Knights of America shared with us some of his perceptions of the contemporary white man's struggle. Rather than criticizing Marxism as utopian, he expressed concern with the lack of racial analysis in Marxian thought. Mehus explained:

> I think that we can make inroads into the working class because we are working class. . . . That's our lot in life, but that lot does not mean that we should not be able to afford medical care—not be able to afford to feed our families. Yes, I believe that there is a struggle of the classes and if that sounds Marxist, once again. But, you see the problem is that Marxists want the whole worldwide working class and the international proletariat. What National Socialism does is it wants basically to create an Aryan State for the Aryan Race. It's our working class that we're concerned about.

In keeping with a National Socialist platform, he combined a social class analysis with racialism.

Despite Metzger's view of the left as utopian, he also integrates a class analysis into his brand of white separatism. For example, Metzger was critical of Pat Buchanan's "border tour,"[5] which was not going to lead to restricting immigration "because a big share of the Republican Party's making a fortune off of illegal aliens . . . and a big portion of the Democratic Party's making a fortune off the illegal aliens, too." Although Buchanan spoke out against immigration, legal and illegal, from Central America, Metzger recognized Buchanan's establishment ties to the wealth and power of the Republican Party.

Since Metzger defines his "third position" as not being on the right-left continuum by blending racialism with more "progressive" ideas, he was encouraged to see that

> Finally some of these fellows are beginning to see that it's time to put the Klan to rest, bury it and remember it as a kind of an institution at one time, but it's through. Its time is done. We're going international, we are encouraging the religious fanatics out. . . . A person can be religious but he has to leave it, keep

his religion to himself or at home or whatever. Originally I was called a Red Klansman when I started this which was communist and, uh, of course, the left called me a fascist. I figured I was pretty close to the right spot you know.

He said, "I've read Mao Tse Tung front to back and I don't care what a person's ideology is, I'm interested in his tactics and techniques. What works I would use and what doesn't work, I get rid of." He suggested that the organization of the far right has much in common with the left in the 1960s: loose networking, no memberships, and no dues. Metzger was critical of the intense factionalization on the right and left. Solidarity would create the power to take care of societal ills. Speaking of the left, he said: "They are divided into a million different groups; they don't go anywhere and they fight each other. The only time they agree to get together is when I come to town." He was equally critical of those conditions on the right.

You have either got guys promoting the Russians are coming through Alaska on horses or 'Chinese Communists are in Mexico or there's atomic bombs in the bays and there's no gold in Ft. Knox and Jesus is coming and I mean they've got just as many kooky positions as the left.

While white power figures are critical of the "pie in the sky" left, a few of them we interviewed originated in left-wing ideologies and shifted to the far right over the life course. The Detroit Skins in Ezekiel's study (1995:183) showed left-wing influence when they re-wrote a phrase shouting "White people/United/Can never be defeated."

Metzger, Beam, Baumgardner, and others in the white power movement have borrowed "leaderless resistance" from the left. Public rallies and Aryan festivals are considered dangerous by many movement leaders who would rather avoid the police and informants who come in and try to set things up. Baumgardner (*Florida Interklan Report,* 1995b:1) published a "militia warning" that urged people to be leery of militia groups that are "being investigated by the BATF baby killers and other federal agencies." He encouraged "militias to organize in a very strict cell-type structure and stay out of the public view. The government knows the American people are preparing to meet force with force." Florida Klansmen were invited to participate in the "Klan Christian Militia which had acquired 300 acres of secluded woodlands to conduct survival and defensive training operations" (*Florida Interklan Report* 1995e:3).

In preparation for the race war, WAR speaks to "lone wolves" and encourages them to remain hidden so that they can penetrate all aspects of society. In a taped speech played at a 1993 Homecoming Rally in Pulaski, Tennessee, Metzger urged skins to grow out their hair and cover their tattoos.[6] Metzger told us:

> Leaderless resistance was actually put together by a Cuban many years ago. Louis [Beam] borrowed it from him and I've used it but it's pretty popular. We don't believe that a monolithic structured organization is viable at this time. So we don't want people joining things and getting membership cards and certificates, anything that would identify you to the government.
>
> Besides we feel more and more that we're behind the lines of operation so that we can operate in a lot of ways in the open. I do [work in the open] as a representative but I tell all new people not to go to meetings, not to have a lot of contact with me and study and educate yourself and become what we call a member of the leaderless resistance. Once you know the program, you don't have to go to meetings to find things out.

Metzger was particularly sensitive to this issue in the aftermath of the civil trial in which he and his son, John, were found guilty of inciting skinheads to kill Seraw in Portland, Oregon. They lost their home and other material possessions and may be paying for this conviction for the next 15 years. After the financial losses from the law suit, Tom Metzger received government assistance for a short time, but the activities of WAR continued.

The cell model is seen as a way to protect the white power movement as a whole as well as individuals who would be more vulnerable with membership in an organization. They fear the access that the government has to surveil white rights activists as well as the potential for entrapment. Metzger said:

> We used to think as long as you maintained legality that you wouldn't have problems and I operated with that idea for sometime, but now I know that they can set you up and lie about you and the juries will believe them. And so it's not safe, you have to keep these kind of people out if you can at all. And the only way you can keep them out is to have cell structures so that they can cause one little group problems but they don't infect the rest.

Metzger said, "We've got one thing in common [with the left], we all hate the government."

Michael Storm (NSDAP/AO)[7] spoke of the future and was encouraged by the hard economic times. He predicted that more people are "groping for solutions" as the "misery index goes up." He credited capitalism with the malaise, as "pure capitalism" intensified in the 1980s and 1990s. People focused on the quest for money, which was not satisfying. He attributed divorce, child abuse, and other social ills to the increased economic stress of our times and looked forward to National Socialism, which would provide state support for white families. Storm viewed the communists being voted back into the eastern bloc as beneficial to the white power movement. He said, "political instability is good for us" as people shift between communism and capitalism, which, he predicted, would lead to eventually becoming disillusioned with both political and economic models.

White separatism is seen as a response to the declining economic conditions and growing political alienation. Robertson (1992) saw "ethnostates" as the only way to provide a safe world for the white race. He advocated:

> Separation and reduction into small-scale political units, not accelerated coagulation into ever larger nations, empires and spheres of interest, should be the political prescription for the future. But since this goes against the grain of globalist thinking, which still holds sway in most Western power centers, devolution will only become mainstream politics after a revolutionary shift in popular attitudes. (Robertson 1992:9–10)

The breakdown into "disparate geographical racial and cultural divisions" was seen as a way to "put back together a whole that is both healthier and greater than the sum of its parts" (p. 10).

Social Class and the White Separatist Movement

What are the social class characteristics of white separatists? We asked people in the white racialist movement, many of whom were leaders in a variety of groupings, what social class was most represented in their organization. The working class was the one most typically named, although many suggested how the movement cut across classes. A third of those we asked mentioned the middle class. Michael Storm told us that the NSDAP/AO targets the middle class based on a theoretical position about "how revolutions take place." In our interview, he explained that in revolutions: "One group displaces another group, but in the ladder of social structure you never jump more than one place. . . . The people who are going to take them [the government] out are going to be middle class people." Movement members have also suggested that William Pierce's National Alliance appeals more to middle-class people due to its more intellectual orientation and serves as a common point of entry for them into the movement.

Moore's (1991:9) study of the Indiana Klan in the 1920s found that they "represented a wide cross section of society" originating from the working class, middle class, and professional occupations. Vander Zanden (1960) found that Klan members tended to be skilled workers, small-business men, marginal white-collar employees, such as gas station attendants, and transportation workers. Goldberg (1991:219) claimed that the KKK has historically attracted members across class lines. Seltzer and Lopes (1986:100) found that supporters of the Klan's racial policies who were most likely to mention disliking blacks, tended to be "male, younger, more educated, unemployed, Fundamentalist, members of labor unions and NOT in blue collar occupations." It is well known that an intelligentsia exists within the movement, which is most visible in historical revisionism that has produced numerous "holohaux" books (Mintz 1985). While most of the people with whom we spoke were working class or lower middle class, some said that there were middle- and upper-class people in the movement, many of whom choose to remain "invisible."[8]

Shaw (1995:42) saw skinheads as primarily working-class factory types frustrated by deteriorating community conditions. He found a "thriving Skinhead scene" in cities like Detroit with a "crumbling poor black center surrounded by middle class suburbs." Ezekiel (1995) studied skinheads in Detroit and characterized them as "people who at a deep level felt terror that they were about to be extinguished. They felt that their lives might disappear at any moment. They felt that they would be blown away by the next wind." Why join a skinhead group to cope with that reality? Ezekiel (1995:156–57) concluded that "joining a tough group made sense on the face of it if you were afraid for your survival." He found personal abandonment experiences troubled many of the skins. As American society has abandoned poor people of color in our cities, white youth have also become disenfranchised, falling into the cracks of despair, hopelessness, and anger. They are the last urban whites living in ghettoized neighborhoods who are not able to connect with the suburban middle class or people of color in the surrounding urban community. Day of the Sword, a popular racist skinhead band, expressed the anger and fear of skins over an uncertain future in "No Crime Being White":

A young Klanswoman with a sign suggesting that "immigrants steal jobs." Public rally, Gainesville, Georgia, September 5, 1992.

> The birthplace is the death of our race.
> Our brothers being laid off is a truth we have to face.
> Take my job, it's equal opportunity.
> The least I can do, you were so oppressed by me.
> I've only put in twenty years now.
> Suddenly my country favors gooks and spicks and queers.
> Fuck you, then, boy I hope you're happy when your new employees
> are the reason why your business ends.

A skin in Ezekiel's (1995:275) book said, "I don't care about your ass. I don't care if you care about my ass. But I do care about poor people in this country."

While the skinheads in Coplon's (1989b) study tended to come from broken homes and have been victims of child abuse, he found that they were as likely to be middle class as poor. The "Burger King" economy provides no room at the top, so "many youngsters see themselves as being forced to compete with nonwhites for the available minimum wage, service economy jobs that have replaced their parent's unionized industry opportunities" (Coplon 1989b:84). Sears (1989:25), a program associate for CDR, suggested that our youth are alienated as they realize that, unlike prior generations, "there is no guarantee that life will be better for the younger generation."

A quiet skinhead we interviewed from the Northwest painted a biographical portrait of disenfranchisement that supports the aforementioned studies. Although not from a poor family, he told the story of a Japanese American stepfather who physically abused him until he ran away, preferring the greater safety of life on the streets. After quite some time, he met a group of skins who offered him shelter, so he entered into their white separatist reality. He wondered what else a homeless white teenager could have done? Although his entry to the movement occurred through personal circumstances, he has maintained Christian Identity beliefs. His only regrets were the tattoos that will mark him for life, leading to fear and loathing in the eyes of "nonmovement" people wherever he goes.

The Effects of the Economic Downturn on the Recruitment of White Separatists

Some (Berlet 1995; Coplon 1989b; Ezekiel 1995; Hardisty 1995; Shaw 1995) suggest that the movement has the potential to grow due to the long-term economic deterioration that Americans have been experiencing. In the past, the working class experienced the brunt of economic ills, while the middle class enjoyed greater economic security and hopes for the future. As mentioned, the white power movement has primarily attracted people from the working and middle classes. The declining economic conditions at this point in America's history have come to affect a larger cross section of Americans, with the middle class increasingly feeling the pinch. Since many movement members are attracted to white racialist philosophies as an explanation of their economic woes, declining middle-class incomes extend the recruitment ground for the movement. In this section, general economic changes in the United States will be discussed. Those changes will then be linked to the effects of those economic changes on whites and a discussion of how economic downturn serves as fuel for the white power movement.

The decline in spendable income has been a reality for millions of people here in the United States. *Dollars and Sense* (1992:23) reported that inequality in the United States was among the worst in the industrialized world during the 1980 to 1988 period.[9] "Among twenty-one top industrialized countries, only Australia has a higher rate of income inequality than the United States." While Hungary and Poland, former Eastern Bloc countries, ranked lowest in inequality, "the poorest 40 percent of U.S. households earn only 16 percent of national income. The richest 20 percent of U.S. households make about 10 times as much as the poorest." When the share of total wealth owned by the top one-half of 1 percent of Americans is examined, the growing gap between rich and poor is even more dramatic with those extremely wealthy families increasing their share from 24 to 29 percent from 1983 to 1988.

Where did their increased wealth come from? The Census Bureau (cited in *Dollars and Sense* 1992:23) reported that from 1979 to 1989 "the percent of full-time year round employees earning 'low wages,' defined as less than $12,195 a year, increased from 12% to 18% of the total work force." Cassidy (1995:118) put the transfer of wealth in real dollars, showing that the "increase in the share of the top quintile involved an *annual transfer* [emphasis added] of income from the middle to the rich of about $275 billion or roughly $4,500 per middle-class household" from 1973 to 1993. Although some attributed declining wages to low worker productivity, numerous reports have shown a negative relationship between falling wages and productivity (*Dollars and Sense* 1992:23). From 1979 to 1989 real hourly earnings for manufacturing workers fell by 8.3 percent despite growth in output per hour of 26.3 percent. In past decades, increased productivity was reflected in wage gains. Shapiro (1992:552) asked, "We're number one! (Really?)." From a review of labor force statistics (1979–1990), he concluded that we have the highest percentage of our "economically active population" working as managers (12 percent), yet we have the lowest growth in productivity among industrialized countries. Chief Executive Officers (CEOs) of American corporations earned 25 times more than the average manufacturing employee, which was the most inequitable in the first world. Cassidy (1995:120) cited studies that suggest that 20 years ago a "typical" CEO earned 40 times as much the average worker, which has increased to 190 times as much. Sklar (1992:21) presented statistics that CEOs "earned as much as 42 factory workers in

1980, 93 factory workers in 1988 and 104 factory workers in 1991." Meanwhile, the average American employee has the fewest paid vacation days in the industrialized world (11 in the United States compared with Spain's 32 days per year) (Shapiro 1992:552).

The middle class "Fear of Falling" discussed by Ehrenreich (1989) in the 1980s has translated into real deterioration in the quality of life. Even the middle class who once experienced a moderate and stable standard of living has been victimized by "downsizing" and "outplacement." A large percentage of those white-collar and managerial workers lived in the suburban serenity of a growth economy of days gone by. Now, they face early retirement, job training, or attempting to start a home business in the midst of a fragile economy (Petersen 1993:11). At the same time, social benefits for the elderly are under assault in the mainstream political arena, making those midlife course families also assume more responsibility, both social and economic, for their aging parents.

In the 1992 film *Falling Down,* Michael Douglas played a middle-aged man who was divorced and living with his aged mother. On the heels of the divorce, which did not grant him custodial rights, he gets fired from his engineering job. While all of those devastating personal losses accumulate into a rage, it is a Los Angeles traffic jam that begins his day of terror as he walks through neighborhoods finding no social support from anyone. The Korean grocery store owner would not give him change for a dollar bill to make a telephone call, two members of a Latino gang wanted to rob him as he rested in an open field on "their turf," and the middle-class white golfers wanted him off of their golf course. Although his violent behavior is inexcusable, social conditions created this man and continued to fan the flames of his rage. One has to wonder how many Americans are one straw away from the one that breaks their backs at a time when policymakers are decreasing social supports to catch people when they fall. Although the character rejected a neo-Nazi who hid him from the police, it is clear that those vigilantes shared some common ground.

By the mid-1970s, the Keynesian solutions of postwar America began to "unravel due to the loss of United States world hegemony, increased international economic competition, rising national indebtedness, declining corporate profitability, chronic economic stagnation and active resistance from organized popular movements" (Abramovitz 1992:100–101). As a response to the deterioration, the conservative agenda supported austerity and the redistribution of income to the wealthiest of Americans. Along with the economic assault on our populace, the government broke the "labor, race and gender accords" developed earlier in the century. The "new austerity program" maintained corporate profit margins at the expense of human need. Those "Reaganite programs directed 60 percent of marketable gain to the top 1 percent of income recipients while the bottom 40 percent suffered an absolute loss of net worth in real terms" (Chomsky 1995:28). The consequences of economic deprivation and the political dramas that fanned the flames of race and gender wars were "fear, chaos, poverty, social decay, and loss of communal solidarity that now plagues our nation" (Abramovitz 1992:107). Although those social conditions were created by the policies of the powerful, the elite placed the blame for social ills on the people at the bottom, the greatest percentage of whom are racial minorities.

As a result of the economic decline that began in the 1970s and was enhanced dramatically by the conservative agenda of the 1980s, social critics of the 1990s are sensing a real change in the socioeconomic relationship of large segments of the population to society's mainstream institutions. Cassidy (1995:88) said, "At the top there is an immensely wealthy elite, which has never had it so good. At the bottom, there is an underclass, which is increasingly divorced from the rest of society." A polarized and rapidly shrinking middle class consists of an "upper echelon of highly skilled and educated professionals who are doing pretty well; and a vast swatch of unskilled and semi-skilled workers, who are experiencing falling wages, stagnant or declining living standards, and increased economic uncertainty" (Cassidy 1995:88). Cassidy argues that this group is not "middle class," since they are not experiencing "rising living standards and a high degree of economic security," characteristics that typified the "middle class." Some "middle-class" families managed to maintain their standard of living because of women working in the paid labor force. While women's wages increased, they did not raise enough to offset the decline in male wages during the 1980s. *Dollars and Sense* (1987:10–11) reported that young men (ages 20–24) were hit hard economically from 1973 to 1984, which was reflected in lower rates of marriage. Young men across racial categories all suffered from rapidly declining wages, but "the real earnings of black men declined by almost 50%." In the past, young men, particularly whites, were optimistic about their economic futures, but the report found that was no longer the case. "Middle-class" families felt the "squeeze" when faced with the necessity of spending an increased proportion of the family income on the three "basic necessities: housing, utilities, and health care" (p. 89).

Cassidy (1995:122) noted the conclusions of the New York Fed conference held in November of 1994 that attributed 60 percent of the fall in wages to the "rise of technology, 10 percent on trade and 30 percent on other factors, among them immigration[10] and the decline of labor unions." Snyder (1993:7) argued that the current move to increase productivity has led to layoffs as businesses replace workers with high-tech equipment to lower labor costs. Not only have corporations increased technological production but in many instances even the high-tech production, which is not labor intensive, has been shifted to third world countries. After a careful examination of the structural changes in the nature of production, why are economists baffled by America's "jobless recovery?" (Petersen 1993:12).

Stephen Roach, the chief economist at Morgan Stanley, was concerned about the "new populist movement on the horizon: anti-capitalism," which he feared would lead to "worker backlash" in the upcoming presidential election. Roach said that "workers want more—not less. New wave Republicanism is starting to feel like a great short" (cited in Cassidy 1995:124). Despite a rigorous review of the statistics on the declining middle class and a recognition of the "rise in anti-immigration, anti-affirmative action, and anti-incumbency rhetoric," Cassidy (1995:124) concluded that "this is nobody's fault; it is just how capitalism has developed. Once this is accepted, maybe the political debate can move away from mutual recrimination and on to ways of governing a less homogeneous and more inequitable society."

Is the declining economy with its devastating impact on the middle class, working class, and poor something that simply happened to a nameless, faceless capitalism? Rather than revert back to outdated explanations like Adam Smith's "invisible hand" of the marketplace, Noam Chomsky (1995:2) argued that "a deliberate policy is driving the country toward a kind of third world model, with sectors of great privilege, growing numbers of people sinking into poverty or real misery, and a superfluous population confined in slums or expelled to the rapidly expanding prison system." *Fortune 500* companies are generating "revenues close to two thirds of the gross domestic product," leading to the creation of antidemocratic "unaccountable private tyrannies" wielding incredible power in the global economy (Chomsky 1995:30).

As mentioned, technological innovation has flourished at the expense of workers and middle management, who experienced massive layoffs. Peery (1995:111) discussed the development of a new class through the shift from industrial to high-tech production. The industrial period earlier in this century needed literate workers and maintained "relative health" of the unemployed through marginal social welfare programs making them available to work during periods of economic expansion. However, the shift to high-tech production made "the expanding sections of the working class superfluous to production," and the reserve army of unemployed are no longer needed. "The structurally unemployed" are a "new, growing, permanently unemployed sector created by economic foundations" (Peery 1995: 112). This emerging new class was driven out of industrial production and society in general (Peery 1995:113). Rifkin (1995), Aronowitz and DiFazio (1994), and others (Alkalimat 1994; Harris and Davidson 1994) are examining the implications of technology and the possibility of "the end of work." What relationship do societal members have to a society that does not employ them? Rifkin (1995) predicts long-term job displacement in all sectors of the labor force as a consequence of technological innovation that has and will continue to replace human labor. He said that the middle class was once the "voice of reason and moderation in the political life of industrialized nations" (Rifkin 1995:289). However, they are feeling "squeezed" by reduced wages and unemployment leading them to

> search for quick solutions and dramatic rescue from the market forces and technological changes that are destroying their former way of life. In virtually every industrial nation, fear of an uncertain future is driving more and more people from the mainstream to the margins of society, where they seek refuge in extremist political and religious movements that promise to restore public order and put people back to work (Rifkin 1995:289).

In the aftermath of current federal cuts and the dismantling of the welfare state, the newly disenfranchised will not be tied to the system by even the marginal and inadequate social welfare programs that have been used historically to control and pacify the poor (Piven and Cloward 1971). Aronowitz and DiFazio (1994:357–58) recognize the potential for workers to gain true citizenship in our "jobless future" resulting from the demise of "work without end." People could become "emancipated from labor to become social agents" with the newly found time for decision making required for the "self management of society," complete democratic governance. However, this cannot occur without a comprehensive political and economic restructuring.

Cassidy (1995:88) said the people in the underclass[11] are not "plugged into society" through social controls in the world of work or governmental programs, such as Aid to Families with Dependent Children (AFDC) or general assistance. As the actual unemployment and underemployment in our society grows, so does the lack of a concerted national effort to reintegrate the "castaways" through a real jobs creation program or a comprehensive reorganization of the political and economic relations in society. In addition, many middle-class Americans have experienced loss, yet are not served by social assistance programs. While they do not earn enough income to enjoy societal opportunities such as college attendance for their children, they do not receive any support to assist them and their progeny in their quest for a secure future. With continued economic downturn, many former middle-class people will experience the misfortune of being pushed out of the system. These two sectors, the political and economic "outsiders" along with the declining middle, will become increasingly susceptible to alternative explanations, to include white power philosophies.

The future of this mass of people pushed out of the system is uncertain, but it is clear that those people will have nothing to lose. Michael Moore interviewed members of the Michigan Citizens Militia in a segment of "TV Nation" (1995). As victims of the last recession they had lost jobs, a business, and their "freedoms." Norm Olson said, "You get to the point where you got nothing left and they can't take anything away from you." They signaled an impending "civil war" and warned, "either you listen to us or you destroy us."

The Posse Comitatus, a tax resistance movement, grew during the 1980s farm crisis. Farmers were displaced from their land, which they considered their birthright, at an alarming rate. In keeping with the populist history of the Great Plains, farmers like Gordon Kahl resisted the collection of federal taxes in a last-ditch effort to maintain their agrarian lives and attempt to disengage from an economy and society that no longer valued or supported the family farm (Corcoran 1990).

Clarence Lusane (1991) has attributed the devastation of drugs and gang wars on the ghettos of urban America to the political economy of racism. Although inner-city violence appears irrational, Upton (1985:256) concluded that urban riots are "politically meaningful acts in a struggle between power holding groups and powerless blacks" who question "the legitimacy of public authority" demanding "greater political participation." Studies have shown that economic inequality has been related to arrests for "violent crimes" among blacks but not whites. That has been explained by the fact that whites have experienced a higher standard of living than blacks (Skogan 1989:243). If violence is generated through economic structures in the black community as studies suggest, the increasing percentage of poor whites experiencing similar employment patterns and opportunities will most likely result in higher rates of violent crime. Although poverty among people of color has been studied,[12] poor whites, both urban and rural, are often not even seen, much less understood. If minority residents of Chicago's Cabrini Green resort to violence and gangs as a way to "survive" in an "insane" world, then we should not be surprised to see similar behaviors among poor whites and others perceiving the threat of economic loss and political disenfranchisement. Milton Kleim (1996), a former white power advocate, wrote on the Progressive Sociologists Network:

> Most of the people who join the "movement" are not evil, though they may be violent. They are lost kids, like myself once was, bitter at a society they perceive as betraying them, very similarly to how many black youth perceive their betrayal by a racist society that has little or no place for them.

White supremacy is diverse in its expression, which can provide a haven for those seeking an explanation of the social conditions of white disenfranchisement along with a call to action. The "new rural ghetto" consists of formerly middle-class people who had achieved "American cultural goals" and lost it. Often forgotten, they are filled with rage as they "watch in hunger" as others eat at tables that not long ago were their own. Filled with "resentment and rage," these people are eager to find a leader who can provide hopes that they will return to their American dream (Davidson 1990:118).

Raphael Ezekiel (author of *The Racist Mind*), Jack Levin (Northeastern University), and James Corcoran (author of *Bitter Harvest*) appeared on "The 20th Century: Hate Across America" (aired October 11, 1995, A&E). They concluded that the social, political and economic conditions in the United States have provided the climate for white separatist and other antigovernment groups, such as the citizens militias,[13] to flourish. The A. W. Mann cartoon in figure 14 provides a graphic depiction of the way that the movement depicts whites as oppressed by ZOG protecting minorities at the expense of whites. Zald (1987:324–25) suggested that the growing number of people at risk as a result of changes in social institutions, like the labor force, provides "grist for the social movement machine."[14]

The children of middle-aged parents, commonly referred to as Generation X, the "baby bust," or the "Armageddon generation," suffer from the uncertainty of diminishing employment prospects, increased tuition for higher education nationwide, and generalized alienation (Gaines

Figure 14. WAR Cartoon of Economic and Political Squeeze by A. Wyatt Mann (n.d.n.p.)

1991:237–38). Sears, a CDR associate, suggested that the current generation "coming of age" are cynical and materialistic, ascribing to upper-middle-class values that set goals well beyond their reach (Sears 1989:25). In line with Sears's assessment, we talked to three young Odinists attending a Klan rally in Ohio who expressed their frustration over trying to get a college education without help. They expressed anger over the fact that poor minorities can get government assistance to attend college. Since their parents' incomes were considered too high by the federal government, they could not afford to help their sons attend the university. Only one of them had been able to stay in college. The other two were working in blue-collar jobs with the hopes of saving up to attend college so that they could one day climb the ladder of upward social mobility.

Social theorists have been examining the effects of economic downturn. Wellman (1993) provides an extensive review of the literature. He suggested that racism, in the past, was primarily linked to the working class since studies showed that middle-class people with a degree of economic security were shielded, to some extent, from policies aimed at reducing racial inequality. The working class was affected by integration more quickly than the middle class because African Americans were more likely to hold working-class occupations, which led to interracial competition for employment. It was easier for the middle class to say that "on the job equality had an 'All American' sound to it, especially if there were very few blacks in one's occupation" (Wellman 1993:52). Over time, Wellman argued that the demands of black people have started to affect the middle class who "start sounding less tolerant and acting more like" the lower-class whites. Middle-class people are experiencing real loss in their standard of living and erosion of the moderate security they once enjoyed. "The concrete problem facing white people is how to come to grips with the demands made by blacks while at the same time avoiding the possibility of institutional change and reorganization that might affect them" (Wellman 1993:59–60).

The expression of racism takes on a different flavor among middle-class whites as they attempt to maintain their "egalitarian" ideals, yet maintain their status position. The middle-class person would tend to say "I'm not opposed to busing; I'm opposed to the time it involves" or indicate they "don't object much to blacks like themselves living 'next door.' " They assert egalitarianism related to race but inegalitarianism related to class (Wellman 1993:53). During a period of increased demand for admission, students at the University of California were more likely to argue that affirmative action perpetuates the stereotypes of black students or that black students were less qualified and would not benefit from the Berkeley experience as much as one of the 2,300 straight-A students who were denied admission (Wellman 1993: 226–30). The structural relationship in which one racial group is subordinated to another remains. Since the expression of racism has a different flavor, Wellman argues that studies of prejudice have not detected middle-class racist sentiments, even though "the consequence of their opposition are the same as if it were the result of prejudice" (Wellman 1993:53). As the middle class continues to "feel the squeeze" economically, the symbolic racism of David Duke (discussed in chapter 5) and other like-minded politicians will probably become more popular.

The Political Process Model and New Social Movements

McAdam's[15] (1982) political process model suggests that broad socioeconomic processes influence both the political opportunities and the organizational strength that shape social movements. To put it another way, these socioeconomic processes restructure existing power relations, which in turn can influence movement emergence, development, and decline. Numerous studies have noted how external or internal socioeconomic forces and political opportunities have shaped movements. For example, the general political instability in Germany after World War I facilitated the Nazi rise to power while economic trends and political realignments changed the political environment in such a way to aid the success of the farm workers movement in the 1960s (Jenkins and Perrow 1977:267; McAdam 1988). In his chapter "To the Reshaping of the New Right and the Rise of the Militia Movement, 1987–1995," Bennett (1995:464) maintained that significant reasons for the rise of that new movement could "be found in the end of the Cold War and the social as well as economic upheavals which are affecting all Americans." According to Tarrow (1994:83–84), the economic depression of the 1930s led to several movements in the United States and Europe. After World War I there were numerous movements, including women's suffrage, factory occupations, and attempts at revolution that "were the joint outcome of economic pressures, the release of pent up political energy and increased political opportunities" (Tarrow 1994:84). The downturn in American economic life over the last 25 years has shifted the balance of power and thus could enhance the position of the movement. To give the concept "political opportunities" more conceptual precision, McAdam (1996) identified four key dimensions. More specifically, the component of political opportunity referred to as "the relative openness or closure of the institutionalized political system" (McAdam 1996:27) is being altered. Rubin (1994:39) pointed out that 20 years ago David Duke and Pat Buchanan would not have been taken seriously in their campaigns. While "economic discontent was the bedrock on which these votes were cast . . . it's also true that for a considerable number of American voters this discontent found expression in the racist and xenophobic campaigns of these candidates." As McAdam (1988:128) has suggested, challengers are typically excluded from meaningful participation in institutionalized politics but "this unfavorable structure of political opportunities is hardly immutable."

Two weeks before Duke's gubernatorial election, Ezekiel (1995: 324–26) spoke with a 65-year-old supporter whose comments demonstrate the connection between the economy and the political values of right-wing populism. The supporter said that "everyone is so mad . . . so disgusted. People are not going to take it. There is going to be a revolution." He was impressed with Duke's "truths," as he had never owned a new truck or new house. He had raised four children with "the wife" scraping by on a $30,000-dollar-a-year job with the telephone company. As a senior, he was working part-time to make ends meet. He was angry about forced integration, busing, and the lack of choices turning him into a second-class citizen. Tax dollars spent on public education did not assist him in providing a parochial education for his children, nor were his financial aid applications accepted when his children went to college. Although he could not afford to send them to college, his earnings were too high, disqualifying them from means-tested programs. The Duke supporter resented tax spending on programs, like welfare, that he did not want or benefit from. In the end, he said, "I want everybody to get what I got: Nothing!"

Croteau (1995) examined the relationship between the working class and participation in social movements, especially leftist movements and unions. He considered the possibility that those workers who were not satisfied with the electoral system or did not feel comfortable in left movements or the labor movement could turn to the right for support (pp. 213, 195). However, he believed that the right is not likely to be effective in attracting the working class because its "economic policies contradict working class realities" (p. 195) even though the right's cultural position may have some appeal. However, the white separatist movement may be attractive to some whites precisely because of their perceived connection of economics with race. The social and economic realities of working class life "form the backdrop against which racial and ethnic discord has escalated over the last two decades" (Rubin 1994:27). At least some of the white working class believe they are experiencing poor economic conditions because the benefits have shifted to minorities.

Two other dimensions of political opportunity are the "stability or instability of that broad set of elite alignments that typically undergird a polity" and "the presence or absence of elite allies" (McAdam 1996:27). Tarrow (1994:87) points out that one element of the opportunity structure that facilitates movements is unstable political alignments that in "liberal democracies" manifest themselves in electoral instability. One could argue that while racial politics has always been used by elites, including the major political parties, since 1968 "it has been central to the Republican and conservative resurgence" (Dionne 1991:78). Dionne continues:

> It is a simple and undeniable truth of American politics that the Republicans gained a great deal both in the South and in white enclaves of Northern big

cities because of the reaction against the Democratic Party's stand in favor of civil rights. The race issue also helped Republicans and conservatives indirectly, by providing them with yet another way of casting liberals as "elitists" who were indifferent to the concerns of average (white) Americans. Indeed, racial politics allowed the Republicans to take advantage of the very class inequalities that their laissez-faire economic philosophy defended. (p. 78)

The upper echelons of the Democratic Party as well as the Republicans had to share responsibility for the political realignment that has occurred:

> Democrats and liberals were complicit in this transformation of American politics. Above all, they failed to understand that the burdens of achieving racial justice were being borne disproportionately by their traditional supporters among the less affluent whites (p. 80)....
> liberals made a difficult political situation a great deal worse by fundamentally misunderstanding the dilemmas that the civil rights revolution posed to members of the white working and lower middle classes. (Dionne 1991:81)

This shift in the association of lower-middle and working-class whites toward the Republican Party signals a somewhat unstable political environment in which various movements could advance their causes. It has also helped legitimize the coupling of race with economics and politics, and the movement can potentially take advantage of this. It is, however, extremely unlikely that any elite who engages in the discourse of racial politics wants to be publicly recognized as an ally of the white separatist movement. At the same time, it does not mean that elites would reject the tacit support of some movement groups. As noted before, Reagan did not reject support from the Klan until it became publicized.

The fourth dimension of political opportunity involves the state's capacity and propensity for repression. McAdam (1996:28) points out "the unpredictable nature of repression and the complex social processes that structure its operation." The interaction of government, movement, and antimovement groups are extremely difficult to predict. Marx and McAdam (1994) identified numerous ways that the federal government can damage a movement, including harassing, intimidating, or imprisoning movement leaders and surveilling movement activists to obtain information that would harm or discredit them and to infiltrate and disrupt the groups. These things have certainly been used against the white separatist movement. COINTELPRO is probably the best example of much of this. Legal cases have also been initiated by the government or by groups opposed to the movement against movement organizations and/or their leaders because of activities of members or associates. In general it appears that the less the state engages in repressive activities, the more helpful this is to the movement. Often government repression intimidates potential activists (Andrain and Apter 1995:6). On the other hand, though, it is possible that excessive government repression or the inappropriate use of it can generate sympathy and support for the movement (Marx and McAdam 1994). The siege of Ruby Ridge may be one example of this. Also, as seen in the cases of Greensboro, North Carolina, the Order, Gordon Kahl, and Ruby Ridge, different branches or units of the government may have differing agendas that influence the movement. The BATF raids on Ruby Ridge and Waco highlighted the potential for government atrocities and provided fuel for white separatists and other segments of our population holding antigovernment sentiments. The interaction between those social, economic, and political situations produced fertile ground for the Aryan seed.

Rather than dealing with problems in our political, economic, and sociocultural reality that fuel the white resistance movement, the government continues to focus on containment. The repression of McCarthyism has been revived in the 1980s and 1990s, targeting the far right with surveillance, infiltration, entrapment, and arrests. One of the most dramatic examples was the Fort Smith Sedition trial in which 14 movement members were charged with conspiracy to overthrow the U.S. government. They were acquitted in 1988 after "heavy expenditures of time, money, and energy" (Goldberg 1991:221). McCarthyism did not rid our society of communism, the witch-hunts did not prevent the development of feminism, and incarceration will not end white separatism. These movements are built on ideological belief systems that will not be eliminated by witch-hunts of any kind. As beliefs are delegitimatized and stigmatized, organizations may go underground, but the belief system will not die. The law enforcement orientation is compatible with state interests to maintain the status quo, which often results in the proliferation of the forces it attempts to contain through the inevitable production of martyrs such as Robert Mathews of The Order, the Weavers, Gordon Kahl, and the Waco Branch Davidians. Ironically, there are times when the authoritarian governmental stance toward the containment of social movements *mirrors and nurtures* the authoritarianism within domestic out-groups like white separatists. In the name of stopping domestic terrorism and ending violence, citizens are killed, many of whom are innocent. As the government attempts to contain the fire, flames are fanned, with sparks shooting out to further the cause.

Another important component of the political process model is indigenous organizational strength. The political opportunities for the movement may be increasing due to broad socioeconomic processes, but the movement at this point is still plagued by numerous organizational concerns and split between the leaderless resistance strategy and the desire for formal hierarchical organizational structure. Concerns have been cited earlier about both the quantity and quality of leaders and members or associates. The movement is extremely factionalized, and although there is general agreement about the importance of race, religious concerns especially divide the movement, and some resist the identification of the movement with Hitler and National Socialism. The concern about the future of the white race does, however, unite the movement, and the identification with like-minded people in the white race results in a sense of community. From the movement's point of view, one very positive development has been the movement's use of the Internet and the implementation of various World Wide Web pages to facilitate communication and to attract new members.

"Mediating between opportunity and action are people and the subjective meanings they attach to their situations" (McAdam 1988:132). Increasing political opportunities in this movement could provide the impetus for cognitive liberation. This would involve changes in people's consciousness that includes their questioning of institutional arrangements, the assertion of their "rights," and the belief that they have the capacity to improve their situation (Piven and Cloward 1979:3–4; McAdam 1988:132). In her study of the working and lower class, Rubin (1994:39) argued that at the subjective level (in spite of the objective class situation), there is "declining significance of class in favor of the increasing salience of race" (p. 39) and "racial identity" or "racial consciousness" has become prominent (p. 195). She perceives this growing racial consciousness developing among white students on college campuses and in society in general in order for whites to connect themselves to a community.

Although many Americans appear alienated, it is important to recognize that the feelings of alienation tend to be directed toward the American government and the state of the economy, questioning those structural arrangements. Rifkin (1995:290) said that the growing numbers of "destitute and desperate human beings" are the "potential levelers . . . whose cries for justice and inclusion have gone unheard and unaddressed." Our political leaders speak of jobs and crime as if they are only remotely related and have refused to acknowledge "the growing outlaw class for whom crime is the last means to secure a piece of a shrinking economic pie" as they find "themselves pink-slipped and suddenly and irrevocably locked outside the gates of the new high-tech global village" (Rifkin 1995:290). Growing numbers of people in our country are feeling politically disenfranchised by governmental programs and expenditures that they do not support. They are angry and confused as the social world collapses (Chomsky 1995:25). Survey data suggest that 80 percent of Americans are aware that our economic system is "inherently unfair" and the government does not serve the majority of the people. Chomsky (1995:28) said that "functioning civil society has been dismantled" to such an extent "that Congress can now ram through programs opposed by large majorities who are left in fear, anger, and hopelessness." A primary ingredient of cognitive liberation is this questioning of the legitimacy of "politics as usual" and the economic system, but the hopelessness or fatalistic outlook should be rejected.

Although alienation may be great, Hamm (1993:166) reported some intriguing differences in types of alienation. He found that the racist skinheads he studied were very alienated regarding politics and economics but not about the future. Most of the skinheads had joined their groups to fight for the survival of their race and had overwhelmingly disagreed with the statement "It's hardly fair to bring children into the world with the way things look for the future." This could be construed as illustrating hope for the future. As we noted from our interviews and other sources, those in the movement question the legitimacy of the current government and/or the entire political system, but they do not appear "fatalistic." The alternative that they have framed is a "white separatist" future with love for the white race. They often tend to believe the movement is growing in size and influence and seem to feel that some form of racial separation will improve their situation. Some see an impending racial struggle while others believe it will be some time before it comes to a head. Thus we believe these people feel that significant change is possible through white separatism.

Croteau (1995) believed that deindustrialization, suburbanization, and the "proliferation of mass-media entertainment" (p. 213) has devastated working-class communities. The white working class now lacks strong institutional supports that allow for a sense of community or solidarity. The white separatist movement could provide support by offering identification with the white race and an ideology of white separatism. Segré (1993:296) has pointed out that fascism can appeal to people's deep-seated longings for community, safety, and solidarity.

Chomsky (1995) was alarmed by the potential growth of fascist movements rooted in the history of American populism and religious extremism.

At the subjective level it would seem that cognitive liberation and the development of a sense of collective identity are closely tied together. New social movement theory helped reintroduce the importance of "the collective search for identity" (Johnston, Laraña, and Gusfield 1997:279) and may be partially applicable to this "old" white racialist social movement. As Buechler (1997) points out, there are actually several theories of new social movements, including a division between political and cultural dimensions. McAdam (1994) acknowledges that the resource mobilization and political process models have not devoted much attention to the cultural or ideational dimensions of collective action. New social movements tend to offer subcultural orientations that challenge the dominant system. Those using new social movements' frameworks often assume that people seek collective identity due to "an intrinsic need for an integrated and continuous social self," and this is especially the case when ethnic, separatist, and nationalist movements are analyzed (Johnston et al. 1997:279). There tends to be a set of beliefs, values, symbols, and meanings that are associated with the feelings of belonging to a differentiated social group.

The new social movements tend to draw on three particular groups: (1) the "new middle class," which includes those who have been employed in advanced technological sectors, the public sector, and human service professions (e.g., social workers, educators, bureaucrats, and those who have high levels of education); (2) those in marginal labor market positions (e.g., students, unemployed); and (3) parts of the traditional petite bourgeoisie or the old middle class who were independent workers (farmers, craftsmen) (Melucci 1988:344). Unlike Peery's (1995) disenfranchised new class, Melucci (1988:344) suggests the "new middle class would be well integrated into society" and contribute most to the "activist" and militant core group. Little evidence exists to support the presence of the "new middle class" in this movement. Metzger stressed the importance of having certain movement members become "embedded" in major institutions (taken from Dees and Fiffer 1993:273), but it is unclear how many movement supporters have penetrated the system. According to Melucci (1988:343–4), "Individuals belonging to marginal, deprived, or declining social groups . . . become involved at a later stage, for shorter periods of time, and at levels of participation with lower costs." This may help explain our belief that some individuals were involved in the movement for only a short time. For example, we would write to a number of addresses that had been listed in recent movement publications but then find their post office boxes were closed and our mail returned. Other times we would be corresponding with someone and then find our letters being returned by the post office. (We recognize some of these people may have moved or have been harassed or pressured to move as well, but the number of times this occurred was considerable.)

Johnston et al. (1997:292) note that new social movements have typically been regarded as creative forces of change identifying directions for cultural innovation, but there may be a less promising face that considers collective identity associated with totalitarianism: "Surely the rise of nationalist movements and ethnic hatred also go to the core of how social actors think about themselves" (Johnston et al. 1997:292). Race is clearly salient in American society and an important basis for identification (Marx and McAdam 1994; Omi and Winant 1996; Rubin 1994). We have pointed out that many people of various classes are being affected by social, political, and economic developments and thus may be searching for a sense of identity. Such developments may contribute to their willingness to participate in a movement even if it is stigmatized. White separatists have framed their ideology in terms of preserving the white race. The identification with the in-group of the white race can provide feelings of solidarity, community, and loyalty. Maintaining the white race through white separatism is both a cultural and political issue for people in this movement.

Conclusions

In this book, we have given an overview of the development of the white racialist movement over the past century. Although general societal forces are recognized by some movement members, it has evolved into a highly factionalized racial movement with a variety of philosophies emphasizing race and culture first. However, it is clear that there are other societal factors that have influenced the growth and development of this movement. As noted in chapter 4, political mobilization and protest have occurred as members of this movement perceive government oppression symbolized by tragedies such as the Weaver one at Ruby Ridge. The white power movement has also opposed governmental social programs, such as busing in the 1960s and contemporary affirmative action, that posed a threat to white privilege. They feared the loss of their white ethnic identities, homogeneous neighborhoods, and potential economic loss as they became less highly favored in an increasing number of social arenas. Most of these people, like a cross section of Americans, are not people who originated with much social, economic, or political power. They have not been brokers in the political process capable of shaping our future. Bound for Glory, a popular skinhead band, expressed anger over the economic loss and political alienation of our times in "Still Standing Here."

> Somedays I think of a farmer who is distraught
> And look at the politician whose position has been bought.
> Foreclosures set in and one has lost his land
> While the other sits back on his ass and claims that he understands.
> One has spent his life working to put food on your table,
> While the other has gotten rich on promises turned to fables.
> Tell me who dictates, tell me who has the upper hand.
> Equality is a myth in this so-called democratic land.

While the political alienation and economic insecurity that they face is a reality shared by most Americans, people in the white separatist movement argue that their deteriorating socioeconomic conditions are a consequence of racism against whites more than the result of general social processes that negatively affect most of us.

Economists have debated whether whites have been experiencing increased absolute or relative deprivation.[16] Rubenstein (1989:323) argued that "relative deprivation" does not by itself produce "mass political violence." Revolt is likely when identity groups expect improvements in their standard of living, yet perceive "attack by competition groups or by powerful outsiders," which leads to their development of "defensive" rebellion strategies. Americans are doubting the efficacy of strategies for political mobilization that have been tried in the past while threats to "group identity and welfare have intensified." Rubenstein (1989:323–25) warned that these societal conditions are ripe for "the politics of vengeance and despair." He suggested that "domestic violence" addresses the "interests and needs of specific identity groups" without broad-based national or international linkages. These groups target their specific enemies instead of the "powers that be." He also argued that this form of rebellion does not develop "plans for a transformation of politics or economics at the national level," and the ideological explanations and solutions generally followed the revolt (Rubenstein 1989:314–15).

This may be true of some domestic groups, but the white separatist movement is far more complicated, with both a national and international orientation exemplified by the cry for whites to unite around the globe. Earlier in this chapter, we presented some views of movement leaders and members. From those comments, there is an ideology of racial identity that has been developed through several generations. While white separatist organizations may have been more organized on local or regional levels in the past, it is clear that the contemporary movement, although factionalized, consists of linkages through joint memberships, organizational mergers, and cooperative action symbolized by white "unity rallies" that have made Pulaski, Tennessee, a popular meeting place and by World Congresses held at AN. Movement organizations propose a number of solutions such as the "Northwest Homeland" (The Order and AN), racial tribalism (WAR), and Hitlerian National Socialism (NSDAP/AO and AN). Although most Americans feel uncomfortable with white separatist visions of the future, the ideology has been developed through several generations and reflects historical changes in organizational structures, strategies, and goals.

Instead of examining the role of capitalism in the development of social classes and the social construction of scarcity, we have been programmed in this society, through institutionalized white supremacy and the ideology of anticommunism, to seek racial solutions over proposals for a deep political and economic restructuring that would benefit us all (Feagin and Vera 1995:33). In our society, civil rights reforms have been enacted without addressing class inequality. Bowser and Hunt (1996:xv) said:

> With a "race problem," the subordination of whole classes of people based on color is justified and competition is reduced. If the "race problem" disappeared tomorrow, however, with people of color still a significant portion of the U.S. population, approximately one in five whites would have real competition from a minority person with whom they did not have to compete before. The odds of white people being displaced from good jobs, housing, educational achievement, recognition, privilege, and income would be higher.

For example, affirmative action may "address or ameliorate the effects of past discrimination and racism" for people of color, while, at the same time, it leads to the "displacement of people, who according to their race and group preference, are displaced from opportunities which their backgrounds and racial norms suggest they are entitled" (Jones and Carter 1996:22).

If we continue to pursue increased opportunities for racial minorities without altering the class structure, racial tensions will be intensified rather than resolved. Whites are less likely to accept civil rights reforms that threaten their own economic security and hopes for the future. Without a dramatic decrease in income inequality and the creation of jobs at livable wages, racial equality only means a declining standard of living for whites with some people of color moving up the class system and most remaining at the bottom. Ironically, greater racial polarization feeds the acceptance of right-wing conservative agendas that support "greater class inequality and a restructuring of the political economies of the advanced capitalist countries at the expense of the working classes" (Kushnick 1996:49), both whites and people of color alike.

However, increased economic equality would not signal an immediate end to racism, since institutionalized racism is deeply embedded in American culture. Interviews with members of The Order on ABCs "Turning Point" (August 20, 1995) revealed the depth of belief that core white separatist movement members maintain. Facing sentences totaling 442 years in Federal Penitentiaries (Flynn and Gerhardt 1989:466, 469), Bruce Carroll Pierce and David Lane[17] still hold on to their belief in "The 14 Words: We must secure the existence of our people and a future for white children." It is clear that incarceration has *not* "rehabilitated" those white warriors so that they would express attitudes that the state would find acceptable. After serving a prison sentence and being disbarred in the 1980s, J. B. Stoner told us in our interview, "They sent me over to prison in Alabama where they rehabilitated me, so I no longer criticize Jews and niggers anymore." Racism, the domination by whites, and the appeal of separatism are age-old. People who are attracted to the movement's philosophy are unlikely to be "rehabilitated" out of their core beliefs by a prison sentence, nor is their incarceration likely to be a significant deterrent to others.

Many members of the movement truly believe that destruction of the white race is inevitable without an apocalyptic race war. They look at multicultural America and fear the loss of their ethnic identity. Robertson (1992:20) wrote:

> The word "alienation," a favorite of Hegel and Marx, adequately describes the pessimistic mood of the majority of whites in the largest Western cities, which have become refuges for myriads of immigrants who neither look, speak nor act like their hosts, the numbers of whom are now declining as fast as the numbers of newcomers are multiplying. When strangers comprise a significant portion of the population of a country, when outsiders form their own neighborhoods in what was once "our" neighborhoods, we start to have doubts about who we are.

He predicted eventual problems of governing such a highly fragmented nation "as the centrifugal forces that pull nations, neighborhoods and families apart grow stronger and the centripetal forces that bind them together grow weaker" (p. 20). It is clear that people gain a sense of identity in a variety of ways, and members of the white separatist movement consider racial identity to be a primary source of their self-definition and self-esteem, hence, the title of this book.

Although political and economic equality would not eliminate the ideology of white racialism or the social psychological need to maintain white ethnic identity, it would allow democratic discourse, which would be much more likely to lead to a greater understanding and the potential resolution of our cultural wars. Some members share a belief in the "core" movement ideology as expressed by the "14 Words" and resent the loss of the political and social opportunities because of their racial values. Others fall into the movement due to economic circumstances and political disenfranchisement and would not be as attracted to white racialism if they could sustain belief in a future where their human needs could be secured. Our cultural differences will not be resolved by simply dismissing some ideas as "bad" with the hope of converting or forcing people to accept status quo multiracial attitudes.

It is impossible to address America's cultural crises when our political and economic institutions perpetuate inequality in all forms. Berlet (1995:41) argued that

> racism, anti-Semitism, and other forms of supremacy are not the exclusive domain of marginal extremist groups but are also domiciled in mainstream culture and politics. Most mainstream human-rights groups still use the rhetoric flowing from pluralist/extremist theory: "radical," "extremist," "fringe." These are terms favored by a group of people who want dissidents to shut up and sit down.

If anything, the consequence of inequality is the blending of economic concerns with a broad base of political support among mainstream citizens, such as fear over unemployment and the declining standard of living, with ideological beliefs like white separatism that are held by a much smaller segment of the population.

The voices of white power figures presented earlier in this chapter demonstrated the reframing of white racialism, redefining and integrating more left-wing concerns into the preexisting ideology. In response to the political and economic crises of our times, "people who would have been working to build the CIO [Congress of Industrial Organizations] 60 years ago are now joining paramilitary organizations" (Chomsky

1995:25). Hardisty (1995:10) linked the "alienation created by a restructuring of the economy that is negatively affecting large numbers of workers" to the "backlash fueled by anger—in the form of resentment, spite, vengeance, envy, loss and bitterness over declining status—on the part of those who feel that they have not benefitted from the changes of the last 30 years." Hardisty (1995:1) argued that U.S. history has more often as not run counter to "democratic values" (Hardisty 1995:1; Zinn 1993, 1980). Under these social conditions, dialogue concerning America's "racial divide" only occurs among people with divergent types of self-interest reflective of their different political and economic positions in our inequitable social system. Berlet (1995:42) also warned that the "free market" of global "neocorporatism" will not lead to democratic outcomes. Instead, hard socioeconomic times will cause people to "turn toward swift, simple solutions and the strong leadership of the 'man on the white horse.' "

Kushnick (1996:9) exclaimed that it is "more necessary than ever for the relationship between racism and capitalism to be put on the political agenda." Bowser and Hunt (1995:248) suggested that we must address racism at the individual, institutional, and cultural levels or racism will just be translated into a new expression without resolution. A reorganization of the United States toward a more politically and economically democratic society could open the door to public discussion and the possibility of resolving our racial conflict. Without that restructuring, the struggle to obtain material necessities and political empowerment will cloud social discourse and perpetuate our cultural wars.

Notes

1. Introduction

1. To study this movement in-depth, we decided to attend rallies and interview leaders of the movement. Among the events we attended were the following: KKKK, Dubuque, IA, rally, May 29, 1992 and Janesville, WI, rally, May 30, 1992; Gainesville, GA, march and rally of various KKK and Skinhead groups, September 5, 1992; Pulaski, TN, rally and march led by Richard Ford's Fraternal White Knights, January 9, 1993; Pulaski, TN, rally and march, evening cross lighting of Thom Robb's Knights of the Ku Klux Klan, January 23, 1993; interview with Tom Metzger in Fallbrook, CA, March 20, 1993; Chicago, IL, Populist Party Conference, May 22, 1993; Chicago, IL, private dinner of Knights of the Ku Klux Klan, May 22, 1993; Springfield, TN, private rally, May 9, 1993; Pulaski, TN, Fraternal White Knights rally and march, January 8, 1994; Coshocton, OH, Klan and SS Action march and rally, April 9, 1994; Rockford, IL, Knights of Ku Klux Klan rally, June 11, 1994; Portage and Culver, IN, American Knights of Ku Klux Klan public rally and private gathering, May 11, 1996; rural area of Paintsville, KY, private celebration of Adolf Hitler's birthday sponsored by White Aryan Legion, April 19, 1997; Hayden Lake, ID, Aryan Nations World Congresses, July 15–17, 1994, July 21–23, 1995, and July 19–21, 1996, and Aryan Youth Assembly April 19–21, 1996; a Federation of Klans' private dinner, March 25, 1995 in Chicago, IL; and the Patriot's Day Picnic, the Church of Jesus Christ in Harrison, AR, May 27, 1995. It should be pointed out that these episodes gave us a great deal of insight into the movement but were

not as long or as penetrating as what sociologists would do in a participant observation study.

2. Ninety of the interviews were coded; these are the ones referred to in our statistical discussion, which typically has 10 people or so with missing data. Throughout the book we use the names and affiliations that people gave us when we interviewed them or when they filled out questionnaires if they gave us permission to do so. Some people did ask to remain anonymous or to use pseudonyms.

3. Holland was convicted of perjury on June 3, 1992, and received "two years' probation, including six months' home confinement, and ordered to pay $911.50 in restitution" along with 250 hours of community service (SPLC, August, 1992a:4). He was accused of concealing monetary resources and attempting to avoid paying damages of $50,000 in personal money and his Klan was fined $400,000 in restitution. Holland appealed the conviction "saying that errors had been made in the trial. The federal government cross appealed," maintaining that his sentence in district court was too lenient (*Marietta Daily Journal,* May 26, 1994; Rankin 1994). Holland eventually went to prison, and later to a halfway house according to the WAR Hotline.

4. We did, for example, observe Dr. Ed Fields use segregation as a key concept in his presentation at a Federation of Klans dinner in March 1995. Like most issues in this movement there is not complete consensus. Some may still be more inclined toward the term *segregation* but our impression is that this is more likely to be advocated by people who are older, have been in the movement for some time, and are less militant.

5. In fact Massey and Denton (1993) maintain that although the word *segregation* disappeared from the American vocabulary during the 1970s and 1980s, urban America remains extremely segregated. They argue "that racial segregation—and its characteristic institutional form, the black ghetto—are the key structural factors responsible for the perpetuation of black poverty in the United States" (Massey and Denton 1993:9).

6. Berlet (1995:40) notes two different uses of the term *white supremacy*. The narrower definition refers to "race-hate groups" but the broader one also includes "the entire superstructure of oppression erected during European colonialism to justify domination of so-called inferior peoples who were identified and made the 'other' by assigning the idea of race to skin color."

7. Diani (1992) is critical of a number of characteristics used to define social movements, including the use of noninstitutionalized behavior and the distinction between public protest and conventional political participation. His synthetic definition of social movement is "a network of informal interactions between a plurality of individuals, groups and/or organizations, engaged in a political or cultural conflict, on the basis of a shared collective identity."

8. An open-systems framework examines both variables within the organization or movement and variables about the organization's or movement's relationship with the external environment. For discussion of the open- and closed-systems models, see Zey-Ferrell (1979).

9. Two criticisms of labeling theorists are that they do not consider the seriousness of certain acts committed by the deviants, and they do not pay attention to the interaction between controlled and controller (Davis and Stasz 1990:48–49). Labeling theorists tend to be more sympathetic to the deviants who they feel are underdogs than to the controllers.

10. Although terms like *upper class, middle class, working class,* and *poor* mask important differences and interests among groups of people, these subjective class labels are reasonably associated with objective measures of socioeconomic status such as education, income, and occupational skill level (Kerbo 1991:192–93). At the same time there seems to be stigma associated with the label "working class," and, for some, calling themselves "middle class" makes them feel better about themselves and their social situation (Rubin 1994:30). The 1988 Survey Research Center national election survey asked respondents if they called themselves middle class or working class. Forty-four percent indicated middle class, 50 percent working class, 4 percent volunteered don't know or other, and only 1 percent rejected the idea of class (Gilbert and Kahl 1993:235).

2. Historical Overview

1. Some sources use 1866 as the date of the founding.

2. With various changes in staff, the death of Richard Butler's wife, Betty, late in 1995, and his own health possibly questionable, Butler announced at the April 1996 Aryan Youth Assembly that he was making plans for a transition to future leadership. No transition was forthcoming, however, at the July 1996 World Congress. Law enforce-

ment seemed more watchful at that World Congress as Dobratz was stopped for driving too slow shortly after leaving AN the first evening of the Congress. Also two participants at the Congress, who were among the 25 or so marching down the sidewalks of Coeur d'Alene, "were arrested halfway into the march for spitting on the sidewalk" (Hopfinger 1996). We are deeply indebted to Pastor Butler and the staff at AN for allowing us to attend three of their World Congresses and one Aryan Youth Assembly.

3. *The Northwest Imperative* by Crawford et al. (1994) is published by CHD and Northwest Coalition Against Malicious Harassment. It provides an extensive and timely consideration of movement groups, especially in the Northwest. One of its three main chapters is entitled "Christian Identity: Kingdom of Hate."

4. Although Metzger, Mahon, Baumgardner, and others see themselves as outside the right-wing movement, we include the resistance under our broad umbrella of the white separatist movement because of their focus on the white race and separatism. We acknowledge major ideological differences between what some might label the traditional right-wing racialist movement and the resistance.

3. Ideology

1. Mr. Sigler requested that we make it clear that whenever he is quoted, he is giving his personal opinions only and they do not necessarily represent those of the Hammerskin Nation or any other individual of the Hammerskin Nation.

2. There are other important aspects of ideology that we do not discuss here, including views toward other minorities than blacks and Jews.

3. Kühl considers the links among German National Socialism, eugenics, and American racism. He (1994:110) points out that since the 1940s eugenicists have exercised more restraint in using the words *superior* and *inferior*.

4. For several social scientific reviews of *The Bell Curve,* see the symposia in the March 1995 (Volume 24, #2) issue of *Contemporary Sociology* (pp. 149–61) and the Winter 1995 (Volume 25, #1) issue of *The Black Scholar* as well as the review essay by Douglas Massey in *American Journal of Sociology* November 1995, Volume 101, #3, pp. 747–53. Massey (1995:747) is critical of the field of sociology because

in certain ways it "actively discouraged the examination of social differences with respect to culture and intelligence." Also of interest are *The Bell Curve Debate* edited by Jacoby and Glauberman (1995), *Measured Lies: The Bell Curve Examined* edited by Kincheloe, Steinberg, and Gresson (1996), and *Inequality by Design: Cracking the Bell Curve Myth* by Fischer et al. (1996). For a pro-movement review of the controversy between race and intelligence, including a discussion of *The Bell Curve,* see "The Illusion Is Over: Race and Intelligence" by George Eric Hawthorne in *Resistance Magazine,* Issue 3, Winter 1995, pp. 7, 26.

5. This was an undated form letter enclosed with a *WAR* newsletter sent to subscribers.

6. As the October–December 1993 *NSV Report* noted, Klan groups could be supporting what it calls separate but equal policies and what the mainstream might call segregation. This article gives an insider history of the recent movement, including discussions of key figures.

7. According to Marger (1987:56), Michels's Iron Law of Oligarchy refers to the "seemingly unavoidable emergence of elite rule created by the structure of modern social organizations."

8. Pettigrew challenges the assumptions in part by pointing out the negative consequences of racial isolation, including that separateness hinders each group from finding out about the values and beliefs they do share and that isolation would facilitate the evolution of differences in values and beliefs, leading to greater difficulties in achieving contact.

9. Joe Rowan was killed in October 1994 in what appears to be a racial incident at a convenience store after his band Nordic Thunder had given a concert in Racine, WI. A black man believed to be the killer was never charged. Major Clerkin of Euro-American Alliance tried to get the legal system to bring charges against the man but was not successful. The Blue Eyed Devils is the new band that has some members from Nordic Thunder.

10. There is an abundance of books on National Socialism such as Ramon Knauerhase's *An Introduction to National Socialism, 1920 to 1939* (Columbus, OH: Charles E. Merrill, 1972), Franz Neumann's *Behemoth: The Structure and Practice of National Socialism 1933–1944* (New York: Harper & Row, 1944), George L. Mosse's *The Crisis of German Ideology* (New York: Grosset, 1964) and *Toward the Final Solution: A History of European Racism* (Madison: University of Wisconsin Press, 1985).

11. Aryans are defined as white people of Baltic, Celtic, Nordic, or related descent, who have no nonwhite ancestry (NSWPP, Koehl, 1980:1).

12. A *Newsweek* article (Leland and Beals 1997:60) reported that interracial marriages have increased considerably since the 1960s and now consist of more than 2 percent of all marriages in the United States.

13. The material that the movement tends to cite for support against the Holocaust can be found in various publications including Richard Harwood, *Six Million Lost and Found* (also titled *Did Six Million Really Die?*) (Chapel Ascote, Ladbroke, Southern, Wasks, Historical Review Press, n.d.); Fred A. Leuchter Jr., *The Leuchter Report: The End of a Myth* (Toronto: Samisdat Publishers Ltd., n.d.); Michael A. Hoffman II, *The Great Holocaust Trial* (Dresden, New York: Wiswell Ruffin House, 1995); and Arthur Butz, *The Hoax of the Twentieth Century* (Chapel Ascote: Historical Review Press, 1976). For material challenging the revisionist version, see *Hitler's Apologists: The Anti-Semitic Propaganda of Holocaust "Revisionism"* (ADL 1993b) and the sections on the Holocaust in the latest *Material Resource Catalog* of ADL.

14. For information on fundamentalism, see *Fundamentalisms Observed,* edited by Martin E. Marty and R. Scott Appleby (Chicago: University of Chicago Press, 1991) and *Religion and Politics in a Comparative Perspective* edited by Broneslaw Misztal and Anson Schupe (Westport, CT: Praeger, 1992).

15. See Aho (1990) for a discussion of the international banking conspiracy.

16. Mark Thomas was implicated in a series of bank robberies associated with the Aryan Republican Army. After he was indicted as an Aryan Republican Army conspirator in Philadelphia, he pleaded guilty in February 1997 (Martin 1997:12). There have been rumors in the movement that Thomas may have been supplying the government with information about movement activities for a long time.

17. Some movement members would object to being labeled politically conservative and part of the right wing. They may believe political conservatives have sold them out and/or may be worse than liberals.

18. For much greater discussion on the differences between Odinism and Ásatrú and the various organizations, see Kaplan's (1994–1995) five-part series in *THEOD Magazine.*

19. The Odinist Fellowship is no longer being published. In 1993 Else Christensen was sentenced to five years and four months for her involvement in a drug smuggling case. She evidently drove the car across state lines but claimed she did not know drugs were in the trunk (Sannhet 1993).

20. According to Berlet and Quigley (1995:40), the Third Position renounces democratic capitalism and communism while supporting a stance based on a Strasserite interpretation of National Socialism, claiming to surpass Nazism. The politics of the Third Position combines a strong antagonistic racial nationalism with purported advocacy of the dignity of labor and environmentalism.

21. Stern (1996:245–46) believes that the statistics that suggest only certain militias may have ties to neo-Nazi and white supremacist groups miss the point as he argues that "racism, especially anti-Semitism, was essential to the [militia] movement." He does, however, believe that the "organizing principle of the militias was that the government had been taken over by evil forces and could not be reformed, that it had to be combated—with arms" (Stern 1996:246).

22. Ken Petersen defected from the National Knights, but later his movement status was not clear.

23. "G. Raubal" has written material favorable to Hitler including "Haus Wachenfeld."

4. Protest and Violence

1. Some residents in Dubuque responded to the Constructive Integration Plan on the basis of fear, rumor, and resentment, and the plan was never put into practice. A Council for Diversity was created by business leaders and others to counteract the negative publicity the community had received from cross burnings and Klan demonstrations. It was more of a public relations endeavor promoting multiculturalism than an attempt to attract minority professionals and executives.

2. For a brief case study of the Klan rallies we attended in Pulaski, Tennessee, in 1993, see Dobratz and Shanks-Meile 1995.

3. Later due to a split in the KKKK, McGiffen became part of Neumann's KKKK.

4. For an interesting movement discussion of the positive and negative aspects of leaderless resistance, see *The WAR Eagle* Volume 1, Issue 2, pp. 3–6.

5. For much greater detail on these cases and on the Klan violence in general during the 1960s and 1970s, see Chalmers 1981, Wade 1987, SPLC 1991, and George and Wilcox 1992.

6. Aho (1990:78–84) points out that symbols represent things other than themselves and play a significant role in constructing our social world. He provides an excellent discussion on heroes and symbols, including how the term *hero* is both a neutral social scientific concept and a label of honor. Also see Aho (1994:chapter 2) for a discussion of heroism and the social construction of the enemy. WAR publishes an Aryan Martyr and POW collage and an Aryan Martyr's Map giving tribute to nine Silent Brotherhood members as well as others like Gordon Kahl, John Singer, Kathy Ainsworth, and Arthur Kirk who died in shoot-outs.

7. John W. DeCamp was a member of the Nebraska state legislature and is author of the book *The Franklin Cover-up: Child Abuse, Satanism, and Murder in Nebraska*. "The Franklin Credit Union scandal, centered in Omaha, opens a window into the hideous world of child abuse, and of organized, illegal drug peddling, patronized and protected by powerful figures in politics and business" (DeCamp 1992:xxi).

8. Leonard Peltier was the American Indian Movement leader accused of killing two FBI agents in a gun battle at Pine Ridge Indian Reservation in 1975. Interestingly, Lynn Crooks, who had assisted a Justice Department attorney in the Peltier case, was the chief prosecutor for the murder trial of Yorie Kahl and Scott Faul (Corcoran 1990). DeCamp (1996b:18) argues that Crooks was a good friend of the two marshals who were killed and thus should have disqualified himself.

9. We wish to thank Mrs. David (Katja) Lane for providing material on this issue.

10. We can only highlight selected parts of this story, but we recommend the book *Every Knee Shall Bow* by Jess Walter (1995). Our interpretation is mainly based on this book, the testimony before the Senate Subcommittee on Terrorism, Technology, and Government (shown on C-Span) in September and October 1995, and our informal discussions in Spokane with Tom Grant of KREM TV 2 and Bill Morlin and Jess Walter of the *Spokane Spokesman-Review* and in Sandpoint, Idaho, with Kevin Keating of the *Idaho Spokesman-Review*. The Bock (1995) book is also a valuable source on Ruby Ridge. Walter's book provided the basis for the CBS miniseries "Ruby Ridge: An American Tragedy." Johnson (1996:3) favorably reviewed the mini-

series, including the following statement about the screenwriter; Randy Quaid, who portrayed Randy Weaver; and Laura Dern as Vicki Weaver: "It is a measure of the skills of Dern and Quaid, and the careful storytelling of screenwriter Lionel Chetwynd and director Roger Young, that even when the couple have their children march like little Nazis in front of the house of neighbors they're feuding with, you never see them as anything less than human." Some movement supporters, on the other hand, were critical of how members of the Weaver family were portrayed, including the children's "march" on their neighbors' house. Randy Weaver (Jubilee Radio Network Newslight Program 1996) expressed his concern over this and commented that the movie had just enough truth in it to legitimize the entire program. He is planning to work with someone on a book giving his portrayal of what happened.

11. The Department of Justice hasn't released significant reports or documents to assess responsibility. However, according to CS (1995), the internal Justice Department investigation done by representatives of the Office of Professional Responsibility and the Criminal Division was acquired by *Legal Times* and posted on the Internet. It evidently indicated BATF was not involved in entrapping Weaver and that there was no proof the shooting of Sammy Weaver was more than an accident. The report also concluded that "certain portions of these rules [of engagement issued at Ruby Ridge] not only departed from the FBI's standard deadly force policy but also contravened the Constitution of the United States." The rules were imprecise and "may have created an atmosphere that encouraged the use of deadly force thereby having the effect of contributing to an unintentional death." Further, the firing of the bullet that killed Vicki Weaver did not meet the "objective reasonableness" standard and the "internal FBI review of the shooting incident has not been sufficiently thorough and reached incorrect conclusions about the second shot" (CS 1995:16).

12. See Walter (1995) also for a discussion of the excellent legalwork not only of Gerry Spence but also of Chuck Peterson, Gary Gilman, and Kent Spence for Weaver and of David Nevin and Ellison Matthews for Kevin Harris. One can only speculate whether the outcome would have been different if these particular lawyers had not been involved in the case.

13. It was not until October 22, 1996, that a one-count felony information was filed against a former high-ranking FBI official, E.

Michael Kahoe, accusing him of obstructing justice by obliterating all signs of an internal "after action" critique of the events at Ruby Ridge. Kahoe pleaded guilty about one week later (Jackson 1996:A16). Gerry Spence, Weaver's attorney, commented: "The government needs to prosecute those who issued the rules of engagement that resulted in the death of these people" and "The federal government is good at diverting our attention from the real case and directing it toward the cover-up" (Associated Press 1996b:3A).

14. For example, Miller et al. (1993) found in their 1992 American National Election Study that to the question "How much of the time do you think you can trust the government in Washington to do what is right?," 71 percent said only some of the time, 25 percent said most of the time, and less than 3 percent said just about always. Less than 2 percent volunteered none of the time (n = 1,339). Almost two-thirds agreed somewhat or strongly that "public officials don't care much what people like me think" and more than half indicated "quite a few" of the people running the government are crooked. A smaller number (n = 683) were asked questions related to race. About 42 percent disagreed somewhat or strongly with the statement "Over the past few years, blacks have gotten less than they deserve" while about 35 percent agreed strongly or somewhat, and the other 22 percent neither agreed nor disagreed. Two-thirds of those surveyed agreed somewhat or strongly with the statement "Irish, Italians, Jewish and many other minorities overcame prejudice and worked their way up. Blacks should do the same without any special favors."

5. Political Mainstreaming: An Alternative to Protest and Violence

1. Dubiel (1986) discusses the difficulties of defining *populism,* which has become a "catch all" phrase for reactionary and grassroots movements.

2. We use the term *far right* interchangeably with the *racist right.*

3. See our earlier article (Dobratz and Shanks-Meile 1988) for a discussion of the linkages of white supremacy to American populism.

4. Phillips (1993:234–35) cites studies that suggest that Wallace's popularity in 1968 tripled and doubled from the 1972 figure to 35 percent in 1974 (18 percent supported Wallace for president and 17 percent would have been willing to cast a protest vote for Wallace).

The findings of Caddell, George McGovern's and Jimmy Carter's pollster, signaled the rise of "frustration politics" as a "growing number of people simultaneously favored radical socialist economic positions while backing a hard-line, even authoritarian position on social issues."

5. The White Citizens' Council was formed in the mid-1950s to fight integration (Zatarain 1990:77).

6. The White Citizens' Councils, like the John Birch Society, did not want to be associated with the Klan, so the regionwide Association of Citizens' Councils formed a separate branch from Asa Carter's Alabama Citizens' Council (Diamond 1995:70).

7. For a detailed account of the roles that George Wallace and the Klan played in fighting the racial integration at the University of Alabama, see Clark's *The Schoolhouse Door* (1995). Actions taken by Asa Carter and the Klan during the mob action against Autherine Lucy, the first African American to be admitted to the University of Alabama, are chronicled on pages 71–74.

8. Wallace and Carto denied their association through Asa Carter in public (Carter 1995:297). For the presidential election of 1968, Carto formed a "front group" called "Youth for Wallace," which was renamed the National Youth Alliance in 1969. It was an unsuccessful attempt by Carto to organize a "pro-Nazi campus" group (Diamond 1995:153).

9. Richard Nixon had Wallace and his associates investigated for corruption in an attempt to remove Wallace as a political contender. That investigation revealed that Asa Carter and Robert Shelton were paid through "a series of noncompetitive contracts with state government" (Carter 1995:300).

10. The White Citizens' Council supported Barry Goldwater as the Republican nominee in the 1964 presidential campaign (Zatarain 1990:81).

11. Since much of Duke's support came from white Democrats, the closed Republican primary process did not promote him as a candidate (Rose and Esolen 1992:243).

12. Gerhard Lauck had been extradited from Denmark and found guilty of disseminating illegal propaganda in Germany.

13. Conservatism, like liberalism, has had numerous variations over time and across societies. The dominant strain of conservatism in the mid-1900s opposed the New Deal. Two important recent varieties of conservatism that differ from each other in significant ways

are the New Right and the neoconservatives. Many of the neoconservatives are former New Deal Democrats and academics while New Rightists are "dyed-in-the-wool conservatives—though ones who are determined to appeal to wider constituencies than did the 'old' Right" (McKenna and Feingold 1995:xviii). The New Right maintains that they focus on the concerns of ordinary people and operate at the grassroots level. The New Right concentrates on family and moral issues such as abortion, pornography, and prayer in public schools. They believe the nation is in danger due to a breakdown in morals. Neoconservatives, on the other hand, concentrate more on global strategies and political economic structures. They support social reform but believe it has gone too far creating an "arrogant bureaucracy." They support the concept of equal opportunity but not equality of results (McKenna and Feingold 1995:xviii–xix). Shapiro (1986) pointed out that neoconservatives want to make government more cost-effective while old conservatives are interested in the nature of government and the meaning of documents like the Constitution. Traditional conservatives consider man's relationship to God and the truth of religion while neoconservatives view religion as needed for social stability. Both are concerned about the state encroaching on the private sector, favor broad distribution of private property and free enterprise, and support traditional morality.

14. The article was, by and large, sympathetic toward much of Buchanan's conservative agenda, since Judis is a senior editor for *The New Republic,* a long-standing New Right magazine.

15. In "We're Grass Roots People," *The Spotlight* referred to the article by Judis. "*The Spotlight* is a newspaper of choice among grassroots Buchanan supporters and Buchanan signals 'his sympathy if not his agreement' with the views of the Liberty Lobby" (*The Spotlight* 1995e:2). Judis (1995:234) noticed that *The Spotlight* was distributed at information tables that included Buchanan campaign workers selling T-shirts and his autobiography during rallies around the country.

6. Toward a Political Economy of White Supremacy

1. Though it can be said that the movement is potentially resurging, the suggestion that there is a great wave of movement activity and influence can also be questioned. Certainly racial issues and concerns are significant in this country, and the movement plays

a role in this. Yet this movement is so greatly stigmatized that one could argue it is currently difficult for it to attract a great deal of support. As Feagin and Vera (1995:161) point out, most white people reject that their views are similar to those of members of movement organizations: "One mechanism of sincere denial is distancing oneself from those whites who are considered to be racist, such as Klan members or skinheads, who are viewed as uneducated or psychologically disturbed." Staying in this stigmatized movement certainly requires a great deal of dedication and perseverance.

Numerical strength of the movement is difficult to evaluate. Some groups may well be growing and attracting new people, but others are fading. The harsh economic realities for a number of people and questionable governmental policies can provide a fertile ground for this movement to grow, and most of our movement participants believed that the movement was growing. Yet in any movement, supporters and members are often prone to exaggerate the impact of their movement. According to Goode and Ben-Yehuda (1994:120), "Exaggeration is a great deal more effective as a movement strategy than the complex task for literal, point-for-point truth telling." The opposition may also engage in such exaggeration to generate fear of and opposition to the movement itself. Such attention may detract from consideration of the broader issues concerning the racism that exists in our everyday lives and in our major institutions and the overall quality of life in our society.

2. "Security" for the 1993 Populist Party Conference in Chicago was provided by members of Thom Robb's KKKK. Art Jones of the ANP also tried to attend, but the Klan "security" denied him entry, which led to an altercation outside of the conference room. Some skinheads and members of other street brigades also attended the conference.

3. Diamond (1995:53) said that the John Birch society has been criticized as "extremist," but its "actual program was prototypically both right-wing and system supportive." However, John Birchers are opposed to government civil rights programs. From our interviews with white power activists, we found that some had participated in the John Birch society in the past. Since it shares some values with the far right and has served as a starting point for some movement members, we consider the John Birch Society and other similar groups as "bridger organizations" that link mainstream conservatism to the far right.

4. Metzger has added a videotape of Chomsky lectures to his sales list. It was highlighted in a flier that accompanied the October 1995 issue of *WAR*.

5. Pat Buchanan brought an entourage to the U.S.-Mexico border as a media event during his presidential campaign to present his anti-immigration views. Metzger said that he decided to join Buchanan on "his tour of the border." Buchanan and his aides, "dressed like Mormon missionaries from the Young Americans for Freedom, went crazy." Metzger said that Buchanan was "just trying to con us again like every politician who comes to the border." WAR produced a videotape of Buchanan's "border tour" that showed Metzger blocked from any real discourse as Buchanan's aides kept him in abeyance. They appeared angry at Metzger's persistence and frightened by the possibility of being seen as an ally.

6. At first, we did not recognize Tom Metzger because he was not wearing his toupee, which he had often worn for public appearances such as the filming of "Race and Reason" programs that air on public access channels across the country. Metzger commented that his now-deceased wife had preferred the toupee. It was ironic that as he was encouraging "lone wolves" to let their hair grow out to infiltrate "mainstream" society, he had shaved off what hair he had left.

7. The NSDAP/AO also utilizes the cell model with recognition by merit, not rank.

8. A few powerful people have been attracted to the movement throughout history. After receiving unmarked boxes of videotapes, cassettes, and reading materials, we learned that some people of means support the movement and wish to remain anonymous. One white separatist informant called them "subcomandos."

9. The rankings utilized the United Nations Development Programme's "Human Development Index," which measures social and economic well being.

10. Cassidy suggested that rising immigration was difficult to assess. He mentioned a 1990 study by Borjas that concluded that immigrants were one-fourth of high school dropouts. From that Cassidy (1995:122) argued that the growing supply of unskilled workers increased "downward pressure on the low paid."

11. The term *underclass* can be distinguished from the *new class*. Peery (1995:112) said that "those who coined the term underclass perhaps thought this was a group unable to keep up, and once falling behind and supported by welfare, consciously accepted an existence

outside" of employer and employee relations. However, the emerging definition of a "new class" argues that the unemployed were created by robotics, which led to "structural, permanent joblessness."

12. We are not suggesting that the plight of poor whites is greater than that of people of color, although there are a greater number of whites living in poverty. African Americans and Latinos receive attention from the media and social scientists, and the gross stereotypes generated about poor people of color are detrimental. However, we argue that poor whites in this society go largely unnoticed despite their large numbers, which is, in part, due to the invisibility of poverty in rural America.

13. The militia movement is often equated with white supremacy in popular press reports. SPLC (1994g:1, 4–8) reports have linked militia in some states to Klan, neo-Nazi, and skinhead organizations. While it is clear that overlapping memberships do exist, the militia movement prefers to identify itself as part of the growing "Patriot's" movement, which brings together a broader collection of ideologies and organizations to include some segments of the white power movement. Media images often equate organizations that, from the outside, appear to have much in common. However, in some cases, fine distinctions are made by insiders in terms of ideology and strategy that prohibit association with those out-groups.

14. Zald also predicted that economic decline would feed the antitax and antiwelfare movements on the "fringe of the Republican party and outside of it." What he did not expect was that the "fringe" would become mainstream Republicanism in the 1990s.

15. McAdam's work focuses especially on emerging social movements, but we believe these concepts are applicable as the white racialist movement has experienced cycles of growth, decline, and resurgence throughout history. He also stresses long-term socioeconomic changes, whereas we argue here that the changes in last 25 years or so have significantly influenced people and politics. For example, there has been no improvement in real median family income between 1969 and 1985. Although some indicators showed a movement toward greater equality after World War II, the 1970s marked the beginning of a reversal in these trends (Thompson 1990:88–89).

16. Relative deprivation can be defined as "deprivation or disadvantage measured not by objective standards but by comparison with the relatively superior advantages of others, such as members of a

reference group whom one desires to emulate" (Theodorson and Theodorson 1969:343).

17. David Lane was interviewed for more than two hours, yet none of his interview was aired in the television program. 14 Word Press distributed the full interview, which illustrated his remaining commitment to the ideas promoted by the Order during the 1980s.

Bibliography

Abramovitz, Mimi. 1992. "The Reagan Legacy: Undoing Class, Race and Gender Accords." *Journal of Sociology and Social Welfare* 19:91–110.

Ackridge, W. Lee. 1978. *The Ku Klux Klan: A Pictorial History*.

Adler, Margot. 1986. *Drawing Down the Moon*. Boston: Beacon Press.

Aho, James A. 1990. *The Politics of Righteousness: Idaho Christian Patriotism*. Seattle: University of Washington Press.

———. 1994. *This Thing of Darkness: A Sociology of the Enemy*. Seattle: University of Washington Press.

Alkalimat, Abdul. 1994. "Information Empowerment and Democracy in the 21st Century." *CYREV* Issue 1:12–14.

All the Way. 1996. "Buchanan, McManus Lean Toward Nationalist Views." February, 10 (2):2.

Allen, Paul. n.d. Untitled Letter That Accompanied Issue 68 of *NAAWP News*.

America First Party Inc. n.d. "Platform-America First Party." Smyrna, GA: America First Party Inc.

American Front. n.d.a. "Some Facts about Blacks."

———. n.d.b. "Whites Must Arm! It's a Jungle Out There."

———. n.d.c. "Capitalism Is Jewish and the Truth Is Anti-Semitic."

———. n.d.d. "Commonly Asked Questions and Answers Concerning the American Front."

———. n.d.e. "White Workers Who's on Your Side?"

American Research Institute. 1994. *The ARI Report: A Detailed Report of the American White Separatist Movement*. Knox, IN: American Research Institute.

Andrain, Charles and David Apter. 1995. *Political Protest and Social Change*. New York: New York University Press.

Anti-Defamation League. n.d.a. "Computerized Networks of Hate." New York: ADL.

———. n.d.b. *Extremist Groups in the United States: A Curriculum Guide*. New York: ADL.

———. 1982. *Hate Groups in America: A Record of Bigotry and Violence.* 1st ed. New York: ADL.
———. 1983. "The 'Identity Churches': A Theology of Hate." *ADL Facts* 28(1).
———. 1985a. "Propaganda of the Deed: The Far Right's Desperate Revolution." New York: ADL.
———. 1985b. "The Populist Party: The Politics of Right-Wing Extremism." *ADL Facts* 30, 2 (Fall).
———. 1987. "An ADL Special Report: The Hate Movement Today: A Chronicle of Violence and Disarray." New York: ADL.
———. 1988a. *Hate Groups in America: A Record of Bigotry and Violence.* 2d ed. New York: ADL.
———. 1988b. *Extremism on the Right.* New York: ADL.
———. 1990a. *Neo-Nazi Skinheads: A 1990 Status Report.* New York: ADL.
———. 1990b. "Pulpit of Bigotry: Ben Klassen and his Anti-Semitic 'Church.' " June, ADL.
———. 1993a. *Young Nazi Killers: The Rising Skinhead Danger.* July, New York: ADL.
———. 1993b. *Hitler's Apologists: The Anti-Semitic Propaganda of Holocaust "Revisionism."* New York: ADL.
———. 1993c. "The Church of the Creator: Creed of Hate." New York: ADL.
———. 1995. *The Skinhead International: A Worldwide Survey of Neo-Nazi Skinheads.* New York: ADL.
———. 1996. *Danger: Extremism.* New York: ADL.
Applebome, Peter. 1995. "Radical Right's Fury Boiling Over." *The New York Times,* April 23, p.13.
Army of Israel. n.d. "Smash the New World Order."
———. 1995a. "Life-The White Choice." *True Israelite* January 27 (5):1.
———. 1995b. "Price of Beans." *True Israelite* February 16 (6):2.
Aronowitz, Stanley and William DiFazio. 1994. *The Jobless Future.* Minneapolis, MN: University of Minnesota Press.
The Aryan Militant. n.d. "The Difference" (quotation of Joseph Tommasi).
Aryan Nations. n.d.a. "Aryan Nations."
———. n.d.b. "Theopolitical Platform."
———. n.d.c. "Platform for the Aryan National State."
———. n.d.d. "This Is Aryan Nations."
Aryan Youth Movement White Student Union. n.d. "Our New President." p. 3.
Ash, Roberta. 1972. *Social Movements in America.* Chicago: Markham Publishing Company.
Associated Press. 1995. "Neo Nazi from Nebraska Arrested in Copenhagen." *Rockford Register Star,* March 24, p. 5A.
———. Berlin (Nexus). 1996a. "Jewish Groups Criticize Judge." January 12.
———. 1996b. "Ex-FBI Manager Accused of Destroying Key Memo Evaluating Weaver Siege." *Des Moines Register,* October 23, p. A3.

Atkins, Stephen. 1992. *Terrorism: A Reference Handbook*. Santa Barbara, CA: ABC-CLIO, Inc.

Barker, William E. 1993. *Aryan America: Race, Revolution, and the Hitler Legacy*. St. Maries, ID: Falcon Ridge Publishing.

Barkun, Michael. 1989. "Millenarian Aspects of White Supremacist Movements." *Terrorism and Political Violence* 1:409–434.

———. 1990. "Racist Apocalypse: Millennialism on the Far Right." *American Studies* 31 (Fall):121–40.

———. 1994. *Religion and the Racist Right: The Origins of the Christian Identity Movement*. Chapel Hill, NC: The University of North Carolina Press.

Barney, Doug. 1996. "Web of Hate: White Separatists Leap on the 'Net." *Network World* January 8, 13 (2):1, 8.

Barnum, David. 1982. "Decision Making in a Constitutional Democracy: Policy Formation in the Skokie Free Speech Controversy." *Journal of Politics* 44:480–507.

Bates, Eric. 1989. "New Blood for the Old Order." *Southern Exposure* Spring, 53–54.

Baumgardner, John. n.d. "The Movement and the Resistance."

Baxter, William. n.d. "Unlikely Alliance: Black Activist and Klan Unite against the System." *The Klansman* 1 (1):1–13.

Beam, Louis R. 1982. *The Klansman's Handbook*. Hayden Lake, ID: Aryan Nations.

———. 1983. *Essays of a Klansman*. Hayden Lake, ID: A.K.I.A. Publications.

———. 1992. "Leaderless Resistance." *The Seditionist* February 12:1–7.

Becker, Howard. 1963. *Outsiders*. New York: Free Press.

Bell, Leland. 1973. *In Hitler's Shadow: The Anatomy of American Nazism*. Port Washington, NY: National University Publications Kennikat Press.

Bellant, Russ. 1991a. *The Coors Connection*. Boston: South End Press.

———. 1991b. *Old Nazis, the New Right, and the Republican Party*. Boston: South End Press.

Benford, Robert D. 1994. "Social Movements." Pp. 1880–87 in *Encyclopedia of Sociology*, vol. 4, edited by Edgar F. Borgatta and Marie L. Borgatta. New York: Macmillan.

Bennett, David H. 1995. *The Party of Fear*. 2d ed. New York: Vintage Books.

Berlet, Chip. 1992. "Right Woos Left." Political Research Associates: Cambridge, MA.

———. 1995. "Anatomy of the Right." *The Progressive* 59 (12):40–42.

Berlet, Chip, and Matthew N. Lyons. 1995. "Militia Nation." *The Progressive* 59 (6):22–25.

Berlet, Chip and Margaret Quigley. 1995. "Theocracy & White Supremacy: Behind the Culture War to Restore Traditional Values." Pp. 15–43 in *Eyes Right! Challenging the Right-Wing Backlash*, edited by Chip Berlet. Boston: South End Press.

Best, Joel. 1989. *Images of Issues*. New York: Aldine De Gruyter.

Betz, Hans-Georg. 1994. *Radical Right-Wing Populism in Western Europe*. New York: St. Martin's.

Billig, Michael. 1978a. "Patterns of Racism: Interviews with National Front Members." *Race and Class* 20 (2):161–79.

———. 1978b. *Fascists: A Social Psychological View of the National Front*. London: Academic Press.

Blair, Mike. 1996. "Rules Were Stacked against Buchanan." *The Spotlight* 22 (12):5.

Blee, Kathleen. 1991. *Women of the Klan: Racism and Gender in the 1920s*. Berkeley: University of California Press.

Blood and Honor. n.d. No title, Issue 1, p. 2.

———. 1994a. "Interview with George Hawthorne of RAHOWA." Mar/Apr., 5:4–5.

———. 1994b. "Interview with Bill Farley of New Minority." July/August, 7:9.

———. 1994c. "Interview with Joe of Nordic Thunder." Mar/Apr., 5:9.

Blood and Honour. 1994. "The Cause Continues in the Name of Ian Stuart." Spring, 16:n.p.

Blum, John, Bruce Catton, Edmund Morgan, Arthur Schlesinger Jr., Kenneth Stampp, and C. Vann Woodward. 1963. *The National Experience*. New York: Harcourt, Brace and World, Inc.

Blumberg, Rhoda Lois. 1984. *Civil Rights: The 1960s Freedom Struggles*. Boston: Twayne Publishers.

Bobo, Lawrence. 1983. "Whites' Opposition to Busing: Symbolic Racism or Realistic Group Conflict." *Journal of Personality and Social Psychology* 45:1196–210.

Bock, Alan. 1995. *Ambush at Ruby Ridge*. Irvine, CA: Dickens Press.

Boggs, Carl. 1986. *Social Movements and Political Power: Emerging Forms of Radicalism in the West*. Philadelphia: Temple.

Booth, William. 1994a. "Surprise Testimony Finishes Prosecution's Beckwith Case." *The Washington Post* February 2, vol. 117, p. A2.

———. 1994b. "Beckwith Convicted of Murdering Evers." *The Washington Post* February 6, vol. 117, pp. A1, A21.

Bowser, Benjamin P. and Raymond G. Hunt. 1996. *Impacts of Racism on White Americans*. 2d ed. Thousand Oaks, CA: Sage.

Brake, Mike. 1974. "The Skinheads: An English Working Class Subculture." *Youth and Society* 6:179–200.

Bridges, Tyler. 1994. *The Rise of David Duke*. University Press of Mississippi: Jackson, MS.

Brogan, Robert "The Celt". 1995. "Skinhead Idealism." *Rise* Summer/Fall, IV:4.

Brown, Richard Maxwell. 1989. "Historical Patterns of Violence." Pp. 23–61 in *Violence in America Protest, Rebellion, Reform*, vol. 2, edited by Ted Robert Gurr. Newbury Park: Sage.

Buechler, Steven M. 1993. "Beyond Resource Mobilization? Emerging Trends in Social Movement Theory." *The Sociological Quarterly* 34:217–35.

———. 1997. "New Social Movement Theories." Pp. 295–325 in *Social Movements: Perspectives and Issues,* edited by Steven M. Buechler and F. Kurt Cylke Jr. Mountain View, CA: Mayfield Publishing Co.

Butler, Richard. n.d. " 'Christian Identity'—'National Socialism' 'Odinism': Is There a Connection? Essay Introduction." *Aryan Nations Newsletter* 83:1.

Butz, Arthur. 1976. *The Hoax of the Twentieth Century.* Chapel Ascote: Historical Review Press.

Canedy, Susan. 1990. *America's Nazis: A Democratic Dilemma.* Menlo Park, CA: Markgraf Publications Group.

Carter, Dan T. 1995. *The Politics of Rage: George Wallace, the Origins of the New Conservatism, and the Transformation of American Politics.* New York: Simon & Schuster.

Carto, Willis A. (ed.) 1996. *Populism vs. Plutocracy: The Universal Struggle.* Washington, DC: Liberty Lobby.

Cassidy, John. 1995. "Who Killed the Middle Class?" *The New Yorker,* October 16, pp. 113–14, 116, 118–24.

Cell, John W. 1982. *The Highest Stage of White Supremacy: The Origins of Segregation in South Africa and the American South.* Cambridge: Cambridge University Press.

Center for Democratic Renewal. n.d.a. *Ballot-Box Bigotry: David Duke and the Populist Party- Background Report #7.* Atlanta, GA.

———. n.d.b. *Internal Document.*

———. 1992. *When Hate Groups Come to Town: A Handbook of Effective Community Responses.* 2d ed. Atlanta, GA.

———. 1996. *The Changing Faces of White Supremacy.* Atlanta: CDR.

Chalmers, David M. 1981. *Hooded Americanism.* New York: New Viewpoints.

———. 1987. *Hooded Americanism: The History of the Ku Klux Klan.* Durham, NC: Duke University Press.

Chapman, Stephen. 1992. "Pat Buchanan in Hot Pursuit of the Segregationist Vote." *Chicago Tribune,* March 8, section 4, p. 3.

Chomsky, Noam. 1995. "Letter from Noam Chomsky." *Covert Action Quarterly* 54(2):25–30.

The Christian Guard. n.d. "Who Is Legitimate Israel." *Dispatch 76.*

Clan Rook. n.d. "Clan Rook."

Clark, E. Culpepper. 1995. *The Schoolhouse Door: Segregation's Last Stand at the University of Alabama.* New York: Oxford University Press.

Clerkin, Major Donald V. 1989. "Essay—The Coming Aryan Republic." *Euro-American Quarterly* X(3):1–6.

———. 1996. "ANTI-TERRORISM." *The Talon* 20 (236, June):1–3.

Clinard, Marshall B. and Robert F. Meier. 1992. *Sociology of Deviant Behavior.* Fort Worth, TX: Harcourt Brace Jovanovich College Publishers.

Coates, James. 1987. *Armed and Dangerous*. New York: Hill and Wang.

Colvin, Rod. 1992. *Evil Harvest*. New York: Bantam Doubleday Dell Publishing Group.

Comparet, Bertrand L. n.d.a. *Your Heritage: An Identification of the True Israel through Biblical and Historic Sources.*

———. n.d.b. *The Cain-Satanic Seed Line*. Hayden Lake, ID: Church of Jesus Christ Christian.

Cooper, Marc. 1995. "Montana's Mother of All Militias." *The Nation* 260 (20):714–21.

Coplon, Jeff. 1988. "Skinhead Nation." *Rolling Stone*, December 1, pp. 50–65, 94.

———. 1989a. "The Skinhead Reich." *Utne Reader,* May/June, pp. 80–89.

———. 1989b. "The Roots of Skinhead Violence: Dim Economic Prospects for Young Men." *Utne Reader,* May/June, p. 84.

Corcoran, James. 1990. *Bitter Harvest: Gordon Kahl and the Posse Comitatus: Murder in the Heartland*. New York: Penguin Books.

Crawford, Robert, S. L. Gardner, Jonathan Mozzochi, and R. L. Taylor. 1994. *The Northwest Imperative: Documenting a Decade of Hate*. Portland, OR: Coalition for Human Dignity.

Crenshaw, Martha. 1992. "Current Research on Terrorism: The Academic Perspective." *Studies in Conflict and Terrorism* 15:1–11.

Croteau, David. 1995. *Politics and the Class Divide*. Philadelphia: Temple University Press.

Crusade Against Corruption. n.d. "Who Needs AIDS-Carrying Haitian Niggeros?" Marietta, GA: Crusade Against Corruption.

CS. 1995. "Justice at Ruby Ridge." *Liberty* September:15–16.

David Duke Report. 1993a. "Boas, Too, Had a Dream!" *David Duke Report,* February:4–5.

———. 1993b. "Best Laid schemes o' Liberals and Lobbyists." January:1.

Davidson, Osha Gray. 1990. *Broken Heartland: The Rise of America's Rural Ghetto*. New York: Free Press.

Davis, James F. 1978. *Minority-Dominant Relations: A Sociological Analysis*. Arlington Heights, IL: AHM Publishing Corporation.

Davis, Nanette J. and Clarice Stasz. 1990. *Social Control of Deviance: A Critical Perspective*. New York: McGraw-Hill.

DeCamp, John W. 1992. *The Franklin Cover-Up: Child Abuse, Satanism, and Murder in Nebraska*. Lincoln NE: AWT, Inc.

———. 1996a. "Statement of Facts to Supplement Motion Under 28 U.S.C. Section 2255 to Vacate, Set Aside, or Correct Sentence." *United States of America vs. Yorie Von Kahl, Movant*. United States District Court for the District of North Dakota.

———. 1996b. "Docket No. C3–83–16(3) Motion Under U.S.C. Section 2255 to Vacate, Set Aside, or Correct Sentence." *United States of America vs.*

Yorie Von Kahl, Movant. United States District Court for the District of North Dakota.

———. 1996c. "Memo from John W. DeCamp, Attorney." April 19.

Dees, Morris and Steve Fiffer. 1993. *Hate on Trial*. New York: Villard Books (Division of Random House).

della Porta, Donatella. 1992. "Introduction: On Individual Motivations in Underground Political Organizations." Pp. 3–38 in *International Social Movement Research,* edited by Donatella della Porta. Greenwich, CT: JAI Press.

DeSilva, Frank. 1996. "Staying the Distance." World Wide Web Aryan Re-education Links, Independent White Racialist Home Page (copied June 22).

Diamond, Sara. 1995. *Roads to Dominion: Right-Wing Movements and Political Power in the United States*. New York: Guilford Press.

Diani, Mario. 1992. "The Concept of Social Movement." *The Sociological Review* 40:1–25.

Dixon, Th.D., Richard. 1996. Personal Correspondence Dated March 18.

Dionne Jr., E. J. 1991. *Why Americans Hate Politics*. New York: Simon & Schuster.

Dobratz, Betty A. and Stephanie L. Shanks-Meile. 1988. "The Contemporary Ku Klux Klan and the American Nazi Party: A Comparison to American Populism at the Turn of the Century." *Humanity and Society* 12:20–50.

———. 1995. "Conflict in the White Supremacist/Racialist Movement in the U.S." *International Journal of Group Tensions* 25:57–75.

Dollars and Sense. 1987. "Even Young Men Feel the Pinch." *Dollars and Sense,* November:10–11.

———. 1992. "U.S. Among Worst in Inequality." *Dollars and Sense,* July/August:23.

Doridio, John F. and Samuel L. Gaertner. 1986. *Prejudice, Discrimination, and Racism*. Orlando: Academic Press, Inc.

Dubiel, Helmut. 1986. "The Specter of Populism." *Berkeley Journal of Sociology* 31:79–91.

Duke, David. 1996. "Duke U.S. Senate correspondence." May 6 (personalized form letter).

Dutt, R. Palme. 1934. *Fascism and Social Revolution*. New York: International Publishers.

Easterbrook, Gregg. 1994. "The Case against the Bell Curve." *The Washington Monthly,* December:17–25.

Eastern Hammer Skinheads. n.d. "Definitions Every White Man Should Know."

Egerton, John. 1994. *Speak Now against the Day: The Generation Before the Civil Rights Movement in the South*. New York: Knopf.

Ehrenreich, Barbara. 1989. *Fear of Falling*. New York: HarperCollins.

Eisinger, Peter K. 1973. "The Conditions of Protest Behavior in American Cities." *American Political Science Review* 67:11–28.

Empire Publishing. n.d. “An Introduction to the Invisible Empire Knights of the Ku Klux Klan.” Denham Springs, LA.

Esolen, Gary. 1992. “More Than a Pretty Face: David Duke's Use of Television as a Political Tool.” Pp. 136–55 in *The Emergence of David Duke and the Politics of Race*, edited by Douglas Rose. Chapel Hill, NC: University of North Carolina Press.

Everett, Kevin Djo. 1992. “Professionalization and Protest: Changes in the Social Movement Sector, 1961–1983.” *Social Forces* 70:957–75.

EXTRA! 1992. “Buchanan and Duke: Playing the Same Hand.” EXTRA! March:11–12.

Ezekiel, Raphael S. 1995. *The Racist Mind: Portraits of American Neo-Nazis and Klansmen*. New York: Viking/Penguin.

Feagin, Joe R. 1971. “White Separatists and Black Separatists: A Comparative Analysis.” *Social Problems* 19:167–80.

Feagin, Joe R. and Hernán Vera. 1995. *White Racism*. New York: Routledge.

Federation of Klans (FOK). n.d. “An Introduction to the Federation of Klans, Knights of the Ku Klux Klan.”

Fields, E. R. 1983. “Dr. Fields' Economic Plan to Save the American Standard of Living, Jobs, and Prosperity.” *Thunderbolt* 288 (May):10.

Finch, Phillip. 1983. *God, Guts, and Guns*. New York: Seaview/Putnam.

Fischer, Claude S., Michael Hout, Martin Sánchez Jankowski, Samuel R. Lucas, Ann Swidler, and Kim Voss. 1996. *Inequality by Design: Cracking the Bell Curve Myth*. Princeton: Princeton University Press.

Fisher, Robert. 1984. *Let the People Decide*. Boston: Twayne Publishers.

Fishman, Walda Katz. 1981. “Right-Wing Reaction and Violence: A Response to Capitalism's Crises. *Social Research* 48:157–82.

Florida Black Knights of the KKK. n.d. “Florida Black Knights of the KKK: United Brotherhood of Unreconstructed Klansmen 10%ers.”

Florida Interklan Report. 1995a. “A People Without Hate Cannot Triumph Over a Brutal Enemy.” April:1–2.

———. 1995b. “Militia Warning.” January:1.

———. 1995c. “Garcia Truckin' On.” September:3.

———. 1995d. “Quotes from Che.” January:4.

———. 1995e. “Klan Militia Acquires Training Ground.” September:3.

———. 1996a. “Klansmen Attend Black Radical Meeting.” June:1–2.

———. 1996b. “More Criticism.” June:3.

Flowers, Stephen E. 1981. “Revival of Germanic Religion in Contemporary Anglo-American Culture.” *The Mankind Quarterly* 21:279–94.

Flynn, Kevin and Gary Gerhardt. 1989. *The Silent Brotherhood: Inside America's Racist Underground*. New York: The Free Press.

———. 1995. *The Silent Brotherhood: The Chilling Inside Story of America's Violent Anti-Government Militia Movement*. New York: The Free Press.

Frank, Arthur W. III, Richard Lachmann, David W. Smith, Janice V. Swenson,

Richard Wanner, and Alan Wells. 1986. *The Encyclopedic Dictionary of Sociology*. Guilford, CT: Dushkin Publishing.

Fried, John H. E. 1980. "Swastika." P. 677 in *Colliers Encyclopedia,* vol. 21, edited by William D. Halsey and Emanuel Friedman. New York: Macmillan.

Fruhling, Larry. 1992. "Klan Polishes a New Image to Sell Message in TV Age." *Des Moines Register,* January 19, p. 5A

Fyfe, Hamilton. 1994. "The Holocaust and the New World Order." *America's Promise Newsletter* May:37–41.

Gaines, Donna. 1991. *Teenage Wasteland*. New York: Harper Perennial.

Gamson, W. 1975. *The Strategy of Social Protest*. Homewood, IL: Dorsey.

George, John and Laird Wilcox. 1992. *Nazis, Communists, Klansmen, and Others on the Fringe*. Buffalo, NY: Prometheus Books.

———. 1996. *American Extremists: Militias, Supremacists, Klansmen, Communists, and Others*. Amherst, NY: Prometheus Books.

Gibson, James William. 1994. *Warrior Dreams*. New York: Hill and Wang.

Gilbert, Dennis and Joseph Kahl. 1993. *The American Class Structure*. Belmont, CA: Wadsworth.

Gill, Molly. 1993. "Racism Is Not a Bad Word." *Anarchy: A Journal of Desire Armed* Spring:77–78.

Gilliam, Dorothy. 1984. "KKK Support." *Washington Post,* April 23, p. D1.

Gladwell, Malcolm. 1995. "Fundamental Ignorance about Numbers." *Washington Post National Weekly Edition,* October 16–22, pp. 7–10.

Glock, Charles and Rodney Stark. 1966. *Christian Beliefs and Anti-Semitism*. New York: Harper & Row.

Goffman, Erving. 1959. *The Presentation of Self in Everyday Life*. Garden City: Doubleday.

———. 1963. *Stigma*. Englewood Cliffs: Prentice-Hall.

Goldberg, Robert A. 1981. *Hooded Empire: The Ku Klux Klan in Colorado*. Urbana: University of Illinois Press.

———. 1991. *Grassroots Resistance: Social Movements in Twentieth Century America*. Belmont, CA: Wadsworth.

Goldstick, Danny. 1991. "Defining Terrorism." *Nature, Society, and Thought* 4:261–66.

Goode, Erich and Nachman Ben-Yehuda. 1994. *Moral Panics*. Cambridge, MA: Blackwell Publishers.

Goodman, Walter. 1968. *The Committee: The Extraordinary Career of the House Committee on Un-American Activities*. New York: Farrar, Straus and Giroux.

Gordon, Paul and Francesca Klug. 1985. *New Right New Racism*. London, England: Searchlight Publications.

Gove, Philip Babcock, ed. 1967. *Webster's Third New International Dictionary*. Springfield, MA: G. & C. Merriam Company.

The Governor's Racial, Religious and Ethnic Intimidation Advisory Committee, National Institute Against Prejudice and Violence, Maryland State Police, Coalition Opposed to Violence and Extremism, and Community Relations Service. U.S. Department of Justice. 1990. "Report on Roundtable Discussion on Skinheads." November 20.

Graham, Hugh Davis and Ted Robert Gurr, eds. 1979. *Violence in America.* Beverly Hills: Sage.

Grassley, Charles E. 1995. "Statement of Senator Charles E. Grassley Senate Committee on the Judiciary Subcommittee on Terrorism, Technology and Government Information, 'Ruby Ridge Investigation' " September 6 (obtained from Senator Grassley's office).

Griffin, Roger. 1995. *Fascism.* New York: Oxford University Press.

Grill, Johnpeter and Robert Jenkins. 1992. "The Nazis and the American South in the 1930's: A Mirror Image?" *The Journal of Southern History* 58:668–94.

Guillory, Ferrel. 1992. "David Duke in Southern Context." Pp. 1–11 in *The Emergence of David Duke and the Politics of Race*, edited by Douglas Rose. Chapel Hill, NC: University of North Carolina Press.

Gurr, Ted Robert. 1989a. "The History of Protest, Rebellion, and Reform in America: An Overview." Pp. 11–22 in *Violence in America: Protest, Rebellion, Reform*, vol. 2, edited by Ted Robert Gurr. Newbury Park: Sage.

———. 1989b. "Political Terrorism: Historical Antecedents and Contemporary Trends." Pp. 201–230 in *Violence in America: Protest, Rebellion, Reform*, vol. 2, edited by Ted Robert Gurr. Newbury Park: Sage.

Hairston, Julie. 1989. "Southern Skinheads." *Southern Exposure* Spring:61–63.

Hale, Matt. n.d. "White Struggle Show #28 Creativity Not Nazism." Audiotape available from World Church of the Creator, East Peoria, IL.

———. 1995a. "A Hand Extended to All White Racial Comrades." *The Struggle* 2 (1) (July):1–3.

———. 1995b. "Creators Distribute Literature at Klan Rally." *The Struggle* 2 (5) (November):5.

———. 1996a. "It's Decided! MATT HALE—our Pontifex Maximus." *The Struggle* 9 (May):1.

———. 1996b. COTC Hotline, July 14.

———. 1996c. " 'The Right to Vote:'—The Most Ineffectual 'Right' We Have." *The Struggle* XV (September):1.

Hall, Paul. 1994. "The Way I See It . . . 'Hate Is Hate.' " *Jubilee* 7 (2) (September/October):2–3.

Hall, Stuart and Tony Jefferson, eds. 1976. *Resistance through Ritual: Youth Subcultures in Post War Britain.* London: Hutchinson.

Hamm, Mark S. 1993. *American Skinheads: The Criminology and Control of Hate Crime.* Westport, CT: Praeger.

Hardisty, Jean. 1995. "The Resurgent Right. Why Now?" *Public Eye* 9 (3/4):1, 3–13.

Harrington, W. 1992. *A White Man's Journey into Black America*. New York: HarperCollins.

Harris, Jerry and Carl Davidson. 1994. "The Cybernetic Revolution and the Crisis of Capitalism" *CYREV* 1:4–12.

Harris, Patricia Roberts. 1980. "Reagan, the Klan and a Critical Debate." *New York Times,* October 17, p. A30, Col. 5.

Harrison, Eric. 1990. "Diaries: Racist Fantasy or Primer for War of Hate?" *Los Angeles Times,* February 18, pp. A1, A25, A26.

———. 1994. "Beckwith's Fate Now in Hands of 3rd Jury." *Los Angeles Times,* February 5, p. A26.

Harwood, Richard. n.d. *Six Million Lost and Found* (also titled *Did Six Million Really Die?*). Chapel Ascote, Ladbroke, Southern Wasks: Historical Review Press.

Hawthorne, George Eric. n.d. "History in the Making." *Focus Fourteen* 611:1–3.

———. 1994. "Join the Resistance." *Resistance Magazine,* Spring: Inside front cover.

———. 1995. "The Illusion Is Over: Race and Intelligence." *Resistance Magazine,* Issue 3 (Winter), pp. 7, 26.

Hayhow, Matt. 1996. "False Ideas." *The Struggle* XIV (August):2.

Heberle, Rudolf. 1951. *Social Movements: An Introduction to Political Sociology*. New York: Appleton-Century-Crofts, Inc.

Hicks, John D. 1961. *The Populist Revolt: A History of the Farmer's Alliance and the People's Party*. Lincoln, NE: University of Nebraska Press.

Hill, Lance. 1992. "Nazi Race Doctrine in the Political Thought of David Duke." Pp. 94–111 in *The Emergence of David Duke*, edited by Douglas Rose. Chapel Hill, NC: University of North Carolina Press.

Hoffman, Bruce. 1989. "Terrorism in the United States: Recent Trends and Future Prospects." *Terrorism, Violence and Insurgency Report* 8:4–11.

Hoffman, Michael A. II. 1995. *The Great Holocaust Trial*. Dresden, NY: Wiswell Ruffin House.

Hofstadter, Richard. 1955. *The Age of Reform*. New York: Alfred A. Knopf.

Holocaust News. n.d. " 'Holocaust' Story an Evil Hoax." *'Holocaust' News* 1:1.

Hopfinger, Tony. 1996. "March Sparks Spectacle." *The Coeur d'Alene Press,* July 20, p. 7.

House on Un-American Activities Committee (HUAC). 1965. Hearings Before the Committee on Un-American Activities, House of Representatives First and Second Sessions. Washington D.C. (Microfilm supplied by U.S. Senator Grassley of Iowa.)

Howell, Susan E. and Sylvia Warren. 1992. "Public Opinion and David Duke." Pp. 80–93 in *The Emergence of David Duke*, edited by Douglas Rose. Chapel Hill, NC: University of North Carolina Press.

Hraba, Joseph, Richard Brinkman and Phyllis Gray-Ray. 1995. "A Comparison of Black and White Prejudice." Iowa State University, Ames, IA. Unpublished manuscript.

Instauration. 1992. "When Will We Get with It? Majority Vote Splitting Wins for Clinton." *Instauration* 18 (1):5.

International Separatist Front (ISF). n.d. Cards defining segregation and separation.

Invisible Empire, KKKK. n.d. "An Introduction to the Invisible Empire KKKK." (S. Vineland, NJ).

Jackson, Robert L. 1996. "FBI Official Pleads Guilty in Ruby Ridge Case." *Los Angeles Times,* October 31, p. A16.

Jacoby, Russell and Naomi Glauberman, eds. 1995. *The Bell Curve Debate.* New York: Random House.

Jenkins, Craig J. 1995. "Resource Mobilization Theory and the Study of Social Movements." Pp. 289–305 in *American Society and Politics: Institutional, Historical and Theoretical Perspectives*, edited by Theda Skocpol and John L. Campbell. New York: McGraw-Hill.

——— and Charles Perrow. 1977. "Insurgency of the Powerless: Farm Workers Movements (1946–1972)." *American Sociological Review* 42:249–68.

Jenkins, M. M. [1991] 1992. "Introduction." Pp. xi–xxvii in *Siege* by James Mason. Denver: Storm Books.

Jew Watch. n.d. "Negro Charged in 'Hate-Crime' Murders." *Jew Watch* Issue 45:1–4.

Johnson, Steve. 1996. "TV Review a Raspberry, She Gave." *Chicago Tribune,* Section 5 Tempo, May 17, pp. 1, 3.

Johnston, Hank, Enrique Laraña, and Joseph Gusfield. 1997. "Identities, Grievances, and New Social Movements." Pp. 274–319 in *Social Movements,* edited by Steven M. Buechler and F. Kurt Cylke Jr. Mountain View, CA: Mayfield Publishing Company.

Jones, Arthur J. 1993. "Leaderless Resistance: A Way to Fill ZOG's Jails." *The WAR Eagle* 1 (2):5–6.

Jones, James M. and Robert T. Carter. 1996. "Racism and White Racial Identity." Pp. 1–23 in *Impact of Racism on White Americans*, edited by Benjamin P. Bowser and Raymond G. Hunt, 2d ed. Thousand Oaks, CA: Sage.

Jordan, Colin. n.d. *A Great Idea-National Socialism Then and Now*. Lincoln, NE: New Order Publications.

Jost. 1993. "Revolutionary Fantasies." *The WAR Eagle* 1 (2):6.

Jubilee. 1996a. "Glossary of Lies." 8 (6):19.

———. 1996b. "The Mad Patter." 8 (4):6.

Jubilee Radio Network. 1996. "Interview with Randy Weaver on CBS Miniseries: Ruby Ridge, An American Tragedy." Newslight Program 103, May 25 (audiotape).

Judis, John B. 1995. "Taking Pat Buchanan Seriously. Seriously." *Gentlemen's Quarterly* 65(12):230–37, 250–52.

Jung, C. G. [1936] 1947. "Wotan." Pp. 1–16 in *Essays on Contemporary Issues,* by C. G. Jung. London: Kegan Paul.

Kahl, Yorie Von. 1989. "Yorie Von Kahl the Son of Martyred Hero Gordon Kahl Writes the Most Damning Indictment Ever Written to the Jew-Rented Prostitutes Called Senators and Congressmen of the USSA." *Aryan Nations Newsletter* 72:1–19.

Kaldenberg, Wyatt. 1996. "Cyber Hate Racism on the Internet: Editorial." *WAR* August:1–2.

Kaplan, Jeffrey. 1993. "The Context of American Millenarian Revolutionary Theology: The Case of the 'Identity Christian' Church of Israel." *Terrorism and Political Violence* 5:30–82.

———. 1994–1995. "The Reconstruction of the Ásatrú and Odinist Traditions." Parts 1–6. *THEOD Magazine* vol. 1 (2):10–13; (3):36–39; (4):28–33; vol. 2 (1):34–40; (2):36–45; (3):10–15.

Katz, Irwin, Joyce Wackenhut, and R. Glen Hass. 1986. "Racial Ambivalence, Value Duality, and Behavior." Pp. 35–60 in *Prejudice, Discrimination, and Racism*, edited by John F. Dovido and Samuel L. Gaertner. Orlando: Academic Press.

Katz, William Loren. 1986. *The Invisible Empire of the Ku Klux Klan: Impact on History*. Seattle: Open Hand Publishing Inc.

Kazin, Michael. 1992. Review Article "The Grass-Roots Right: New Histories of U.S. Conservatism in the Twentieth Century." *American Historical Review* 97:136–55.

———. 1995. *The Populist Persuasion: An American History*. New York: Basic Books.

Kerbo, Harold. 1991. *Social Stratification and Inequality*. New York: McGraw-Hill.

Kerling, Edward. 1995. "Whitey Revolutionary—An Incredible Journey." *WAR* December:8–9.

Kincheloe, Joe L., Shirley R. Steinberg, and Aaron D. Gresson III, eds. 1996. *Measured Lies: The Bell Curve Examined*. New York: St. Martin's Press.

Kinder, Donald R. and David O. Sears. 1981. "Prejudice and Politics: Symbolic Racism versus Racial Threats to the Good Life." *Journal of Personality and Social Psychology* 40:414–31.

King, Ronald. 1992. "On Particulars, Universals and Neat Tricks." Pp. 242–52 in *The Emergence of David Duke*, edited by Douglas Rose. Chapel Hill, NC: University of North Carolina.

King, Wayne. 1985. "Computer Network Links Rightist Groups and Offers 'Enemy' List." *New York Times*, February 15, p. A17.

Kitsuse, John I. 1980. "Coming Out All Over: Deviants and the Politics of Social Problems." *Social Problems* 28:1–13.

Klandermans, Bert. 1991. "The Peace Movement and Social Movement Theory." Pp. 1–39 in *International Social Movement Research*, vol. 3. Greenwich, CT: JAI Press Inc.

The Klansman. n.d. "The Ku Klux Klan Emerges Unified." *The Klansman* 2 (new format):1.

Klassen, Ben. 1973. *Nature's Eternal Religion*. Lighthouse Point, FL: The Church of the Creator.

———. 1992. *The White Man's Bible*. Milwaukee, WI: The Milwaukee Church of the Creator.

Klee, Earl. 1989. *Politics: An American Perspective*. Lake Oswego, OR: Circa Press.

Kleim, Milton. 1996. Communication on the Progressive Sociologists Network, September 26.

Kluegel, James R. 1990. "Trends in Whites' Explanations of the Black-White Gap in SES." *American Sociological Review* 55:513–25.

Kluegel, James R. and Lawrence Bobo. 1993. "Opposition to Race-Targeting." *American Sociological Review* 58:443–64.

Kluegel, James R. and Eliot R. Smith. 1982. "Whites' Beliefs about Blacks' Opportunity." *American Sociological Review* 47:518–32.

———. 1983. "Affirmative Action Attitudes: Effects of Self-Interest, Racial Affect, and Stratification Beliefs on Whites' Views." *Social Forces* 61:797–824.

———. 1986. *Beliefs about Inequality: Americans' Views of What Is and What Ought to Be*. New York: Aldine DeGruyter.

Knauerhase, Ramon. 1972. *An Introduction to National Socialism, 1920–1939*. Columbus OH: Bell & Howell Company.

Knights of the Ku Klux Klan (Harrison, AR). n.d.a. "Knights of the Ku Klux Klan."

———. n.d.b. "*An Introduction to the Knights of the Ku Klux Klan*."

Koehl, Matt. 1980. *Official Program National Socialist White People's Party*. Cicero, IL: National Socialist Publications.

Kourier 1993. "*Non Silba Sed Anthar!*" 3 (8):n.p.

Kühl, Stefan. 1994. *The Nazi Connection*. New York: Oxford University Press.

Kushnick, Louis. 1996. "The Political Economy of White Racism in the United States." Pp. 48–67 in *Impact of Racism on White Americans*, edited by Benjamin P. Bowser and Raymond G. Hunt. 2d ed. Thousand Oaks, CA: Sage.

Lane, David. n.d.a. "White Genocide Manifesto." St. Maries, ID: 14 Word Press.

———. n.d.b. "Dissension Within the Resistance." *Focus Fourteen* 506:1–2.

———. n.d.c. "Wotan's Volk." *Focus Fourteen* 509:1–2.

———. n.d.d. *Revolution by Number*. St. Maries, ID: 14 Word Press.

———. n.d.e. "Universalist Imperialism." *Focus Fourteen* 610:1–4.

———. n.d.f. "Untitled Speech Before Aryan Youth Assembly Given by Mrs. David Lane on April 20, 1996." *Focus Fourteen* 605:1–4.

———. n.d.g. *Wodensson in Verse*. St. Maries, ID: 14 Word Press.

———. n.d.h. "Now or Never." *Focus Fourteen* 609:1–5.

———. 1994a. *The Mystery Religions and the Seven Seals*. St. Maries, ID: 14 Word Press.

———. 1994b. *Auto-Biographical Portrait of the Life of David Lane and the 14 Word Press*. St. Maries, ID: 14 Word Press.

———. 1995. "Interview with Meredith Vieira, ABC News." August 30 (videotape provided by Mr. and Mrs. David Lane, 14 Word Press).

Langer, Elinor. 1990. "The American Neo-Nazi Movement Today." *The Nation* 251(3):82–107.

Langmuir, Gavin. 1990. *Toward a Definition of Antisemitism*. Berkeley and Los Angeles: University of California Press.

Larson, Viola. 1992. "Identity: A Christian Religion for White Racists." *Christian Research Journal* (Fall): 20–28.

Lauck, Gerhard (interview with Lars-Göran Hedengård). 1991. "*The NSDAP/AO and the National Socialist Movement in Germany Today.*" NSDAP/AO.

Lay, Shawn (ed.) 1992. *The Invisible Empire in the West: Toward a New Historical Appraisal of the Ku Klux Klan of the 1920s*. Urbana and Chicago: University of Illinois Press.

Leland, John and Gregory Beals. 1997. "In Living Colors." *Newsweek,* May 5, pp. 58–60.

Leuchter, Fred A. Jr. n.d. *The Leuchter Report: The End of a Myth*. Toronto: Samisdat Publishers Ltd.

Levin, Jack and Jack McDevitt. 1995. "Landmark Study Reveals Hate Crimes Vary Significantly by Offender Motivation." *Klanwatch Intelligence Report* August 79:7–9.

Lixfield, Hannjost. 1994. *Folklore and Fascism*. Edited and translated by James R. Dow. Bloomington and Indianapolis: Indiana University Press.

Lo, Clarence Y. H. 1982. "Countermovements and Conservative Movements in the Contemporary U.S." *Annual Review of Sociology* 8:107–34.

Lofton, John. 1985. *Protest: Studies of Collective Behavior and Social Movements*. New Brunswick: Transaction.

Lusane, Clarence. 1991. *Pipe Dream Blues*. Boston, MA: South End Press.

Lutz, Chris and Leonard Zeskind. 1987. *They Don't All Wear Sheets: A Chronology of Racist and Far Right Violence, 1980–1986*. The Division of Church and Society of the National Council of the Churches of Christ in the U.S.A.

Lyons, Matthew N. 1995. "What Is Fascism?" Pp. 244–45 in *Eyes Right! Challenging the Right Wing Backlash*, edited by Chip Berlet. Boston: South End Press.

Macdonald, Andrew. 1980. *The Turner Diaries*. Arlington, VA: National Vanguard Books.

MacLean, Nancy. 1994. *Behind the Mask of Chivalry: The Making of the Second Ku Klux Klan*. New York: Oxford University Press.

Mahon, Dennis. n.d. "Why I Indict Capitalism." *Race and Reality* 2 (1):5.

———. 1993. "Will God Save the Aryan Race?" *Race and Reason* Jan/Feb. 1 (3):1–11.

———. 1994. "What's All This C.R.A.P.?" *WAR* June:6.

Mann, A. W. n.d. *A. Wyatt Man Super Art Book.* Fallbrook, CA: White Aryan Resistance.

Marger, Martin N. 1987. *Elites and Masses: An Introduction to Political Sociology.* Belmont, CA: Wadsworth Publishing Company.

———. 1991. *Race and Ethnic Relations: American and Global Perspectives.* Belmont, CA: Wadsworth Publishing Company.

Margolis, Diane Rothbard. 1985. "Redefining the Situation: Negotiations on the Meaning of 'Woman'." *Social Problems* 32:332–47.

Marietta Daily Journal. 1994. "Resentencing Ordered for Former Klan Leader." May 26, Marietta, GA.

Martin, David. 1997. "The Midwest Bank Bandits." (Des Moines) *City View,* March 12, pp. 9–12.

Marty, Martin E. and R. Scott Appleby, eds. 1991. *Fundamentalisms Observed.* Chicago: University of Chicago Press.

Marx, Gary T. and Douglas McAdam. 1994. *Collective Behavior and Social Movements: Process and Structure.* Englewood Cliffs, NJ: Prentice-Hall.

Mason, James. 1992. *Siege.* Denver: Storm Books.

Massey, Douglas. 1995. "Review Essay of the Bell Curve: Intelligence and Class Structure in American Life." *American Journal of Sociology* 101:747–53.

Massey, Douglas S. and Nancy A. Denton. 1993. *American Apartheid.* Cambridge: Harvard University Press.

Mathews, Mitford M. (ed.) 1951. *A Dictionary of Americanisms.* Chicago: University of Chicago Press.

McAdam, Doug. 1982. *Political Process and the Development of Black Insurgency, 1930–1970.* Chicago: The University of Chicago Press.

———. 1988. "Micromobilization Contexts and Recruitment to Activism." Pp. 125–54 in *International Social Movements Research,* vol. 1, edited by Bert Klandermans, Hanspeter Kriesi, and Sidney Tarrow. Greenwich, CT: JAI Press.

———. 1994. "Culture and Social Movements." Pp. 36–57 in *New Social Movements,* edited by Enrique Laraña, Hank Johnston, and Joseph R. Gusfield. Philadelphia: Temple University Press.

———. 1996. "Conceptual Origins, Current Problems, Future Directions." Pp. 23–40 in *Comparative Perspectives on Social Movements,* edited by Doug McAdam, John D. McCarthy, and Mayer N. Zald. Cambridge, England: Cambridge University Press.

McAleer, Tony. 1995. "Plug into the Freedom of the Internet." *Resistance* 4 (Spring):13.

McClendon, McKee J. 1985. "Racism, Rational Choice, and White Opposition to Racial Change: A Case Study of Busing." *Public Opinion Quarterly* 49:214–33.

McConahay, John B. and Joseph C. Hough Jr. 1976. "Symbolic Racism." *Journal of Social Issues* 32(2):23–45.

McCullough, David. 1992. *Truman.* New York: Simon & Schuster.

McLaughlin, John. 1993. "Publisher's Note." *The WAR Eagle* 1 (2):6.

McKenna, George and Stanley Feingold. 1995. *Taking Sides: Clashing Views on Controversial Political Issues.* Gulford, CT: Dushkin Publishing.

McMahon, William B. 1992. "David Duke and the Legislature: 'A Mouth That's Different.' " Pp. 112–35 in *The Emergence of David Duke*, edited by Douglas Rose. Chapel Hill, NC: University of North Carolina Press.

McNallen, Stephen. 1994. "The Red Tribes Speak." *The Runestone* 9(Fall): 2–4.

Meet the Press. 1992. Interview with Pat Buchanan. January 12, volume 92. Silver Spring, MD: Kelly Press, Inc.

Mehus, David. 1992. "From the Dragon." *The Barricade* December, IV:1–2.

Melucci, Alberto. 1981. "Ten Hypotheses for the Analysis of New Movements." Pp. 173–194 in *Contemporary Italian Sociology,* edited by Diana Pinto. Cambridge, England: Cambridge University Press.

———. 1988. "Getting Involved: Identity and Mobilization in Social Movements." Pp. 329–348 in *International Social Movement Research*, vol. 1, edited by Bert Klandermans, Hanspeter Kriesi, and Sidney Tarrow. Greenwich, CT: JAI Press.

———. 1989. *Nomads of the Present.* London: Hutchinson Radius.

Metzger, Tom. n.d. White Aryan Resistance form letter to those receiving *WAR.*

———. 1993a. Hot Line (February 7).

———. 1993b. Hot Line (February 21).

———. 1995. "Editorial by Tom Metzger." *WAR* (July):2.

———. 1996a. "Racism and Racial Separation." *WAR* (May):11.

———. 1996b. Hot Line (June 9).

———. (assisted by Jack Carter). 1996c. *Biography of Tom Metzger.* (Obtained from Fallbrook, CA: White Aryan Resistance).

———. 1996d. Hot Line (May) (no date given on hot line).

———. 1996e. Hot Line (August 4).

Michels, Robert. 1959. *Political Parties.* New York: Dover Publications, Inc.

Miles, Robert. n.d.a. "The Identity of Dualism and the Duality of Identity." n.p.

———. n.d.b. *The Birth of a Nation: Declaration of the Existence of a Racial Nation within Confines of Hostile Political State.* Cohoctah, MI: Mountain Church.

———. 1983. "33/5 A Guide to Ritual with Proposed Adaptations to Fit the Needs of the Order in the 5th Era." *Mountain Church of Northern Ohio.*

Miller, Dean. 1992. "FBI Links Bullet That Killed Degan to Harris' Rifle." *The [Spokane] Spokesman Review,* September 16, pp. A1–A6.

Miller, Warren E., Donald R. Kinder, Steven J. Rosenstone, and the National Election Studies. 1993. AMERICAN NATIONAL ELECTION STUDY, 1992: PRE- AND

POST-ELECTION SURVEY [ENHANCED WITH 1990 AND 1991 DATA] [Computer file]. Conducted by University of Michigan, Center for Political Studies. ICPSR ed. Ann Arbor, MI: University of Michigan, Center for Political Studies, and Inter-university Consortium for Political and Social Research [producers], 1993. Ann Arbor, MI: Inter-university Consortium for Political and Social Research [distributor].

Mintz, Frank P. 1985. *The Liberty Lobby and the American Right: Race, Conspiracy, and Culture*. Westport, CT: Greenwood Press.

Misztal, Bornislaw and Anson Schupe, eds. 1992. *Religion and Politics in Comparative Perspective: Revival of Religious Fundamentalism*. Westport, CT: Praeger.

Moore, Jack B. 1993. *Skinheads Shaved for Battle: A Cultural History of American Skinheads*. Bowling Green, OH: Bowling Green State University Popular Press.

Moore, Leonard. 1990. Review Essay "Historical Interpretations of the 1920's Klan: The Traditional View and the Populist Revision." *Journal of Social History* 24:341–57.

———. 1991. *Citizen Klansmen*. Chapel Hill: University of North Carolina Press.

———. 1992. "Historical Interpretations of the 1920s Klan: The Traditional View and Recent Revisions." Pp. 17–38 in *The Invisible Empire in the West*, edited by Shawn Lay. Urbana and Chicago: University of Illinois Press.

Moore, William V. 1992. "David Duke: The White Knight." Pp. 41–58 in *The Emergence of David Duke and the Politics of Race*, edited by Douglas Rose. Chapel Hill, NC: University of North Carolina Press.

Morganthau, Tom, Michael Isikoff, and Bob Cohn. 1995. "The Echoes of Ruby Ridge." *Newsweek*, August 28, pp. 24–28.

Mosse, George L. 1964. *The Crisis of German Ideology*. New York: Grosset.

———. 1985. *Toward the Final Solution: A History of European Racism*. Madison: University of Wisconsin Press.

Murray, Valgard. 1995a. "An Open Letter to the Asatrú Community." *Vor Trú* 53:42–43.

———. 1995b. "Asatrú Is Not Universalist" (letter). *Vor Trú* 54:34–35.

National Alliance. n.d. "Information for Prospective Members of the National Alliance." Hillsboro, WV: National Alliance.

National Association for the Advancement of White People (NAAWP). 1980. "The NAAWP Program-Equal Rights for Whites." (flier): New Orleans, LA: NAAWP.

———. 1992a. "Why Is the NAAWP Necessary?" *NAAWP News* July, 66:6.

———. 1992b. "NAAWP vs. NAACP." *NAAWP NEWS* July, 66:6.

———. n.d.a. " 'Love' and 'Hate,' " *NAAWP NEWS* 41:1.

———. n.d.b. "100 Radio and Television Talk Shows Completed Since September." *NAAWP Action*:2–4.

———. n.d.c. "An Interview with David Duke." *NAAWP NEWS* 49:1, 8–9.

———. n.d.d. "Commentary." *NAAWP NEWS* 52:1

National Office of the National Alliance. 1993. "What Is the National Alliance?" Hillsboro, WV: National Vanguard Books.

National Socialist Front. 1992. "The Agenda." *The Barricade* (December) 4:2–3.

National Socialist Vanguard. 1989a. "Management About National Socialism (Naziism)." *NSV Report* 7 (4):1–2.

———. 1989b. "Operations: Louisiana." *NSV Report* 7 (1):1–3.

———. 1990. "Operations: Louisiana." *NSV Report* 8 (1):4–5.

———. 1993. "Brief History of the White Nationalist Movement." *NSV Report* 11 (4):1–8.

National Socialist White People's Party (NSWPP) (Copyrighted by Matt Koehl). 1980. *The Program of the National Socialist White People's Party.* Cicero, IL: NS Publications.

National Vanguard. 1994. "The New World Order, 'Free' Trade, and the Deindustrialization of America." *National Vanguard* (March-April) 113:3–12.

National Vanguard Books. 1991. "Who Rules America? The Alien Grip on Our News and Entertainment Media Must Be Broken." Catalog No. 13, Hillsboro, WV: National Vanguard Books:16–20.

———. 1993. "New World Order Comix #1." Hillsboro, WV: National Vanguard Books.

Neumann, Franz. 1942. *Behemoth: The Structure and Practice of National Socialism 1933–1944.* New York and Evanston: Harper & Row.

The New Christian Crusade Church. n.d. "Land of the ZOG: What Is ZOG?" *The CDL Report* 137:1–16.

———. 1992a. "Conflict at the Top: Who Will Control the New World Order?" *The CDL Report* 154:1–7.

———. 1992b. "The North American Free Trade Agreement: A Step Toward One World Government." *The CDL Report* 156:1–4.

———. 1993. "Order Extra Copies of This Issue." *The CDL Report* 160:16.

———. 1994. "Despite Mid-Term Election Results U.S. Congress and President Still Subservient to Israel." *The CDL Report* 174:1–3.

New Order (organization). n.d.a. "Principles of National Socialism."

———. n.d.b. "Help Save This Endangered Species."

———. 1992a. "Born-again Duke Rejects 'Nazism.'" *NS Bulletin* 327:1–6, 8.

———. 1992b. "No Compromise." *NS Bulletin* 327:1, 7–8.

Newton, Michael and Judy Ann Newton. 1991. *The Ku Klux Klan: An Encyclopedia.* New York: Garland Publishing.

Northern Hammer Skinheads (NHS). n.d. no title. *The Hammerskin* February, 3:n.p.

NS Kindred. n.d. "What Is National Socialism?" NSJ, CA: NS Kindred.

NSDAP/AO. n.d. "White Man, Fight Back! Join the NSDAP/AO."

———. 1989. “Action Program for Aryan Skinheads: Dedicated to David Lane.” *New Order* 82:1–10.

———. 1994a. “White Man, Fight Back! Join the NSDAP/AO.” *New Order* 111:8.

———. 1994b. “More Nigger Terror.” *New Order* 108:1.

———. 1995. “Free Gerhard!” *New Order* 116:1–2.

———. 1996. “Third Party Run?” *New Order* 123:4.

NSLF (National Socialist Liberation Front) Headquarters. n.d. “The Black Plague.” Metairie, LA.

Oklahoma WAR. 1992. “It’s Now WAR!” *The Oklahoma Excalibur* Mar./May:1–2.

Omi, Michael and Howard Winant. 1996. *Racial Formation in the United States: From the 1960s to the 1990s.* 2d ed. New York: Routledge.

O’Reilly, Kenneth. 1989. *“Racial Matters” The FBI’s Secret File on Black America, 1960–1972.* New York: The Free Press.

Peery, Nelson. 1995. Untitled Plenary Speech on a Panel called “Moving Forward: Seizing the Future.” Pp. 110–116 in *Job-Tech: The Technological Revolution and Its Impact on Society,* edited by Abdul Alkalimat, Douglas Gills, and Kate Williams. Chicago: Twenty-First Century Books and Publications.

People Against Racist Terror (PART). 1994. “Eco-Fascism: Environmentalism as Racism.” *Alternative Press Review* Winter:28--29.

Peters, Pete. n.d.a. “The Bible—Handbook for Survivalists, Racists, Tax Protestors, Militants and Right-Wing Extremists.” LaPorte, CO: Scriptures for America.

———. n.d.b. “The Real Hate Group.” LaPorte, CO: Scriptures for America.

———. n.d.c. “White Crime in America.” LaPorte, CO: Scriptures for America.

———. 1991. *America the Conquered.* LaPorte, CO: Scriptures for America.

Petersen, David. 1993. “Triumph of Capital.” *Z Magazine* 6(5):11–15.

Pettigrew, Thomas F. 1971. *Racially Separate or Together?* New York: McGraw-Hill.

Phillips, Kevin. 1993. *Boiling Point.* New York: HarperCollins.

———. 1994. *Arrogant Capital.* Boston: Little, Brown.

Pierce, William. 1991. Introduction and Afterward to “A Call to Arms” speech by Robert Mathews. Tape recording by National Vanguard Books, Hillsboro, WV.

———. 1993. “One More Word on ‘Leaderless Resistance.’ ” *The WAR Eagle* 1 (2):4.

———. 1996. “Why They Hate Pat Buchanan.” *Free Speech* 2 (3):1–5.

Piper, Michael Collins. 1996. “Buchanan Racks GOP’s Foundation.” *The Spotlight* 22 (8):1, 3.

Piven, Frances Fox and Richard Cloward. 1971. *Regulating the Poor.* New York: Vintage Books.

———. 1979. *Poor People's Movements*. New York: Vintage Books.

———. 1989. *Why Americans Don't Vote*. New York: Pantheon.

"Politicians Who Are Owned by 'The Jewish Lobby.' " n.d. distributed by The Christian Guard; for more information write *The Truth at Last*.

Populist Party. n.d. "The Populist Party of America: A Platform for the 1990s." Ford City, PA.

Powell, Lawrence N. 1992. "Slouching Toward Baton Rouge: 1989 Legislative Election of David Duke." Pp. 12–40 and 59–79 in *The Emergence of David Duke and the Politics of Race*, edited by Douglas Rose. Chapel Hill, NC: University of North Carolina Press.

Quinley, Harold E. and Charles Glock. 1979. *Anti-Semitism in America*. New York: Free Press.

Rackleff, Robert B. 1989. "Republicans and Racism: The GOP's Strategy Led Right to David Duke's Doorstep." *Washington Post,* February 26, p. C5, Col. 1.

Randal, Jonathan. 1996. "Germany Sentences U.S. Nazi to 4 Years." *Washington Post,* August 23, pp. A23–A24.

Rankin, Bill. 1994. "White Supremacist Faces Resentencing." *Atlanta Constitution*, May 25.

Rejai, Mostafa. 1984. *Comparative Political Ideologies*. New York: St. Martin's Press.

Remak, Joachim. 1957. " 'Friends of the New Germany' The Bund and German-American Relations." *Journal of American History* 29:38–41.

Resistance Magazine. 1994a. "Unstoppable. Resistance Records Forging a New Destiny for White Power Music." Spring, unnumbered:n.p.

———. 1994b. "A Word on Violence." Summer, 2:17.

———. 1995. "Band Sales Report." Fall, 5:49.

Revolutionary Nationalist. n.d. "The Decline of Western Civilization." Pp. 9, 12.

Reynolds, Ed. 1995. "The Future Awaits . . ." newsletter, January 11.

Ribuffo, Leo P. 1983. *The Old Christian Right: The Protestant Far Right from the Great Depression to the Cold War*. Philadelphia: Temple University Press.

Rice, Arnold S. 1972. *The Ku Klux Klan in American Politics*. New York: Haskell House Publishers Ltd.

Richert, Paul. 1993. "Vote Totals In—Gritz and Populist Party Soundly Defeat All Other Third Parties." *The Populist Observer* 83:1–3.

Rickey, Elizabeth A. 1992. "The Nazi and the Republicans: An Insider View of the Response of the Louisiana Republican Party to David Duke." Pp. 59–79 in *The Emergence of David Duke and the Politics of Race*, edited by Douglas Rose. Chapel Hill, NC: University of North Carolina Press.

Ridgeway, James. 1990. *Blood in the Face: The Ku Klux Klan, Aryan Nations, Nazi Skinheads, and the Rise of a New White Culture*. New York: Thunder's Mouth Press.

Rifkin, Jeremy. 1995. *The End of Work*. New York: G. P. Putnam's Sons.
Riley, Michael. 1992. "White & Wrong: New Klan, Old Hatred." *Time,* July 6, pp. 24–27.
Right as Reina. 1995. "Separatist Family Persecuted by Media in Rockford, IL." June:1.
Robb, Thom. 1990. "Is the Negro to Blame? An Editorial by Pastor Thomas Robb." *The Torch* April:3.
Robertson, Wilmot. 1992. *The Ethnostate*. Cape Canaveral, FL: Howard Allen Enterprises, Inc.
Rockford Register Star. 1994. "Cleaning Up After the Klan." June 13, p. 5A.
Rockwell, George Lincoln. 1966. "The Battle of Chicago." *The Rockwell Report* September/October:2–24.
———. 1977. *White Power*. Second printing.
Romine, Mr. and Mrs. W. B. 1934. "A Story of the Original Ku Klux Klan." Pulaski, TN: *The Pulaski Citizen*.
Rose, Douglas. 1992. "Six Explanations in Search of Support: David Duke's U.S. Senate Campaign." Pp. 156–196 in *The Emergence of David Duke*, edited by Douglas Rose. Chapel Hill, NC: University of North Carolina Press.
Rose, Douglas and Gary Esolen. 1992. "Duke for Governor: 'Vote for the Crook.'" Pp. 197–241 in *The Emergence of David Duke*, edited by Douglas Rose. Chapel Hill, NC: University of North Carolina Press.
Rosenthal, Steven J. 1994. "The Global Danger of Fascist Resurgence." *East-West Review* 1:14–27.
Ross, Jeffrey Ian. 1994. "The Psychological Causes of Oppositional Political Terrorism: Toward an Integration of Findings." *International Journal of Group Tensions* 24:157–85.
Ross, Loretta. 1995a. "Militia Nation: Saying It with a Gun." *The Progressive* 59 (6):26–27.
———. 1995b. "White Supremacy in the 1990s." Pp.166–81 in *Eyes Right! Challenging the Right Wing Backlash*, edited by Chip Berlet. Boston: South End Press.
Rubenstein, Richard E. 1989. "Rebellion in America: The Fire Next Time?" Pp. 307–28 in *Violence in America, vol. 2: Protest, Rebellion, Reform,* edited by Ted Gurr. Newbury Park, CA: Sage.
Rubin, Lillian B. 1994. *Families on the Fault Line: America's Working Class Speaks about the Family, the Economy, Race, and Ethnicity*. New York: Harper Perennial.
Ryan, Vince. 1995a. "America's True Beliefs." *The Spotlight* November 6:11.
———. 1995b. "Shame on Nord." *The Spotlight* December 25:14–15.
———. 1996a. "Reassessing Pat." *The Spotlight* 22 (22):18–19.
———. 1996b. "Pat: Form a New Party." *The Spotlight* 22 (13):17.
———. 1996c. "Plutocrats and Politics." *The Spotlight* 22 (6):18, 22.

Saloutos, Theodore. 1968. *Populism Reaction or Reform?* Huntington, NY: Robert E. Krieger Publishing Co.

Sannhet, Thor. 1993. "An Interview with Else Christensen and Postscripts Regarding Her Prison Sentence and the Demise of Her Publication *The Odinist.*" *Vor Trú* 49:5–30.

Savage, Rick (compiler). 1995. "Frequently Asked Questions and Answers on Israel-Identity," transmitted on the Internet February 27.

Schier, Frank. 1994. "A+ for Police F- for Protesters." *Rock River Times* June 16, vol. II (35):1–8.

Schmidt, Hans. 1993. "The Holocaust Museum: An Album of Agony." *GAN-PAC Brief* 129 (July):1–6.

Schulman, Steven. 1989. "Racism and the Making of the American Working Class." *International Journal of Politics, Culture, and Society* 2:361–66.

Schuman, Howard, Charlotte Steeh, and Lawrence Bobo. 1985. *Racial Attitudes in America.* Cambridge, MA: Harvard University Press.

Schur, Edwin. 1980a. "Comments and Postscript." Pp. 393–404 in *The Labelling of Deviance Evaluating a Perspective,* 2d ed., edited by Walter R. Gove. Beverly Hills, CA: Sage.

———. 1980b. *The Politics of Deviance: Stigma Contests and the Use of Power.* Englewood Cliffs: Prentice-Hall.

Schwartz, Mildred A. 1990. *A Sociological Perspective on Politics.* Englewood Cliffs, NJ: Prentice-Hall.

Scutari, Richard. 1995. "Hail the Order." *Focus Fourteen* 508. St. Maries, ID: 14 Word Press.

Sears, Eva. 1989. "Skinheads: A New Generation of Hate Mongers." *USA Today,* May, pp. 24–26.

Segré, Claudio G. 1993. "Fascism." Pp. 294–96 in *The Oxford Companion to Politics of the World,* edited by Joel Krieger. New York: Oxford University Press.

Seliger, M. 1976. *Ideology and Politics.* New York: The Free Press.

Seltzer, Rick and Grace M. Lopes. 1986. "The Ku Klux Klan: Reasons for Support or Opposition Among White Respondents." *Journal of Black Studies* 17(1):91–109.

Seymour, Cheri. 1991. *Committee of the States.* Mariposa, CA: Camden Place Communications, Inc.

Shapiro, Andrew L. 1992. *The Nation.* "We're Number One! (Really?)" April 27:552.

Shapiro, Edward. 1986. "Conservatism and Its Discontents." *The World and I* 1 (9):565:72.

Shaw, William. 1995. "Hate, Rattle and Roll." *Details* July:38–40, 42, 44, 47–48, 157.

Shibutani, Tamotsu and Kuan M. Kwan. 1965. *Ethnic Stratification: A Comparative Approach.* London: The Macmillan Company Collier-Macmillan Limited.

Sifry, Micah. 1993. "Anti-Semitism in America." *The Nation* 256(3):92–96.
Simpson, George and J. Milton Yinger. 1972. *Racial and Cultural Minorities: An Analysis of Prejudice and Discrimination*. New York: Harper & Row Publishers.
Simpson, J. A. and E. S. C. Weiner (preparers). 1989. *The Oxford English Dictionary*. Oxford: Clarendon Press, Volume XX.
"Skinheads." n.d. Obtained from archives, Political Research Associates dated 1989.
Sklar, Holly. 1992. "Imagine a Country." *Z Magazine* 5(11):21–23.
Skocpol, Theda and John L. Campbell, eds. 1995. *American Society and Politics: Institutional, Historical, and Theoretical Perspectives*. New York: McGraw-Hill.
Skogan, Wesley G. 1989. "Social Change and the Future of Violent Crime." Pp. 234–50 in *Violence in America, vol. 1: The History of Crime,* edited by Ted R. Gurr. Newbury Park, CA: Sage.
Smith, Bradley. n.d. *The Holocaust Controversy: The Case for Open Debate*. Visalia, CA: Committee for Open Debate on the Holocaust.
Smith, Brent L. and Kathryn D. Morgan. 1994. "Terrorists Right and Left: Empirical Issues in Profiling American Terrorists." *Studies in Conflict and Terrorism* 17:39–57.
Smith, Robert C. 1995. *Racism in the Post-Civil Rights Era: Now You See It, Now You Don't*. Albany: State University of New York Press.
Sniderman, Paul M. and Thomas Piazza. 1993. *The Scar of Race*. Cambridge, MA: Harvard University Press.
Snow, David A., E. Burke Rochford Jr., Steven Worden, and Robert D. Benford. 1986. "Frame Alignment Processes, Micromobilization, and Movement Participation." *American Sociological Review* 51:464–81.
Snow, David A. and Robert D. Benford. 1988. "Ideology, Frame Resonance and Participant Mobilization." *International Social Movement Research* 1:197–217.
———. 1997. "Master Frames and Cycles of Protest." Pp. 456–72 in *Social Movements: Perspectives and Issues*, edited by Steven M. Buechler and F. Kurt Cylke Jr. Mountain View, CA: Mayfield Publishing.
Snyder, Bryan. 1993. "Pop Austerity." *Dollars and Sense,* July/August, pp. 6–7, 20.
Southern Poverty Law Center. 1989. *A Decade Review 1980–1990 Hate Violence and White Supremacy*. Montgomery, AL: Southern Poverty Law Center.
———. 1991. *The Ku Klux Klan: A History of Racism and Violence*. Montgomery, AL: Southern Poverty Law Center.
———. 1992a. "Holland Gets Probation for Perjury Convictions." *Klanwatch Intelligence Report* August, 62:4.
———. 1992b. "Aryan Nations Showing Ominous Signs of Life." *Klanwatch Intelligence Report* April, 60:1–6.

———. 1992c. "Parade Permits: Message Cannot Dictate Cost." *Klanwatch Intelligence Report* August, 62:9.

———. 1993. "Church of the Creator In Turmoil Over Leadership Change." *Klanwatch Intelligence Report* April, 66:1–4.

———. 1994a. "A Neo-Nazi Legend Gears Up for One Last Hurrah." *Klanwatch Intelligence Report* April, 72:4–5, 8.

———. 1994b. "Law Enforcement Strategy." *Klanwatch Special Report* Spring:1–ix.

———. 1994c. "Federal Judge Breaks Up James Farrands' New Klan." *Klanwatch Intelligence Report* October, 75:7.

———. 1994d. "National Alliance Fastest Growing Neo-Nazi Organization in North America." *Klanwatch Intelligence Report* April, 72:1–6.

———. 1994e. "Aryan Nations Youth Festival Draws Largest Crowd of Skinheads in Years." *Klanwatch Intelligence Report* June, 73:7–8.

———. 1994f. "Ten Ways to Fight Hate." *Klanwatch Special Report* Spring:1–11.

———. 1994g. "Racist Extremists Exploit Nationwide Militia Movement." *Klanwatch Intelligence Report* December, 6:1, 4–8.

———. 1995a. "1994 Hate Group Count: Neo-Nazi Groups Multiply, Skinhead Groups Decline." *Klanwatch Intelligence Report* March, 77:10–11.

———. 1995b. "Neo-Nazi Skinhead Movement Declines in U.S." *Klanwatch Intelligence Report* March, 77:3.

———. 1995c. "Aryan Nations: A Long History of Hate and Violence." *Klanwatch Intelligence Report* March, 77:7.

———. 1995d. "Aryan Nations Stages Alarming Comeback in 1994." *Klanwatch Intelligence Report* March, 77:1, 5–7.

———. 1995e. "Over 200 Militias and Support Groups Operate Nationwide." *Klanwatch Intelligence Report* June, 78:1–2.

———. 1995f. "Pierce Sued for Profit from COTC Headquarters Sale." *SPLC Report* June, 25(2):4.

———. 1995g. "Hate Movement Shifts Tactics in 1994." *Klanwatch Intelligence Report* March, 77:9–11.

———. 1996a. "Active Hate Groups in 1995." *Klanwatch Intelligence Report* February, 81:4–7.

———. 1996b. "National Alliance: North America's Largest Neo-Nazi Group Flourishing." *Klanwatch Intelligence Report* May, 82:5–8.

———. 1996c. "Center Wins Judgment Against Neo-Nazi Leader." *SPLC Report* June, 26(2):1, 2.

———. 1996d. "Identity Rallies Draw Antigovernment Extremists." *SPLC Report* June, 26 (2):1, 3.

———. 1996e. *False Patriots*. Montgomery, AL: SPLC.

———. 1997a. "Too Busy to Hate." *Klanwatch Intelligence Report* 85 (Winter):17–18.

———. 1997b. "Active Hate Groups 1996." *Klanwatch Intelligence Report* 85 (Winter):19–22.

———. 1997c. "Skinhead Violence 'It's Come Back Again.' " *Klanwatch Intelligence Report* 85 (Winter):14–16.

Spector, Malcolm and John I. Kitsuse. 1977. *Constructing Social Problems.* Menlo Park, CA: Cummings.

Spence, Gerry. 1993. *From Freedom to Slavery.* New York: St. Martin's Press.

The Spotlight. 1995a. "Know-How Is Key to Victory." 21(52):6

———. 1995b. Untitled ad for Hot Bumper Stickers. 21(52):6.

———. 1995c. "Advertising Policy." 21(52):15.

———. 1995d. "Candidate Scares Elitists." 21(48):2.

———. 1995e. "We're Grassroots People." 21(52):2.

———. 1996. "Duke Makes Bid for Senate Seat as Johnson Retires." 22 (19):14–15.

SS Action Group. n.d.a. "Why We Use the Swastika." Levittown, NY.

———. n.d.b. "Who We Are and What We Are All About." *Aryans Awake!*

———. n.d.c. "We Are For . . . We Are Against."

SS Race Theory and Mate Selection Guidelines. 1990. Translated by Karl Hammer. (No city or publisher).

Stern, Kenneth S. 1996. *A Force Upon the Plain.* New York: Simon & Schuster.

Storm, Michael. 1983. "America the Beautiful?" *New Order* 52:2.

———. 1996. "Editorial." *New Order* 123:2.

Strom, Kevin Alfred. 1995. "Two Nations, Not One." Hillsboro, WV: National Vanguard Books.

———. 1996. "Facing Racial Realities." *Free Speech* 2(7):1–4.

Subcommittee on Terrorism, Technology and Government Information of the Senate Committee on the Judiciary. n.d. *Ruby Ridge: Report of the Subcommittee on Terrorism, Technology and Government Information of the Senate Committee on the Judiciary.* (Obtained from Senator Specter's Office: Washington D.C.)

The [Spokane] Spokesman Review. 1992. "The Weaver Cabin Shooting." *The Spokesman Review,* August 22, p. A1.

Tanner, Julia. 1978. "New Directions for Subcultural Theory." *Youth and Society* 9:343–72.

Tarrow, Sidney. 1994. *Power in Movement.* Cambridge, England: Cambridge University Press.

Taylor, Samuel. 1992. "Race and Intelligence: The Evidence." *American Renaissance* 3 (11):1, 3–6.

Taylor, Verta and Nancy E. Whittier. 1995. "Collective Identity in Social Movement Communities: Lesbian Feminist Mobilization." Pp. 344–57 in *American Society and Politics: Institutional, Historical, and Theoretical Perspectives,* edited by Theda Skocpol and John L. Campbell. New York: McGraw-Hill.

Theodorson, George A. and Achilles G. Theodorson. 1969. *A Modern Dictionary of Sociology*. New York: Barnes & Noble Books.

Thomas, Mark. 1993. Untitled article. *The Watchman* October.

Thompson, Grahame. 1990. *The Political Economy of the New Right*. London: Pinter Publishers.

Thompson, Jerry. 1980. "Alabama Doctor's Home Klan Recruiting Station." *The Tennessean*, Dec. 8, 1980, reprinted in *My Life With the Klan* by Jerry Thompson, from the Pages of *The Tennessean*, n.d.:9.

Thornton, Jeannye, David Whitman, and Dorian Friedman. 1992. "Whites Myths about Blacks." *U.S. News and World Report,* November 9, pp. 41–44.

"Thorsson." 1996. "Cyber Nazis: Racial Socialists on the Internet." *Blood and Honor* 16 (Spring):9.

Throckmorton, Robert. 1993. "Contradictions Galore in the Left-Right Business." *Instauration* (9):10–11.

Thunderbolt. 1983a. "Gang of Four Asian Nations Stealing Your Job." August, 291:1.

———. 1983b. "No 'Gas Chambers' Were Ever Found." June, 289:1.

———. 1983c. "Survey Shows Blacks Avoid Work." August, 291:1.

———. 1983d. "Kennedy Attacked Mississippi Not Cuba." August, 291:14.

Tilly, Charles. 1978. *From Mobilization to Revolution*. Reading, MA: Addison-Wesley.

Toy, Eckard V. Jr. 1989. "Right-Wing Extremism from the Ku Klux Klan to the Order, 1915 to 1988." Pp. 131–52 in *Violence in America: Protest, Rebellion, Reform*, vol. 2, edited by Ted Robert Gurr. Newbury Park: Sage.

The Truth at Last. n.d. #350. "Negro Crime Wave Sweeps America." 350:10.

———. n.d. #355. "Future White Minority." 355:10.

———. n.d. #356a. "Duke Fought Against All Odds." 356:8.

———. n.d. #356b. "Why People Like Pat Buchanan." 356:5.

———. n.d. #364. "Anheuser-Busch Dumps Whites Gives Jobs to Non-Whites." 364:1.

———. n.d. #365. "Holocaust Museum Is Biggest Fraud in History—Already Cost Taxpayers 33 Million." 365:8–10.

———. n.d. #366. "Patriots Launch—America First Party!" 366:1, 8.

———. n.d. #368. "Jewish Influence Is Awesome Makes Up 56% of Clinton's Appointees." 368:1.

———. n.d. #371. "Adopting Blacks into White Families Does Not Raise Their IQ." 371:1.

———. n.d. #373a. "Clinton Names Two Jews to Federal Reserve Board—Discriminates Against Christians." 373:1.

———. n.d. #373b. "Media Suppresses News That Second Court Nominee Is a Jew. Clinton—First President to Nominate * Two Jews to the U.S. Supreme Court—and**Two Jews to the Federal Reserve Bank Board." 373b:1.

———. n.d. #374a. "Negro Crime Out of Control." 374:10.

———. n.d. #374b. "Nicole Simpson Would Be Alive Today Had She Married a White Man! Simpson Case Proves That Interracial Marriage Violates the Laws of Nature." 374:1.

———. n.d. #376a. "Holocaust Story Used to Exploit Taxpayers." 376:1.

———. n.d. #376b. "Schindler's List Suppresses Fact That Germans Prosecuted Camp Head." 376:4.

———. n.d. #376c. "Jews Admit 1.8 Million, Yet Tell World 6 Million!" 376:5.

———. n.d. #378. "Book Threatens Liberal's Line on Racial Equality." 378:1.

———. n.d. #387. "Buchanan Running Second as Dole Falters!" 387:14.

Tucker, James P. Jr. 1995. "Populism Sweeping America: Democrats Jump Ship." *Spotlight* 21(50):1.

Tucker, Richard K. 1991. *The Dragon and the Cross*. Hamden, CT: Archon Book.

Turner, Capstan with A. Jay Lowery. 1985. *There Was a Man: The Saga of Gordon Kahl*. Nashville, TN: Sozo Publishing Co.

Turque, Bill with Ginny Carroll, Vern E. Smith, Clara Bingham, Adam Wolfberg, Patrice Johnson, Susan Miller, and John McCormick. 1991. "The Real David Duke." *Newsweek,* November 18, pp. 24–28.

Upton, James N. 1985. "The Politics of Urban Violence." *Journal of Black Studies* 15(March):243–58.

Vander Zanden, James W. 1960. "The Klan Revival." *American Journal of Sociology* 65:456–62.

Vor Trú. 1993. "By Laws of the Asatrú Alliance." 49:37.

Wade, Wyn Craig. 1987. *The Fiery Cross: The Ku Klux Klan in America*. New York: Simon & Schuster.

Walter, Jess. 1995. *Every Knee Shall Bow: The Truth and Tragedy of Ruby Ridge and the Randy Weaver Family*. New York: HarperCollins.

Walter, Jess and Bill Morlin. 1992. "Weaver Wouldn't Spy for Feds." *The [Spokane] Spokesman Review,* September 13, pp. A1, A16.

Walton, J. 1979. "Urban Political Economy." *Comparative Urban Research* 7:1, 9.

Walsh, Tom. 1996. "Odinism, Friend or Foe?" *The Struggle* XV (September):3.

"Warrior Weekend Grows Popular, Effective: Eyes of World Focus on Youth Training, BBC to Cover Convention." 1987. *All The Way* April 3 (4):1 (Archives of Political Research Associates 4/18/89).

Wasserman, Ira M. 1979. "A Reanalysis of the Wallace Movement." *Journal of Political and Military Sociology* 7:243–56.

Watson, Thomas E. n.d. *The African*. Marietta, GA: Thunderbolt, Inc.

We Are The Law. n.d. "We Are The Law." 4: unnumbered.

Weber, Mark. n.d. *The Holocaust: Let's Hear Both Sides*. Costa Mesa, CA: Institute for Historical Review.

Wellman, David T. 1993. *Portraits of White Racism*. New York: University of Cambridge Press.

"What We Stand For . . . Goals and Objectives of the Nazi Party of the New Order." n.d. Penland, NC.

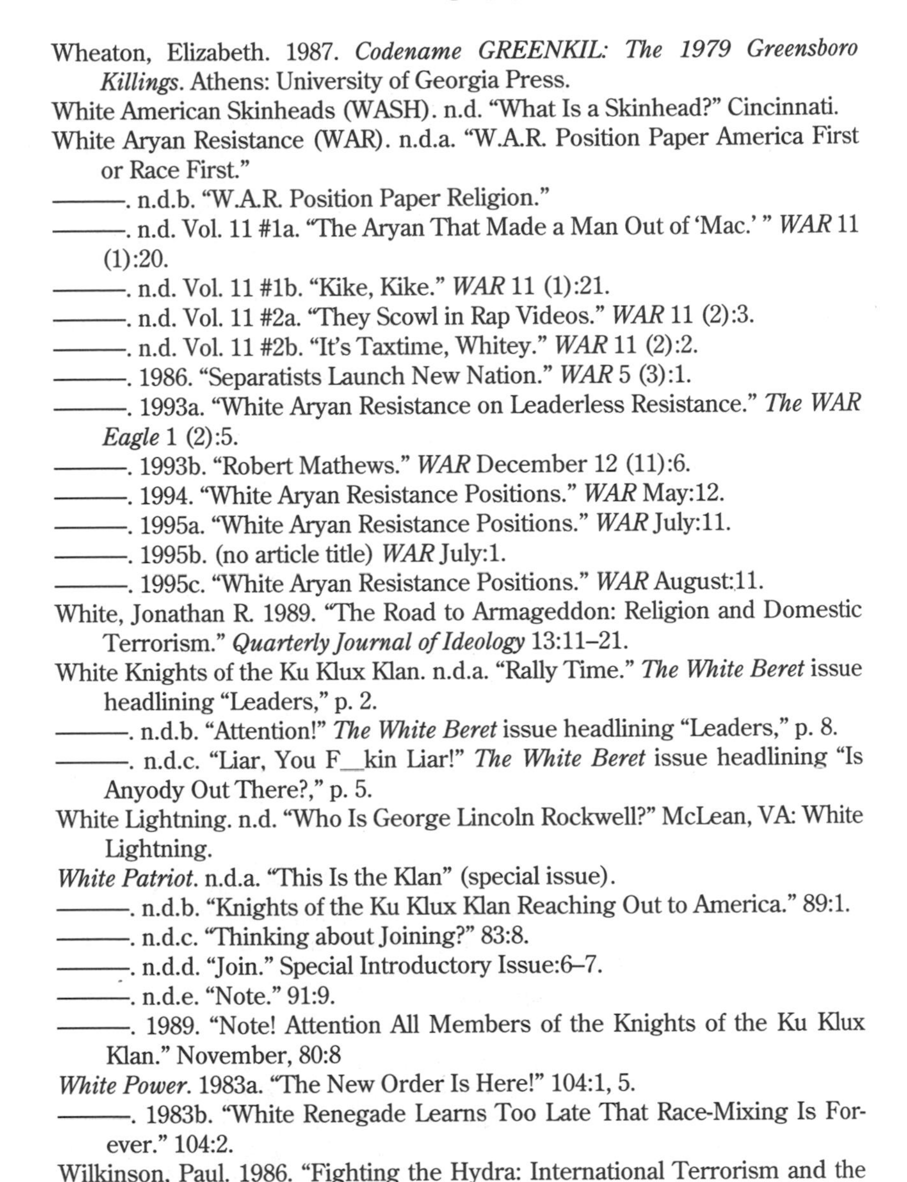

Wheaton, Elizabeth. 1987. *Codename GREENKIL: The 1979 Greensboro Killings*. Athens: University of Georgia Press.
White American Skinheads (WASH). n.d. "What Is a Skinhead?" Cincinnati.
White Aryan Resistance (WAR). n.d.a. "W.A.R. Position Paper America First or Race First."
———. n.d.b. "W.A.R. Position Paper Religion."
———. n.d. Vol. 11 #1a. "The Aryan That Made a Man Out of 'Mac.' " *WAR* 11 (1):20.
———. n.d. Vol. 11 #1b. "Kike, Kike." *WAR* 11 (1):21.
———. n.d. Vol. 11 #2a. "They Scowl in Rap Videos." *WAR* 11 (2):3.
———. n.d. Vol. 11 #2b. "It's Taxtime, Whitey." *WAR* 11 (2):2.
———. 1986. "Separatists Launch New Nation." *WAR* 5 (3):1.
———. 1993a. "White Aryan Resistance on Leaderless Resistance." *The WAR Eagle* 1 (2):5.
———. 1993b. "Robert Mathews." *WAR* December 12 (11):6.
———. 1994. "White Aryan Resistance Positions." *WAR* May:12.
———. 1995a. "White Aryan Resistance Positions." *WAR* July:11.
———. 1995b. (no article title) *WAR* July:1.
———. 1995c. "White Aryan Resistance Positions." *WAR* August:11.
White, Jonathan R. 1989. "The Road to Armageddon: Religion and Domestic Terrorism." *Quarterly Journal of Ideology* 13:11–21.
White Knights of the Ku Klux Klan. n.d.a. "Rally Time." *The White Beret* issue headlining "Leaders," p. 2.
———. n.d.b. "Attention!" *The White Beret* issue headlining "Leaders," p. 8.
———. n.d.c. "Liar, You F__kin Liar!" *The White Beret* issue headlining "Is Anyody Out There?," p. 5.
White Lightning. n.d. "Who Is George Lincoln Rockwell?" McLean, VA: White Lightning.
White Patriot. n.d.a. "This Is the Klan" (special issue).
———. n.d.b. "Knights of the Ku Klux Klan Reaching Out to America." 89:1.
———. n.d.c. "Thinking about Joining?" 83:8.
———. n.d.d. "Join." Special Introductory Issue:6–7.
———. n.d.e. "Note." 91:9.
———. 1989. "Note! Attention All Members of the Knights of the Ku Klux Klan." November, 80:8
White Power. 1983a. "The New Order Is Here!" 104:1, 5.
———. 1983b. "White Renegade Learns Too Late That Race-Mixing Is Forever." 104:2.
Wilkinson, Paul. 1986. "Fighting the Hydra: International Terrorism and the Rule of Law." Pp. 205–24 in *Terrorism, Ideology, and Revolution*, vol. 1, edited by Noel O'Sullivan. Great Britain: Wheatsheaf Books.
Williams, David R., Risa Lavizzo-Mourey, and Reuben C. Warren. 1994. "The Concept of Race and Health Status in America." *Public Health Reports* January/February, 108:26–41.

Williams, Leonard. 1987. "Ideological Parallels Between the New Left and the New Right." *Social Science Journal* 24(3):317–27.

Wisdom from the Edda. 1996. Harrisburg PA: White House Press and Graphics Service (revised edition, first printing by The Giallerhorn Book Service 1981).

"Why Asatru." n.d. Obtained from Stephen McNallen, Asatru Folk Assembly.

Woodward, C. Vann. 1966. *The Strange Career of Jim Crow*. London: Oxford University Press.

Worsley, Peter. 1993. "Populism." Pp. 730–31 in *The Oxford Companion to Politics of the World*, edited by Joel Krieger. New York: Oxford University Press.

Wotansvolk. n.d. "Flags." St. Maries, ID: 14 Word Press.

———. 1995. *Wotanism in Today's World*. St. Maries, ID: 14 Word Press.

Yeboah, Samuel Kennedy. 1988. *The Ideology of Racism*. Great Britain: Hansib Printing Limited.

York, Michael. 1995. *The Emerging Network: A Sociology of the New Age and Neo-Pagan Movements*. Lanham, MD: Rowman & Littlefield.

Zald, Mayer. 1987. "The Future of Social Movements." Pp. 319–36 in *Social Movements in an Organizational Society: Collected Essays*, edited by Mayer Zald and John D. McCarthy. New Brunswick, NJ: Transaction.

Zatarain, Michael. 1990. *David Duke: Evolution of a Klansman*. Gretna, LA: Pelican Publishing Company.

Zerzan, John. 1993. "Rank-and-file Radicalism within the Ku Klux Klan." *Anarchy: A Journal of Desire Armed* (Summer):48–53.

Zeskind, Leonard. 1984. *It's Not Populism, America's New Populist Party: A Fraud by Racists and Anti-Semites*. Atlanta, GA: Center for Democratic Renewal and Southern Poverty Law Center.

———. 1985. "The Far Right." *Schmate* Summer, 11–12:25–32.

———. 1986. *The "Christian Identity" Movement*. The Division of Church and Society of the National Council of the Churches of Christ in the U.S.A.

Zey-Ferrell, Mary. 1979. *Dimensions of Organizations*. Santa Monica, CA: Goodyear Publishing Co.

Zia, Helen. 1991. "Women in Hate Groups: Who Are They? Why Are They There?" *MS,* March/April, pp. 20–27.

Zinn, Howard. 1980. *A People's History of the United States*. NY: Harper and Row.

———. 1993. *Failure to Quit*. Monroe, ME: Common Courage Press.

Zuo, Jiping and Robert D. Benford. 1995. "Mobilization Processes and the 1989 Chinese Democracy Movement." *The Sociological Quarterly* 36:131–56.

Note: The a,b, etc. are assigned to the references by the order in which they appeared in the text. "No date" is indicated by n.d. "No page" is indicated by n.p.

Index

The Authors

Betty A. Dobratz received her Ph.D. from the University of Wisconsin and is a professor of sociology at Iowa State University. Her major research interests are in political sociology, social movements, and social inequality. She was secretary-treasurer of the political sociology section of the American Sociological Association from 1996 to 1999. She was awarded a NATO postdoctoral fellowship for the study of Greek politics during the Papandreou era and did research in Greece for about 10 months in 1988 and 1989. She has authored and coauthored numerous articles on Greek politics. With Stephanie Shanks-Meile, she is studying the white separatist movement in the United States and conducting interviews with movement participants. She received a grant from the American Philosophical Society to visit library collections to obtain research materials about that movement.

Stephanie L. Shanks-Meile received her Ph.D. from the University of Nebraska-Lincoln and is a professor of sociology at Indiana University Northwest. Her major research interests are political sociology, social movements, race relations, gender, social organization, and medical sociology. She has served as an associate editor for *Humanity and Society* and a reviewer for *Human Relations* of the Tavistock Institute. She has published research on disability organizations and the social psychology of "blindness." Her other publications focus on women's labor force participation in health care occupations and professions. She has been conducting primary research with Betty Dobratz on the white separatist movement for many years, culminating in this monograph.